THE REVIVAL OF NATURAL LAW

Natural law theory has been enjoying a significant revival in recent times. Led by Germain Grisez in the USA and John Finnis in the UK, one school of thinkers has been articulating a highly developed system of natural law built upon a sophisticated account of practical reasoning and a rich and flexible understanding of the human good. However, long-standing prejudices against old-style natural law among moral philosophers and Protestant ethicists, together with the new theory's appropriation by conservatives in the impassioned debate between the Vatican and dissenting theologians in the United States, have prevented the Finnis-Grisez version from being adequately appreciated.

Providing a clear and substantive introduction to the theory for those who are new to it, this book then broadens, assesses, and advances the debate about it, examining crucial philosophical, theological and ethical issues and opening up discussion beyond the confines of the Roman Catholic Church.

Part I, on philosophical issues, starts with two broad chapters that locate the Grisez school in relation to modern moral philosophy and the Roman Catholic philosophical tradition of Thomism, and then follows these with further chapters on two crucial issues: the possibility of consensus on the human good, and the nature of moral absolutes. Part II, on theological dimensions, begins with a Lutheran critique of Grisez, locates him in relation to the ethics of two very prominent 20th century Protestants, Karl Barth and Stanley Hauerwas, and then explores the major area of theological controversy within the Roman Catholic community—how to conceive of the 'Church's' authority with regard to moral matters. Part III subjects the school's thought to critical examination in a broad range of ethical fields: bioethics, gender, sex and the environment. A concluding chapter then develops eight topics that recur in the course of the book: the status of ethical realism in the contemporary intellectual climate; whether realism is best conceived in rationalist or naturalist terms; whether marriage should be counted as a basic good; whether physical pleasure should not be counted a basic good; whether it is always wrong to act deliberately against a basic good; the problems of moral certainty and authority; the *rapprochement* between Protestant and Roman Catholic ethics; and, finally, whether ethical understanding is really independent of one's anthropological point of view.

Drawing together North American, European and Australian contributors from moral philosophy and Protestant ethics as well as from Roman Catholic moral theology, this book opens up the debate about the Finnis-Grisez theory, highlighting its strengths and weaknesses, in order to advance current discussion about natural law in moral theology and in moral and legal philosophy.

The Revival of Natural Law

Philosophical, theological and ethical responses to the Finnis-Grisez School

Edited by

NIGEL BIGGAR
University of Leeds, England

RUFUS BLACK
United Faculty of Theology, Melbourne, Australia

Routledge
Taylor & Francis Group

LONDON AND NEW YORK

First published 2000 by Ashgate Publishing

2 Park Square, Milton Park, Abingdon, Oxon OX14 4RN
711 Third Avenue, New York, NY 10017, USA

Routledge is an imprint of the Taylor & Francis Group, an informa business

First issued in paperback 2016

Copyright © Nigel Biggar and Rufus Black 2000

British Library Cataloguing in Publication Data
The revival of natural law : philosophical, theological and
    ethical responses to the Finnis-Grisez school
    1. Natural law - Moral and ethical aspects 2. Ethics
    3. Religion and ethics
    I. Biggar, Nigel II. Black, Rufus
    340.1'12

Library of Congress Control Number: 00-108135

ISBN 13: 978-0-7546-1262-9 (hbk)
ISBN 13: 978-1-138-25671-2 (pbk)

Contents

List of Tables

List of Abbreviations

CMP	Germain Grisez, *The Way of the Lord Jesus*, vol. 1: *Christian Moral Principles* (Chicago: Franciscan Herald Press, 1983)
DMQ	Germain Grisez, *The Way of the Lord Jesus*, vol. 3: *Difficult Moral Questions* (Quincy, Illinois: Franciscan Press, 1997)
FE	John Finnis, *The Fundamentals of Ethics* (Oxford: Clarendon Press, 1983)
LCL	Germain Grisez, *The Way of the Lord Jesus*, vol. 2: *Living a Christian Life* (Quincy, Illinois: Franciscan Press, 1993)
LDLJ	Germain Grisez and Joseph M. Boyle, *Life and Death with Liberty and Justice: a Contribution to the Euthanasia Debate* (Notre Dame and London: University of Notre Dame Press, 1979)
MA	John Finnis, *Moral Absolutes: Tradition, Revision, and Truth* (Washington, D.C.: Catholic University of America Press, 1991)
NDMR	John Finnis, Joseph M. Boyle, and Germain Grisez, *Nuclear Deterrence, Morality, and Realism* (Oxford: Clarendon Press, 1987)
NLNR	John Finnis, *Natural Law and Natural Rights* (Oxford: Clarendon Press, 1980)
PP	Germain Grisez, Joseph Boyle, and John Finnis, "Practical Principles, Moral Truth, and Ultimate Ends", *The American Journal of Jurisprudence*, 32 (1987), pp. 99-151
ST	Thomas Aquinas, *Summa Theologiae*

List of Contributors

SABINA ALKIRE holds a D.Phil. from Oxford University, England, where she has tutored in both economics and theology. She now works for the World Bank in Washington, D.C.

GÖRAN BEXELL is Professor of Ethics in the Department of Religious Studies at the University of Lund in Sweden. He is author of *Teologisk etik —en introduction* (Stockholm: Verbum, 1997), and has written on the encounter between Roman Catholic and Lutheran ethics.

NIGEL BIGGAR is Professor of Theology at the University of Leeds, England, where he directs the Institute for the Advanced Study of Religion, Ethics, and Public Life. He is author of *The Hastening that Waits: Karl Barth's Ethics* (Oxford: Oxford University Press, 1993, 1995).

RUFUS BLACK is Associate Lecturer in Christian Ethics in the United Faculty of Theology, Melbourne, Australia; and the author of *Christian Moral Realism* (Oxford: Oxford University Press, forthcoming).

LISA SOWLE CAHILL is Professor in the Department of Theology at Boston College, Boston, USA, and author of *Sex, Gender and Christian Ethics* (Cambridge: Cambridge University Press, 1996).

TIMOTHY CHAPPELL is Lecturer in Philosophy in the University of Dundee, Scotland, and author of *Understanding Human Goods: a Theory of Ethics* (Edinburgh: Edinburgh University Press, 1998).

BERNARD HOOSE is Lecturer in Christian ethics at Heythrop College, London, England. He is author of *Proportionalism* (Washington, D.C.: Georgetown University Press, 1987) and *Received Wisdom? Reviewing the Role of Tradition in Christian Ethics* (London: Geoffrey Chapman, 1994).

DAVE LEAL is Lecturer in Philosophy and Moral Theology at Regent's Park College, Oxford, England.

RALPH McINERNY is Michael P. Grace Professor of Medieval Studies at Notre Dame University, USA, and author of *Ethica Thomistica: the Moral Philosophy of Thomas Aquinas* (Washington, D.C.: Catholic University of America Press, 1982, 1998).

GARETH MOORE is Prior of the Communauté Dominicaine, Rixensart, Belgium, and author of *The Body in Context: Sex and Catholicism* (London: SCM, 1992).

MICHAEL NORTHCOTT is Senior Lecturer in the Department of Christian Ethics and Practical Theology at the University of Edinburgh, Scotland, and author of *The Environment and Christian Ethics* (Cambridge: Cambridge University Press, 1996).

OLIVER O'DONOVAN is Regius Professor of Moral and Pastoral Theology at the University of Oxford, England, and author of *Resurrection and Moral Order* (Leicester and Grand Rapids: IVP and Eerdmans, 1986).

Acknowledgements

The editors and publishers wish to thank T. & T. Clark for permission to reprint Oliver O'Donovan's article, "John Finnis and Moral Absolutes", which was first published in *Studies in Christian Ethics*, 6/2 (1993), pp. 50-66.

The editors also wish to thank Virginia Dunn for her indispensable and characteristically unstinting help in producing this book.

Preface

This book is a response to the revival of natural law theory. After a punishing century for moral realism, such a revival is perhaps the last thing that we would have expected. Yet it may be precisely adversity that has stimulated it. For the vigorous attack on moral realism —of which natural law theory is a form *par excellence*— produced significant clarifications of the philosophical deficiencies of existing realist theories. Armed with these clarifications and an awareness of its current inadequacies, Germain Grisez began his own restatement of natural law theory in the mid-1960s. Since then, his project has drawn sympathisers and collaborators to its cause, to such an extent that one may speak of a Grisez School. With the School's restatement now in a mature form, far more highly developed than any of its rivals, and worked through in relation to a wide range of practical moral questions, a broad assessment of its achievements, problems, and possibilities is timely.

Such an assessment of this new natural law theory is also important, because many substantial gains remain to be made from engaging with it. Unfortunately, much of its value has been obscured by the highly-charged church-political context, and consequently polemical manner, in which it has been debated within (largely American) Roman Catholic academia. What is more, the School's own rhetoric and conclusions on particular questions such as abortion, contraception, euthanasia, and divorce have often had a defensive character that has deterred many from a deeper inquiry into its work. The main aim of this book, therefore, is to reopen discussion by assembling responses from a wider-than-usual range of commentators, bringing the School into dialogue with fresh philosophical, social-scientific, and theological interlocutors, and somewhat broadening its application to moral issues.

The scope and depth of the Grisez School's work is such that it has the potential to attract and reward attention across a wide front. Aristotelians may well be drawn to its central concern to develop a rich and sophisticated account of human flourishing or *eudaimonia*. Kantians, on the other hand, are likely to find themselves absorbed in the substantive account of practical reasonableness which the School develops in its sympathetic dialogue with Kant.[1] Some might even spy the silhouette of reconciliation between these hitherto polar oppositions. For those concerned with virtue ethics, the Grisez School presents a sophisticated theory of character in which reason and emotion together play an integral part in decision-making; and it offers a satisfying resolution of the false, but all-too-conventional dichotomy between the concerns 'What should I do?' and 'Who should I be?'. Moral philosophers in the analytical tradition will probably gravitate toward the School's attempt to develop a form of moral realism that respects a version of the claim —one which explicitly incorporates key features of R.M. Hare's analysis— that one cannot derive an 'ought' from an 'is'. Theologians, especially Protestants, will be curious to explore the relationship between the 'natural' and the theological dimensions of Grisez's ethic. And finally, at the demanding point of ethical application, there should be much to occupy those engaged in trying to negotiate a way through the complex issues raised by care for human life, sexual relations, gender roles, and responsibility toward the non-human world.

With one exception, all the chapters in this book are freshly commissioned pieces written by those who have engaged critically with the work of the Grisez School. The authors represent a range of disciplines (philosophy, theology, and the behavioural sciences), a number of countries (the United Kingdom, Sweden, Belgium, Australia, as well as the United States), and several Christian traditions (Lutheran, Reformed, Anglican, as well as Roman Catholic). The broad provenance of these contributions testifies to the impact and significance of Grisez and his colleagues.

The first stirrings of the development of a new school of thought about natural law began in 1963-64, when Grisez prepared an entry for the *New Catholic Encyclopedia* on "Man, Natural End of".[2] In this article he began to explore the limitations of Aquinas' account of the natural end of human persons. Then, in his rather technical-sounding "First Principle of Practical Reason: A Commentary on the *Summa Theologiae*, 1-2, Question 94, Article 2",[3] his exegesis drew out the way in which practical reason operates in the foundation of Aquinas' ethics. After this beginning in Thomistic exegesis, Grisez moved on to articulate a form of natural law theory which, while claiming to be founded upon a more accurate interpretation of Aquinas than rival scholastic theories, is nevertheless free-standing. The early versions of this theory appeared in *Contraception and the Natural Law* (1964)[4] and *Abortion: the Myths, the Realities, and the Arguments* (1970),[5] which were published in the vortex of highly politicised debates about these controversial questions. Although these accounts have since been superseded, their criticisms of the then-existing natural law theories still hold. Then, in 1974, Grisez presented his new theory in the first of three editions of a popular textbook, *Beyond the New Morality: the Responsibilities of Freedom*,[6] written with Russell Shaw, a professional writer who has collaborated with Grisez on a number of projects to make his work more widely accessible.

Before his theory reached its mature expression, Grisez produced two important works that furnished the necessary metaphysical foundations for the School's ethics: *Beyond the New Theism: a Philosophy of Religion* (1975)[7] and *Free Choice: a Self-Referential Argument* (1976).[8] The second of these books was co-written with Joseph Boyle and Olaf Tollefsen. The fruits of Boyle's collaboration with Grisez, which began in 1970, had already emerged during the previous year in an important article, "Aquinas and Prescriptive Ethics", where Boyle demonstrated that one could accept key insights in Hare's prescriptivism without endorsing a non-realist approach to ethics.[9] The next major product of Grisez and Boyle's collaboration was *Life and Death with Liberty and Justice: a Contribution to the Euthanasia Debate* (1979).[10] Meanwhile, Grisez also began a sustained attack on consequentialist theories in general,[11] later focusing his criticism on Roman Catholic 'proportionalists' such as Richard McCormick and Bruno Schüller, whose views, in his opinion, undermined traditional teachings. These and other more liberal Catholic writers were also in Grisez's sights as he responded to challenges to Rome's traditional teaching on subjects such as contraception.[12] Eventually, these exchanges between Grisez and his opponents developed into clashes over the question of dissent within the Church.[13] Whatever the relative merits of the opposing sides, this heated conflict with popular Catholic writers greatly alienated Grisez and his thought from important liberal Catholic academic circles in the United States and the United Kingdom. In our opinion, this resulted in a significant hindrance of the advancement of ethical understanding.

The next major development in the Grisez School's project came with the publication in 1980 of John Finnis' *Natural Law and Natural Rights*, where the theory of natural law was advanced by applying it to important jurisprudential questions concerning the nature of justice, rights, authority, law, and obligation. This work attracted a great deal of attention and critical comment. Unfortunately, and perhaps because of the charged ecclesial-political environment, many of the ensuing criticisms were based on serious misunderstandings.[14] Finnis went on to provide a further restatement of the core of the School's theory in *The Fundamentals of Ethics* (1983), which brought it into dialogue with contemporary Anglo-American moral philosophy, as well as with Aristotle and Kant.

The publication in 1982 of the nearly one-thousand pages of Volume 1 of *The Way of the Lord Jesus —Christian Moral Principles—* marked the next major landmark in the evolution of the thought of the Grisez School. Its origins lie back in 1977 when Grisez began on the project which has structured his life and work since that date: answering Vatican II's call for a renewal of moral theology. Carried out from his specially endowed chair at Mount Saint Mary's College in Maryland, this project has now yielded three volumes: *Christian Moral Principles*, which sets out the philosophical basis of the natural law ethic, and its theological qualifications; *Living a Christian Life* (1992), which deals with the specific spheres of moral responsibility common to all people; and *Difficult Moral Questions* (1997), which tackles particular moral quandaries. These vast volumes have drawn a large number of collaborators into the project, although among these Boyle and Finnis have remained intellectually predominant.

These three main collaborators, Grisez, Boyle and Finnis, worked together to produce a comprehensive restatement of the core of their new natural law theory in an extremely dense and tightly argued article, "Practical Principles, Moral Truth, and Ultimate Ends" (1987). To date this article remains the central point of reference for analysing their theory.[15] 1987 also saw the publication of Russell Hittinger's book, *A Critique of the New Natural Law Theory*.[16] Unfortunately, this book —which was quite influential in propagating the impression that the Grisez theory suffered from serious inadequacies— was, like so many other attacks on it, based on serious misunderstandings. However, the debate took a more constructive turn in the early 1990s, with the publication of a collection of essays on the theory by Robert George.[17] By this stage, George, who had contributed to *Living a Christian Life*, had become another important figure in the School —a significance firmly established by the publication of his application of the theory to the question of legislation on morals, *Making Men Moral* (1993).[18]

The present book seeks to take a further step in the constructive assessment and development of the Grisez School's new natural law theory. In order for this critical development to occur across the breadth of the School's thought, we have divided the work into three parts. After the Introduction, where the systematic core of the theory is presented for those who are either new to the discussion or who seek a concise statement of its key features, Part I treats some of the central philosophical issues involved in the School's work and locates it in contemporary discussion. In Part II we move to a discussion of the theory's theological dimensions. Then, in Part III, we turn from systematic questions to the theory's application to the important issues involved in bioethics, sexual ethics, gender relations, and the treatment of the non-human world. Finally, we conclude with a set of reflections on some of the main themes running through the preceding essays. It is our hope that those who read this book will find the thought of the Grisez School as worthy of response and development as those who have contributed to it.[19]

Nigel Biggar and Rufus Black   *April 2000*

NOTES

1   Finnis, *FE*, pp.107-35.
2   A work not actually published until 1967. Germain Grisez, "Man, Natural End of", *New Catholic Encyclopedia*, vol. 9 (New York: McGraw-Hill, 1967), pp.132-38.
3   Germain Grisez, "First Principle of Practical Reason: a Commentary on the Summa Theologiae 1-2, Question 94, Article 2", *Natural Law Forum*, 10 (1965), pp.168-201.
4   Germain Grisez, *Contraception and the Natural Law* (Milwaukee, Wisconsin: Bruce, 1964).
5   Germain Grisez, *Abortion: the Myths, the Realities, and the Arguments* (New York and Cleveland: Corpus Books, 1970).
6   Germain Grisez and Russell Shaw, *Beyond the New Morality: the Responsibilities of Freedom* (Notre Dame and London: University of Notre Dame Press, 1974).
7   Germain Grisez, *Beyond the New Theism: a Philosophy of Religion* (Notre Dame and London: University of Notre Dame Press, 1975).
8   Joseph M. Boyle, Germain Grisez, and Olaf Tollefsen, *Free Choice: a Self-Referential Argument* (Notre Dame and London: University of Notre Dame Press, 1976).
9   Joseph M. Boyle, "Aquinas and Prescriptive Ethics", *Proceedings of the American Catholic Philosophical Association*, 49 (1975), pp.82-95.
10   Germain Grisez and Joseph M. Boyle, *Life and Death with Liberty and Justice: a Contribution to the Euthanasia Debate* (Notre Dame and London: University of Notre Dame Press, 1979).
11   The most complete account of this attack on consequentialism was delivered in Germain Grisez, "Against Consequentialism", *American Journal of Jurisprudence*, 23 (1978), pp.21-72. It had, however, already taken its mature form in Germain Grisez, "Choice and Consequentialism", *Proceedings of the American Catholic Philosophical Association*, 51 (1977), pp.144-52.
12   G. Grisez and J.C. Ford, "Contraception and the Infallibility of the Ordinary Magisterium", *Theological Studies*, 39 (1978), pp.258-312; Germain Grisez, "Infallibility and Specific Moral Norms: a Review Discussion", *The Thomist*, 49 (1985), pp.248-87; Germain Grisez, "Infallibility and Contraception: a Reply to Garth Hallett", *Theological Studies*, 47 (1986), pp.134-45.
13   See, for example, Grisez, *CMP*, pp.871-98; Germain Grisez, "History as Argument for

Revision in Moral Theology: a Review Discussion", *The Thomist*, 53 (1991), pp.103-116.

14   Important instances of these misunderstandings occur in, Ralph McInerny, "The Principles of Natural Law", *American Journal of Jurisprudence*, 25 (1980), pp.1-15; to which a specific reply was made in John Finnis and Germain Grisez, "The Basic Principles of Natural Law: a Reply to Ralph McInerny", *American Journal of Jurisprudence*, 26 (1981), pp.21-31. Similar misunderstandings to McInerny's also occur in V. Bourke, "Review of J. Finnis, *Natural Law and Natural Rights*", *American Journal of Jurisprudence*, 26 (1981), pp.243-47; and H. Veatch, "Review of J. Finnis, *Natural Law and Natural Rights*", *American Journal of Jurisprudence*, 26 (1981), pp.247-59. Further significant misunderstandings may also be found in Brian Johnstone, "The Structures of Practical Reason: Traditional Theories and Contemporary Questions", *The Thomist*, 50 (1986), pp.417-46; J. Schultz, "Is-Ought: Prescribing and a Present Controversy", *The Thomist*, 49 (1985), pp.1-23; P. Simpson, "St Thomas and the Naturalistic Fallacy", *The Thomist*, 51 (1987), pp.51-69 (Grisez replied to Johnstone, Schultz, and Simpson in Germain Grisez, "The Structures of Practical Reason: Some Comments and Clarifications", *The Thomist*, 52 [1988], pp.269-91); and in D. Flippen, "Natural Law and Natural Inclinations", *New Scholasticism*, 5 (1986), pp.284-316 (to which Grisez responded in Germain Grisez, "Natural Law and Natural Inclinations: Some Comments and Clarifications", *New Scholasticism*, 6 [1987], pp.307-20, which also included a further response to Shultz).

15   Germain Grisez, Joseph Boyle, and John Finnis, "Practical Principles, Moral Truth, and Ultimate Ends", *American Journal of Jurisprudence*, 32 (1987), pp.99-151.

16   Russell Hittinger, *Critique of the New Natural Law Theory* (Notre Dame and London: University of Notre Dame Press, 1987). For the problems with Hittinger's account, see Robert George, "Recent Criticism of Natural Law Theory", *The University of Chicago Law Review*, 55 (1988), pp.1371-1429; and Germain Grisez, "A Critique of Russell Hittinger's Book, *A Critique of the New Natural Law Theory*", *New Scholasticism*, 62 (1988), pp.438-65.

17   Robert George (ed.), *Natural Law Theory: Contemporary Essays* (Oxford: Clarendon Press, 1992).

18   Robert George, *Making Men Moral* (Oxford: Clarendon Press, 1993).

19   Some of our contributors are accustomed to using British spelling conventions, others to using American ones. Since the divergence between them is not great, and their differences are well known and easily intelligible, we have seen no good reason to insist on standard practice throughout this volume. Our only requirement has been consistency within each chapter. Quotations, however, have been allowed to retain their original style.

Introduction: The New Natural Law Theory

Rufus Black

The natural law theory developed by the Grisez School is a sophisticated and supple moral theory. Yet its very complexity and comprehensiveness makes obtaining an appreciation of it something of a challenge. Simply coming to terms with the systematic core of the theory can be daunting. This chapter will attempt to introduce this core by dividing the task into three more manageable stages.

The *first stage* is to reflect on the background and conceptual framework which have shaped the theory. Central to this background are the inadequacies and failures of previous natural law theories, which were negative, proscriptive, and possessed of too limited an account of what brings fulfilment into a human life. An important feature of this conceptual framework is the distinction between the practical reason we use to make ethical decisions and the theoretical reason we use —in disciplines including science, history and metaphysics— to inquire into the nature of reality. An awareness of this distinction will help to make it clear why the Grisez School does not think that one can argue from a statement about how the world 'is' to a statement about what one 'ought' to do.

The *second stage* is to ask 'What are the objects and objectives that bring meaning, fulfilment and wholeness into a human life?' What, in other words, are the things we pursue that enrich our lives and the lives of others? Once we are aware of the horizon of things, from knowledge and friendship to inner peace and skills in play, which we might pursue in order to bring fulfilment into our lives, the question for the *third stage* will be 'What should guide my choices about which good thing(s) to pursue, and how should I pursue them?'

Over the years, the Grisez School has produced various formulations of their theory. The most philosophically precise account of their mature work is Grisez, Boyle, and Finnis' extremely dense fifty-page article, "Practical

Principles, Moral Truth, and Ultimate Ends".[1]   This article, fleshed out by John Finnis' *Natural Law and Natural Rights* (which combines clarity, accessibility, and philosophical precision most helpfully), forms the basis of the account that follows.

Stage 1: The Background and Conceptual Framework

The Problems with Scholastic Natural Law Theory and Classical Moral Theology

The Grisez School's theory developed in response to what they perceived as the problems and inadequacies of scholastic natural law theory and the classical Roman Catholic moral theology that it underpinned.   While some protest that their characterisation is too generalised and their criticisms too sweeping, these resonate with the concerns of others, especially various Protestant critics; and, at the very least, they give a clear indication of what the School is seeking to avoid. The forms of natural law theory which Grisez describes as 'scholastic' are those that direct people in the manner of 'Here you are —here is your nature— now be what you are', and which account for morality in terms of conformity or otherwise to some "built-in pattern".[2]   While "[s]uch advice can have a true sense . . . unless human persons have possibilities which are not yet defined, there is no room for them to unfold themselves through intelligent creativity and freedom".[3]   The result, he argues, is that this approach tends to produce a negative and minimalist ethic, since:

> What does not conform to human nature can be forbidden absolutely.   What does conform cannot be absolutely required, since people cannot possibly do everything which is permissible ....   Thus scholastic natural-law theory is far more adept at issuing a few prohibitions than at directing people's lives toward growth and flourishing.[4]

It is on the doorstep of this type of theory that Grisez lays the blame for what he identifies as the three key failings of classical moral theology.   First, "[c]lassical moral theology tends to reduce Christian moral life to a means of gaining heaven and avoiding hell".[5]   As a result, moral theology has apparently little to say about the meaning and value of the present life.   This problem arose because scholastic natural law theories did not identify an intrinsic relationship between human nature and the worthwhile, meaningful, fulfilling activities of life.

According to Grisez, classical moral theology's second failing is its "static character".[6] While he agrees that human nature does not change, he maintains that history constantly opens up new possibilities for action. By defining human nature in very limited terms, and as possessing only a limited range of principles to guide action, scholastic natural law theory has little capacity to offer a positive vision of how to respond to these new possibilities in human life.

Thirdly, because scholastic natural law theory does not identify the human fulfilment to be gained from living the moral life, and because of its static character, Grisez also argues that classical moral theology succumbs to the life-denying strictures of legalism. People come to obey rules simply for fear of punishment or the promise of reward, and not because they are guides to living truthfully and living well.[7] Almost inevitably, this means that the final failing of classical moral theology is that "it is too much concerned with laws and too little concerned with persons".[8] Put simply, on Grisez's account, classical moral theology failed because it was unable to identify a sufficiently rich conception of a person's well-being (i.e., the good) to which moral principles would direct her.

The Key Conceptual Presuppositions of the New Natural Law Theory

Even more significant than these distortions of moral theology, is what Grisez holds to be "a logically illicit step" at the heart of scholastic natural law theory: the attempt to move deductively "from human nature as a given reality, to what ought and ought not to be chosen".[9] In holding that this move from 'fact' to 'value', from 'is' to 'ought', is logically illicit, the Grisez School takes an important stand in one of the central debates of twentieth-century moral philosophy. While they hold that Hume can be interpreted as articulating the logic underlying this position,[10] and they acknowledge certain important affinities between their position and that of R.M. Hare,[11] the foundation of their argument is the logical distinction between theoretical reason and practical reason. Both the distinction and the carefully articulated relationship between these two forms of reason are key organising ideas in the systematic foundations of their natural law theory.

The use of *theoretical reason*, Grisez and Finnis argue, *is to pursue knowledge about aspects of reality*.[12] It seeks to establish the truth of a proposition by testing the conformity of its content with some *prior reality*.[13] Theoretical reason can establish this conformity by both deductive and inductive forms of reasoning. The product of such reasoning is theoretical knowledge. A wide range of forms of intellectual inquiry produce this sort of knowledge, including history, science, and metaphysics. While theoretical reason establishes truthfulness against prior realities, we should note that it can employ these observations to formulate scientific laws (e.g., in the fields of physics and chemistry) and semi-scientific 'laws' (e.g., in the fields of economics and psychology) by which to predict the future.

In contrast to theoretical reason's function of pursuing knowledge in relation to prior realities, Grisez emphasises that the function of *practical reason* is actually *to bring realities into being*.[14] It is *the form of reason that we use to make choices about what we should do*. These choices will range from the commitments that structure our lives, such as 'What career should I pursue?', to very daily decisions like 'What should I eat for dinner?' Practical reason, first, identifies what is attractive in the different options that present themselves for choice; and second, provides us with reasons upon which we can base our actions. So, for example, in making a career choice, practical reason will enable us to recognise the different appealing features of being an artist (the opportunity to develop skills of creative expression) or a nurse (the opportunity to help bring people health) and provide us with reason(s) to guide our decision (choose the career that fits best with all the different dimensions of your person). In deciding to become an artist, a person actually acts to bring a new reality into being (i.e., her particular skills of artistic expression).

Practical reason does not work alone. It also operates in conjunction with theoretical reason. In deciding what to eat for dinner, we need the theoretical knowledge of what will actually provide nourishment. Faced with many options for a meal, practical reasons —such as, 'that we should pursue health' and 'that we should seek harmony with our feelings'— will help guide our choices. Practical reason will also rule out some nourishing candidates from consideration as food, such as other people[15] and, some would argue, other animals.

It should be evident that the operation of practical reason assumes the possibility that a person can make choices that are sufficiently free for her to call them her own. The architectonic importance of free choice in Grisez, Finnis, and Boyle's analysis of practical reason is emphasised by their observation that '[p]erhaps the most important presupposition [of their ethical framework] from philosophical anthropology is that human persons can make free choices'.[16] Central to what makes choice so important is that they hold it to be significantly constitutive of both a person's character and human fulfilment.[17]

Employing the distinction between practical and theoretical reason, Grisez, Finnis, and Boyle formally express the claim that one cannot derive an 'ought' from an 'is' in the following terms:

> ...from a set of theoretical premises, one cannot logically derive any practical truth, since sound reasoning does not introduce what is not in the premises. And the relationship of principles to conclusions is a logical one among propositions. Therefore, the ultimate principles of morality cannot be theoretical truths of metaphysical and/or philosophical anthropology.[18]

The insight to which the Grisez School is pointing here may be clearer to some in an alternative formulation. If it is borne in mind that they describe practical reason as 'reasons for acting', then their argument can be formulated in the following terms: the way human nature (or any other aspect of reality for that matter) *is*, cannot function to provide a reason why, where choice exists, a person should bring one reality into being and not another. That is, where there is a desire or a necessity to make a choice about which option to pursue, then to make a statement simply about the way the world 'is', does not provide a reason why one option should be chosen rather than another. Put baldly, a fact alone does not provide a reason to act. The inability of theoretical statements to function in this way should be no surprise given that they refer to prior realities and not to bringing future realities into being.

This insistence by the Grisez School that it is not logically possible to derive an 'ought' from an 'is' has caused some to ask how their theory could be a *natural* law theory, if we cannot derive moral conclusions from the nature of things as they are.[19] Yet the subtle —and often misunderstood— means whereby the School is able to make both these affirmations is basic to their restatement of the natural law theory; and it opens up a significant challenge to those moral philosophers who believe that the naturalistic fallacy denies the possibility of moral realism. In the next stage of our introduction, we will see how our reasons for doing what we do, in fact correspond to our human nature.

Stage 2: Determining What Brings Fulfilment in a Human Life

Basic Human Goods

How do we discover the worthwhile or fulfilling object(ive)s that we offer as reasons for what we do? To avoid the naturalistic fallacy, the Grisez School formulates this question as an inquiry into our *reasons* rather than merely into our object(ive)s. The most straightforward way to discover these reasons is to ask ourselves 'Why do I do what I do?', and 'Why do other people do what they do?'[20] For example, I might ask 'What are you doing this evening?', to which you might reply, 'I am going out for dinner with my friends tonight'. I might push the issue by asking again, 'Why?' You might reply —knowing I was a philosopher because only philosophers ask such obvious questions— 'Because I haven't seen them for a while and it would good to catch up'. Again, I could ask, 'Why do you want catch up with them?', to which the response would doubtless come, 'Because I want to maintain my friendship with them'. Finally I would ask, again, 'Why?' And to this your reply is likely to be simply, 'Because I value my friendship with these people'. Here you are offering 'friendship' as a practical reason which explains and justifies what you are doing. Although such interrogation may feel conversationally contrived, it is nevertheless helpful to think back through such an instance of practical reasoning, because it reveals that the pursuit of friendship can be *a reason for acting* that requires no further reason to justify it.

We could ask the same sort of series of questions about all the activities we (and others) pursue in our daily lives. Finnis, Grisez, and Boyle suggest that, if we did so, we would arrive at a list of our 'most basic' or ultimate reasons for doing things. They call these ultimate reasons for acting 'basic human goods'. These are listed in Table 1.1 below.

Table I.1   The basic human goods

The General Categories of Basic Human Goods	Dimensions of Human Nature to Which these Goods Correspond
Substantive Goods (goods in which people can participate without deliberately pursuing them):	Human beings ...
1. 'life itself —its maintenance and transmission— health and safety';[21]	'as animate ... organic substances';[22]
2. 'knowledge and [a]esthetic experience';[23]	'as rational beings capable of knowing and experiencing reality';[24]
3. '[s]ome degree of excellence in work and play'.[25]	'as simultaneously rational and animal';[26]

Reflexive Goods (goods pursued through choice):

4. '[h]armony between and among individuals and groups of persons —living at peace with others, neighbourliness, friendship';[27] as 'agents through deliberation and choice'.[29]
5. harmony between the different dimensions within the self, including one's feelings, emotions, judgements and choices;[28]
6. Harmony between the dimensions within the self and a person's acts: 'harmony among one's judgements, choices, and performances —peace of conscience and consistency between one's self and its expression';[30]
7. '[h]armony with some more-than-human source of meaning and value'.[31]

The Grisez School argue that the reason everyone will arrive at this particular list and not some other, is that the different goods *correspond to* different dimensions of human nature. It is crucial to note that the concept here is 'correspondence to', not 'derivation from'.[32] For example, the good of harmony between our emotions and our choices corresponds to the fact that humans are beings that are capable of experiencing feelings, including emotions. This correspondence indicates that the foundations of moral reasoning are grounded in the reality of human nature, although the logical process for identifying these foundations has not involved deriving them from the facts about human nature to which they correspond. The nature of practical reasoning's 'grounding' in the reality of human nature is particularly apparent, if one considers the way in which the basic human goods would be different if human nature were different. For example, if humans were not, in fact, able to feel emotions —like Vulcans in *Star Trek* (!)— 'inner harmony' would never be a reason for justifying why do what we do.

The necessary connection between the basic goods and human nature provides the basis for the Grisez School's claim that a person's 'inclinations' (e.g., curiosity) and 'dispositions' (e.g., affection) provide important experiences or data for the task of determining what are the goods.[33] For example, when curiosity is prompting us to seek knowledge about something, reflection on that experience, whether to explain it to oneself or to others, is likely to lead us to recognise that the pursuit of knowledge *in itself* is the reason that explains what we are doing.[34]

The Nature of Basic Human Goods

Once we have determined the list of basic goods, we can enhance our understanding of their nature by considering the various features which they possess. Their first characteristic is that they are *pre-moral goods*.[35] Simply acting for one of these reasons does not make our behaviour moral.[36] In fact, because they offer a general explanation of why people do what they do, the goods will also explain what people are pursuing when they make immoral choices. For example, we might find that terrorists, in blowing up innocent civilians, were ultimately seeking justice as a means of establishing a secure foundation for harmony between people. They might reason that we cannot live peaceably or in harmony with our neighbours if there are serious, outstanding justice-claims between us; and that terrorism is the only (or most effective) way to obtain such justice. But merely because they act for *a* reason does not make their action morally right. More commonly, people often seek the good of harmony between feelings and choices when they choose some harmful course of action which gives vent to emotions like anger (e.g., by hitting someone), fulfils prejudicial feelings (e.g., by unreasonably discriminating against someone), or satisfies an emotional desire (e.g., by stealing something one covets).[37]

The second feature of these goods is that they are *incommensurable*.[38] By 'incommensurable' the Grisez School means that the goods themselves do not possess properties or qualities that enable a comparison to be made between them. Basic human goods are, in other words, distinct reasons for doing something. They are incommensurable in that each is an ultimate reason for acting. There are no reasons more basic than friendship or knowledge that we can use to compare their relative value. We are aware of this incommensurability in the tension we experience between two options that embody different goods; for example, between staying at home to seek knowledge by studying and going out to enjoy the company of friends. We need an external principle to judge which good to choose; we cannot make that judgement by considering the goods alone.

It is important to observe that the Grisez School insists, not only that different goods —like friendship and knowledge— are incommensurable, but that different *instances* of the same good are also incommensurable.[39] Consideration of friendship alone will not enable me to choose which of two friends I should see, if I want to see them both. I might be able to find a reason to choose, such as that one friend is only in town today while the other lives around the corner; but the very need to find a reason demonstrates that the value of friendship alone does not provide me with the basis for making my choice.

A third feature of basic human goods, which arises from the fact that they are incommensurable, is that they are *non-hierarchical*.[40] We cannot, in other words, order them in a *permanent* hierarchy. There will always be situations in which we could prefer one good to another. Often people will say, 'Well, surely life takes preference over the other goods'. Yet, when we acclaim those who suffer martyrdom for the sake of truth or justice, we recognise that there are times when life is not the highest good. After all, 'greater love has no one than to lay down her life for her friends'. 'All right', a sceptic might say, 'there are certain goods —perhaps life, knowledge, and friendship— which might not be capable of hierarchical arrangement. Yet surely these form a class of goods which will always take precedence over others like the excellence of skills in play or aesthetic experience'. In response, one can only observe that, if this were actually the case, no one should risk his or her life in sports such as mountain climbing, which people do just for the joy of the excellence of climbing; nor should war photographers risk their lives to get an aesthetically better photograph.

Fourthly, basic human goods are all *constituent elements of human fulfilment*.[41] In establishing the full range of possible justifications for a person's action, the basic human goods define the possibilities that a human being can pursue through choice. Human fulfilment comes as a person pursues those possibilities. We need to recognise that it is not some more fundamental category to which we can reduce the basic human goods. Rather, the basic human goods *taken together* define and constitute human fulfilment.

A fifth feature of basic human goods is that they are *always culturally embodied*. Although the Grisez School does not draw out this feature, it is clear from their analysis that to talk of goods is to discuss realities that always and only exist in the particularity of lives that are shaped by the community and culture in which they are embedded. This is an important feature to highlight, because claims for *a* set of goods can appear to express a questionable Enlightenment universalism, even of a cultural imperialism. In the case of the Grisez School, the combination of the diversity of goods, their incommensurability, and their non-hierarchical relationship provides both an explanation of cultural diversity and a strong basis for affirming its value. The non-hierarchical nature of the wide range of goods, made wider by the incommensurable forms that each good can take, means that one would expect communities to pursue the goods according to different rankings and in an indefinite number of forms. What is more, given that these diverse pursuits are incommensurable and distinctive expressions of the good, there is a strong case for the value of this diversity and the importance of preserving it. Because different cultures give particular expression to universal goods, it is possible to make a global claim for the importance of valuing the local, the contextual, and the particular. Significantly, this cultural diversity will also involve moral plurality. For example, differing selections about how, and in what order of priority the various goods should be pursued, mean that some societies have strong moral norms for the maintenance of community, while others have norms that promote individual autonomy. Although arising from different cultural priorities, both sets of norms have objective value. Therefore, contrary to many perceptions of natural law theory, this new account provides a basis for explaining and affirming moral diversity, rather than a target for it. Nonetheless, alongside its valuing of cultural diversity, the theory retains a capacity to provide a universal moral critique of extreme behaviour or cultural practices such as genocide, apartheid, or female circumcision.[42]

A sixth feature, which the Grisez School claims that basic human goods possess, is that they are *self-evident*.[43] This does not mean that everyone actually recognises the particular list of object(ive)s as goods; but rather that, once a person has understood what is meant by a good, in the light of the sort of reflection necessary to identify it, she will recognise it as a basic justificatory reason for action.[44] In answering the series of questions posed earlier about seeing friends, by saying that we see them simply because we value friendship and that we can give no more basic explanation, we thereby *recognise* friendship as a basic human good. This non-inferential exercise of reason, which is the skill of recognition or —in Finnis' terms, "grasping"[45]— is an often overlooked capacity of reason that is essential to the task of doing ethics. There is nothing particularly odd about it, because all forms of reasoning, including scientific reason, rely upon certain principles and categories that one simply recognises non-inferentially as self-evident —that is to say, concepts which, once one understands their content, one recognises to be true.[46] As Finnis points out, theoretical inquiry, whether in the science or the humanities, relies upon the principle that "forms of deductive inference, are to be used and adhered to in all one's thinking, even though no non-circular proof of their validity is possible (since any proof would employ them)".[47]

This use of the notion of self-evidence tends to be one of the major stumbling-blocks to the acceptance of the Grisez's School's natural law theory.

For it can seem implausible that one simply apprehends such a range of substantive claims about what is of value, rather than arriving at them through the analysis of evidence and argument. Some might even think that what is being offered is simply a sophisticated form of intuitionism. Central to the School's response to these concerns about self-evidence is their argument that, although we simply recognise the logical foundation of a train of practical reasoning in the set of basic human goods, it is still possible to produce evidence and argument to *support* the claims made about them.[48] Such support begins, as we have seen, by correlating the goods with the dimensions of the human person. Then it develops with the suggestion that a careful examination of the data of anthropological and empirical psychology, taken as a whole, indicates that the behaviours observed in different peoples and cultures express the diverse ways in which humans pursue a common set of goods.[49] What is more, the very possibility of anthropology as a science is dependent upon some, usually implicit, account of basic human goods; for without such an account it would be impossible to render explicable (in the sense of understanding the reason for) the behaviour of people in other societies and cultures. If no reason could be provided for why someone did what they did, then one would have to look to a psychiatric explanation for his behaviour.[50]

Along with presenting empirical evidence in support of their list of basic human goods, the Grisez School also provides other forms of argument for the inclusion or exclusion of various putative goods. The arguments, which we might usefully consider here, are those they employ against the two items most often claimed as omissions from their list: pleasure and freedom 'or autonomy'.

Why Pleasure is not a Basic Human Good

We need to be clear here about the sort of pleasure to which we are referring. There are satisfying and enjoyable (i.e., pleasurable) states of feeling that are integral to our participation in various of the basic human goods.[51] For example, being in the company of friends, which is participating in the good of friendship, often involves pleasurable feelings of affection. The achievement of a physical feat in sport, such as scoring a goal in football, brings the pleasurable feeling of elation. If we had the space, we could go on to detail a wide range of pleasurable feelings that are *integral* elements of the pursuit of those basic human goods.

The kind of pleasure such an analysis might leave as a distinct basic human good, is purely physical pleasure. This might arise from eating food simply for the resultant pleasurable sensation rather than for the satisfaction of hunger, some psychological need, or delight in the excellence of culinary skill. Central to the Grisez School's argument against purely physical pleasure being a basic good is the thought-experiment of Robert Nozick's 'experience machine'. Grisez states Nozick's experiment in the following terms:

> Suppose a device were invented which could create experiences somewhat like a motion picture, but communicated directly to the brain, so as to make the experience a total one in which the individual's awareness of being a spectator was eliminated. Suppose, further, that one could select a lifelong program on this device and consign oneself —or one's child or best friend— to this pleasurable and all absorbing existence. Would there be any point to doing so?[52]

The answer, Grisez and Finnis assert, is 'No, because the result would not really be the living of a life'.[53] What makes something we pursue worthwhile is that we have invested something of ourselves —our energy and our capabilities— in bringing it about. By making such a commitment, whether to develop real friendships, real skills, knowledge, or to become a more integrated person, these things become an enduring part of our lives. The seeking of pure experiences can be a reason for action; but it is not foundational because it is not consistent with the purpose of practical reasoning, which the basic goods reveal as the intelligent pursuit of genuine human fulfilment.

Why Freedom is not a Basic Human Good

A second common candidate for inclusion in the list of basic human goods is freedom, or more accurately, personal autonomy. In considering the Grisez School's response to this question, it is helpful to draw on the work of Robert George since he has provided its most substantive treatment of this question.[54] George begins by clearly defining personal autonomy as the capacity to exercise "effective freedom (from internal compulsions and neurotic impediments as well as from external constraints) to bring reason to bear in making self-constituting choices".[55] George develops his position in conversation with Joseph Raz's claim that autonomy is intrinsically valuable as "a constituent element of the good life" because it enables a person to be, at least in part, the author of her own life.[56] In making this argument, Raz nevertheless holds that when a person exercises her autonomy to do something harmful, she realises nothing of value. George agrees that this is a sound argument, because otherwise it would be necessary to affirm that there was something intrinsically good about profoundly wicked choices; but he argues that this conclusion also reveals that personal autonomy is not in itself intrinsically valuable.[57] George supports his position by arguing that autonomy is never an ultimate reason for doing something: a person will always choose it because it enables her to participate in some good(s).[58] One could, of course, desire autonomy to satisfy a non-rational force, such as an emotional desire simply to do what one pleases. However, an emotional desire to do something is not a reason *per se* to do anything. Of course, seeking harmony with one's emotions is a reason for acting —even for seeking autonomy— but it is the seeking of harmony within the self, and not the satisfaction of the emotion, that is the *ultimate* reason for acting.[59] Thus, from George's perspective, the value of autonomy arises from its capacity to contribute to the good life. On this account, autonomy would be of no positive value when its use was self-destructive or deliberately harmful to others.

Yet this recognition that autonomy is not a basic human good —i.e., it does not provide an ultimate reason for action— does not imply that it is unimportant or insignificant. On the contrary, as George concludes, personal autonomy is a requirement or condition for being practically reasonable because it enables us to deliberate and to choose. Put another way, autonomy is an integral part of the good of practical reasoning insofar as it contributes to the pursuit of human fulfilment.[60] Beyond its role in practical reason, autonomy is also instrumentally valuable for the pursuit of many forms of the other goods. Without it, for example, artists, poets, and writers would not be able to create works which freely express excellence in the skills of work and play that go into the production of art and its associated goods of aesthetic pleasure and knowledge.[61]

Stage 3: What Principles Should Guide the Pursuit of Human Fulfilment?

The First Principle of Morality[62]

Faced with such a broad horizon of possibilities for humanly fulfilling action, the question arises, 'Which worthwhile goals and objectives should we pursue and how should we pursue them?' Just as seeking to do a scientific experiment requires attention to the principles of scientific reason, so deliberating upon what to do requires us to attend to the principles of practical reasoning.

Fundamentally, the demand of practical reason, as with any other form of reasoning, is to be reasonable. '*Right reason*', as Grisez, Boyle, and Finnis observe, 'is nothing but *unfettered reason*'.[63] To explain the general nature of the demand of this particular form of reason, they consider its key organising principles. The principle that they see as most helpful for this task is the imperative, which they claim to be self-evident, that 'Good is to be done and pursued'.[64] They make several important observations about this first principle of practical reasonableness.[65]

To begin with, Grisez and his colleagues compare this first practical principle to the principle of non-contradiction which operates in every reasoning process. They observe that the principle of non-contradiction is not a basic premise of *any* train of reasoning, but rather operates as a methodological requirement in relation to *all* reasoning.[66] The principle that 'Good is to be done and pursued', they suggest, operates similarly in all practical reasoning.[67] This means that it operates in relation to all the basic human goods in all their forms. In other words, this first principle directs people towards the pursuit of friendship, knowledge, harmony between the different dimensions of the self, and so on.[68] The Grisez School observe that, given that this principle operates to direct people towards human fulfilment in all choices made by practical reason, it is possible to conclude that the point of practical knowledge is "the intelligent direction toward human fulfilment".[69] And although they do not really draw this out, it is this first principle which gives the School's theory its very positive orientation. For its operation with regard to the basic human goods ensures that the first requirement of practical reason is to seek that which is humanly fulfilling.

While the Grisez School holds that the first principle, with its integral directiveness towards the good, is 'self-evident', they also affirm that it is possible to provide theoretical support for it. Indeed, we were moved to inquire about the methodological principles of practical reason in the first place because we were presented with a horizon of worthwhile and desirable objects and objectives (basic human goods). Thus, the task of practical reason is to determine how we are to pursue these worthwhile object(ive)s which are also constituent elements of human fulfilment. It is this basic task which the first principle operates to sustain in all aspects of practical reasoning.

In discussing the emergence of the moral 'ought', however, the Grisez School focuses upon the *negative* function of the first principle: to avert pointlessness or, more specifically, to prevent deviation from the point of practical reasoning. At the same time, the School also recognises that the first principle *alone* will not prevent *all* pointlessness —and thus deviation from the point of practical reasoning— because a choice to pursue one aspect of human fulfilment could unnecessarily impede other dimension(s) of human fulfilment. For example, a person building a house —hereby pursuing the good of life at least— may do so in a needlessly inefficient way. If she had been more efficient, she could have pursued other humanly fulfilling activities and left more resources for others' use. Or a person might seek financial security —hereby pursuing, amongst others, the goods of life and of harmony between the different dimensions of the self (by overcoming feelings of insecurity)— but do so by mugging someone. In this case (presuming there was some other way in which the person could obtain the necessary resources for survival), such an action would unnecessarily harm the victim's human fulfilment.

The Grisez School also suggests that the general demand of practical reason to avoid pointlessness, which the first principle expresses, can be further specified to prevent *all* pointlessness in order to make *all* practical reasoning completely consistent with that general demand. This specification they formulate in the following terms:

> In voluntarily acting for human goods and avoiding what is opposed to them, one ought to choose and otherwise will those and only those possibilities whose willing is compatible with a will toward integral human fulfilment.[70]

It is at this stage in the Grisez School's account that the moral 'ought' emerges: implicit in this first principle of morality is the possibility of making choices that are not in accordance with it. Since this first principle articulates reason's requirement that a particular choice be made, it is making an ought-claim; because an 'ought', in this analysis, is a summary expression of the reason(s) why one course of action should be chosen in preference to some other course(s). Put simply, being moral is nothing less than being completely practically reasonable in the making of decisions about how to pursue human fulfilment.

The Basic Requirements of Practical Reasonableness

The first principle of morality is very general, and in order to actually make decisions, we clearly need to specify its particular requirements. Finnis and Grisez have both done this, although in different ways.[71] Both of them conceive of these requirements generally as the self-evident principles for being reasonable, given human nature and the conditions of human life. More specifically, Grisez conceives of them as the principles necessary to avoid the distortion of human decisions by feelings and emotions; and so they include, for example, that "One should not be deterred by *felt inertia* from acting for intelligible good",[72] and that "One should not, in response to *different feelings* toward different persons, willingly proceed with a preference for anyone unless the preference is required by intelligible goods themselves".[73]

While Grisez's account of the requirements of practical reasonableness focuses primarily upon the nature of humans as beings whose choices are shaped by both reason and feelings, Finnis' approach, which also takes account of human nature, looks more broadly to both the "conditions of human life"[74] and the nature of practical reasoning itself.[75]   So, for example, given that our experience reveals that the pursuit of fulfilling activities requires substantial amounts of time and personal energy, and that human life is limited in these regards, Finnis holds that it is a self-evident requirement of practical reason that a person should make some kind of life-plan to coordinate her time, energy, and commitments. As with the basic human goods, such principles are self-evident in the light of experience, but that experience is not formulated as the factual premises from which the principles are derived.

We can summarise as follows the conditions of human life, the dimensions of human nature, and the knowledge derived from practical reason, which are significant in Finnis' analysis:

1. any significant pursuit of worthwhile activities (or goals) in human life will often involve substantial amounts of time and energy and sometimes material resources;
2. human life is limited by finite time and personal energy;
3. human life is subject to changing circumstances, including the possibility of unpredictable and (highly) disruptive events;
4. the different worthwhile activities of human life are distinct and cannot be compared with one another (i.e., they are incommensurable);
5. integral human fulfilment is constituted by all the basic human goods;
6. the realising of many worthwhile goals in human life will require cooperation with other people;
7. material resources are limited;
8. each person is unique, including in his/her skills, capacities and circumstances;
9. all humans share the same essential nature; and human persons are multi-dimensional beings, having at least rational, emotional, existential (choice-making), inter-personal, and cultural dimensions; and
10. a person's feelings and emotions can be in harmony or conflict with his/her reasoning and choosing. [76]

For Finnis, these are the conditions of human life and dimensions of human nature which the requirements of practical reasoning "respond to".[77] He identifies these corresponding requirements of practical reason:

1. "have a harmonious set of orientations, purposes and commitments";
2. "do not leave out of account, or arbitrarily discount or exaggerate, any of the basic human goods";
3. "do not leave out of account, or arbitrarily discount or exaggerate, the goodness of other people's participation in human goods";
4. "do not attribute to any particular project the overriding and unconditional significance which only a basic human good and a general commitment can claim";
5. "pursue one's general commitments with creativity and do not abandon them lightly";
6. "do not waste your opportunities by using needlessly inefficient methods, and do not overlook the foreseeable bad consequences of your choices";
7. "do not choose directly against any basic human good";
8. "foster the common good of your communities";
9. "do not act contrary to your conscience, i.e., against your best judgement about the implications for your own action of these requirements of practical reasonableness and the moral principles they generate or justify"; and
10. "[d]o not choose apparent goods, knowing them to be only the simulations of real goods, even when simulation brings real emotions or experiences, real satisfactions".[78]

As Finnis points out, most of these principles, sometimes individually, sometimes in various combinations, have been emphasised by philosophers and theologians throughout history as constituting the essentials of morality.[79] This should come as no surprise because they all sought, in their different ways, to articulate what good reasoning itself requires in the face of "human wants and passions and the conditions of human life".[80]

One Should Never Choose Directly Against a Basic Human Good

Of the various principles outlined, the one worth making comment upon within the confines of this discussion, because of its significance in the making of difficult moral decisions, is the requirement that one should not choose directly against any basic human good. This principle responds to the fact that to act in such a way as to deliberately harm or impede human fulfilment would be to act against the very purpose of practical reasoning itself —to further human fulfilment.

It is important to be very clear about what is being claimed by this principle. The operative notion is the 'intentional choice' to harm some basic human good. This means that it is part of one's chosen proposal to achieve some purpose which harms a basic human good(s). In other words, if the good(s) were not harmed, the objective of the proposal would not have been achieved. For example, it would be wrong in a war to bomb a city with the proximate aim of killing its innocent civilians (thus intentionally harming the good of life), even if the ultimate aim of this proposal was the good one of pressuring the enemy government into coming to terms, and thereby shortening the war. The critical significance of this choice to kill the civilians becomes immediately evident, when we recognise that the proposal would fail if the civilians were out of town on the day of the bombing. On the other hand, if the proposal in bombing was to destroy a key military headquarters —located, unfortunately, in an industrial area— in order to weaken the aggressive forces and thereby achieve the good purpose of ending the war, the death of innocent civilians could be foreseen but need not be desired. For instance, these deaths would not be part of the proposal if it did not matter that the civilians were away from the locality of the headquarters at the time of the attack, perhaps because it occurred outside working hours. The requirement to be fair in relation to foreseen side-effects would mean that every attempt to launch the attack at such a time should be made.

At this point some people object, saying that this distinction appears all too fine. In a sense, it appears so only until we realise that we make such distinctions all the time. If I choose to become a lawyer to fight for justice, I necessarily forego the opportunity to prevent deaths by becoming a doctor. I certainly do not want such deaths to occur: it is not part of my proposal in becoming a lawyer that some people should die. It is, however, the inevitable side-effect of my choosing the worthwhile vocation of a lawyer and not a doctor. Similarly, when an ambulance crew arrives at an emergency scene where many people have severe injuries and the crew knows they cannot save them all, they do not desire the deaths of those they do not treat. So long as their choice of whom to save is not arbitrary —for example, it is not a choice to save those who are best dressed or who are of a particular ethnic origin— the crew do nothing wrong in not saving everybody. This may be tragic, but it is not immoral.

A more formal way of making this point is to say that you cannot intend, either as an end or as a means, to harm a basic human good; but you can *within the bounds of fairness* accept a harmful side-effect as a consequence of choosing a good end. This claim might appear similar to what is often called the principle of double-effect. As Grisez clearly explains, this principle claims that,

> One may perform an act having two effects, one good and the other bad, if four conditions are fulfilled simultaneously:
> 1. the act must not be wrong in itself, even apart from the consideration of the bad effect ...;
> 2. the agent's intention must be right ...;
> 3. the evil effect must not be the means to the good effect ...;
> 4. there must be a proportionately grave reason to justify the act ....[81]

Although such a formula might appear attractive, Grisez points out that it has three problems.[82] First, it provides no criteria for determining the limits and nature of an act. Do we define the abortionist's act, for example, by the final outcome (saving a mother's life), by the immediate result of the act (the death of a foetus), or by the immediate act itself (injecting a chemical abortifacient into a woman)? Secondly, it is unclear what counts as a means, in the same way that it is unclear what counts as an act. Finally, it is very unclear what is meant by a "proportionately grave reason". In the end, the principle of double-effect is a rather clumsy version of the intentionality analysis we have been discussing for determining the limits of responsibility.

The Development of Moral Norms

These general principles bring us to the question 'How do we formulate the more specific moral norms that guide our choices in particular kinds of situations?'[83] Such norms can be both positive ('you should') and negative ('you should not') and the process of framing each type, although interrelated, differs.

Positive norms arise from practical reason's essential quality of pointing people towards human fulfilment. Any generic proposal for action that directs a person towards participation in a basic good, which does not violate any of the requirements of practical reason (i.e., that does not deliberately thwart human fulfilment in some other way), can be formulated as a positive norm: 'You should play with your children', 'You should work', 'You should see your friends', 'You should watch films'. Frequently these norms will not be obligatory because one could rightly choose to follow another norm: if a person is following the norm to work, he will not also be able to play with his children.

The specification of these norms is likely to evolve in the light of experience. A parent whose time is being consumed by paid work might well realise that 'You should play with your children' needs further elaboration — 'regularly'. It is an important feature of the Grisez School's natural law theory that norms are capable of such evolution.[84] The development of this particular norm highlights the fact that a person's particular circumstances will often shape the operation of moral norms. For the parent working excessively, the prompting of the positive norm to play with his children becomes an imperative.

Obligatory positive norms —'Always tell the truth'— can also arise as the positive formulation of negative norms —'Never deliberately deceive anyone'. These *negative norms* emerge when a generic proposal for action does violate some requirement of practical reason; in other words, when such a proposal involves unreasonably thwarting human fulfilment. In the case of deliberate deception, in Grisez's analysis, such an act will necessarily involve a choice to impede the basic good of harmony between the different dimensions of the self by deliberately causing a conflict between one's outward expression and inward being.[85]

From Norms to Decisions

The final step in natural law theory occurs when we move from norms to the specific decision which a particular person has to make. It may be that we face a situation with limited options, where a clear norm is operative —'Do not deliberately deceive someone or do not break your promises'— and the decision we should make is clear. However, many choices will require further reflection in which we have to take into account our particular circumstances. Our response to the norm, 'You should choose a career', which specifies an aspect of the basic requirement of practical reason —'Have a harmonious set of orientations, purposes and commitments'— provides a good illustration of a choice that will require such deliberation. If we have strong existing commitments to the struggle for social justice, we might contemplate becoming a lawyer, a political activist, or an aid worker. If we are contemplating a commitment to raise a family, we should limit our choice of career paths to those compatible with fulfilling the norms that specify such a commitment. As we proceed with this deliberation, we are likely to face the common situation in which two or more good options present themselves to us and we have no reason to prefer one to another. In these cases, Grisez proposes that we seek "to determine how well possibilities otherwise judged good comport with the rest of one's individual personality".[86] This means that we need to discern which option best harmonises with all the other dimensions of our being. An important consideration here is likely to be our feelings. In such a situation, if we had clear feelings of preference for a particular choice —say, for being an aid worker instead of a lawyer— that would be a good reason for choosing that option, because it would further the basic human good of harmony between our different dimensions.

The Grisez School's Natural Law Theory and Virtue Ethics[87]

This affirmation of emotions and feelings in the natural law theory of the Grisez School provides a substantial point of contact with virtue ethics; for it is an important concern of key virtue theorists that emotions and feelings be given an appropriately positive place in moral theory. According to the Grisez School, all decisions, moral and immoral, involve feelings (which include emotions) as motives; and, as has just been observed, feelings will at times rightly guide decision-making. This account of the ethical role of feelings is integral to the Grisez School's conception of ethics as centrally about the formation of character; an understanding which, of course, also lies at the heart of virtue ethics. Tellingly, Grisez himself recognises the connection between his account of natural law and the ethics of a pre-eminent virtue theorist in his little-commented-upon observation that "Stanley Hauerwas [in] *Character and the Christian Life* ... provides an analysis of character very close to mine".[88]

At the heart of both Grisez's theory and Hauerwas' ethics lies the same reciprocal relationship between choice and character that Grisez describes succinctly in the following terms:

> Once the choice is made, a certain aspect of one's self is involved in the good one has chosen which is not involved in the alternative. One is as one has chosen to be. If the very same alternatives were to present themselves again —everything one judges good or bad being the same— one could have no reason for choosing otherwise. And so no new choice would be necessary. This is why previous choices provide fixed points of reference to resolve further situations without new choices ....[89]

Building upon this analysis, Grisez then articulates the same essential definition of virtues as Hauerwas:

> Virtues and vices are considered to be both the residue of one's previous acts and dispositions to engage in further acts similar in moral quality to those which gave rise to the dispositions.[90]

As with Hauerwas, Grisez concludes that character is the general disposition that arises from the individual dispositions summarised by the notions of virtue and vice.[91] For both writers, this summation will be more than the sum of the parts because there will be times when the particular combination of virtue and vice —

of honesty and cowardice for example— will produce a disposition described by neither quality.

Virtue theorists are not simply concerned that there be an adequate account of character. They also seek to persuade us that who a person is, plays a central role in shaping the decisions he or she makes.[92] While this is not the place for a lengthy discussion of that issue, we may usefully observe that Grisez's notion of 'vocation' in his theological rendering of this theory, suggests that who a person is, plays a central role in shaping their moral life.[93] This notion has its secular analogy in Finnis' requirement of practical reason that a person develop a 'life plan'. When we consider the important role ascribed to character by the Grisez School, we are bound to agree with Grisez that those who set natural law theory against theories of character are establishing a serious false dichotomy.[94]

Conclusion

In concluding with the importance for the Grisez School of the development of virtue, we are reminded that the core of the theory is a framework for reasoning that will assist people to live life —and to live it to the full— in community with one another. Despite its concern with human fulfilment, it is not a call to an egoistical or selfish life, for practical reason requires that we cooperate with one another for the common good. At times this requirement will have us choose against a narrow conception of self-interest, and sometimes it will require a very high degree of self-sacrifice —such as when reason demands that we refuse to cooperate with totalitarian acts. Ultimately, however, the new natural law theory assures us that ethics is about the enhancement of human life.

NOTES

1   Germain Grisez, Joseph Boyle, and John Finnis, "Practical Principles, Moral Truth, and Ultimate Ends", *American Journal of Jurisprudence*, 32 (1987), pp.99-151.
2   *CMP*, p.105.
3   Ibid.
4   Ibid., p.105-6.
5   Ibid., p.106.
6   Ibid.
7   Ibid.
8   Ibid.

9   Ibid., p.105.
10   *NLNR*, pp.36-42.
11   Joseph M. Boyle, "Aquinas and Prescriptive Ethics", *Proceedings of the American Catholic Philosophical Association*, 49 (1975), pp.82-95.
12   *FE*, p.2.
13   *PP*, p.115.
14   Ibid., pp.115-17.
15   Cf., Oliver O'Donovan, "John Finnis and Moral Absolutes", ch. 4 of this volume.
16   Grisez, *PP*, p.100. For Grisez's defence of free choice see Joseph M. Boyle, Germain Grisez and Olaf Tollefsen, *Free Choice: a Self-Referential Argument* (Notre Dame: University of Notre Dame Press, 1976); and in shortened, less rigorous form, *CMP*, pp.41-72.
17   This claim will be considered below.
18   *PP*, p.102.
19   For an account of these objections and a response to them see Robert George, "Human Nature and Natural Law", in *Natural Law Theory*, Robert George (ed.) (Oxford: Clarendon Press, 1992).
20   Ibid., pp.106-107.
21   *PP*, p.107.
22   Ibid.
23   Ibid.
24   Ibid.
25   Ibid.
26   Ibid.
27   Ibid., p.108.
28   Ibid.
29   Ibid., p.107.
30   Ibid., p.108.
31   Ibid.
32   Ibid., p.107.
33   Ibid., pp.108-9; *NLNR*, pp.60-2.
34   *NLNR*, pp.60-1.
35   *NLNR*, p.59.
36   *PP*, pp.123-5.
37   Ibid.
38   Ibid., p.110.
39   Ibid.
40   *NLNR*, pp.92-5; *PP*, pp.139-40.
41   *PP*, pp.114-5.
42   The notion of the culturally-embodied nature of basic human goods is explored more fully in Sabina Alkire and Rufus Black, "A Practical Reasoning Theory of Development Ethics: Furthering the Capabilities Approach", *Journal of International Development*, 9 (1997), pp.263-79.
43   The claim that the basic goods and the basic requirements of practical reason are self-evident is one of the most contentious features of the theory. In *Christian Moral Realism* (Oxford University Press, forthcoming), I argue that the truth value of these first principles can be established without an appeal to self-evidence (ss. 2.2, 2.3.3.3 and 2.4).

44   *NLNR*, pp.64-5.
45   Ibid., p.34.
46   Ibid., pp.68-9.
47   Ibid., p.68.
48   *PP*, pp.111-3.
49   *NLNR*, pp.83-5, 97-8. See also Sabina Alkire, "The Basic Dimensions of Human
        Flourishing", ch. 3 of this volume.
50   *PP*, p.113.
51   *NLNR*, pp.96-7.
52   *CMP*, p.121.
53   Ibid. and *NLNR*, pp.95-6.
54   Robert George, *Making Men Moral* (Oxford: Clarendon Press, 1993).
55   Ibid., p.177.
56   See, for example, Joseph Raz, *The Morality of Freedom* (Oxford: Clarendon Press,
        1986), p.408.
57   George, *Making Men Moral*, pp.175-6.
58   Ibid., pp.178-9.
59   Ibid.
60   Ibid., p.181.
61   Ibid., p.180.
62   This section is drawn from my *Christian Moral Realism*, s. 2.3.2.
63   *PP*, p.121.
64   Ibid., p.119.
65   It is important to note that the first principle is only first in the sense that it expresses the
        general orientation of practical reasonableness (ibid., p. 120).
66   Ibid.
67   Ibid., pp.119-120.
68   Ibid., p.120; *CMP*, pp.180-1.
69   *PP*, p.120.
70   Ibid., p.128.
71   *CMP*, pp.205-28; *NLNR*, pp.100-33.
72   *CMP*, p.205 (italics added).
73   Ibid., p.211 (italics added).
74   *NLNR*, p.101.
75   *FE*, pp.75-6.
76   For the discussion from which these elements are distilled see *NLNR*, pp.103-26.
77   *FE*, p.75.
78   The list is taken from Finnis' own summary (*FE*, pp.75-6) of the requirements
        which he articulates at length in *NLNR*, pp.103-26. It should be noted that (10) was
        not added until *FE*.
79   *NLNR*, p.102.
80   Ibid., p.101.
81   *CMP*, pp.307-8.
82   Ibid., p.308.
83   For Grisez's discussion of the process of norm formulation see *CMP*, pp.254-6.

84 An important discussion of the development of moral norms in the Grisez School's theory is found in O'Donovan, "John Finnis and Moral Absolutes", ch. 4 of this volume.

85 *LCL*, p.405.

86 Ibid., p.292.

87 The relationship between natural law theory and virtue ethics is developed at greater length in Black, *Realism*, Chapter 5.

88 *CMP*, p.71.

89 Ibid., pp.51-2; cf. Stanley Hauerwas, *Character and the Christian Life: a Study in Theological Ethics* (San Antonio: Trinity University Press, 1975), pp.112-5.

90 *CMP*, p.58; cf. Hauerwas, *Character*, p.71.

91 *CMP*, p.59; cf. Hauerwas, *Character*, pp.75-6.

92 See, for example, Stanley Hauerwas with David Burrell, "From System to Story: an Alternative Pattern for Rationality in Ethics" in Stanley Hauerwas, Richard Bondi and David B. Burrell, *Truthfulness and Tragedy* (Notre Dame and London: University of Notre Dame Press, 1977), p.17.

93 *CMP*, pp.637-44, 555-65. See also Germain Grisez, "Personal Vocation: a Key to Authentic Renewal of the Church", *Homiletic and Pastoral Review* 85 (April 1985), pp.10-20.

94 *CMP*, p.194.

Part I:

Philosophical Issues

1 Natural Law Revived:[1] Natural Law Theory and Contemporary Moral Philosophy

Timothy Chappell

Natural Law Theory as a Moral Theory: an Outline

Begin by reflecting on what motivates (or can motivate) any and every sort of human agent, at all times and in all places, in their actions. Such reflection reveals a definite variety (as opposed to an indefinite variety) of real basic intelligible goods or values, which are available to or attainable by all humans in all societies and cultures.[2] These basic goods are kinds of goods that we can intelligibly conceive any or every human agent as acting *towards* or *for the sake of*, in and of themselves, and with no further objective beyond those goods in mind.[3] Examples of such intelligible[4] goods include: life itself, knowledge and aesthetic experience, friendship, and peace with God or 'religion'.[5]

The basic goods are known to be *goods* simply because they are objects of pursuit. They are known to be *basic* simply because they, unlike other possible objects of pursuit, are objects of pursuit in themselves. No deductive argument can show that the basic goods are either goods or basic —precisely because of their basicity. One cannot appeal to any deeper reason why someone might want to participate in some basic good: the basic goods themselves provide the deepest reasons that there are for wanting anything. On the other hand, one can show that there would be something deeply irrational about rejecting a basic good or goods. To do so is a kind of incoherence. In another formulation, the basic goods are *self-evident —per se nota*.[6]

Different basic goods suggest different possibilities for humans, and make different demands on them. So we need a way of understanding how to relate our living and our choices to these goods, and in particular to the occasions on which their demands conflict or seem to conflict, by pulling us in different directions at once. This way is to be specified by *practical reasonableness*.

Practical reasonableness, as grasped by humans, is both itself a form of basic good, and so one of the ultimate reasons for acting. But it is also the ability to interrelate or 'integrate' the other basic goods in a morally adequate way.[7] Its requirements can be summed up in one very simple principle, "the first principle of practical reasoning". This is St. Thomas's formula —another self-evident truth[8]— "that good is to be done and pursued, and evil to be avoided".[9]

The central question of ethics, properly so called, is then the problem which practical reasonableness is meant to solve: the problem, namely, of how the basic goods, "the principles that express the general ends of human life", are to be "brought to bear upon definite ranges of project, disposition, or action", or instances of these,[10] in a way which leads towards "integral human fulfilment".[11]

Reflection on this problem suggests a number of further amplifications or specifications of the first principle of practical reasoning or of morality.[12] These further amplifications form "the basic requirements of practical reasonableness", or "the modes of responsibility which specify the first principle [that is, of morality]".[13]

These specifications include such things as the following norms: no arbitrary preferences between persons or goods;[14] reasonable resistance both to the pushing and the pulling of inappropriate emotions, and to the lack of such impulsions where they are appropriate;[15] and a preference for solidarity and community rather than individualism.[16]

The most important further specification is this thesis: that individuals have three possible attitudes towards any good —they may (i) *pursue* it or (ii) *honour* it (without actually pursuing it), or (iii) *violate* it. Of these three attitudes, actions chosen under attitudes (i) and (ii) are (other things being equal) permitted; but those chosen under attitude (iii) are absolutely forbidden.[17]

Given these goods and these norms, it is possible to begin the work of *casuistry* —of applying one's moral philosophy to particular problems and cases.

Here is a very brief and simplified, but still (I hope) accurate, summary of what the natural law theory expounded by Grisez, Finnis, Boyle and their associates ('the Grisez School') comes to, when it is considered as a theory of ethics.[18] How might contemporary moral philosophers of other allegiances respond? What might they learn from the Grisez School? And what might the School learn from them?

These questions are real and pressing ones, partly because of the disappointing lack of overlap which is still evident between the agendas of the Grisez School and what I shall call 'mainstream' contemporary moral philosophy in the analytical tradition. That mainstream includes, and discusses the works of, consequentialists and contractarians, Humeans and Kantians, neo-intuitionists and Aristotelians, virtue ethicists and Nietzscheans.[19] But, despite the remarkable flourishing of the School in the last few years, mainstream ethics[20] still does not usually involve it in its discussions. Nor conversely does the Grisez School always draw on or contribute to the mainstream's discussions as profitably as it might.[21]

To set up, or widen the range of, useful communication between the two sides, this chapter will consider some of the objections to the Grisez School's theory which will naturally seem pressing to anyone who works within that mainstream. Such objections are likely to include questions about its relationship to the Aristotelian and Thomist tradition(s), and in particular to that tradition's allegedly discredited teleological biology; about the School's understanding of objectivity; about their conceptions of nature (is theirs a *naturalistic* ethical theory, like Cicero's or the Stoics'?) and of reason (or is theirs a *rationalistic* ethical theory, like Kant's?); and about its attitude to the (alleged) gap between 'facts' and 'values'.

It is possible to answer (or suggest answers to) these questions by exploring the natural law theory of the Grisez School under three main headings. First I shall offer two brief criticisms of its conception of reason. Then I shall review its account of the basic goods (which I believe amounts to a conception of nature). This will lead me, at the end of the paper, to suggest an amendment to its account of the distinction between facts and values.

The tone of my comments here will, inevitably, be a critical one. That critical tone should not be thought to betray a lack of sympathy or engagement with the project. On the contrary: it is because I find the Grisez School's project so appealing that I think it is necessary to subject it to a particularly close scrutiny. It is not every day that someone achieves what they have achieved: that is, to propose a whole new genus of moral theory. Just as it stands, at the point to which it has by now progressed, their theory is a remarkable philosophical achievement. The purpose of my criticisms is not to knock it down, but to facilitate further progress.

Is the First Principle of Practical Reasonableness Self-Evident?

The Grisez School claims that its "first principle of practical reasonableness" is "self-evident". Yet famously (or notoriously), they reach some highly controversial ethical conclusions —apparently just by developing and applying that notion. In particular, they conclude that there are some absolute moral prohibitions on certain sorts of action-type. The key to their prohibition of, for example, killing one person to save seven other people from being killed, lies in its insistence on what Grisez calls the seventh and eighth modes of responsibility:

> One should not be moved by hostility to freely accept or choose the destruction, damaging, or impeding of any intelligible human good.... One should not be moved by a stronger desire for one instance of an intelligible good to act for it by choosing to destroy, damage or impede some other instance of an intelligible good.[22]

These modes of responsibility are supposed to be no more than 'specifications' of the first principle of morality. And that is supposed to be closely logically related to the 'self-evident' first principle of practical reasonableness.[23] What is going on here? How can we be moving so easily from 'self-evident' first principles, to claims about what must never be done that are, to put it mildly, far from self-evident?

One worry which is raised by this apparently over-easy progress is the cynical one that the modes of responsibility have simply been generated *ad hoc* to give certain conclusions in applied ethics —so that it is hardly surprising if they do. Another worry is that, in fact, not even this much adhockery will suffice to give the Grisez School the conclusions it wants about, for example, moral absolutism —unless we have a clear and unequivocal understanding of precisely what is meant by the notion of "destroying, damaging or impeding" "an instance of an intelligible good". But this understanding is far from easy to obtain.[24]

Moreover, even the first principle of practical reasonableness —let alone the other principles to which it supposedly leads us— does not seem self-evident. St.Thomas's formula tells us (T) "that good is to be done and pursued, and evil to be avoided". We are instructed by the Grisez School to view this as a claim the truth of which is to be known just by understanding the terms of the claim. But there are other claims of similar format which might equally be thought to have a claim to self-evidence, if (T) has. For example, these: (U) good is to be done and pursued; (V) evil is to be avoided; (W) good is to be pursued.

Now (U), (V) and (W), taken separately, are not consistent with (T).[25] (U) does not prohibit an agent from pursuing good by evil means — as (T) does. (V) does not prohibit an agent from doing nothing —as T does. (W) does not prohibit an agent from doing *nothing but* evil, provided all he does is done (in some more or less nebulous sense) *in pursuit of* good —as (T) does. Therefore (U-W) are, logically, real alternatives to (T). So (T) is not self-evident, if by that it is meant that anyone is bound to accept (T) as soon as they understand it. After all, it is in effect true that plenty of people do not accept (T), but accept (U) —or, even worse, (W)— instead. That is what it means to be a consequentialist.

It follows that, to rebut consequentialism, we do not merely need to be able to argue for (something like) Grisez's seventh and eighth modes of responsibility. We need to be able to argue for the "first principle of practical reasonableness" on which they are founded. I do not suggest that this cannot be done.[26] But I do submit that the Grisez School —inclined as they are to miss the real and crucial content of St.Thomas's practical formula— have not yet done it.

Sensible Goods, Intelligible Goods, and Pain

Leaving reason aside, I turn to nature, as this notion occurs in the Grisez School's theory; that is, I turn to their account of the basic goods. Why should we think that there are any basic goods? And even if there are, why should we accept the School's account of which are the basic goods? How might one account of the basic goods be justified against another? What is the role of claims about objectivity in a theory of the basic goods? And what is the role of claims about self-evidence and incoherence?

The notion of a 'basic good' —something which puts an end to chains of explanation of human actions by being pursued in its own right, and not for the sake of anything beyond it— is of course an old one, going back at least to Plato's early dialogues.[27] Famous uses of the notion have also been made by Aristotle, Hume and Mill:

> Suppose that, in our actions, there is some objective which we want for its own sake, while everything else we want only because of that objective; and suppose that it is false that everything is chosen for the sake of something else. (For if that were true, then X would be wanted only for the sake of Y, and Y only for the sake of Z, and Z for the sake of something else again –we would face an infinite regress, and our wishes would be empty and vain.) On these conditions it is clear that the good and the best will be that objective which is chosen in its own right. [Aristotle][28]

It appears evident that the ultimate ends of human actions can never, in any case, be accounted for by *reason*, but recommend themselves entirely to the sentiments and affections of mankind, without any dependence on the intellectual faculties. Ask a man *why he uses exercise;* he will answer, *because he desires to keep his health.* If you then enquire, *why he desires health,* he will readily reply, *because sickness is painful.* If you push your enquiries farther, and desire a reason *why he hates pain,* it is impossible he can ever give you any. This is an ultimate end, and is never referred to any other object. [Hume][29]

The theory of life on which this theory of morality is grounded [states that] pleasure, and freedom from pain, are the only things desirable as ends; and that all desirable things (which are as numerous in the utilitarian as in any other scheme) are desirable either for the pleasure inherent in themselves, or as means to the promotion of pleasure and the prevention of pain. [Mill][30]

There is then some philosophical consensus about the idea that, on pain of infinite regress, *some* good(s) must be basic goods. What is more problematic is to say which. The difficulties involved in this should be sufficiently indicated by the very different uses to which Aristotle, Hume, and Mill put the notion of a basic good in our three quotations.

Aristotle apparently[31] wants to show that there is only one basic good —*eudaimonia* as he calls it— by reference to which all explanations of motivation must terminate if we are to avoid the threatened regress, and render our ethics rational. Mill too thinks that there is only one basic good, by reference to which the rationality of ethics is defined. But his basic good is pleasure (in some sense), which Aristotle specifically denies is the same thing as *eudaimonia.*[32] Moreover, Mill never *argues* that pleasure is the basic good, either by threatening a regress or by any other means. He only *asserts* that it is so; indeed he actually says that it is impossible to argue for the basic goodness of pleasure.[33] Compare Hume, who would agree with Aristotle and Mill that arrival at a reference to some basic object of desire is arrival at a terminus of reasoning. But for two reasons this fact does not, in his view, imply anything very interesting about the necessary shape of moral theory. First, it is unclear whether, in Hume's view, there can be any serious moral theory at all. Second, he thinks that it is purely a contingent matter that human desires have the objects they happen to have.[34]

These three other accounts of the basic goods are, then, very different from each other. The Grisez School's account of the basic goods can be assessed by contrasting it with them. The first contrast which I shall note is this: like Aristotle, and unlike Mill and Hume, the Grisez School rejects any sort of hedonism. For them pleasure is not only not the good (as it is for Mill); it is not a basic good, or basic object of desire, at all (as it is for Hume). As they would put it, (physical)[35] pleasure is not an 'intelligible good', but merely a 'sensible good'; and sensible goods are not basic goods.

The Grisez School's rejection of hedonism seems like a good move. It is now generally accepted, even by utilitarians, that the thesis that all motivation to act ultimately depends on the pleasure anticipated from one's action is clearly false, and a source of gross distortions in moral psychology —both because of its hedonism and because of its monism. That Mill himself felt some discomfort about this —originally Benthamite[36]— thesis seems clear from his hasty insistence, in the quotation above, that "desirable things ... are as numerous in the utilitarian as in any other scheme".[37]

However, to go from that claim to the claim that pleasure is not a basic good at all is a further and more controversial step. To facilitate this move, the Grisez School introduces (as we have seen) a distinction among the goods that motivate, between sensible goods and intelligible goods. The theory then claims that pleasure is not an "intelligible good", and therefore not a basic good (though it is, apparently, a "basic motive"[38]). This claim does not mean, as it might appear to, that the motivation of actions done solely in pursuit of pleasure is not fully explicable. (If it did, there would be a severe problem for the School's account of the explicability of wrong actions.) Rather it means that (physical) pleasure does not necessarily contribute to "integral human fulfilment"[39] as (say) health and the absence of depression do: "pain does not have the character of a privation, and so it is not intelligibly bad".[40] But these moves not only take the Grisez School several crucial steps away from (what seemed to be) the original, simple vision[41] of correlating *everything* that is actually desired in its own right with *everything* that is basically good, and several steps in what seems to be the unhelpful direction of Cartesian dualism.[42] They also introduce profound complications and difficulties into the School's thought.

In particular it is, apparently, claimed that merely sensible evils cannot deprive us of integral human fulfilment. Thus Grisez is happy to remark that "pain is no less beneficial to the organism than pleasure".[43] As a matter of physiology, this remark is just wrong, since pain (unlike pleasure) can in itself be a cause of physical trauma and even, in severe cases, of death.[44] Quite apart from that, it is surely true that pain of any considerable intensity, while it lasts, deprives humans of any chance of integral human fulfilment. (If not, why else would it be the case —as it presumably is— that there couldn't be toothache in heaven?) Consider, then, Grisez's comments on the matter:

> If one confuses sensible and intelligible sources of motivation and takes pleasure and pain to be basic principles of human action, one's conception of action will be distorted. There is an intelligible aspect under which one can choose pleasure and

seek to avoid pain, namely, the lessening of tension or increase in harmony among various parts of oneself. [But] emphasis upon pleasure and pain tends to focus concern upon oneself and to distract attention from the larger possibility of finding one's fulfilment by participation in community, ultimately the heavenly fellowship.[45]

First, Grisez begs the question here: no one who "takes pleasure and pain to be basic principles of human action" is guilty of *confusing* "sensible and intelligible sources of motivation" unless those types of motivation are genuinely distinct —which is what we are waiting to see proved.[46]

Second, the above passage follows up the claim that taking pain and pleasure to be intrinsically motivating distorts one's conception of action, with a point about pain making one self-centred —as if the latter proved or established the former. But it does nothing of the kind. Self-centredness is a distortion *of character*: a distortion in "one's conception of action" would have to be a distortion of one's *theory of action*.

Third, it is hardly plausible to think that "the lessening of tension or increase in harmony among various parts of oneself" is the *only* "intelligible aspect under which one can choose pleasure and seek to avoid pain". Presumably the Grisez School would deploy something like this claim to answer my toothache question above; but it seems awkward to take such an indirect route when a direct one is available. I might choose pleasure by stepping into a coffee shop, breathing deeply of the aroma of coffee, and immediately stepping out again. It seems a bit much to be obliged to say that this action of mine is either unintelligible or else aimed at lessening my internal tension and increasing my psychic harmony. Why might it not simply be understood as *chosen because pleasant*?

Fourth, it may be true that "pain tends to focus concern upon oneself": but it is still absurd to blame someone with raging toothache for not being able to think about anything except his pain.[47] It is equally absurd to suppose that there would be something wrong, "distorted", or self-centred about his wish to be free of the pain unless he wished to be free of the pain *for some further reason*, such as "so as to have greater internal harmony" or "for the sake of participating in community". It is not, as Grisez seems to think, that there is something self-centred about being prepared to attend to pain. On the contrary, the impossibility of attending to anything *else* during severe pain is —partly— what makes pain such a bad thing.

So we can and do seek freedom from pain as a good in and of itself, and pain can be a real source of "privations" (if I understand this murky term aright) of "integral human fulfilment". On the Grisez School's own principles, these two points ought to show that (some) basic good is located in the area of pleasure and freedom from pain. The School's account of this distinction between sensible and intelligible goods is quite unsatisfactory as it stands, and has a dismaying tendency to lead it both into embarrassing epicycles, and also into a rather callously breezy asceticism.

Could the distinction between sensible and intelligible goods just be abandoned? That might have the consequence that there was a moral absolute concerning pleasure and pain (perhaps, for example, a prohibition against torture). But that consequence is a welcome one. Unless there is something intelligibly wrong with pain in its own right, it seems that the Grisez School will be obliged to say that all that is *directly* morally wrong with cruelty or torture, is that it is an offence against justice or sociability. That, however, only captures part of the badness of cruelty, which surely has something directly to do with the pain involved. I conclude that the contortions about pain and pleasure which the Grisez School is forced into by its distinction between sensible and intelligible goods are simply an unnecessary blemish on their theory, and that that distinction ought therefore to be given up, along with the related, and equally distorting, distinction between 'emotional' and 'rational' motivation. [48]

Listing the Basic Goods

I turn to a second point of contrast between the Grisez School's and others' accounts of the basic goods. As is already clear, the School are like Hume, and unlike Aristotle or Mill, in positing a plurality of different basic objects of desire or goods. And as already commented, this seems a good move. It does just seem wrong to think that there is or could be any *one* objective which sane human beings are *always* pursuing, whatever they do — whether that single objective is supposed to be pleasure, utility, *eudaimonia*, or anything else.

Which are the basic goods? Finnis lists the following seven: life, knowledge, play, aesthetic experience, sociability, practical reasonableness, religion. In *Christian Moral Principles*, Grisez lists these seven:[49] self-integration; practical reasonableness; justice and friendship; religion or holiness; life and health; knowledge and aesthetic appreciation; and activities of skilful work and of play, "which in their very performance enrich those who do them". [50]

A similar sevenfold list to this last occurs, in reverse order, in "Practical Principles";[51] the main difference here is that "practical reasonableness" seems to have been replaced by a reference to "peace of conscience and consistency between one's self and its expression", which is intended to play the same general role in the theory as practical reasonableness (and "authenticity"[52]) did in earlier formulations.

I have already noted and criticised one way in which goods are discriminated by the Grisez School —as "sensible" or "intelligible". A second discrimination is also made, between properly basic goods and merely instrumental goods, which are good only insofar as they help you to achieve the basic goods.[53] A third distinction occurs in "Practical Principles" (and something similar is suggested in other writings). This is between the "reflexive" intelligible goods —those of which it is true that "the instantiations of these goods include the choices by which one acts for them"[54]— and the "substantive" goods —those of which this is not true. The substantive goods correspond closely to humans' nature as a particular kind of mortal animal. The reflexive goods reflect a different aspect of being human: that it involves rational agency "through deliberation and choice".[55] In "Practical Principles", the substantive intelligible goods are life, knowledge and aesthetic experience, and excellence in work and play; the remaining four intelligible goods are reflexive. (This should make it clear how one might apply the substantive-reflexive distinction to the other lists of goods.)

Now one might scent something suspiciously schematic in the notion that there are exactly seven basic goods —just as there are seven virtues and gifts of the Spirit in Aquinas, and seven churches and a sevenfold Spirit in the Book of Revelation, and indeed seven rings for the dwarves in *The Lord of the Rings*. Finnis remarks that "there is no magic in the number seven".[56] For all that, it keeps cropping up —or has done until *Living a Christian Life* appeared. This does not operate a sevenfold scheme of basic goods, since Grisez now claims that there is an eighth basic good, that of *marriage*.[57]

But this suggestion, I fear, does not improve the theory of the basic goods. In fact so long as one keeps in view what the role of a basic good was originally supposed to be according to the Grisez School, the suggestion must seem extraordinarily unpromising. It is plausible to claim that there is no more explaining an action once one has explained that it is aimed at achieving the good of, say, friendship or knowledge. By contrast, the suggestion that *marriage* is an intrinsically intelligible end of action in anything like the same way seems quite hopeless. We do not complete any action-explanation by saying that the action to be explained is aimed *at marriage*. It is perfectly intelligible to go on and ask why marriage is a good thing, in a way that it is arguably not intelligible to go on and ask why friendship or knowledge are good things. Moreover, what makes marriage a good thing is nothing separate from its instantiation of other basic goods, such as, say, friendship, self-integration, play, aesthetic good (given a partner attractive either in body or in *epitêdeumata*, or in both), physical health and well-being —and even, dare one say it, *physical pleasure*.

Indeed, Grisez himself as good as admits that marriage is a good because it instantiates other basic goods when he writes that "marriage is a special kind of open ended community".[58] But to admit this is, surely, just to admit that marriage is *not* a basic good, but a case of the basic good of sociability.

If Grisez still insisted, despite this, that marriage is a basic good in its own right, that would still raise the questions of why it has not been universally found among human societies; and which of the very different *conceptions* of marriage found among those societies that have recognised it, is *the* "basic good of marriage". Is the Bedouin conception of marriage, or the Trobriand Islanders', the one that represents the basic good? Was Solomon partaking of the basic good of marriage when he took his seven-hundredth wife?

The Objectivity of the Basic Goods

I have been testing out the Grisez School's account of the basic goods in the obvious way: by asking whether everything in its list of basic goods is *necessary* —whether that list includes anything that is not in fact a basic good (for example, perhaps, marriage); and by asking whether the list as a whole (or something like it) is *sufficient* —whether there are genuine basic goods which that list does not include (for example, perhaps, pleasure).

However, a crucial difficulty with this test which I have not yet attended to is simply this: What sort of a test is it? By that I do not just mean, 'What questions does it involve?'; for we know that. It involves asking which of the objectives of action that humans pursue are intelligible in their own right, and why. Any such objective —if it can stand up to further "examination and sifting",[59] and provided it is not merely a sensible or an instrumental good— will turn out to be an intelligible basic good, or some aspect of such a basic good. What I mean by asking what sort of a test this is, is rather the following question: *'From what standpoint* is the test to be applied?'. More specifically: 'Whose motivations are we examining? And who are the 'we' to whom some of these motivations are intelligible in their own right, while others are not?'.

To take a well-known example of Donald Davidson's: "If you tell me you are easing the jib because you think that will stop the main from backing, I don't need to be told that you want to stop the main from backing".[60] Here the explanation of why the speaker is 'easing the jib' (whatever easing the jib may be) is completed very quickly indeed. Anyone who shares the context of the explanation, that of sailing, will find it fully intelligible without any further addition. So why not say that 'stopping the main from backing' (whatever that is) is a basic good?

A second example: one mafioso asks a second, 'Why did you kill Fingers Marciano?', to which the reply is 'Because I have a vendetta against the Marcianos'. Once again, anyone who shares the context of these gangsters will find this a fully intelligible reply, with no need for any further addition. So why not say that vendetta is a basic good?

And a third: I ask you 'Why did you buy that ticket?' You reply 'To win the lottery —it's a lottery ticket'. Once again, I find this fully intelligible in and of itself. So why not say that winning the lottery is a basic good?

How are the Grisez School to prevent the —presumably absurd— conclusions that such familiar exchanges as these three give us complete explanations of action, and that each refers us back to some basic intelligible good? They might try suggesting that the goods mentioned in the last three paragraphs are merely instrumental, or else merely aspects of other, more broadly defined and more basic goods. But both moves face difficulties. The 'merely-an-aspect' move faces the general, and very difficult, question of 'How much generality is enough?'. The 'instrumental-goods' move faces the objection that, although it is true that people *often* use monies they win on the lottery as instruments for furthering a basic aim such as their friendships, it is also nonetheless true that they sometimes use their friendships as instruments for furthering a basic aim such as winning the lottery.

Still, the Grisez School may suggest that one can reasonably ask why vendetta, or winning the lottery, or easing the jib, should be thought to furnish an agent with an intelligible good in and of itself. It makes sense to ask 'But why do you want to fulfil your vendettas?', even if that is not a normal question for a gangster to ask. That is to say: the explanation which refers us back to the notion of vendetta is complete *in the context*, but that does not mean it is complete *tout court*.

But now we need to know what my phrase 'complete *tout court*' means. The answer to this question cannot be what a follower of Mill might suggest: that an action-explanation is complete *tout court* if and only if it is intelligible to every human (or every human who is sane and over a certain mental age). For action-explanations referring back to vendetta satisfy that requirement. Anyone who is sane and over a certain mental age can be taught about the concept of vendetta, and taught that in Sicily and elsewhere vendetta is counted as a reason for (often pretty drastic) action. Apparently one needs to know nothing more than this —in particular, one does not need to *accept* the concept of vendetta— to find the gangster's action in killing Fingers Marciano completely intelligible.[61] But that, surely, cannot be enough to make vendetta a basic good.

A second possible answer, prompted by Hume's remarks, would be that an action-explanation is complete *tout court* if and only if it is impossible intelligibly to carry that explanation any further. This suggestion faces the problem that, on this issue, the Grisez School seems to stand in the same relation to monistic theories of the good, as 'anarchistic pluralist' explanations —terminating in concepts like vendetta— stand in relation to it. The School denies that anarchistic pluralist action-explanations are complete, because we can intelligibly carry them on by showing that such objectives as vendetta are only desirable because they instantiate (or fail to instantiate) certain sorts of more basic good. But *pari passu*, monistic theories of the good like utilitarianism deny that explanations of the sort offered by the Grisez School are complete, because we can intelligibly carry them on by showing that such objectives as friendship or knowledge are only desirable because they instantiate (or fail to instantiate) the *single* sort of most basic good of all —utility, pleasure, *eudaimonia*, or whatever.

A substantive account is still needed of what makes references to 'friendship' or 'knowledge' (etc.) more intelligible as a sort of completion of action-explanation than either of the other two suggested sorts of completion. As we have already seen, the Grisez School deals quite well with the challenge from the side of monism about the good. But then monism was never an especially plausible one anyway. On the other side —the side of anarchistic pluralism— it is still less clear how we are to be sure that we have not reached a basic good when we arrive at a reference to, for example, vendetta.

So here is a third possible answer to the question of what makes an action-explanation complete *tout court*. This is suggested by Finnis's "rather confident assertions" about "all human societies", and about the "universality of those basic value judgements that are manifested not only in various moral requirements and restrictions but also in the many forms of human culture, institutions, and initiative".[62] The answer runs like this: an action-explanation is complete *tout court* if and only if it refers us back to motivations which are intelligible to *humans just as such*; that is, intelligible to humans considered simply as humans, and apart from any particular historical or social context which they might occupy.

Clearly this suggestion has its problems too. Since we evidently never do meet, and never can hope to meet, humans 'just as such' in this sense, it is far from clear what is going to be intelligible (or, for that matter, self-evident) to them,[63] and what is not, and why. It might be said that, in the explanation of actions, context is everything; but what the Grisez School offers is precisely an abstraction from any particular context. The danger is, then, that the notion of humans 'just as such' will turn out to be at best an ideal construct;[64] and at worst a way of begging the question, or a metaphysical mummy to go on the shelf in the Museum of Ethics, in the bay next to Kant's transcendental conception of the person.[65]

In any case, there is another instructive question we should ask about Finnis's "rather confident assertions" about all human societies. The question is 'So what?', and it brings out a third point of contrast between the Grisez School's account of the basic goods and the others which we have been considering.

Finnis evidently thinks it important to instance similarities between all human societies. But we should ask why it is important. Suppose it is true, as it no doubt is, that "all human societies show a concern for the value of human life", or of truth, or of friendship: what does that prove? And why would it matter if such claims were shown to be false? (Compare a claim that in all human societies, the word for 'great-uncle' contains three syllables. What does that prove? And what does it matter if the claim is false, as it presumably is?)

What Finnis's "rather confident assertions" are meant to prove, I think, is that generalisations about all human societies can get us some way towards an account of what humans 'just as such' take to be basic goods. And this suggests why Finnis needs some such claims to be true: because he is moving from generalisations across actual human societies, to generalisations which are supposed to be essentially true of humans. To put it another way, he is moving from the normal, the universal-but-contingent, to the normative, the universal-and-so-necessary.

Like Mill's and Aristotle's accounts, and unlike Hume's, the Grisez School's is an account of the basic goods, and not merely of the basic objects of desire. The School must (and does)[66] claim that the basic objects of human desire are in some sense naturally or necessarily objects of desire. For if it were true, as Hume thought, that it was purely a contingent matter what humans typically desired, then —as Hume also thought— there would be no particular ethical significance in finding out what humans do in fact typically desire, any more than there would be in finding out how many syllables there are in the words which humans do in fact typically use for 'great-uncle'.

The obvious question to ask here is of course: 'But can the Grisez School make this sort of move without fallaciously moving from an Is to an Ought?'. I think that they are themselves in some doubt about that question. On this matter Finnis's assertions are a good deal less confident, and he is more inclined to insist, sometimes by appeal to Aquinas' authority, that ethics should begin, not from 'nature', but from 'reason'.[67] However, I believe that the answer to the question should be 'Yes'. The School's (tentative and intermittent) appeals to what is natural, seen as a way of getting from the normal to the normative, need involve no fallacious moves. But —I shall now suggest— to be sure of avoiding fallacious moves at this point, they need to make an addition to their theory.

We may put the point like this: One of the most attractive prospects which the Grisez School open up is the possibility of a *via media* between Kant and Hume on practical and moral reasoning. On one side, we have Kant's top-down anti-naturalism. Kant's "pure practical rationality" alone provides reasons for action which can be counted as moral reasons. In the genesis of moral motivation and action, natural reasons ("inclinations") can have no part to play whatever. On the other side, we have Hume's bottom-up naturalism. Hume's faculty of reason, considered alone, is "entirely inert": so the only possible source of motivations for any action, moral or otherwise, is "the sentiments and affections of mankind, without any dependence on the intellectual faculties" —whatever those "sentiments and affections" may actually happen to be.

Now the Grisez School might comment that Hume and Kant are arguing to opposite conclusions *ex eodem medio*. Both assume without argument that the direction of our natural inclinations, as they actually are, must be a motley rabble, arbitrary, contingent, and undirected. From this assumption, Hume concludes that ethics itself must be arbitrary and contingent; whereas Kant concludes that, since ethics *cannot* be either arbitrary nor contingent, it cannot be founded on our natural inclinations.

But the Grisez School rejects the shared assumption. It claims, and tries to illustrate the claim in detail, that our natural inclinations are neither arbitrary nor contingent. Therefore, it says, they can furnish us with some foundations for ethics —namely, an account of the basic goods, of the goods which are recognised as goods by humans 'just as such'. Consequently, the School wants to conclude, ethics need not be limited either to Kantian apriorism or to Humean scepticism. In a fully developed Grisez-style theory, both reason and nature can be given their due: neither need be rejected, subordinated to some schematism, or pressed into a distorted parody of the other's role; for both have a part to play. The *is* of nature and the *ought* of ethics are different, but there are ways of getting from one to the other. In particular, the *is to be* of (sub- or pre-moral) practical reason has a crucial intermediary role.

This is indeed an enticing prospect. But the point of my 'So what?' argument above was precisely to raise the question of whether the Grisez School can realise that prospect, given their present resources. The crucial difficulty, as I have already pointed out, is to get from the normal, the universal-but-contingent, to the normative, the universal-and-so-necessary. Unless we can provide an account of that transition, it is not clear why claims about what humans typically desire or don't desire should matter for ethics.

Without such an account, the School faces an unpleasant dilemma. On the one hand, they may choose to accommodate naturalistic data. But, as argued above, on its present resources their theory can only do this by moving directly from nature —an account of human desires as they happen to be— to the foundations of practical reasoning —an account of human desires as they necessarily and naturally are (cp. Finnis's "rather confident assertions"). At the moment, this move looks very much like some form or other of the fallacy of confusing the descriptive and the evaluative. On the other hand, they may choose a wholesale rejection of the data about actual human desires which Humean naturalism takes as read, and retreat into quasi-Kantian rationalism (a retreat which, in practice, is all too frequently evident).

How is the Grisez School to avoid this dilemma? The answer, I believe, is that they should grasp the first horn of the dilemma, by providing an account of how we may validly (or, better, intelligibly) get from the normal to the normative. As their theory stands, it recognises distinctions between the moral and the practical, and the practical and the natural: between *ought*, *is to be*, and *is*:

> The moral *ought* cannot be reduced to the *is to be* of practical truth without eliminating the distinction between the directiveness of a practical judgement that something immoral is to be done and the normativity of the moral truth that it ought not to be done. The *is to be* of practical truth cannot be reduced to the *is* of human nature without eliminating the distinction between, on the one hand, action and fulfilment through it, and on the other, what persons are by nature, prior to their exercise of free choice. [68]

We want the account of "the *is to be* of practical truth" to be intelligibly grounded in "the *is* of nature". And we want to avert the danger that the Grisez School's appeals to nature turn out to be either merely fallacious, or else merely irrelevant. (Here I am disagreeing with Finnis: appeals to nature, I suggest, should *not* be merely "a speculative appendage, added by way of metaphysical reflection", to an otherwise rationalistic ethics.) If we are to achieve these ends, then besides the distinctions and transitions which the theory recognises between *is*, *is to be*, and *ought*, there is a further distinction and transition which the theory should also recognise. This is the distinction and transition between the natural in the sense of the normal and the natural in the sense of the normative: as one might also put it, between the *is* of descriptive biology and the *should be*[69] of teleological biology.

The key notion which mediates this transition is the notion of an *essential function* or *tendency*. For any biological kind of thing X, 'X's essential function(s) and tendency (or tendencies)' means: what X characteristically does or is just in virtue of being an X. For example, the essential function of a spermatozoon is to fuse with an ovum to create a zygote. That, as we say, is what a spermatozoon is *for*. As we also say, anyone who fails to understand this, does not understand what a spermatozoon is.

Consequently, to say that some particular Y is an example of some kind of thing licenses certain inferences; in particular, this one: from 'Y *is* a (healthy) spermatozoon in favourable circumstances' we are entitled to infer that 'Y *should be* attempting to fuse with an ovum to create a zygote'. This is a valid inference from (descriptive biology's) categorical *is*, via the notion of an essential function, to (teleological biology's) defeasible *should be*. Or again, this one: from 'Y is a heavy object close to the earth, with nothing supporting it' we are entitled to infer that 'Y *should be* falling towards the centre of the earth'. This is a valid inference from (descriptive science's) categorical *is*, via the notion of an essential tendency, to (teleological science's) defeasible *should be*.

This sort of transition from descriptive to teleological claims is a pervasive feature of scientific discourse, and indeed of causal and scientific explanation in general. Notice three points about such transitions from *is* to *should be*.

First, the possibility of executing such transitions is in general an ineliminable part of scientific understanding. As I put it above, to be ignorant of what a spermatozoon is for, is to be ignorant of what a spermatozoon is. Similarly, to be ignorant of what heavy objects tend to do (that is, fall towards the strongest available gravitational centre), is to be ignorant of what heaviness is. Despite the long tradition in post-Renaissance natural science[70] of (usually rather vague) denunciations of 'Aristotelian teleological science', it remains true that there is not the slightest possibility that a science which does any explaining at all could be anything but teleological in (at least) the sense just outlined.

Second, claims about the essential functions or tendencies of things are empirically based, but they are not statistically reducible to empirical data collected in the past. The claim that the essential function of a spermatozoon is to fuse with an ovum to create a zygote obviously does not mean that that is what all or most spermatozoa do. For only a tiny minority of spermatozoa manage to fulfil their essential function. Likewise, the claim that 'unsupported heavy objects fall towards the strongest available gravitational centre' is based on experience, but it is not based on experiment. Claims about essential functions or tendencies are not then statistical.

Third, claims about essential functions and tendencies are not, as they might appear to be, reducible to expectations about the future either. On the contrary, they are the ground for (reasonable) expectations. 'The kettle is very light, so it should be easy to lift' is not simply equivalent to 'The kettle is very light, so I expect it to be easy to lift'. The former offers (the beginnings of) an explanation of what makes the latter's expectation a reasonable one.

I hope I have now done enough to suggest that there can, in general, be a defensible account of transitions from the natural-as-normal to the natural-as-normative. So what is the application of this point to the Grisez School's theory?

The answer is that it puts us in a position to ask whether there are any functions or tendencies which are *essential to humans*. If there are, then we will be entitled to make some inferences about humans of the same form as those made above about spermatozoa and heavy objects. For certain fillings of F, a categorical claim in descriptive anthropology of the form 'X is a human' will entail a defeasible claim in teleological anthropology of the form 'X should be (that is, will have a tendency or disposition to be) F'. What is more: if the functions or tendencies essential to humans include dispositions towards certain sorts of things as basic objects of desire, then it will be clear what it means to say that there are basic goods in the sense in which the Grisez School means that claim. For from 'X is a human', what will follow will be 'X should be (that is, will have a tendency or disposition to be) concerned about the value of life'.

If any normative claims of this sort are true about humans, notice three points about such claims. First, such claims will be a crucial part of our understanding (including our scientific understanding) of humans, and of what it is to be humans. Yet, second, such claims are neither merely statistical nor merely predictive claims. They go rather deeper than that. For, third, they pick out the most salient facts or characteristics of humans. That is, they pick out what we must, *pace* Hume, see as important or essential about human beings if we are to understand humans just as such (in what is now quite a precise sense of 'humans just as such'). But salience in this sort of description is not to be understood as a function of salience in any lower-order description, for instance of the sort that a head-count or opinion poll, or any other sort of mechanical repetition of a simple experimental test, might provide. 'Humans should be (that is, will have a tendency or disposition to be) concerned about the value of life' can still be true even in the unpleasant case where, actually, most humans are not concerned about the value of life.

The *should be* of teleological science is then both essentially distinct from and essentially related to the *is* of descriptive science. It has been my claim that scientific explanation, indeed most sorts of explanation, cannot get along without both description and teleology. *Should be* is also essentially distinct from the *is to be* of practical truth, and the *ought to be* of moral truth.[71] On the other hand, *should be* is essentially related to *is to be*, just as *is to be* is essentially related to *ought to be*. For *is to be* is given prior to *ought to be*, and provides the 'substrate matter' out of which that new sort of judgement is formed, by synoptic integration across all the diverse sorts of direction that practical truth may give.[72] Just likewise, the teleological *should be* is given prior to *is to be*, and provides the 'substrate matter' out of which that new sort of judgement is formed, by synoptic integration across all the diverse sorts of direction that teleological truth might give. (To put it another way, there is something that "persons are by nature, prior to their exercise of free choice". Necessarily, human nature equips us with certain desires and not others; but until our free choice is exercised, none of human nature's desires will be voluntarily pursued.) Finally, the same sort of relationship of actuality to substrate can also be discerned between the teleological *should be* and the descriptive *is*. For as already explained, salience in a teleological account is not to be understood as a function of salience in any lower-order, descriptive, account; even though it is true that that teleological account is based, empirically, on the descriptive account, it is not reducible to that account. Something like this structure, I suggest, is what we need to answer the 'So what?' question raised above, and put the theory of the Grisez School on a firmer basis by showing how the appeals to nature that it tentatively makes —and ought to make with much greater confidence— can be fully justified as earning the fundamental place in ethical theory that the School should give them.

Summary and Conclusions

After outlining the Grisez School's ethical theory (as I understand it), and suggesting a problem or two about its conception of reason, this essay has argued against the distinction between intelligible and sensible motivations which they are currently disposed to make, but which I think represents a false turning. I have criticised them on one score directly related to this, the question of the place of *pleasure* in the theory of human motivation, and one rather different score, namely Grisez's rather odd claim that marriage is a basic good. Then I have pointed to a fundamental difficulty facing the School about the idea of ascribing any desires for basic goods to 'humans as such'. The last few pages have argued, in effect, that the School could solve this problem, and (into the bargain) could achieve a much smoother account of the essential distinctions and relations between what it calls 'the theoretical' and 'the practical', if it rejected the common but mistaken modern view that any theoretical account, for example a scientific one, is purely descriptive and entirely lacking in evaluative qualities. I have suggested that it could usefully put to work the very weak and loose sense of evaluation which is involved in teleological accounts of the sort I have described. The proposal is that the recognition of what I have been calling the possibility of valid moves from the natural-as-normal to the natural-as-normative would enable the Grisez School to fill in a blank area between the theoretical and the practical that it is currently rather inclined to shy away from, but about which it might easily have something to say that would prove to be interesting, worthwhile, and theoretically fruitful for the future development of what is already an impressively rich and comprehensive moral theory.[73]

NOTES

1   "Natural law could not rise, decline, be revived, or stage 'eternal returns'..." (Finnis, *NLNR*, p.24). But, as Finnis notes, "discourse about natural law" could —and has.

2   Cp. Grisez, *PP*, pp.106-7.

3   *PP*, p.103; *NLNR*, ch. IV; Grisez, *CMP*, ch. 5.

4   Intelligible goods and bads are distinct from sensible goods and bads (the obvious pair of the latter being pleasure and pain): *CMP*, ch. 5B; *PP*, p.112.

5   *PP*, pp.107-8; different lists may be found in *NLNR*, ch. IV and *CMP*, ch. 5D.

6   *PP*, pp.106-9; *CMP*, ch. 7, Appendix.1; *NLNR*, ch. III.

7   *NLNR*, pp.101-2: "Reasonableness both is a basic aspect of human well-being and concerns one's participation in all the (other) basic aspects of human well-being".

8   *CMP*, ch. 7C, p.179.

9   "*Bonum agendum et persequendum, et malum vitandum*": St.Thomas Aquinas, *Summa Theologiae* (Madrid: Bibliotéca de Autores Christianos, 1951), IaIIae, q.94, a.2.

10   *NLNR*, p.101; cp. p.59. *CMP*, ch. 7E, p.183: "The principles of practical reasoning ... do not tell us what is morally good. Rather, they generate the field of possibilities in which choices are necessary.... Evidently, then, there is a need for moral norms which will guide choices toward overall fulfilment in terms of human goods".

11   Grisez's phrase: *CMP*, ch. 7F. Cp. *NLNR*, p.96: in "participating in [the basic values] in the way one chooses to, one hopes ... for 'happiness' in the deeper, less usual sense of that phrase in which it signifies, roughly, a fullness of life, a certain development as a person, a meaningfulness of one's existence".

12   Plainly distinct in *CMP*, ch. 7D-E; less so in *NLNR*, ch. V.

13   *NLNR*, ch. V; *CMP*, ch 8.

14   *NLNR*, ch. V.3-4; Grisez's fifth and eighth modes of responsibility, *CMP*, ch. 8E, H.
15   *NLNR*, ch. V.5. Rational resistance to unreasonable emotion is, evidently, implicit in every one of Grisez's modes of responsibility: *CMP*, ch. 8.
16   *NLNR*, ch. V.8; Grisez's second mode, *CMP*, ch. 8B.
17   *NLNR*, ch. V.5 ("detachment and commitment"), V.6 ("the (limited) relevance of consequences: efficiency, within reason"), and V.7 ("respect for every basic value in every act"); Grisez's seventh and eighth modes, *CMP*, ch. 8G and H.
18   I consider 'natural law' as a theory of ethics. In a connected sense, but one which does not concern me here, the phrase also names a theory of law.
19   Some crude pigeonholing may help to clarify, by examples, what I mean by the mainstream. Consequentialism: Shelly Kagan, *The Limits of Morality* (Oxford: Clarendon, 1989); Derek Parfit, *Reasons and Persons* (Oxford: Clarendon, 1987); and James Griffin, *Well-Being* (Oxford: Clarendon, 1986). Contractarianism: John Rawls, *A Theory of Justice* (Oxford: OUP, 1971); and David Gauthier, *Morals by Agreement* (Oxford: Clarendon, 1986). Humeanism: Annette Baier, "Moral Sentiments and the Difference they Make", *Proceedings of the Aristotelian Society*, Supplement, LXIX (1995); and Simon Blackburn, *Essays in Quasi-Realism* (Oxford: OUP 1993). Kantianism: Onora O'Neill, *Constructions of Reason* (Cambridge: CUP 1989); and Thomas Nagel, *Mortal Questions* (Oxford: OUP 1984). Neo-intuitionism: Jonathan Dancy, *Moral Reasons* (Oxford: Blackwell, 1991). Aristotelianism: Sarah Broadie, *Ethics with Aristotle* (Oxford: OUP 1991). Aristotelian neo-intuitionism: John McDowell, "Virtue and Reason", *Monist*, 62 (1979). Virtue ethics: Philippa Foot, *Virtues and Vices* (Oxford: Blackwell, 1978); Alasdair MacIntyre, *After Virtue* (London: Duckworth, 1991); and Michael Slote, *From Morality to Virtue* (Oxford: OUP 1992). Nietzsche's influence (even if only as an irritant) is pervasive, and especially clear in the work of Foot (as cited), and of Bernard Williams, particularly *Ethics and the Limits of Philosophy* (London: Penguin, 1985).
20   Again, a different situation obtains in contemporary analytical philosophy of law (where Finnis' work in particular has had a notable impact), just as it does in contemporary moral theology.
21   Here I should declare myself as a writer sympathetic to the Grisez School, who has himself consciously tried to bridge the gap in question: see Timothy Chappell, *Understanding Human Goods* (Edinburgh: Edinburgh UP, 1998). Another is Hayden Ramsay, *Beyond Virtue: Integrity and Morality* (London: Macmillan, 1997).
22   *CMP*, ch. 8G and H.
23   See, for example, *PP*, p.121: "*Right reason* is nothing but *unfettered reason*" –a phrase which implies that anyone who sees clearly will see the truth of the Grisez School's theory.
24   As I know from my own efforts to clarify that notion: see Chappell, *Understanding Human Goods*.
25   *Pace PP*, p.115, where (U) simply replaces (T)!
26   In fact I have tried to do it: Chappell, *Understanding Human Goods*, ch.3.
27   See Plato, Euthydemus 278e-282c (ed. W. Lamb, Loeb Classical Library [London: Heinemann, 1962]), for an argument eliminating all proposed basic goods except wisdom.
28   Aristotle, *Nicomachean Ethics*, Bk.I, ch.ii, 1094a19 ff. (my own translation).
29   David Hume, *Enquiry concerning the Principles of Morals* [1777], ed. L.A.Selby-Bigge (Oxford: Clarendon, 1988), Appendix.1.
30   John Stuart Mill, *Utilitarianism*, ed. M.Warnock (London: Fontana, 1962), ch.2.

31   The Grisez School has consistently taken Aristotle to be a monist about value (*PP*, p.101); but in fact, the texts do not show this uncontroversially. Despite *Nicomachean Ethics*, I.ii (ed. Bywater, Oxford Classical Text [Oxford: Oxford UP, 1890]) it seems possible to interpret Aristotle's theory as being, like the Grisez School's, a sophisticated value pluralism: see Chappell, *Understanding Human Goods*, ch.1.1. In which case, the relation between Aristotle's *eudaimonia* and the different sorts of more particular good that he recognises may be, not so much like that between Mill's "desirable things" and the pleasure which makes them desirable, as like that between the different goods recognised by the Grisez School, and their concept of "integral human fulfilment".

32   See Aristotle, *Nicomachean Ethics*, X.2.

33   See Mill, *Utilitarianism*, ch.4.

34   Hume would have agreed with Thomas Hobbes' sweeping denials in *Leviathan* (ed. E.Curley [Indianapolis: Hackett, 1994], I.6.7, 11.1) that there are any necessary objects of desire: "Whatsoever is the object of any man's appetite or desire, that it is which he for his part calleth good.... There is no such *finis ultimus* (utmost aim) nor *summum bonum* (greatest good) as is spoken of in the books of the old moral philosophers".

35   The qualification is necessary because of the extreme ambiguity of 'pleasure' (and 'pain'). I can describe many things as pleasures (or pains), which involve no particular physical sensation at all —for example, reading Aristotle (or Derrida), or going to a wedding (or a funeral). These experiences count as pleasures or pains in a very broad sense, which can perfectly well include the experience of other sorts of basic goods described by the Grisez School. The same is not inherently true of physical pain and pleasure.

36   See Jeremy Bentham, *Introduction to the Principles of Morals and Legislation* (ed. M.Warnock [London: Fontana, 1962]), ch.I.1: "Nature has placed mankind under the governance of two sovereign masters, *pain* and *pleasure*. It is for them *alone* to point out what we ought to do, as well as to determine what we shall do".

37   Nowadays it is commonly denied by his admirers that Mill so much as held the hedonist-monist thesis: a conclusion apparently deduced from the premiss that great philosophers don't hold obviously false views. This premiss appears to be false, and is certainly question-begging.

38   *PP*, pp.111-2.

39   "Integral human fulfilment" means the envisaged ideal state of human life by reference to which the Grisez School assesses practical actions as morally good or bad.

40   *CMP*, p.120.

41   Of course, it is true that Grisez says (*CMP*, p.124) that "the results of this sort of inquiry cannot be accepted uncritically. The raw data must be examined and sifted". But one needs *principles* for selection between the data, if that examining and sifting is itself not to be a rather uncritical process. In the case of pleasure, it seems that the Grisez School are bypassing their own principles.

42   *Pace* the disclaimer at *PP*, p.100.

43   *CMP*, p.120.

44   See *The Concise Medical Family Handbook* (London: Harper-Collins, 1981), s.v. 'Pain'.

45   *CMP*, p.121.

46   Cp. *PP*, p.137: "Any basic good is an aspect of the fulfilment of the person as such, and so is superior to sensible goods, each of which as sensible can fulfil only the

sentient nature of a person". *Only* the sentient nature? What more is there to a 'person as such' besides sentience? ("Intelligence" cannot be the answer —unless we already accept that this is something quite difference from "sentience"; an idea which seems to fly in the face of normal English usage.)

47   And anyway, preoccupation with *my pain* is distinct from preoccupation with *myself*.

48   *PP*, p.104.

49   *CMP*, ch. 5D.

50   *NLNR*, pp.86-9.

51   *PP*, pp.103-4.

52   Ibid., p.140.

53   Ibid., p.113.

54   Ibid., p.107.

55   Ibid.

56   *NLNR*, p.92.

57   Grisez, *LCL*, pp.555-69, esp. p.568.

58   Ibid., p.569.

59   *CMP*, p.124.

60   Donald Davidson, *Essays on Actions and Events* (Oxford: Clarendon, 1984), p.6. Davidson makes a different point with this example.

61   Cp. the remarks on comparative anthropology in *PP*, p.113: "Accepting the list of basic goods as first principles of action explains how the anthropological enterprise is possible, whereas claiming that all human values are culturally conditioned renders the enterprise inexplicable". The argument here seems to be (i) that an anthropologist A cannot understand some other society S's practice P unless A shares with S some broad conception of what the point(s) of P might be; but (ii) there can be no such shared conception of pointfulness without some conception of basic goods which is shared between A and S; *therefore* (iii) there is *one* conception of the basic goods shared by any anthropologist and *any* society. The truth of (ii) is contestable, as my Mafiosi example shows; the move from (ii) to (iii) is a specimen of the quantifier-shift fallacy.

62   *NLNR*, pp.83-4.

63   I pay little attention in this discussion to another suggestion that is made by the Grisez School (it appears, for example, in my opening summary of their theory): that the basic goods are self-evident goods. This is for a simple reason, which my discussion has to cover anyway: that self-evidence is always self-evidence *to someone*. Consequently one cannot escape the problems about context by this route. If "G is a self-evident good" means, roughly, that "G is understood to be a good as soon as 'G' is understood", the relevant question is "Understood *by whom*?". Perhaps Sicilian toddlers 'understand' vendetta to be a good as soon as they understand 'vendetta'.

64   Cp. *PP*, p.113: "Accepting the list of basic goods is supported by the data; rejecting it is at odds with the data". Which data? The data of "empirical psychology and philosophical anthropology" —except, that is, for "Freudian psychology, structuralist anthropology, behaviourism, and dualistic philosophies of the person". But how much data does that leave?

65   Cp. Williams, *Ethics and the Limits of Philosophy*, pp.55 ff.

66   *PP*, p.107: "The diversity of the basic goods is neither a mere contingent fact about human psychology nor an accident of history".

67   For example *NLNR*, p.36: "For Aquinas, the way to discover what is morally right (virtue) and wrong (vice) is to ask, not what is in accordance with human nature, but what is reasonable. And this quest will eventually bring one back to the *underived* first principles of practical reasonableness, principles which make no reference at all to human nature, but only to human good. [Question: How does Finnis suppose we can know what human *good* is, without knowing anything about human *nature*?] From end to end of his ethical discourses, the primary categories for Aquinas are the 'good' and the 'reasonable': the 'natural' is, from the point of view of his ethics, a speculative appendage added by way of metaphysical reflection, *not* a counter with which to advance either to or from the practical *prima principia per se nota*".

68   *PP*, p.127.

69   This sort of *should be* is not a near-synonym of (the moral) *ought to be*. The sense of *should be* I have in mind is best shown by examples like: "He is a carpenter, so he *should be* good with his hands".

70   It is, incidentally, mere prejudice to think that post-Renaissance natural science is the only natural science there is. See, for example, Norman Kretzmann, Anthony Kenny, and Jan Pinborg (eds.), *The Cambridge History of Later Mediaeval Philosophy* (Cambridge: CUP, 1982), ch. VII.

71   This can be stated schematically by pointing out that, in the Grisez School, the truth-conditions of moral, practical, teleological, and theoretical claims may all be given differently (see *PP*, p.115 ff.). Moral truths, according to the Grisez School, are "adequated" to their anticipated realisation in "integral human fulfilment"; practical truths are adequated to the anticipated "realisation of that which is possible through acting in conformity with" such practical truths; and theoretical truths are adequated to "prior reality, actual and possible". Teleological truths are adequated in none of these ways; their truth conditions are rather to be found in the actual or possible realisations of what is possible given actually existing essences, including the human essence.

72   Cp. *PP*, p.126.

73   I am grateful to Nigel Biggar and Rufus Black for their comments on this paper, and to Hayden Ramsay and Christopher Martin for useful discussion of some of the issues it raises. As readers of my *Understanding Human Goods* will see, there is some overlap between it (pp.37-45, 53-57) and the present essay. There are also connections with T.D.J. Chappell, "Why is faith a virtue?", *Religious Studies*, 32 (1996), pp.27-36. Those interested in textual history might like to know that, despite its later appearance, an earlier draft of the present essay is in fact the *Urtext* for the other two.

2 Grisez and Thomism

Ralph McInerny

Germain Grisez has emerged as one of the most important Catholic moralists of our time. He began as a philosopher but along the way retooled himself as a theologian. In his magisterial work in progress, *The Way of the Lord Jesus*,[1] he is engaged in an effort which can be fittingly compared with the moral part of the *Summa theologiae* of Thomas Aquinas. In producing his work, Grisez has been exhibiting the concept of commitment he analyses within it. His influence has been both broad and deep —not to say high. It is often said, sometimes with pride, sometimes with resentment, that his work lurks as a kind of *eminence Grisez* behind certain magisterial pronouncements. He long ago accepted the role of the paladin of the Magisterium, taking on its critics whenever the opportunity presented itself.

It is because the Magisterium continues to recommend Thomas Aquinas as our mentor in philosophy and theology that Grisez often invokes Thomas in the course of developing his moral theology. Volume One of his *chef d'oeuvre*, contains an appendix of some six dense, triple-columned pages recording the references to Thomas —less than half the number devoted to scriptural references, but three times the number of pages recording references to Vatican II. It would be quite wrong, however, to imagine that Grisez is undertaking yet another rethinking of the thought of Aquinas. His is, and is meant to be, an original work. What then is the relationship between Grisez's moral thought and that of Thomas Aquinas?

This question could be addressed in a number of ways. One might review what others have written on the matter, some finding Grisez wanting in thomisticity, others defending him on that score. Or one might independently enumerate all the points on which Grisez is clearly of one mind with Thomas, others where he consciously departs from him, and the grey areas where it is unclear whether a teaching is recognized as the one or the other. I have eschewed both of these approaches here. If there is one thing on which Grisez and Thomas are emphatically at one it is in their insistence on the importance of starting-points, of principles. Principles are important, of course, because they affect everything that follows from them.

53

Now, if there were differences, important differences, in the way Grisez and Thomas understand the starting-points of ethics, clearly this would be more significant than other differences along the way.

Grisez makes it clear that he is not engaged in rewriting traditional moral theology. He is a particularly severe critic of "scholastic natural-law theory", and while he exempts Thomas from some specific criticisms, his dissatisfaction with what he considers the inadequacies of Thomas is not hidden. On the matter of starting-points, it is not always clear whether Grisez considers what he is offering as a version of what Thomas taught, as an improvement on it, or as a replacement of it. Nonetheless, that there are differences between the two men at this liminal level would be clear to anyone comparing them. What may not be clear is the depth of the differences. It has long been my suspicion that the differences between the two men are radical here. This paper attempts to explain why.

The differences in question concern the understanding of the meaning of 'good' and the account given of the first principle of practical reasoning. That the differences are deep becomes clear when one considers the innovation on which Grisez prides himself, the so-called "modes of responsibility". The fact that he does not find such a doctrine in Thomas is a sign of their divergence. Perhaps I should point out that I have written on both Grisez *et sequaces eius* before, but the major points of this article are not a repetition of those earlier misgivings.[2] While my own preference, when the doctrines of Grisez diverge from those of Thomas, will perhaps be clear, my main purpose here is to establish the profound differences between the two men on the nature of the good and the starting-point of practical reasoning, not to argue on behalf of the one or the other. And, once more,   I concentrate on threshold differences since these affect everything that follows.[3]

The Ultimate End of Human Action

It is notorious that Thomas, like Aristotle, sees in the overarching end of human action the starting-point for moral reflection. The moral part of the *Summa* devotes five questions to the treatment of man's ultimate end. Thomas then discusses aspects of voluntariness and goes on to an analysis of the various will-acts —and cognitive acts— that enter into a complete human action. Grisez, in *Christian Moral Principles*, having defined moral theology, discusses choice, then conscience, refutes some rivals and then, in

Chapter 5, begins his discussion of the "goods which fulfill persons". I will first say some things about Thomas' treatment of ultimate end, that is, the human good, and then contrast what he says with Grisez's doctrine on goods and bads.

What Thomas Taught

When the moral reflection that issues in moral philosophy begins, action has of course already been going on. To engage in such reflection is itself a human act. The moralist thus has a vast field before him (in every sense): the countless deeds performed, being performed, but also about to be performed by innumerable human beings, himself included. How on earth can he gain any purchase on so extensive a field of study? Even if he sought to confine himself to his own actions, the matter would seem to be unmanageably manifold. The search for moral principles first asks what all of those actions commonly exhibit, what is true of all of them.

The analogy that Thomas draws is from natural philosophy. Indeed, it is from the outset of the *Physics* that he takes the methodological principle that governs all his own work.[4] It is the nature of the human mind to begin with a first universal grasp of singulars, expressing a formality they all share. Progress amounts to learning more and more specific characterizations of things. Thus, the natural philosopher first asks the most comprehensive questions about things that have come to be as the result of a change (*ta physika*). What is it they all have in common despite their bewilderingly many differences? Aristotle shows us in a magnificent example of philosophical analysis that any such thing must be a compound of subject and property, of matter and form. The great difference between surface and substantial changes of such entities is broached; that they are in place and measured by time, and so on. These things are the least that can be said about physical objects. They are true of all of them despite their further differences.

This same procedure, Thomas observes, is to be found in the practical order.[5] We must first seek truths common to all human acts. The most obvious thing about ourselves and other human beings is that we are doing things. What has been said of physical objects is true of us, so far as it goes, and so is what has been said of living substances. Indeed, in *On the Soul*, Aristotle has said quite a number of things about the specific kind of living substance we are. But that is not the angle of the moralist. The subject matter of moral doctrine is human action, the deeds men do.

How to begin? At the beginning, with what they all have in common. What characterizes a human act is that it is undertaken for some end.

Responsible acts are those to which the question 'Why are you doing that?', can be directed; we are answerable for them. Such acts are in our power and proceed from cognitive awareness and will —the mind sets an end which is willingly pursued. Activities which can truly be ascribed to a human agent but which do not proceed from him in this way —e.g. digesting, balding, tripping— may be called 'acts of a man' but not 'human acts'. Human acts are voluntary, a term meant to cover both the will-act as such and its execution by foot and hand and the like. Raising my hand is voluntary because commanded by the will. What is willed is an end that is or is taken to be the good of the agent. All voluntary acts are for the sake of the end, the good. Moreover, there is an effective identification of human acts and moral acts: "... moral acts are specified by the end, for moral acts and human acts are the same".[6]

This does not mean simply that "for the sake of an end" is predicable of each and every human act. Thomas is after far more than the predicable universality of 'end' and 'good'. He understands the human good as that for the sake of which all human acts are undertaken. This is what he means by the ultimate end of human actions, already mentioned in the opening article. Is there a comprehensive end of human actions? Is there some one good for the sake of which they are all undertaken, and in the absence of which they would be absurd and foolish? Like Aristotle, Thomas observes that we have a word for the ultimate end, namely, "happiness". For Aristotle, the truth that there is an ultimate end is primary and can thus only be defended by reducing to absurdity objections to it.[7] Thomas takes a similar approach[8] and the way he understands it is clear when he explains why there could not be a plurality of ultimate ends:

> *Respondeo dicendum quod de ultimo fine possumus loqui dupliciter: uno modo, secundum rationem ultimi finis; alio modo secundum id in quo finis ultimi ratio invenitur.*
> [I answer that we can speak of ultimate end in two ways, in one way, with reference to its meaning, in another way, with reference to that in which the meaning is taken to be realized.][9]

What is meant by the *ratio ultimi finis?* It is the account or *logos* or definition we give of the phrase. Man's ultimate end is the good that will perfect and fulfill him. Concretely, ultimate end is the application of the formality, what is meant by ultimate end, to something taken to satisfy that meaning —a kind of sandwich, the upper half of which characterizes the lower half. Many things have been thought to satisfy the notion of ultimate end. Classical morality gathers them into large groups: pleasure, wealth, power, fame, and so on. These, or species of them, have been put forward as the point of anything we do. When St. Paul speaks of those *"cuius deus venter est"* ("whose god is their belly"), he is pointing out that some treat food as the be-all and end-all of human life. The question thus becomes: Do all or any of these candidates deserve the characterization? Classical moral philosophy argues that they do not. Thomas will devote the second question of the *Prima Pars* to a similar effort, ticking off eight candidates for ultimate end, and finding all of them wanting. He even adds that the proof that they are wanting is often best grasped when they are had.[10] In short, there can be a plurality of candidates for the role of ultimate end, but only one defensible winner of the role.

I mention these commonplaces because they are important. These are the first steps Thomas takes in moral theology, as they were the first steps Aristotle took in the *Nicomachean Ethics*. One begins with the notion of a comprehensive end. One begins by speaking of the 'good' as common to all good things. Things will be called good insofar as the *ratio boni* is taken to be realized in them. Good is first understood as an end, as what is sought, as the point of action, as something perfect and sufficient. It is not simply that anything we do has some point and aims at some good or other; they are all gathered up at the outset in the community provided by the meaning of 'ultimate end' and of 'good'. How does Thomas reply to the objection that the ultimate end consists of a plurality of things?[11] The formality under which things are brought when they are called good is the *ratio boni perfecti*. This conception of good excludes the possibility of any perfection outside it. Whether he speaks of ultimate end, the human good, or happiness, Thomas always employs this distinction between their meaning and the things in which that meaning is taken to be realized. The *ratio boni* is thus conceptually prior to things called good. The notion of good is not built up from them; they are recognized as good because they save the notion, or at least are thought to.

The good is first recognized as an end, but something may be called good because it is a means to an end and is only so desired. Other things, desirable in themselves, also serve as means to a further end. The ultimate end is never a means. But good is first and primarily to be understood as end, indeed, as ultimate end.

Needless to say, the use of 'good' to talk about morals, in both Thomas and Aristotle, presupposes a vast background of non-moral uses of the term. The change which characterizes the physical world, involves the actualization of a potentiality. Actualization is the completion or perfection of potentiality. The end of any natural process is the good aimed at. Universal teleology is notoriously presumed by Thomas' moral thinking.

From that point of view, human action is a special case —which was the point of the second article of question one of the *Prima secundae*. Non-moral goods function as ends in the various processes Thomas referred to in article one as acts of a man that are not human acts.

But can 'good' be common in this way? Whether taken in all its sweep or as confined to the human good, good is not a genus, it is not something that can be predicated univocally. There are remarks in Grisez that suggest that this consideration plays some role in what he has to say about basic goods.

'Acting according to reason' is often given as an account of the human good. Rational activity is good only insofar as it is well done. It is the adverbial modification of the activity as well or badly done that is of moral importance. After Aristotle and Thomas have argued that rational activity is peculiar to and characteristic of man and that to do it well is a sufficient basis for saying that the agent is good, they immediately point out that 'rational activity' means many things. It is, in Thomas' terminology, analogous. Rational activity can mean either the activity of reason itself or activities which participate in or are governed by reason. Rational activity in the essential sense is subdivided into theoretical and practical. Participative rational activity comes down to the desires following on perception which can come under the sway of reason. If the perfection of an activity is its virtue and if rational activity covers many different kinds, there must be a corresponding plurality of virtues. The human good, it seems, is inescapably multiple.

But things which share a term in this way are ordered. The order among the various kinds of rational activity proposed by Thomas is of two kinds. Objectively speaking, the perfection of reasoning will lie in theoretical knowledge and preeminently in *theoria*, contemplation of the divine. This analysis is the culmination of the unpacking of the ultimate end, a movement from clarifying its *ratio* to finding what most perfectly saves that meaning. Contemplation is the answer and consequently is man's ultimate end. Needless to say, one must distinguish between the subjective side, happiness, and the object of contemplation.

It is of maximum significance that Aristotle postpones the discussion of contemplation until the end of the Nicomachean Ethics. When he turns in Book Two to a discussion of the virtues which constitute the ultimate end, he significantly remarks that one does not become good by philosophizing. The definition of virtue then given establishes another order among the virtues. If virtue is that which makes the agent good and renders his activity good, virtue applies unequally, analogously, to intellectual virtues and moral virtues. Given the recurrence of 'good' in the definition, and given that good is the object of appetite, habits that have their seat in appetite are virtues in a primary sense. Thus temperance is more properly a virtue than science, even the science of metaphysics which is the locus of contemplation. Intellectual virtues give one the capacity to do something well, but since they are not lodged in appetite, there is no inclination or bent actually to do the thing. Intellectual virtues, Thomas notes, give the *facultas* but not the appetitive disposition to use it. Thus a man can be called good only in a sense, *secundum quid*, because he has such virtues. Notoriously, art in the practical intellect and various habits of theoretical intellect, make one having them good only in a sense. One does not become good by philosophizing.[12]

But one can philosophize well or badly in the moral sense of these terms. The intellectual virtues, as they figure in human acts, are directed by practical intellect and will. One undertakes to engage in them and for a purpose which may include gaining truth, but the truth figures in action as a good to be sought. Not simply the good of the intellect, but as good for me to pursue here and now. The unity of the moral life is thus lodged in the virtue directive of practical reason's choices and this virtue presupposes the moral virtues, the virtues of appetite. Moral virtues depend on the direction of prudence and the truth of the judgment of prudence is dependent on moral virtue. This is the rich setting in which the truth that contemplation best saves the notion of ultimate end must be understood.

From good to goods In the *Summa*, IaIIae, q.94. a.2, having established that the first principle of the practical order is "the good is to be done and pursued and evil avoided", Thomas indicates how it is that one passes from the first principle to others. The passage will be one from the most general to the less general. In order to be guided by the first principle, one will have to specify a good that can in fact be chosen. The first principle is foundational with respect to all other principles in the practical order. How are less general principles to be formulated? Everything that practical reason naturally grasps as human goods provides a basis for other precepts:

> *Quia vero bonum habet rationem finis, malum autem rationem contrarii, inde est quod omnia illa ad quae homo habet naturalem inclinationem ratio naturaliter apprehendit ut bona, et per consequens ut opere prosequenda, et contraria eorum ut mala et vitanda.*
>
> [Because good has the note of end and evil has the contrary note, reason naturally grasps as good all those things to which man has a natural inclination and consequently as to be pursued in action, and the contrary of these are grasped as evils to be avoided.][13]

The natural inclinations are ordered, the first being one man shares with all things: the desire to continue in being. The second inclination is one man shares with all animals: the urge to mate and rear young. The third is peculiar to man, an inclination following on his defining difference, reason, thanks to which he seeks to know the truth about God and to live in society. Particular natural law precepts bear on the goods revealed as the ends of these inclinations. On the basis of the first inclination, those things by which man is conserved in being, and their contraries, pertain to natural law. On the basis of the second inclination there are natural law precepts concerning reproduction and the education of children. On the third are based such precepts as that one should shun ignorance, not harm others with whom he must live and the like.

Beginning with the assumption that man seeks his good, we move on to articulate this good, to ask what its constituents might be. Since man is a complex organism comprising many appetites —natural inclinations— his total good comprises a number of constituent goods. A nature as nature is ordered to some end as its good or perfection. Primarily, by 'nature' is meant the intrinsic principle in changeable things, and this nature is either matter or form. But the term 'nature' is extended to cover every substance or being, and then whatever is fitting to the thing given its nature is said to be natural and to belong to it as such (*per se*). In this sense, the principles or starting-points in a thing are called natural. "This is obviously so in the case of intellect: the principles of intellectual knowledge are naturally known. Similarly the principle of voluntary activities must be something naturally willed".[14] What is it that is naturally willed? *Bonum in communi*, the good universally taken. Another name for this good is 'ultimate end', which stands to desirable things in a way analogous to the way the first principles of demonstration stand to intelligible things. This good includes everything that pertains to the one willing according to his nature. That is, we not only will what pertains to the faculty of will but also what pertains to each of the faculties and to the whole man. So it is that a man naturally wills not only the object of will, but also what befits the other faculties, such as knowledge of the truth, which befits intellect, and existing and living and the like which concern natural survival. All these things are included in the object of will as particular goods.[15] Particularizations of the human good presuppose the human good as such, the desire for the ultimate end. Just as the first and most common precept is founded on the most fundamental appetite, the will's desire of the ultimate end —the good is to be done and pursued and evil avoided— so the precepts which bear on the ends of other natural inclinations express their relation to the ultimate end, man's overall good.

Grisez on the Good

When one turns from Thomas to Grisez, one is struck by similarities, but also by differences. It is noteworthy that Grisez prefers to speak of human goods rather than of the human good. He uses the concept of ultimate end sparingly and then not in the sense of *the* ultimate end. The phrase does not even appear in the index of *Christian Moral Principles*. This is no accident.

In developing his account of the central meaning of 'good' and 'bad',[16] Grisez begins with a difficulty. All creation is said to be good, but what of evil? Non-moral evil is a privation, a lack of what would make a thing to be as it ought to be. Goodness, by contrast, is fullness of being. Moreover, it is the fulfillment of potentiality.[17] Of course, there are goods and goods. What are the goods which fulfill human persons? Here Grisez insists on a distinction between two kinds of basic good, reflexive and substantive. The reflexive —also called 'existential'— goods are both reasons for choosing and are in part defined by choosing. The examples of such goods are four: self-integration, practical reasonableness and authenticity, justice and friendship, and religion. There are other non-reflexive or substantive basic human goods in the account of which choice is not included. Although they provide reasons for choosing, choice is not part of their account. Grisez lists three such substantive goods: life and health, knowledge of truth and aesthetic appreciation, play and skill. This listing of seven basic human goods is a central point in Grisez's theory. Human goods are intelligible goods which are distinguished from sensible goods. The latter are characterized by pleasure as opposed to pain. Intelligible goods provide reasons for choice, for acting. The basic human goods are all intelligible goods and thus reasons for acting, but they must be subdivided into reflexive/existential and substantive basic human goods. The latter can be objects of choice, but that fact is not part of what they definitionally are. They are realized states of affairs which result from choices.[18]

It is only by being taken up into reflexive acts, moral acts as such, that the substantive goods take on a moral aspect.[19] The reflexive goods are presented as modes of 'harmony', so much so that 'harmony' and 'moral good' seem to function as synonyms. Could we supply 'moral virtue' as synonymous with these? How do the reflexive goods look under that suggestion? Self-integration is harmony among all the parts of a person which can be engaged in freely chosen acts. Practical reasonableness or authenticity is harmony among moral reflection, free choices and their execution. Justice and friendship is choosing to act in harmony with one another. Religion or holiness is harmony with God.

Now there are several gathering terms involved in this comparison — on the side of existential goods, harmony, but also fulfillment which covers them all: "In sum there are seven categories of basic human goods which perfect persons and contribute to their fulfillment both as individuals and in community".[20]   What is the significance, if any, of such gathering, or common, terms and phrases? Grisez notes that some have used "vague and obscure language" to refer to human fulfillment, speaking for example of "living in accord with reason" or "for self-realization" or "acting out of love". Sometimes, as with 'happiness' it is a summary of the basic goods, or as with 'self-realization' it is simply an articulation of the notion of good itself. He attributes three functions to such talk. It is a way of summarizing all the basic forms of human goodness, as 'happiness' did for the Greeks.[21] How is 'human fulfillment' or 'in accord with human reason' common to all the basic goods? Or, put more simply, how is 'human good' common to all the basic goods? The subdivision of basic goods into existential and substantive indicates that not all basic goods are human goods in the same sense. The substantive seem clearly human goods in a lesser sense than the existential.

From goods to good   Obviously Grisez's discussion of the meaning of 'good' and 'bad' is important for this question: "Goodness lies in a fulfillment of potentialities which leads to being and being more; badness lies in the realization of a potentiality which cuts off further possibilities and tends to limit opportunities for self-realization which would otherwise be open to an entity".[22] It is clear that Grisez is offering what might be called an account of ontological goodness and badness. His use of *Summa,* Ia, q.5, a.1.1 makes that clear. In this sense of them, the terms 'good' and 'bad' presuppose teleology —natures and ends. Like Thomas, accordingly, he sees moral good and bad as special cases of good and bad, those which are peculiar to human agents. In its most general use, "goodness is the fulfillment of potentialities"[23] and not the realization of a possibility for non-fulfillment. Potentiality is directional —toward a corresponding actuality. But the fundamental point is that the fulfillment of a potentiality is good and the thwarting of that potentiality is bad.

Having distinguished good and bad, Grisez goes on to distinguish between sensible goods and bads and intelligible goods and bads: "This complexity in the uses of the words 'good' and 'bad' arises from the complexity of the human person.... [H]uman persons are both sentient and intelligent. Their sentient nature is similar to that of other animals; their intelligence and freedom of choice are distinctive.... Free choices are made on the basis of judgments about what will fulfill or prevent the fulfillment of the person as a whole". Although complex, the acting person is one self: "A person lives in a single world, and the behavior must be adapted to all aspects of the reality of this world". Behavior is usually motivated both by emotion and will, that is, directed to both sensible pleasure and intelligible fulfillment. [24]

"Since human goodness is found in the fullness of human being, one begins to understand what it is to be a good person by considering what things fulfill human persons. Things which do so are human goods in the central sense —that is, intelligible goods".[25] Such goods are aspects of persons, not things. It is not simply things as things, as opposed to say their human possession or use, that Grisez has in mind in denying that things like wealth, fences and locks are basic goods: "They are extrinsic things persons can possess and use, but they do not guarantee personal fulfillment even in the bodily, intellectual, and cultural dimensions, much less in the existential or moral dimension".[26] Grisez speaks of the empty gas tank, and asks if it is good or bad by itself. Surely only in relation to something else —it can prevent a person doing what he wishes. I want to get home and I run out of gas. In the light of my desire, gas is good and no-gas is bad. But this is because it is part of an intelligible chain of purposes, and such a chain always ends in something appealing in itself.

The integration of the basic goods   If the overriding meaning of the human good is self-fulfillment and if there is a plurality of human goods because of the complexity of the human person, the question arises as to how the basic goods come together as the integral human good. It will be noticed that self-integration is one of the basic goods, but by it Grisez does not mean the effort to bring together all the basic goods. The integral human good is not identical with the basic human good of self-integration. The integral human good consists of both existential and substantive goods. How does self-fulfillment cover the bringing together of the basic goods? That is, is there one way of doing this, or is there a plurality of ways which are ranked as good, better, and best, or is there simply no limit to the ways in which the basic goods are to be integrated? In order to appreciate Grisez's response to such questions, it is necessary to examine his *sui generis* interpretation of what precedes the discussion of natural inclinations in the famous article of Aquinas.

The First Principle of Practical Reasoning

What Thomas Taught

The text to which we referred for Thomas' account of natural inclinations, and the way in which their ends ground natural law precepts, actually begins at a prior point. Thomas is asking himself whether there is more than one precept of natural law.[27] His answer is going to be 'Yes and no'. First he develops an analogy to which he has appealed several times prior to this discussion. Precepts of natural law function in practical reasoning the way in which the first principles of demonstration function in theoretical reasoning. Like the latter, the former are *per se nota*. That is, knowledge of their truth is not derived from other truths functioning as premises. These precepts are the starting-points of all practical reasoning, not just an instance of it. Propositions are knowable in themselves when their truth is obvious from the very meaning of their terms. The immediacy of such truths is grounded in reality but is available only to those who understand what is being referred to. This is the basis for the distinction between self-evidence as such and self-evidence for us. Only as expressed in a proposition is there self-evidence in the full sense. And, because not everybody knows everything, some self-evident propositions will not be understood to be such by those who do not understand their terms. But there are some things which no one can fail to know and it is such common self-evident starting-points to which Thomas now refers, using the Latin *dignitates* for the Greek *axiomata*. What is it that no one can fail to know?

Thomas stresses that there is an order to be followed in this discussion: we first speak of what every mind grasps and then we speak of the grasp of practical reason. Further, within reason *simpliciter* —theoretical reason as presupposed by practical reason— there is an order. First, there is the grasp of the simple, then there is judgment about simples. Being, that which is, is what the mind first grasps and on the basis of it forms a first non-gainsayable judgment which Thomas expresses as "the same thing is not to be affirmed and denied at the same time". All other judgments are said to be based on this.

There is a parallel of this in practical reason. Practical reason is ordered to some work (*opus*) and every agent acts for an end which has the note of good, which is the principle of the practical order. The first thing simply grasped is the good, understood as the object of desire (*quod omnia appetunt*). The first precept of the law is based on this concept of the good: the good is to be done and pursued and evil avoided. On this all other precepts of the law of nature are founded. The text continues into the treatment of natural inclinations.

Grisez on the First Principle

Grisez begins his discussion of practical reasoning with a crucial distinction. Practical reasoning, he says, has two phases, a first concerned with what might be done —he calls this its general phase— and another with what ought to be done. General principles of practical reasoning are not moral principles because both good and bad people use them. Grisez understands the first principle Thomas formulated —*bonum est faciendum et prosequendum, et malum vitandum*— to be a general practical principle. It is not, he asserts, a moral principle. 'Good' here means 'whatever can be understood as intelligibly worthwhile'. The principle extends to and governs all coherent practical thinking: "What the first practical principle provides is a foundation for practical thinking".[28] It directs toward a fulfillment to be realized in and through human action. It is self-evident.

Grisez makes it clear that he thinks Thomas would agree that "good is to be done and pursued" is not a moral principle. It is normative, however, "even though it does not specify the relationship of actions to goods in such a way that deliberation and choice among possibilities are at all limited".[29]

The reiterated reason why Thomas' first principle is not a moral principle is that it governs the practical thinking of bad people as well as good. Grisez summarizes his dissatisfaction with "scholastic natural-law theory" by pointing out that it substitutes the imperative "Do good and avoid evil" for the gerundive, thereby trying to turn it into a moral principle.[30] Another reason is that spontaneous action is governed by the first principle but, as not involving choice, is not moral. A further reason, suggested rather than expressed, is that there are actions whose appraisal is not a moral one. One who is said to be a good golfer may or may not be a good person.[31]

None of these reasons convinces. Is his suggestion that *faciendum* could be translated as either 'what might be done' or 'what ought to be done'? And how does the latter relate to the former? By calling the first general, he suggests that the second is a particularization of the first. *Ought* implies *can*? Or are we to think that when we act badly we are merely aiming at something that might be done? Surely 'ought to be done' is common to good and bad action. No more could Grisez mean that the general phrase or understanding of the principle is not moral in the sense that moral is opposed to immoral. His point is rather that the moral realm is not yet in play. But this suggests that one opts into the moral order as if it were a game one might or might not choose to play. It is impossible to think that Germain Grisez would entertain such a possibility. What then does he mean?

Light is cast on his reasons by his discussion of the general determinations of the first practical principle. The principle directs toward fulfillment to be realized in and through human acts. The good is to be done and pursued. But we grasp as goods all the fulfillments to which we are naturally inclined. There is a basic principle of natural law corresponding to each natural inclination. Who in reading this will not think it is simply a restatement of what we read in Thomas? Grisez refers to Thomas on natural inclinations, while pointing out that he himself has discussed basic goods in greater detail than Thomas did: "The general determinations of the first principle of practical reasoning are these basic precepts of natural law".[32] But if the first practical principle is not a moral principle, how can the precepts of natural law be determinations of it? The statement of the first *moral* principle has yet to be made. No small difficulty, but here is the crucial remark about the formation of natural law precepts: "They take the form: Such and such a basic human good is to be done and/or pursued, protected and promoted".[33] This is the key to the fundamental difference between Germain Grisez and Thomas Aquinas.

For Grisez, the form that less general practical principles takes is ' — is to be done and pursued'. The blank is to be filled in with one or the other basic goods which have been identified as the objects of natural inclinations. A practical principle which directs thinking to each basic good is, like the first principle, self-evident. But what would a basic precept of natural law look like on this understanding? There is a natural inclination toward sex. Sexual pleasure, sexual congress is the object of a natural inclination. So: 'Sexual pleasure is to be engaged in and pursued and otherwise protected and promoted'. Is this a mere lapse on Grisez's part?

That it is not can be seen by looking backward and slightly forward in his exposition.

Grisez prefers to talk about the human goods rather than the human good. The 'good' in the first principle functions as a place-marker for any basic human good, a blank that can be filled in with any one of them. It is because of this that he suggests that we formulate determinate principles by substituting a basic good for the place-marker.

By contrast, Thomas holds that natural concupiscence is to be ordered to the common good of our nature, and ordered by reason. Natural law is *aliquid rationis*; it is the direction by practical reason to the good to which we are naturally ordered, the ultimate end which is perfect and sufficient. The goods which are the objects of natural inclination enter into natural law precepts insofar as reason orders them to the good of reason: "Just as in man reason dominates and commands the other powers, so all the natural inclinations pertaining to the other powers must be ordered by reason. Thus this is right for everyone that all man's inclinations should be directed by reason".[34] Natural inclinations pertain to natural law insofar as they are ruled by reason and are thus reduced to the first precept: "In this way there are many precepts of natural law which however share in a common root".[35] The common root is the *bonum universale* grasped by reason. Thus the form of less general precepts of natural law would be ' — should be pursued according to the direction of reason'. And reason orders to the comprehensive good of the agent: that is what *bonum* means in Thomas' formulation of the first precept.

Clearly there is no need of a precept commanding us to pursue goods to which we are naturally inclined. We do not require direction as far as the ends of natural inclinations are concerned. Such ends are givens of human nature: we do not choose to hunger or thirst or to be attracted by the opposite sex. Yet Grisez's understanding of determinations of the first practical principle, which he calls natural law precepts, is precisely the judgment that the ends of natural inclinations are to be pursued, protected, etc. If that is what natural law precepts said, they would be otiose. We do not need to be told to hunger and thirst.

In any case, we can see why Grisez says that he has not yet entered the moral order. The principles of practical reason as he has developed them do not tell us what is morally good. What do they do? They generate the field of possibilities in which choices are necessary. But when choices are made, no one disputes that basic goods are good or their opposites evil. He mentions *Gaudium et spes*, section 35, but says that it, like Thomas' formulation, is unsatisfactory as a moral principle. What we need, over and above the foregoing, is a first principle of morality whose function will be to "provide the basis for guiding choices toward human fulfillment".[36] What does he propose as the first principle of morality? "The basic principle of morality might best be formulated as follows: *In voluntarily acting for human goods and avoiding what is opposed to them, one ought to choose and otherwise will those and only those possibilities whose willing is compatible with a will toward integral human fulfillment".*[37]

What Grisez's moral principle adds is "integral human fulfillment" as the measure of pursuing the basic goods. He has to add this because he does not see that something like that is the meaning of *bonum* in what he calls the first practical principle. That first practical principle, as Grisez envisages it, can be rephrased by putting the ends of natural inclinations in the place of good, one of the basic goods for the place-marker 'good'. This has the unfortunate result of commanding a natural inclination to have the end it has. Moreover, what he means as "integral human fulfillment" seems to continue his assumption that the basic goods are more basic than the notion of good and than the primary practical judgment that the good is to be done and pursued and its opposite avoided. Just as Grisez fragments the principle into a number of injunctions commanding us to pursue the ends of particular inclinations, so when he seeks to put them together in "integral human fulfillment" the task is one of bringing into unity a set of precepts whose particular goods have to be treated in such a way that one of them is not pursued at the expense of the others. Integral human fulfillment, as Grisez understands it, takes as primary obligations the pursuit of the ends of inclinations, the basic goods, and morality involves their orchestration.

The nature of the moral task in Grisez is further clarified by the eight modes of responsibility on which he prides himself as being their first systematic theorist. These modes specify the first moral principle. We are urged not to be deterred from acting for intelligible goods, on the one hand, but not to be impatient or individualistic in pursuing them either. Emotional motivation, positive or negative, is warned against; one must be careful not to prefer one person to another. The human good is the summation of the basic goods, and their integration must avoid giving precedence to one over another:[38] "Integral human fulfillment means a single system in which all the human goods would contribute to the fulfillment of the entire human community".[39]

It is because basic human goods, in the plural, are more basic than any prior orientation toward one's comprehensive good that integral human fulfillment is like establishing a federation between sovereign states. Choice and modes of responsibility must, as it were, respect states' rights.

Conclusion

The radical difference between the moral thought of Germain Grisez and Thomas Aquinas is obscured by Grisez's employment of Thomistic texts to make his points and his apparent belief that Thomas would share his interpretation of those texts. In talking about basic goods, Grisez often refers to the text in which Thomas speaks of the goods revealed by natural inclinations. Particular natural law precepts bear on such goods. So far, Grisez and Thomas are agreed. But Grisez thinks that the form of such particular precepts is 'X should be done, pursued, protected', where X takes as its value one or the other of the basic goods. This has the odd result, *inter alia*, of urging the pursuit of sex as a natural law precept. For Thomas, the form of a particular precept is 'X should be pursued as reason directs the pursuit to one's overall good', where values of X are the ends of natural inclinations.

This striking difference reveals a difference in understanding *bonum* in the first practical principle as formulated by Thomas: *bonum est faciendum et prosequendam*. For Thomas it is the comprehensive good of the agent, *bonum in communi, bonum universale,* the agent's ultimate end. Any object of will must save the *ratio boni*, a formality which relates it to one's overall good. For Grisez, by contrast, 'good' is the disjunction of the basic goods, a place-marker for any of them. But it seems to have no meaning of its own.

Understanding particular practical precepts as he does, Grisez needs a way to relate such reasoning to the moral order. Integral human fulfillment is the means of brokering the various basic goods: "The guidance which the ideal of integral human development offers to choice is to avoid unnecessary limitation and so maintain openness to further goods."[40] Morality consists in not choosing one basic good at the expense of the others and the pursuit of them in such a way that the self remains open and is not needless restricted. The ideal is more and more of the basic goods, a more expansive participation in them, personally and communally.

It has not been my purpose here to argue for or against either of these approaches. My much more modest aim has been to show that

Germain Grisez and Thomas Aquinas differ in crucial ways and at the very outset of moral teaching. These differences doubtless generate others as the teaching of each man moves on from its starting-point.

NOTES

1   *The Way of the Lord Jesus* is a work in progress. For purposes of this study, it is the first volume, *Christian Moral Principles* [*CMP*], that will serve as the basis of the comparison between Grisez and Thomas Aquinas.

2   Benedict Ashley, in "What is the End of the Human Person? The Vision of God and Integral Human Fulfillment", in *Moral Truth and Moral Tradition: Essays in Honour of Peter Geach and Elizabeth Anscombe* (Four Courts Press: Dublin, 1994), pp.68-96, makes different points than I do here.

3   Grisez is a prolific writer and his *magnum opus* does not exhaust his productivity. For purposes of this article, I will concentrate on *CMP*. This is the work that will have been read even by those unacquainted with his other writings. On the points that interest me in this analysis, Grisez wrote prior to *CMP* and he has returned to the topic since alone and in tandem. To the best of my knowledge, there is no significant difference between what he says on these matters in *CMP* and what he has written subsequently. His famous article on *Summa Theologiae* [*ST*], IaIIae, q.94, a.2, which is most easily available in a shortened form in *Aquinas: A Collection of Critical Essays*, edited by Anthony Kenny (New York: Doubleday Anchor, 1969), pp.340-82, a book reissued by the Notre Dame Press, does not figure in my critique here. Some of the matters I previously took issue with in it have disappeared in the account in *CMP*. Of course I am not suggesting anything causal. Grisez has often felt that his critics were insufficiently familiar with his *oeuvre*. This study concentrates on *CMP* for the reasons given.

4   There is a magisterial discussion of this procedure in *ST*, Ia, q.85, a.3 where the influence of the considerations at the outset of the *Physics* is manifest.

5   *ST*, IaIIae, q.94, a.4.

6   *ST*, IaIIae, q.1, a.3.

7   The significance of the fact that Aristotle defends the claim that there is an ultimate end of human action by a *reductio* in *Nicomachean Ethics*, I.2 is not always noticed. Undeniable truths, the kind that can serve as starting-points, can be defended only indirectly. Thomas in his commentary on this passage displays the series of *reductiones* that carry Aristotle's point. The implication is that it is self-evidently true that there is an ultimate end of human acts.

8   *ST*, IaIIae, q.1, a.4.

9   *ST*, IaIIae, q.1, a.7. All translations are mine, made for this essay.

10 *ST*, IaIIae, q.2, a.1: "... *eorum insufficientia magis cognoscitur cum habentur*".

11 He takes the objection from Augustine (*The City of God*, XIX, 3), who is discussing Varro's views: "This is then the life of man which is rightly called happy —a life which enjoys virtue and the other goods of soul and body without which virtue cannot exist". Thomas answers: "It should be noted that all those many things are understood in the notion of one perfect good constituted by them which they [i.e Varro] took to be the ultimate end ..." (*ST*, IaIIae, q.1.a.5.1).

12 This sketch is based on *ST*, IaIIae, qq.55-58.

13   *ST*, IaIIae, q.94, a. 2. Here I use the translation to be found in *Thomas Aquinas: Selected Writings*, edited and translated with an introduction by Ralph McInerny (London: Penguin, 1998), p.645.

14   *ST*, IaIIae, q.10, a.1.

15   *ST*, IaIIae, q.10, a.1: "Et ideo necesse est quod hoc modo accipiendo naturam, semper principium in his quae conveniunt rei, sit naturale. Et hoc manifeste apparet in intellectu: nam principia intellectualis cognitionis sunt naturaliter nota. Similiter etiam principium motuum voluntariorum oportet esse aliquid naturaliter volitum. Hoc autem est bonum in communi, in quod voluntas naturaliter tendit, sicut etiam quaelibet potentia in suum obiectum: et etiam ipse finis ultimus, qui hoc modo se habet in appetibilibus, sicut prima principia demonstrationum in intelligibilibus: et universaliter omnia illa quae conveniunt volenti secundum suam naturam. Non enim per voluntatem appetimus solum ea quae pertinent ad potentiam voluntatis, sed etiam ea quae pertinent ad singulas potentias, et ad totum hominem. Unde naturaliter homo vult non solum obiectum voluntatis, sed etiam alia quae conveniunt aliis potentiis, ut cognitionem veri, quae convenit intellectui, et esse et vivere et alia huiusmodi quae respociunt consistentiam naturalem, quae omnia comprehendunt sub obiecto voluntatis, sicut quaedam particularia bona".

16   The paragraphs that follow summarize the teaching of Chapter 5 of *CMP*.

17   *CMP*, pp.115-19.

18   Ibid., pp.121-25.

19   It is Grisez's account of this 'taking up' that is the object of criticism below.

20   *CMP*, p.124.

21   Ibid., p.125.

22   Ibid., p.117. One could quibble about Grisez's using 'potentiality' both for what is fulfilling and for the opposite. He does not, of course, mean that an entity is equipped with two sets of potentialities, one whose fulfillment increases being and another which thwarts a being. Thomas, following Aristotle, would ascribe the possibility that a thing may cease to be, to its matter and possibilities —potentialities— whose fulfillment increases the intended perfection of the thing. Sometimes potentialities are impeded; and, of course, sometimes faculties or capacities are abused —and this can take us into the moral order. I have in mind such remarks as, "Yet not every fulfillment of potentialities is good. People get sick and die, who make mistakes in reasoning, who burn potatoes, or who hurt others are fulfilling potentialities just as truly as people who live healthily, who think straight, who make good dinners and who help others" (ibid., p.118). Surely this is wrong. The organism does not have a potentiality to get sick in the way in which health is the fulfillment of its potentiality. That the potentiality might not —that it is possible that the potentiality not— be realized, is not the mark of another potentiality of that organism. If it were, calling health good and sickness bad would sound arbitrary —the distinction could no longer be grounded in the fulfillment of potentiality or its opposite.

23   Ibid., p.118.

24   Ibid., p.119.

25   Ibid., p.121.

26   Ibid.

27   *ST*, IaIIae, q.4, a.2.

28   *CMP*, p.179.

29   Ibid., p.180.

30   It is difficult to see why 'Do good' is not equivalent to 'Good ought to be done'. Grisez is aware of *ST*, IaIIae, q.17, a.1. Thomas notes that reason can express its

command either absolutely, by a verb in the indicative mode (e.g., 'This is to be done by you'), or so as to move someone to act (e.g., 'Do this'). The distinction is between modes of reason's command (*imperium*). In any case, we are now interested in Grisez's understanding of Thomas, not his understanding of other interpreters of Thomas.

31   See *CMP*, p.129.
32   Ibid., p.180.
33   Ibid.
34   *ST*, IaIIae, q.94, a.4.3.
35   Ibid., q.94, a.2.2.
36   *CMP*, p.184.
37   Ibid., Grisez's emphasis.
38   Chapter 8 of *CMP* is devoted to these modes of responsibility.
39   Ibid., p.222.
40   Ibid., p.186.

3 The Basic Dimensions of Human Flourishing: A Comparison of Accounts

Sabina Alkire[1]

> A course of reflection is, in a way, an attempt to understand one's own character, or nature. The attempt thus parallels attempts made, in quite another way, by those anthropologists and psychologists who ask (in effect) whether there is a human nature and what are its characteristics. The anthropological and psychological studies ought to be regarded as an aid in answering our own present question —not, indeed, by way of any 'inference' from universality or 'human nature' to values (an inference that would be merely fallacious), but by way of an assemblage of reminders of the range of possibly worthwhile activities and orientations open to one.[2]

Central place is given, in Finnis' and Grisez's reinterpretation of natural law theory, to the role of basic human goods or reasons for action,[3] which they claim form the "evaluative substratum of all moral judgements".[4] The procedure for identifying basic reasons for action as grasped by practical reason is carefully described to avoid the naturalistic fallacy; and ethical analyses which consider each basic human good are claimed to be fuller, more systematic, and more nuanced —more able to guide persons towards flourishing rather than merely prohibit deviance.[5] Despite the centrality of these goods to their natural law theory, Grisez, Boyle, and Finnis are far more tentative about the particular set of reasons for action that they have actually proposed. Finnis writes that there is "no magic number" of basic reasons, and there is "no need for the reader to accept the present list, just as it stands, still less its nomenclature (which simply gestures towards categories of human purpose that are each, though unified, nevertheless multi-faceted)".[6] He still claims that the set they do identify is analytically useful[7] and contains "all the basic purposes of human action".[8]

Given the centrality of the basic reasons for action to the Grisez School's natural law theory, then, this chapter will address the question of whether independent social, psychological, and philosophical research supports Finnis' list. In *Natural Law and Natural Rights*, Finnis refers to some works on anthropology and ethics, and to Davitt's 1968 survey of psychological, anthropological, and philosophical literature on basic values,[9] to suggest that the basic goods are cross-culturally valid. However, anthropological and psychological research on cross-cultural values has advanced significantly in the past three decades, and moral philosophy has never explored more actively the question of whether and to what extent most values are culturally relative and/or objective. There is now a need to revisit the subject.

This chapter will explore the question of how Finnis' set of basic goods or reasons for action compares to other sets of basic human values that have been independently proposed by other authors in several disciplines. It will consider seven sets of dimensions of human value that can be related relatively easily to 'basic reasons for action'. These have been proposed by two other philosophers, James Griffin[10] and Martha Nussbaum;[11] by Milton Rokeach[12] and Shalom Schwartz,[13] two psychologists who have done large-scale, cross-cultural research on values; by Manfred Max-Neef,[14] who has been engaged practically in identifying and meeting basic needs in Latin America; and by Robert Cummins[15] and Maureen Ramsay,[16] who have themselves surveyed and synthesised 'lists' of human needs from different sources. An analysis based upon these sources, however, cannot purport to be a complete treatment of the question of whether the elements of Finnis' basic reasons for action are both universal and sufficient; for the literature on values is vast, multi-lingual, and much of it is not easily available. To restrict one's sources, as we will do, to recent material in the English language available in Britain (though including non-Western work), limits the study arbitrarily; and further research will be needed to check for bias. Also, literature on cross-cultural values often conceives of values as norms, virtues, or attitudes rather than as reasons for action.[17] For example, the majority of work on developing a global ethic that is shared by world religions focuses on principles (not killing the innocent, justice, honesty, environmental sustainability); it does not give a systematic account of the dimensions of human flourishing, and for that reason it is not included here.[18]

Why do we choose to engage such a disparate group of interlocutors, rather than confine our study to discussions among scholars of natural law? Our reasoning is as follows: if Finnis' account of the basic reasons for action is indeed true, then it is reasonable to expect that others would have 'recognised' these reasons independently in the course of their own work, be it philosophical or practical. The authors above have been selected because they represent a spectrum of studies that might be expected to yield such independent confirmation. Griffin and Nussbaum both employ a form of introspection and practical reason to generate a list of universal human values. Rokeach and Schwartz undertake empirical tests to illuminate what people in different cultures actually value both intrinsically and instrumentally. Max-Neef uses a practical classification of human needs to stimulate a holistic discussion of social policies. Cummins classifies literature that has attempted to measure the 'quality of life' in a relatively complete way, and Ramsay classifies the literature in behavioural psychology regarding the needs of human beings. The methods used by these authors differ according to their projects. But all of them have struggled with the same question: what dimensions of human value are valid for everyone? This chapter will use their various answers —arising out of very different methodologies— as "an assemblage of reminders of the range of possibly worthwhile activities and orientations open to one",[19] and analyse their implications for Finnis' list.

Before briefly introducing the seven authors, we would do well to be clear on the set of 'basic reasons for action' in Finnis' account.[20] 'Basic human goods' are reasons for acting which need no further reason.[21] Initially they were referred to as 'basic goods', then as 'basic human goods'; now the preferred nomenclature is 'basic reasons for action'. Finnis has revised his set of basic reasons on several occasions, most recently in an essay entitled "Is Natural Law Theory Compatible with Limited Government?".[22] The list has expanded to include work as well as play, and to include marriage. Knowledge and aesthetic experience, which were distinct initially, have been collapsed together into one reason for action. In the intermediate stage, practical reasonableness was divided into self-integration, inner peace and practical reasonableness, and 'consistency between one's self and its expression'; in the first and final accounts it appears as a single item. Life, friendship or sociability, and harmony with a greater-than-human source of meaning and value, are present in all three sets of basic reasons for action, and are subject to only minor differences in explanation. Hereafter we will use 'basic reasons for action', 'dimensions of value', and 'dimensions of human flourishing' interchangeably.

Table 3.1 Finnis' lists of 'basic reasons for action'

Finnis, 1980: *Natural Law & Natural Rights*	Finnis et al., 1987: "Practical Principles..."	Finnis, 1996: "Natural Law Theory and Limited Government"[23]
1. life 2. knowledge 3. play 4. aesthetic experience 5. sociability (friendship) 6. practical reasonable-ness 7. religion	1. life 2. knowledge, and appreciation of beauty 3. some degree of excellence in work and play 4. friendship 5. self-integration 6. practical reasonableness 7. religion, or harmony with some greater-than-human source of meaning and value	1. knowledge of reality (including aesthetic appreciation) 2. skilful performance in work and play for its own sake 3. bodily life and the component aspects of its fullness: health, vigour, and safety 4. friendship or association and harmony between persons, in its various forms and strengths 5. the sexual association of a man and a woman which, though it essentially involves both friendship between the partners and the procreation and education of children by them, seems to have a point and shared benefit that is irreducible either to friendship or to life-in-its-transmission; and therefore (as comparative anthropology confirms, and Aristotle and the 'third founder' of Stoicism, Musonius Rufus, came particularly close to articulating) should be acknowledged as a distinct basic human good: 'marriage' 6. harmony between one's feelings and one's judgements (inner integrity) and between one's judgements and one's behaviour (authenticity): 'practical reasonableness' 7. harmony with the widest reaches and most ultimate source of all reality, including meaning and value

Partners in Dialogue

We could proceed by lifting the 'names' of different human values from different accounts of human flourishing, sorting these into categories, and then seeing whether or not they can be contained by Finnis' list. But this procedure would fail to take into account the underlying projects of the different authors, each of whom has developed his or her account of human flourishing for different operational purposes. Hence the sets of values that

they propose often represent very different philosophical kinds of things —
not all are 'basic reasons for action— and it would be both disrespectful of
their work, and insufficient to our purposes, not to acknowledge these
differences.

Thus I begin by introducing each author whose list is to be
considered; sketching briefly how the set of needs, values, or domains they
specify has arisen in their own work; gesturing towards the problem for
which the set forms a part of the solution; and then presenting its
components. Because the task of this chapter is to judge the adequacy of
the list Finnis proposed in 1996 against his definition of basic reasons for
action, I mention these other authors' methods so that the reader might bear
them in mind and more fully understand their different accounts. I will not
evaluate any of these other accounts here. Rather, I will describe and then
apply the method for evaluating candidates for the status of 'basic good'
that was set forth by Grisez, Boyle, and Finnis in "Practical Principles,
Moral Truth, and Ultimate Ends" (1987), in order to see which elements of
Finnis's 1996 list are challenged or corroborated by these other accounts.
This method of evaluation does not rely on mere consensus or taxonomy,
but rather on reasoned argument.[24]

James Griffin's Prudential Values

James Griffin, White's Professor of Moral Philosophy at Oxford, has begun
to develop a theory of virtue ethics.[25] He has rejected the 'informed desire'
account, in which desire is itself creative of value; he now sees values as
objective, recognised by the observant actor. His recent work includes an
account of prudential values which, as in Finnis' account,[26] are a limited set
of distinct reasons for action which form the substratum of prudential
reflection. Recognising prudential values "involves recognizing a reason
for action grounded in one's well-being, requires bringing a situation under
some concept —enjoyment, accomplishment, and so on ...". Prudential
values are identified at a sufficiently general level that they are applicable
to anyone. Griffin writes: "For me to see anything as prudentially valuable,
I must see it as enhancing life in a generally intelligible way, in a way that
pertains to human life, not to any one particular person's life".[27]

To illustrate, Griffin puts forward what he refers to as "my own list"
of prudential values. He prefaces it with the qualification that it is "no
doubt incomplete" and will need to be revised when the distinction between

prudence and morality is clarified. His list contains five elements, which are set out below in Table 3.2.

Table 3.2   Griffin's 'prudential values'

1. *accomplishment:* achievement that gives life meaning.
2. *the components of human existence:* "Choosing one's own course through life, making something of it according to one's own lights, is at the heart of what it is to lead a human existence. And we value what makes life human over and above what makes it happy. What makes life 'human' in the special normative sense that the word has here centres on 'agency'. One component of agency is deciding for oneself. Even if I constantly made a mess of my life, even if you could do better if you took charge, I would not let you do it. Autonomy has a value of its own. Another component is having the basic capabilities that enable one to act: limbs and senses that work, the minimum material goods to keep body and soul together, freedom from great pain and anxiety. Another component is liberty: the freedom to read and to listen to others, the absence of obstacles to action in those areas of our life that are the essential manifestations of our humanity —our speech, worship and associations".
3. *understanding:* "Simply knowing about oneself and one's place in the world — certain important anthropocentric knowledge— is part of a good life. We value, not as an instrument but for itself, the authenticity of our experience, life free from illusion and delusion…".
4. *enjoyment:* "We value pleasures, the perception of beauty, the enjoyment of the day-to-day textures of life".
5. *deep personal relations:* "When personal relations become deep, reciprocal relations of friendship and love, then they have a value apart from the pleasure and profit they bring".[28]

Griffin's categories[29] of 'understanding' and 'deep personal relations' (which we may assume includes marriage) find direct parallels in Finnis. The 'components of a human existence' seem to include life and practical reasonableness, but are wider and also include autonomy, basic physical capabilities (limbs and senses that work), minimum material goods, freedom from pain and anxiety, and liberty. The categories of 'accomplishment' and 'enjoyment' have no exact parallel in Finnis' account (although they are related to skilful performance in work and aesthetic appreciation, respectively), and are new propositions to be considered.

Martha Nussbaum's Basic Human Capabilities

Martha Nussbaum, the Ernst Freund Professor of Law and Ethics at the University of Chicago, is developing a neo-Aristotelian account of universal values "as a foundation for basic political principles that should underwrite constitutional guarantees".[30] This account articulates human flourishing in terms of capabilities, which are the set of valuable beings and doings that a person or society has a real (both internal and external) possibility of enjoying. Nussbaum identifies a list of basic capabilities that "have value in themselves" (rather than being merely instrumental), and are specific yet open to plural specification.[31] Her list is incomplete; it identifies only the set of human capabilities that are necessary for a dignified human existence anywhere. She writes, "I believe that we can arrive at an enumeration of central elements of truly human functioning that can command a broad cross-cultural consensus".[32] Indeed she notes that her proposed list has already been revised a number of times and that it thus, in its present state, already represents a kind of "overlapping consensus".[33] By 'overlapping consensus' she intends the same definition as John Rawls: "that people may sign on to this conception as the free-standing moral core of a political conception, without accepting any particular metaphysical view of the world, any particular comprehensive ethical or religious view, or even any particular view of the person or of human nature".[34]

Nussbaum's inquiry produces a set of central human capabilities which "can always be contested and re-made" but which, like Rawls' primary goods, "can be endorsed for political purposes, as the moral basis of central constitutional guarantees, by people who otherwise have very different views of what a complete good life for a human being would be.[35]

She describes her central human functional capabilities in considerable detail (see Table 3.3, below). For Finnis and for Griffin, a one-word or one-phrase description of the elements is sufficient —people can supply the rest by recognising the value from their own experience and reflection. In contrast, Nussbaum's categories specify institutional or legal means that facilitate the concerned capabilities. This marks her approach as significantly different from Griffin's or Finnis', because whereas theirs represent generic dimensions of human value, hers is further downstream the operational process.

Her list of central capabilities are the following: life, bodily health, bodily integrity, senses, imagination and thought, emotions, practical reason, affiliation, other species, play, and control over one's environment.[36] In comparison with Finnis' set of reasons for actions, Nussbaum does not include excellence in work (although she does include play), marriage, or harmony with a greater-than-human source of meaning and value. She separates life from bodily health and bodily integrity, and practical reasonableness from 'control over one's environment'. She also includes categories that have an imperfect overlap with Finnis': 'senses, thought and imagination' (which include some knowledge), and 'emotions'. Her category of 'affiliation' seems roughly parallel to Finnis' 'friendship'. The category 'other species' is a new proposition.

Table 3.3   Nussbaum's 'central human functional capabilities'[37]

1. *life:* being able to live to the end of a human life of normal length; not dying prematurely, or before one's life is so reduced as to be not worth living.

2. *bodily health:* being able to have good health, including reproductive health; to be adequately nourished; to have adequate shelter.

3. *bodily integrity:* being able to move freely from place to place; having one's bodily boundaries treated as sovereign, i.e., being able to be secure against assault, including sexual assault, child sexual abuse, and domestic violence; having opportunities for sexual satisfaction and for choice in matters of reproduction.

4. *senses, imagination, thought:* being able to use the senses, to imagine, think, and reason —and to do these things in a "truly human" way, a way informed and cultivated by an adequate education, including, but by no means limited to, literacy and basic mathematical and scientific training; being able to use imagination and thought in connection with experiencing and producing self-expressive works and events of one's own choice —religious, literary, musical, and so forth; being able to use one's mind in ways protected by guarantees of freedom of expression with respect to both political and artistic speech, and freedom of religious exercise; being able to search for the ultimate meaning of life in one's own way; being able to have pleasurable experiences, and to avoid non-necessary pain.

5. *emotions:* being able to have attachments to things and persons outside ourselves; to love, to grieve, to experience longing, gratitude, and justified anger; not having one's emotional development blighted by overwhelming fear and anxiety, or by traumatic events of abuse or neglect. (Supporting this capability means supporting forms of human association that can be shown to be crucial in its development.)

6. *practical reason:* being able to form a conception of the good and to engage in critical reflection about the planning of one's own life. (This entails protection of liberty of conscience.)

7. *affiliation:* (a) being able to live for and toward others, to recognise and show concern for other human beings, to engage in various forms of social interaction; to be able to imagine the situation of another and to have compassion for them; to have the capability for both justice and friendship. (Protecting this capability means protecting institutions that constitute and nourish such forms of affiliation, and also protecting the freedoms of assembly and political speech.); (b) having the social bases of self-respect and non-humiliation; being able to be treated as a dignified being whose worth is equal to that of others.   (This entails, at a minimum, protections against

discrimination on the basis of race, sex, religion, caste, ethnicity, or national origin.)

8. *other species:* being able to live with concern for, and in relation to, animals, plants, and the world of nature.

9. *play:* being able to laugh, to play, to enjoy recreational activities.

10. *control over one's environment:* (a) political: being able to participate effectively in political choices that govern one's life; having the right of political participation, and protections of free speech and association; (b) material: being able to hold property (both land and moveable goods) not just formally but in terms of real opportunity; having property rights on an equal basis with others; having the freedom from unwarranted search and seizure: having the right to seek employment on an equal basis with others; being able to work as a human being, exercising practical reason and entering into relationships of mutual recognition with other workers.

Manfred Max-Neef's Axiological Categories

Manfred Max-Neef, a Chilean professor and activist, has, together with his associates, developed a matrix of human needs. He uses this matrix practically, to conduct community exercises in rural and urban areas —for example, in Argentina, Bolivia, Chile, Colombia, Sweden, and the UK. The exercises divide participants into groups of ten, who gather for two days. In "an intense process of introspective analysis",[38] each group analyses the needs and 'satisfiers' that have constructive or destructive effects in their society. Their analysis is informed by ten classes of need, each of which has four kinds of expression: being (attributes), having (tools, norms), doing (agency), and interacting (social expressions in time and space). For example, Max-Neef proposes that the human need for 'understanding' has the following expressions:[39]

Table 3.4 Max-Neef's 'expressions' of the 'need' for understanding

Need	Expressions of a need			
	Being	*Having*	*Doing*	*Interacting*
UNDER-STANDING	critical conscience, receptiveness, curiosity, astonishment, discipline, intuition, rationality	literature, teachers, method, educational policies, communication policies	investigate, study, experiment, educate, analyse, meditate	settings of formative interaction, schools, universities, academies, groups, communities, family

Like Finnis' and Griffin's, Max-Neef's classification is generic. He argues that "needs can be satisfied … with different intensities", and at the level of the individual, of the social group, or of the environment.[40] Needs which are not adequately satisfied constitute an aspect of human poverty. In his own work with groups, Max-Neef devotes considerable attention to the thesis that poverty generates social pathology.

Max-Neef presents and describes several criteria he has used in constructing his classification of human needs, so as to be of use to a community that wishes to interpret its own situation holistically. The criteria indicate that this set of needs *is* intended to be exhaustive —to indicate all dimensions of human need that are universal (even though they may not all be observable in every community) and relevant in different cultures. Furthermore, the fact that each need must be "readily recognizable and identifiable as one's own" suggests that persons are understood to be engaging practical reason when they reflect on this list.

Table 3.5   Max-Neef's criteria for the classification of needs

1. *the classification must be understandable:* the needs listed must be readily recognisable and identifiable as one's own.
2. *the classification must combine scope with specificity:* it must arrive at a limited number of needs which can be clearly yet simply labelled but, at the same time, be comprehensive enough to incorporate any fundamental felt need.
3. *the classification must be operational:* for every existing or conceivable satisfier[41] one or more of the needs stated must appear as a target-need of the satisfier (in other words, any action or organisation must be intelligible by reference to the needs as 'reasons for action').
4. *the classification must be critical:* it is not sufficient for the categorisation to relate satisfiers to needs; it is essential to detect needs for which no desirable satisfier exists; it is also crucial to identify and restrain those satisfiers which inhibit the actualisation of needs.
5. *the classification must be propositional:* in so far as it is critical and capable of detecting inadequacies in the relation between the existing satisfiers and the fulfilment of needs, this classification will serve to work out an alternative order capable of generating and encouraging satisfiers for the needs of every man and woman as integral beings.[42]

The ten elements of Max-Neef's matrix are: subsistence, protection, affection, understanding, participation, leisure, creation, identity, and freedom. Interestingly, they form the closest parallel to Finnis' set: subsistence and protection together parallel life; understanding parallels knowledge; creation and leisure parallel work and play; participation and identity parallel practical reason (or, as in Finnis's 1987 formulation, expression and self-integration); and affection parallels friendship. Max-Neef has no distinct category for marriage or religion/transcendence. He writes that he does not think transcendence is a universal need yet, although it may become so.[43]

Rokeach's Value Survey

In the early 1970s, social psychologist Milton Rokeach constructed an account of human values which has informed a substantial body of empirical psychological research on values. Rokeach defined a value as "an enduring belief that a specific mode of conduct or end-state of existence is personally or socially preferable to an opposite or converse mode of conduct or end-state of existence".[44] He assumed that: the total number of values that a person possesses is relatively small; people everywhere possess the same values to different degrees; values are organised into value systems; antecedents of human values can be traced to culture, society and social institutions, and personality; and consequences of human values will be manifested in virtually all phenomena.[45] His account identified two 'kinds' of values: terminal values or ends —which may be personal (salvation, mature love) or social (world peace, brotherhood)— and instrumental values or "modes of conduct". Rokeach described his project as an endeavour to study values in a "value-free" way. This phrase, which brings to mind Finnis' observation that the discussion of reasons for action is pre-moral, indicates that the values are not meant to communicate or advocate a particular moral framework; they are the elements out of which different moralities are constructed.

Rokeach identified eighteen terminal values and eighteen instrumental ones. The terminal values were drawn from several hundred identified in literature and personal experience. The selection of the final list was informed by Rokeach's definition of terminal value and by two empirical studies (one in a hundred American cities; one with thirty graduate students), but was otherwise 'intuitive' (for which it has been criticised subsequently).[46] The original Rokeach Values Survey (1982), which has been extensively applied, required participants to 'rank' each of the eighteen values in importance from 1 to 18, providing separate rankings for the two kinds of values. Modifications were made in the survey's procedure subsequently. For example, participants were asked to rate the strength of the value rather than rank all eighteen (because of complaints that some values seemed equivalent, while others were unrankable).[47]

Finnis' account of reasons for action corresponds, roughly, to Rokeach's category of terminal values or ends, so it is this list that we will consider.[48] They are: a comfortable life, an exciting life, a sense of accomplishment, a world at peace, a world of beauty, equality, family security, freedom, happiness, inner harmony, mature love, national security, pleasure, salvation, self-respect, social recognition, true friendship, and wisdom. There are parallels here with all of Finnis' basic human values, except for (perhaps) marriage and 'life'.[49] Wisdom parallels Finnis' knowledge for its own sake; true friendship parallels friendship; mature love parallels marriage and friendship; inner harmony, freedom, and self-respect may parallel practical reasonableness, albeit imperfectly; and salvation parallels harmony. In addition, like Nussbaum and Griffin, Rokeach includes pleasure (as well as happiness); and like Griffin, he includes 'accomplishment'. The categories 'social recognition', 'an exciting life', and 'family security', represent new propositions.

Shalom Schwartz's Universal Human Values

Shalom Schwartz holds the Clara and Leon Sznajdermain Chair as Professor of Psychology at the Hebrew University of Jerusalem. He has proposed and revised a "theory of the universal content and structure of human values" based on empirical cross-cultural research. In developing a framework for this empirical research, Schwartz has tried to formulate: "the substantive content" of values; the "comprehensiveness" of the values identified; whether the values have some equivalence of meaning across groups of people; and whether there is a meaningful and identifiable structure of relations among different values.

Schwartz defines values as "desirable trans-situational goals, varying in importance, that serve as guiding principles in the life of a person or other social entity. Implicit in this definition of values as goals is that: (1) they serve the interests of some social entity; (2) they can motivate action, giving it direction and emotional intensity; (3) they function as standards for judging and justifying action; and (4) they are acquired both through socialization to dominant group values and through the unique learning experiences of individuals".[50] In contrast to Rokeach and others, Schwartz argues that "there is a values space that can be carved into (arbitrary) categories that relate to one another on a motivational continuum. The latter is why they form a coherent structure".[51]

Schwartz has progressively tested his theory in different countries (on all inhabited continents), regions, religions, and language groups; and he has made adjustments to the list of values along the way. Initially, the respondents were generally university students and school teachers; more recent data includes twelve near-representative national samples, and eight samples using adolescents. Respondents are presented with a list of about thirty terminal values and about twenty-six instrumental values identified (as in Rokeach's study) by two or three brief phrases. They then "set their scale" by choosing and rating the most important value as seven ("of supreme importance"), and the least important value as one. Finally, they rate how each value fares "as a guiding principle in my life" on a scale from negative one to seven.[52]

Schwartz selected fifty-six values by drawing on values literature;[53] and he modified his substantive list of value dimensions in response to evidence from about two hundred surveys in sixty-four countries involving well over 60,000 respondents.[54] His current set of comprehensive[55] value dimensions is set out in Table 3.6 below.

Table 3.6 Schwartz's 'value dimensions'

1. *power:* social status and prestige, control over people and resources.
2. *achievement:* personal success through demonstrating competence according to social standards.
3. *hedonism:* pleasure and sensuous gratification for oneself.
4. *stimulation:* excitement, novelty, and challenge in life.
5. *self-direction:* independent thought and action —choosing, creating, exploring.
6. *universalism:* understanding, appreciation, tolerance, and protection for the welfare of all people and for nature.
7. *benevolence:* preservation and enhancement of the welfare of people with whom one is in frequent personal contact.
8. *tradition:* respect, commitment, and acceptance of the customs and ideas that traditional culture or religion provide.
9. *conformity:* restraint of actions, inclinations, and impulses likely to upset or harm others and violate social expectations or norms.
10. *security:* safety, harmony, and stability of society, relationships, and self.

Schwartz asserts, in defence of this list, that "[i]t is possible to classify virtually all the items found in lists of specific values from different cultures into one of these ten motivational types of values".[56]

Schwartz also tested an eleventh value, 'the goal of finding meaning in life' or spirituality; but he found that, as it is not derivable from universal human requirements,[57] it may not be recognised across cultures.

Schwartz's dimensions do not include life (in the sense of health and reproduction —security is mentioned) or marriage. Achievement appears again as a value which may parallel accomplishment or 'excellence in work and play'. Pleasure and stimulation also appear again. Further, there are new items —power, conformity, tradition, and universalism— that have not been encountered in previous lists.

As these dimensions suggest, Schwartz has tested and rejected Rokeach's separation of terminal and instrumental (mode of conduct) values.[58] This might make his work more difficult to compare with Finnis' than the previous writers, because the dimensions named above conflate principles of practical reasonableness and basic human goods.[59] However, Schwartz claims that *each* of these value areas contains both terminal and instrumental aspects. If that is the case, then one could try to imagine and consider the claimed 'terminal' aspect of each dimension (for example, universalism and benevolence must relate somehow to goods of affiliation or relationship with people and other species).[60] Furthermore, as Schwartz's work has the most substantive empirical grounding of current values research, it seems important to consider it in detail.

Robert Cummins' Quality of Life Domains

Robert Cummins, Professor of Psychology at Deakin University, Australia, has surveyed theoretical and empirical literature on the 'quality of life', and classified "the terminology used by researchers in the social sciences to define domains of subjective well-being". Initially, he reviewed twenty-seven different accounts of 'quality of life' domains (note: this literature does not overlap with the sources of previous authors)[61] and found that a clear majority supported five of his seven domains; 22% and 30% supported the remaining domains of safety and community, respectively.

Subsequently, Cummins 'tested' his seven domains in the following way. Over 1,500 journal articles on the quality of life were identified. To these Cummins applied five criteria for inclusion in his study (i.e., a minimum of three domains, breadth of range, exclusion of happiness criteria, etc.), which thirty-two studies of the (overwhelmingly Western) articles met. Together these proposed 173 names of 'domains' for quality of life indicators (the aggregate number of domains was 351, but there were some repetitions). Cummins either classified each domain into one of the seven categories or else left it unclassified as a residual.[62] His work was checked by two colleagues, and differences of opinion were resolved by discussion. Cummins found that 68% of the 173 values domains (83% of the 351 domains mentioned) could be sorted into the seven headings.[63]

Cummins' seven domains are: material well-being, health, productivity, intimacy/friendship, safety, community, and emotional well-being. Material well-being, health, and safety clearly parallel Finnis' 'life'; productivity may be a sub-set of 'excellence in work and play'; intimacy or friendship parallels Finnis' friendship at least, and probably marriage as well; emotional well-being is a sub-component, perhaps, of practical reasonableness (harmony of thoughts and feelings); the category of 'community' is a new proposition. Missing from Cummins' synthesis (although not from his sources) is knowledge, practical reasonableness in the sense of meaningful choice, and harmony with a greater-than-human source of meaning and value.

Cummins' work is of interest because it aggregates and consolidates empirical work (although entirely on the basis of consensus rather than reasoned argument), and so provides a taxonomy of a different kind of indicator of human flourishing; namely, social indicators of the quality of life. Also, in order to be suitable for surveys asking people how satisfied they are in a certain respect, Cummins' domains have to be accessible to practical reason and appropriate for public discussion.

Maureen Ramsey's Universal Psychological Needs

Another similar exercise in 'list consolidation' was done by Maureen Ramsay. Ramsey was interested in identifying "objective and essential" physical and mental health needs in order to develop empirical indicators of them and identify means of satisfying them. She studied the psychological needs identified by ten authors (not covered by Rokeach):[64] Brentano,[65] Maslow,[66] Fromm,[67] Nielsen,[68] Lane,[69] Davies,[70] Packard,[71] Galtung,[72] Mallman,[73] and Kretch, Crutchfield, and Livson.[74] Based on convergence rather than reasoned argument,[75] she classified their lists into six categories of need: physical survival, sexual needs,[76] security, love and relatedness, esteem and identity, and self-realisation. She drew mainly on clinical studies to substantiate each category as a 'need'.[77]

Ramsay's work is included because it draws on a distinct and well-established literature in behavioural psychology and social theory. Her approach, like Cummins', classifies lists of needs according to the author's taxonomy —which is a distinct exercise from the synthesis project to be discussed shortly, but it is nevertheless useful to study.

Her final list does not include knowledge, harmony with a greater-than-human source of meaning and value, or, possibly, practical reasonableness. However, six of the ten source-lists have elements that, arguably, refer to these dimensions[78] —and these elements may be found scattered around four of her six different categories.

These seven authors, then, provide "an assemblage of reminders of the range of possibly worthwhile activities and orientations open to one". For example, various proposals for new dimensions have been encountered: e.g., other species, enjoyment, novelty, self-respect, social recognition, power, and so on. Partial reformulations or a redrawing of boundary lines might be considered in light of categories such as accomplishment, health and security as distinct from survival, identity or inner harmony as distinct from freedom or participation, etc. The possibility of separating out the social dimension from the personal dimension has been raised repeatedly. The repeated omission of dimensions such as 'knowledge' and 'harmony with a greater-than-human source of meaning and value' should provoke discussion as to whether or not these dimensions are indeed necessary. The second half of this chapter will evaluate these and other considerations which seem to arise from the various lists.

Dialogue with Finnis

Method of Analysis

As may be apparent, the description and consideration of even as few as seven different lists raises more issues than can be adequately addressed here, and there are a variety of ways of organising a discussion about them. This discussion will be divided into three topics: the boundaries and adequacy of the items in Finnis' 1996 list; the proposals of new items to be added; and the relationship between the individual and society vis-à-vis the goods. Our aim is to judge the adequacy of Finnis' list of basic reasons for action against his definition of them. On this basis, we may establish some procedures for inquiry. First, this approach will differ considerably from the aggregation or consolidation exercises of Cummins and Ramsay, because categories which are not basic reasons for action would need to be articulated as reasons for action in order to enter this discussion. Second, while the consensus of a number of writers and empirical studies on the validity of a certain dimension may indicate an additional condition for inclusion, the consensus (or majority-view) of authors cannot be the sole basis on which to modify or append the current list. Third, it must be stated clearly that there will be a different kind of validity to the different formulations of what needs, values or capabilities are; and a judgement that a particular category is not appropriate as a 'basic reason for action' is not a judgement on its appropriateness in the author's own conceptualisation. Fourth, a critical assessment of the empirical studies that are invoked in support of particular lists of values is beyond the scope of this chapter.

In "Practical Principles, Moral Truth and Ultimate Ends", Grisez, Boyle, and Finnis outline criteria for judging whether to add or delete candidates from their set of basic reasons for action. Substituting 'dimension' (of value) for 'basic reason for action' or 'basic good', these may be summarized as follows:

1. the dimension must be based in practical reason.
2. it must be irreducible: dimensions are reasons for action which need no further reason, and they must not include items which are a subset of some other valuable and basic reason for acting.
3. the dimension must represent complete reasons for acting: that is, it cannot be a basic motive (e.g., pleasure, pain) which is valuable only when its pursuit coheres with the pursuit of a valuable reason; further, it must be intrinsically rather than only instrumentally valuable ('only' is an important qualification because some basic items —like life or knowledge— will also have an instrumental dimension).
4. the dimensions are not virtues: dimensions of human flourishing represent the basic values people are seeking when they "be and do and have and interact", morally or immorally; they are neither virtues nor personal qualities (e.g., gentleness, self-respect).[79]

These criteria will inform our discussion below.

The Boundaries and Adequacy of Finnis' Dimensions

A number of dimensions have been presented by these studies as different ways of conceptualising elements shared with Finnis, or as specifications or combinations of items on his lists.   This section will consider the implications of these studies for each of Finnis' basic reasons for action.

Bodily life (health, vigour and safety) This category was present in all but the lists of Rokeach and Schwartz, and their omission of this item has been discussed already. However, five lists distinguished security or safety from life,[80] and at least one distinguished health.   Leaving aside the issue of health, the question is whether security is an intrinsically valuable dimension distinct from physical well-being (subsistence and health).

The ground for seeing security as a facet of bodily life seems to rest on the observation that if one acts for security —for example, in buckling a seat-belt or in reforming a police force or in accepting a less interesting job that will provide economic security— part of the reason for acting is indistinguishable from subsistence or health: if we suffer an accident or attack, our bodies will be damaged; if we do not have an income or our goods are stolen, our health and nutritional status may suffer.

However, there is another aspect to security, which refers to the anxiety induced by danger, by deep uncertainty about the future, and so on. In this framework, one acts for security in order to be able to be free of control by forces beyond oneself (war, poverty, assault, chance).   This possibility-of-not-being-controlled could be phrased positively as the 'possibility of exerting control' or of 'making meaningful choices'.   Put thus, the element of safety or security which is not present in life or health could be viewed as a part of practical reasonableness, or self-determination. So security seems to be a reason for action which pertains to (the preservation of) life, and to some wider reason for action which is related to practical reasonableness; but it is not a distinct reason for action.

Knowledge   Schwartz, Cummins, and Ramsey do not include any dimension which relates to understanding for its own sake.[81] Yet the questions of a three-year-old ('Why is the sky blue?'), or adult curiosity about politicians' personal lives or the zebra's feeding patterns, can be justified by the simple statement, 'I just want to know, that's all'. Nussbaum groups 'thought' with senses and imagination in one category, which is actually the closest parallel to Finnis' aligning aesthetic appreciation with knowledge. Rokeach includes wisdom (an understanding of life); Max-Neef and Griffin include understanding for its own sake. Hence this dimension will be retained, but called 'understanding', since this may express more clearly its 'for-its-own-sake' nature than 'knowledge' (especially when, as now, knowledge and information are most often assumed to be means to an end).

Skilful performance in work and play No other author speaks of skilful performance in work and play for its own sake in their final accounts of value. However, five authors mention accomplishment or achievement or productivity or creation, which raises the question whether any or all of these point to the same basic reason for action.[82]

The ground for accepting this proposition in the case of Schwartz, Max-Neef, and Cummins is the following. Finnis' category is 'skilful performance in work and play for its own sake'. It seems that the terms 'work' and 'play' function to make the reason for action widely applicable to many activities. Hence it might make as much sense to call it 'skilful performance for its own sake'. One instantiates this dimension when one truly exerts oneself in practising the oboe, or in writing, or in preparing a meal, or in doing a good job as a barmaid or surgeon or linesman. In this sense, it seems likely that these different terms are gesturing to the same dimension: the performing of a creative activity with excellence.

The ground for rejecting the proposition is that in some accounts — Griffin's certainly, and perhaps others— the term 'accomplishment' expands beyond work and play and includes excellence in friendship, art, knowledge, and self-understanding. In this sense, 'accomplishment' or 'achievement' would refer to excellence in pursuing *each* dimension —a way of pursuing activities— rather than to a distinct end in itself. Here, David Wiggins' suggestion comes to mind, that what one might seek to maximize is not utility but meaning.[83] This does not make accomplishment at all irrelevant; it merely suggests that to call accomplishment in Griffin's sense a basic reason for action would be a mistake. In Finnis' and Grisez's theory, the work of such a concept is done by one or more of the self-evident 'principles of practical reasonableness'.

Like Finnis in *Natural Law and Natural Rights*, Nussbaum distinguishes play from other dimensions and especially from 'serious' undertakings. It could refer to activities which are not serious —such as comedy, song, game, decoration, or dance. But these could be seen as done for the sake of creative expression —the kind of value someone participates in by singing for fun, even though she is not a great singer and has never considered taking voice lessons. Clearly a professional cricket player might consider a good game to be an 'accomplishment' in the sense mentioned above. But people recognise the difference between playing music or sport 'for fun', or painting and writing 'because they want to', and doing these things as a professional. There is a difference too between this and 'aesthetic appreciation', in the sense of the contemplation of a work of art done by another. Here I tentatively propose play or creative expression as a separate reason for action, but I will return to it when we consider 'enjoyment' and the different aspects of practical reasonableness.

Marriage   No author presented an equivalent of this.[84] The closest is Rokeach's 'mature love (sexual and spiritual intimacy)'. Ramsay identified 'sexual needs', but subsequently discussed these as parts of other domains rather than as a discrete one. Griffin's 'deep personal relationships', Cummins' 'intimacy or friendship', and Max-Neef's 'affection' presumably include marriage as well as other friendships. So one question here is whether this 'reason for action' is sufficiently distinct from friendship in general. The response depends on whether or not affection, sexuality, and intimacy fall on a continuum which parallels the intensity of friendship conceived of as mutual concern and appreciation. If not, and if affection is a basic reason for action, then the distinction should be preserved; there would be two basic reasons for action.

Even if Finnis' dimension were to be recognised, the word 'marriage' may not be the best title for it. While all of the other basic reasons for action are named in such a way that refers the reader to a good, the word 'marriage' to many ears and in many languages connotes a culturally specific ceremony or a social institution or the joining of two families, rather than a pre-moral *value* involving a joining of lives that includes sexual intimacy, a meaningful relationship, and possibly procreation. This is potentially confusing, since reflection on the name of culturally particular institutions may not lead people in one place to recognise the same underlying good(s) which persons in other places recognise and associate with that institution.

Finnis argues that marriage is different in kind from the other reasons for action in that it represents two factors: first, sexual union and possibly procreation and the joint raising of children; and second, friendship or companionship. From these two separable factors, he argues, comes a kind of good which is irreducible to either. Still, it does not quite seem the case that if a person asks, 'Why do I do what I do?', often enough, the *only* reason they will come up with will be, 'Because she's my wife' — another equally simple reason may be, 'Because he's my son'.

The other way of conceiving of the good of marriage would be as a commitment that joins intimate friendship or sexual union with companionship, possibly procreation, and probably other things as well. The difficulty with protecting the sexual commitment as constituent of a distinct, internally plural reason for action (rather than a nexus of basic reasons for action joined by the commitment), is its arbitrariness. It seems arbitrary to grant special status to one joint 'commitment' (in Grisez's and Finnis' sense[85]), when there are other commitments of similar depth that have equal claim to distinction —for example, parenthood, which exceeds the category of 'friendship' into which the theory currently puts it. One might also propose sexual partnership as a distinct reason for action; but this seems an incomplete description of a dimension valued for the depth and duration of human interaction and probably involving significant emotional, intellectual, and spiritual intimacy. A further description of this kind, however, makes this category overlap with friendship, and so does not evade the problem of internal plurality. Therefore, for the moment I will allow —with Griffin, Max-Neef, Ramsay, and Cummins— one reason for action to cover friendship and intimacy.

One could go part of the way towards addressing the above problems by proposing 'family' as a distinctive reason for action. This would include reproduction and the raising of one's children. However, as none of our sources propose this, we will not pursue the matter further here.

Friendship Friendship was present in some way or another in all of the accounts. The question that arises here is whether friendship —the one basic reason for action— can meaningfully cover the full range of relationships and interactions it intends, from family and close friends to pals on the local cricket team, acquaintances, and one-off social encounters. The issue is not whether instantiations of friendship vary in value and intensity —this is the case for all dimensions[86]— but whether they can be conceived as different facets of a single reason for action, or whether more than one dimension is involved here.

Rokeach, for example, identified 'social recognition' and Ramsay identified 'esteem and identity needs' (but *each* of her ten source-materials include esteem, recognition, a sense of belonging, etc., as *distinct from* the needs for identity, self-realisation, and self-actualisation). Cummins identified the category 'community' as distinct from that of intimacy or friendship.[87]   Schwartz's categories of conformity and power and universalism all seem related. One proposition that might arise from this is that there is a dimension of 'community' or 'belonging' that is distinct from friendship —a good of 'being a part of' that is distinct from the individual quest for identity and the achievement of self-respect, but which is realised when a community validates the identity of an individual.

Our discussion of the dimensions of marriage and friendship requires a brief excursus to clarify their applicability to a group rather than an individual. Finnis has framed his basic goods so that they encompass both individual and social flourishing. This is helpful because, as we have seen, some of the proposals for forming 'distinct' categories arise out of a distinction between individual and group expressions of a single dimension; and these may be declined once it is clear that social values are already included. One way to do this is to use Max-Neef's format to highlight the social or 'interacting' aspect of a dimension:

Table 3.7   The social aspect of Finnis' goods

Dimension	Expressions of a dimension			
	Being	*Having*	*Doing*	*Interacting*
LIFE				'world at peace', 'national security', looking after the poor…
FRIEND-SHIP				universalism, general benevolence, community

This may serve to clarify immediately that Rokeach's 'a world at peace' — and indeed all of the terminal values that he considers 'social' rather than 'personal'— should not be considered as distinct dimensions, but rather as social aspects of other dimensions. Peace, for example, is an aspect of life and of practical reasonableness. Accordingly, rather than immediately proceeding to designate 'social recognition' or 'social esteem' as a distinct dimension —although references to it are very prominent in the literature— we will delay consideration until we discuss practical reasonableness, because 'social recognition' is best understood as indicating the social aspect of this basic reason.

Practical reasonableness   All authors except Cummins, Griffin, and possibly Ramsay designated practical reason as a distinct dimension; but among them a number of distinctions were made which bear consideration. Nussbaum separated practical reason ('being able to form a conception of the good and to engage in critical reflection about the planning of one's life') and 'control over one's environment' (one of whose two sub-components is political participation).   Rokeach separated freedom (independence, free choice) from inner harmony (freedom from inner conflict).   Schwartz specified this dimension as 'self-direction'.   Max-Neef presented three related categories: participation, identity, and freedom. Furthermore, as mentioned above, Ramsey's esteem and identity category, and the various other categories related to social recognition and power, may be a social expression of practical reason rather than of friendship. The question to be tackled here is how many irreducible reasons for action this cluster contains.

In response, we begin by classifying the candidates into four basic categories. First of all, comes *identity* (that is, choices related to oneself). There seems to be a widely recognised reason for action which has to do with the choice, construction, and expression of the identity of the individual or community, which may also be termed self-direction or self-determination. Furthermore, when this identity is recognised and affirmed by others, another value (self-respect, social recognition) emerges.[88]

The second category is *inner harmony*. This seems to be closest to what Finnis intended by 'practical reasonableness' in 1996 (harmony between one's feelings, judgements, and behaviour), and 'self-integration' in 1987. It comprises the integration of emotions, thoughts, and actions. People act in part to instantiate this need when, for example, they talk with a friend about a problem that is bothering them, when they take a vacation alone after a time of crisis, or even when they act impulsively.   Social expressions of this dimension might be discussion, participation, consensus-building, and such like.[89]

Then there is *meaningful choice*. We mentioned, in discussing security above, that the possibility of not being controlled by external forces, of exercising some meaningful choices in one's environment, is an aspect of security that might fit into agency. These choices might have to do with one's own personal life-choices, as in self-determination; but more often they might also be choices on behalf of others, or choices about others (which would include Schwartz' dimension of power), or even choices which have but a marginal relation to personal identity.[90]

Griffin and Rokeach also propose 'liberty' as a distinct dimension of human flourishing. However, liberty is not itself a basic reason for action: one requires liberty in order to have the capability to pursue meaningful actions. In that sense, it is instrumental. Liberty which is not instrumental is found in the potential to exercise meaningful choices which constitute one's identity and commitments.

The final potential category is *creative expression*. Finnis' argument against "pleasure being the point of it all"[91] challenges the claims set forward by various authors that 'pleasure', 'enjoyment', and 'hedonism' are self-standing basic reasons for action; and this line of criticism is not refuted by any of the mentioned authors.[92]

As was mentioned in the section on work and play above, there may be a category of creative expression (which may not necessarily be *self*-expression: e.g., playing hockey 'for fun', or making private sketches of flowers, or relating a funny story) that is enjoyable even if not performed 'excellently'; whose value resides in the doing of the thing and not in the decision to do it or the quality of the performance; and which is valuable whether done alone or with others.

Now that I have reduced to four the candidates for the status of a basic reason for action, let me proceed to evaluate them. I propose that identity and meaningful choice be considered expressions of the same basic reason, made on different terrains. The exercise of practical reason —of meaningful choice— creates a personal identity. The exercise of choice in personal commitments not only creates this identity but also determines social and relational identities. And the choice of positions on meaningful issues which seem remote from personal identity —such as political platforms— is nonetheless continuous with the need to fashion and express both a personal and communal identity.

I propose creative expression as a distinct dimension that is the same as 'play'.

I also propose inner harmony or self-integration as a separate dimension, though this may require further review. In Grisez's and Finnis' account, emotions are motives for action that are neither necessarily moral nor necessarily immoral. Since other basic reasons for action make intelligible both moral and immoral actions, this does not rule out emotions as a candidate. Moral action engages appropriate emotional motives. This means that the exercise of practical reason, fully explicated, includes the sifting and engagement of emotions —and of other dimensions as well. Yet in practical reflection, persons commonly can and must distinguish the value of acting to express or satisfy an emotion, from acting for a reason. This distinction is clearly seen when one contrasts acting well out of duty and in spite of one's emotions —where there is inner turmoil and so the need for an exercise of will— from acting well and with passion, when one's emotions, desires, and actions are all aligned. The latter seems more fulfilling; and so I propose it as a separate reason for action.

Harmony with greater-than-human source of meaning and value   Any explicit reference to spirituality, transcendence, or religion as a distinct domain of value was missing from five of the seven lists examined. This would seem to raise doubts about whether this represents a distinct basic reason for acting. However, such a dimension is not so absent as it might appear. Max-Neef omits it, not because he does not consider it valuable, but rather because (in his view) humanity has not yet evolved to the state where the need for 'transcendence' is universal. Most authors distribute factors of religion or spirituality among other dimensions, which is not surprising, given that across cultures faiths, like commitments, combine different elements of human and social life. Nussbaum distributes elements of spirituality among the capabilities of affiliation, emotion, imagination, thought, and so on.[93] Schwartz tested a category called spirituality, and found "that no clear set of at least three values that might be thought to represent spirituality recurs as a group across the majority of nations".[94] Five of Ramsay's ten contributing authors had specific domains that related to faith, and she distributed them among other categories.[95]   Similarly, nearly half of Cummins' sources refer to this: eight of his twenty-seven "lists of quality of life domains" do include 'religion'; one includes 'comfort from religion'; one, 'the spiritual life'; and two, 'psychological or spiritual well-being' (Cummins grouped all of these under 'emotional well-being'). Griffin, in contrast, lacks spirituality either as a domain or a sub-component of a domain, or as a possible eventual domain. So, although there is no consensus here, there is considerably more implicit affirmation of religion or spirituality than first appears.

The outstanding question is whether the dimensions among which religious or spiritual elements are scattered exhaustively represent religion or spirituality, or whether these should be designated an additional 'reason' for action. I will label this candidate 'spirituality', since it should not be assumed to entail theism.

This possible dimension refers to reflection on the overall ends of human life, and to practices such as prayer, meditation, and contemplation by which the self unites with a transcendent reality. It is related to self-integration, although this involves one's personal mixture of emotions — anger, compassion, jealousy, love, competitiveness, disappointment, hope— whereas 'spirituality' is about a more fundamental coherence. It is firmly engaged with the quest for meaning, which has been repeatedly acknowledged ('meaningful choice') and which occurs at both an individual and social level. Certainly, religious persons may understand individual and social choices, relationships, accomplishments, and emotions to have a religious hue, but this hue is not fully explained by the other dimensions taken together.

Therefore, I propose harmony with a greater-than-human source of meaning and value as a distinct basic reason for human action, and one of several dimensions of human flourishing, while acknowledging that further work needs to be done on this.

Addendum: the Natural Environment

Nussbaum proposes "being able to live with concern for and in relation to animals, plants, and the world of nature" as a basic capability. Is this a basic reason for action distinct from those already discussed? Part of the value of harmony with the non-human environment is aesthetic —for example, the beauty of crashing waves or of a soaring heron. Part of the value of the environment to people is that it provides life —nourishment and security— and is also instrumental to work and leisure. Part of the value of animals is instrumental, if they are for food or work or security; and one's relationship to domestic animals also partakes in a limited way of the value of friendship. Part of being at harmony with nature is very much like being at harmony with a greater-than-human source of meaning and value —and, indeed, Finnis earlier described this dimension as "harmony between oneself and the wider reaches of reality".[96] Nevertheless, I would propose harmony with the natural world as a distinct reason for action, since it is not reducible to the other aspects of human relatedness, i.e., harmony between all the dimensions within the self, with other people, and with God.[97]

Conclusion

On the basis of the consideration of seven authors' diverse accounts of basic values, which purport to be exhaustive and cross-culturally valid, this study proposes the following list of basic reasons for action:

1. life (health, security, reproduction);
2. understanding for its own sake;
3. skilful performance and production;
4. creative expression (play, humour, sport);
5. friendship and affiliation;
6. meaningful choice and identity;
7. inner harmony between feelings, judgements, and behaviour;
8. harmony with a greater-than-human source of meaning and value;
9. harmony with the natural world.

The names of the categories are not especially important; indeed, some flexibility in labelling is positively desirable, because people will have different responses to different words, and may need to be reminded of the breadth of territory each reason could encompass.

Further reflection, both philosophical and empirical, is required to take this study forward. In particular, the literature of values research (especially anthropological) in other languages and covering other geographical areas, needs to be reviewed and its data incorporated. The synthesis presented here could be used as a working hypothesis to be tested by empirical studies of global values; and it could offer constructive criticism of the theories of values being used in psychology and in social indicators research. Still, the validity of the dimensions of human flourishing proposed in this chapter needs further scrutiny and development. Further, the distinguishing and designation of basic reasons for action contains a genuine element of ambiguity that must be emphasised over and over again, rather than too quickly hidden. Max-Neef, Grisez, and others have found that the value of having a set of dimensions becomes apparent when it is used practically. Hence, to quote Galtung, this discussion would be satisfactory, not if it were final, but rather if it were fruitful; that is, if it served "to identify problems already known to be important" and if it were able "to guide us further in understanding problems that may become important one day but have not yet crystallized sufficiently".[98]

APPENDIX I

Table 3.8 The dimensions of human flourishing: a summary of the lists

Finnis (1996)	Griffin	Rokeach
bodily life – health, vigour, and safety	accomplishment components of human existence	a comfortable life (prosperous life)
knowledge	deciding for	an exciting life (a stimulating, active life)
skilful perform-	oneself/agency	a sense of accomplishment (lasting contribution)
ance in work	minimum material	a world at peace (free of war and conflict)
and play	goods	a world of beauty (beauty of nature and the arts)
friendship	limbs and senses	equality (brotherhood, opportunity for all)
marriage	that work	family security (taking care of loved ones)
practical	freedom from pain	freedom (independence, free choice)
reasonable-	and anxiety	happiness (contentedness)
ness	liberty	inner harmony (freedom from inner conflict)
harmony with	understanding	mature love (sexual and spiritual intimacy)
ultimate	enjoyment	national security (protection from attack)
source of	deep personal	pleasure (an enjoyable, leisurely life)
reality	relations	salvation (saved, eternal life)
		self-respect (self-esteem)
		social recognition (respect, admiration)
		true friendship (close companionship)
		wisdom (a mature understanding of life)

Nussbaum	Schwartz	Cummins	Max-Neef
life	power	material well-being,	subsistence
bodily health	achievement	health,	protection
bodily integrity	hedonism	productivity,	affection
senses, thought imagination,	stimulation	intimacy/ friendship,	understanding
emotions	self-direction	safety,	participation
practical reason	universalism	community,	leisure
affiliation	benevolence	emotional well-	creation
other species	tradition	being	identity
play	conformity		freedom
control over one's environment	security		

APPENDIX II

Commitment

Commitments are a particular kind of free choice. They are subjective orderings of the basic human goods, executed by repeated free choices (or large organising free choices[99]) to focus legitimately on certain goods or aspects of goods to the exclusion of others —for choices necessarily constrain action to a limited set of objectives.[100] Commitments are not long-term goals which can be accomplished, but are open-ended decisions to pursue a set of goods. Yet like long-term goals, they are to be carried out by many small choices. Commitments are not made by 'commensuration' between basic human goods, nor are they a voluntary 'choosing' certain basic values for oneself. Finnis compares them to weights and measures:

> Just as we adopt systems of weights and measures in terms of which we can *then* carry out commensurations, comparisons and computations of quantities, so we as individuals and societies adopt sets of commitments that *bring* the basic human values into a relation with each other sufficient to enable us to choose projects and, in some cases, to undertake a cost-benefit analysis to identify better and worse (and even, sometimes, best) solutions.[101]

However, any set of weights will not do —commitments are not arbitrary either. Finnis notes that a rational commitment will take account of "one's assessment of one's capacities, circumstances, and even of one's tastes"; and Grisez notes that individual commitment must be in accord with the person's emotions and with "the bodily, organic, and psychic dimensions of the personality".[102] Furthermore, commitments are to be stable —that is, they are to endure in time, and "not be abandoned lightly"; and, because an individual or community will have many commitments of varying breadths, they are to harmonise with other commitments held by that individual or community. Grisez notes that, as a person matures, fewer new commitments are made; and many choices are made without moral reflection, because they are made in the framework of previous choices or commitments with which the person is still satisfied.[103] But on the other hand, commitments are not indelible nor are they necessarily to be conserved. Rather, persons and (especially) societies which have commitments in place must still remain open to the full range of basic human goods and to the possibility that their commitments may rightly change: "[t]he guidance which the ideal of integral human fulfilment offers to choice is to avoid unnecessary limitation and so maintain openness to further goods".[104] The value of commitments is not only that they are necessary for effective actions and introduce the possibility of integrity, but also that they spur innovation: commitments "provide one with the power to creatively think out objectives which one without commitment would not even consider".[105]

Finally, it would be well to be entirely clear as to when commitments which are also moral can or must be made, for the space may be narrower than at first it seems. A possible choice which does not pursue a basic good directly or instrumentally is not a candidate for a freely chosen commitment. Furthermore, a choice which is unreasonable, which does not respect one of the principles of practical reasonableness, is not a candidate for commitment. No commitment is required by reason, and so no commitment itself provides sufficient reason to override the practical principles.[106] As Finnis points out, it is worth the effort, if one doubts the stringency of these principles, to do the thought-exercise of actually taking a particular choice-option through each of the principles and finding out for oneself how demanding they are.[107] The possible commitments which satisfy both of these criteria, and only this range, constitute fully rational or moral options between which a community may freely choose.[108]

NOTES

1 I am grateful to Rufus Black, Robert Cummins, Martha Nussbaum, and Shalom Schwartz for their helpful comments on this article, and to John Finnis, James Griffin, Mozaffar Qizilbash, Amartya Sen, and Frances Stewart for helpful comments on related work.

2 Finnis, *NLNR*, p.81.

3 Throughout this chapter the terms 'basic human good', '[basic] reason for action', and 'dimension [or domain] of value [or human flourishing]' are used synonymously.

4 *NLNR*, p.59.

5 For example, see Grisez, *DMQ;* Grisez, *CMP*, pp.105-6; and the Introduction to this volume.

6 *NLNR*, p.92.

7 *NLNR*, p.91: "In this way we can analytically unravel even very 'peculiar' conventions, norms, institutions, and orders of preference, such as the aristocratic code of honour that demanded direct attacks on life in duelling".

8   *NLNR*, p.92.
9   Davitt's synthesis describes the following value areas: life, sexual union, knowledge, art, communication, meaning, decision-responsibility, title (property), protection and security (T. E. Davitt, "The Basic Values in Law: a Study of the Ethico-legal Implications of Psychology and Anthropology", *Transactions of the American Philosophical Society*, 58/5 [1968]).
10   James Griffin, *Value Judgement: Improving our Ethical Beliefs* (Oxford: Clarendon Press, 1996).
11   Martha Nussbaum and D. Estlund, *Sex Preference and Family: Essays on Law and Nature* (Oxford: Oxford University Press, 1997).
12   Milton Rokeach, *The Nature of Human Values* (New York: Free Press, 1973).
13   Shalom Schwartz and W. Bilsky, "Toward a psychological structure of human values", *Journal of Personality and Social Psychology*, 53 (1987), pp. 550-62; Shalom Schwartz and W. Bilsky, "Toward a Theory of the Universal Content and Structure of Values: extensions and cross-cultural replications", *Journal of Personality and Social Psychology*, 58 (1990), pp. 878-91; S. H. Schwartz, "Are there Universal Aspects in the Structure and Contents of Human Values?", *Journal of Social Issues*, 50/4 (1994), pp.19-45.
14   Manfred Max-Neef, *Human Scale Development: Conception, Application, and Further Reflections* (London: Apex, 1991).
15   Robert Cummins, "Domains of Life Satisfaction: an Attempt to Order Chaos", *Social Indicators Research*, 38/3 (1996), pp.303-28.
16   Maureen Ramsay, *Human Needs and the Market* (Aldershot: Avebury, 1992).
17   See especially the stream of work using Ronald Inglehart's 'World Values Surveys' (*Modernization and Postmodernization: Cultural, Economic, and Political Change in Forty-three Societies* [Princeton: Princeton University Press, 1997]; and *Human Values and Beliefs —a Cross-cultural Sourcebook: Political, Religious, Sexual, and Economic Norms in Forty-three Societies*, Findings from the 1990-93 World Value Survey [Ann Arbor, Michigan: University of Michigan Press, 1998]); and the Chinese Culture Connection, "Chinese Values and the Search for Culture-free Dimensions of Culture", *Journal of Cross-Cultural Psychology*, 18 (1987), pp.143-64. Rokeach calls the definition of value-as-mode-of-conduct, "instrumental" (Milton Rokeach, *Beliefs, Attitudes, and Values* [San Francisco: Jossey-Bass, 1969]; Rokeach, *The Nature of Human Values*). It has been used in psychology by Kohlberg, Piaget, Lovejoy, English, and Scott. Similarly, a strong body of interdisciplinary research has emerged from game theoretic principles (see, for example, Avner Ben-Ner and Louis Putterman (eds.), *Economics, Values, and Organizations* [Cambridge: Cambridge University Press, 1998]; and Herbert Gintis, *Game Theory Evolving* [Princeton: Princeton University Press, 2000]), which likewise test human values described as modes of conduct such as cooperation.
18   Hans Küng, *A Global Ethic for Global Politics and Economics* (London: SCM, 1997); Hans Küng and Karl-Josef Kuschel (eds.), *A Global Ethic: the Declaration of the Parliament of the World's Religions* (Continuum, 1993); and the Dalai Lama, *Ethics for a New Millennium* (New York: Riverhead Books, 1999).
19   *NLNR*, p. 81.
20   For a conceptual introduction to the basic goods and their method of derivation, see the Introduction to this volume.

21   Grisez, Boyle, and Finnis, *PP*, p.103. The term 'reasons for action' is preferred to 'basic goods' or 'basic human goods' and will be used most often in this chapter; but all three terms are synonymous.

22   John Finnis, "Is Natural Law Theory Compatible with Limited Government?", in Robert P. George (ed.), *Natural Law, Liberalism, and Morality* (Oxford and New York: Oxford University Press, 1996).

23   Ibid., pp.4-5.

24   Finnis further clarifies the problem with consensus in a paper on Habermas (John Finnis, "Natural Law and the Ethics of Discourse", paper for the conference on Jürgen Habermas, Florence, June 1998).

25   Griffin, *Value Judgement*, James Griffin, "Virtue Ethics and the Environs", *Social Philosophy and Policy*, 15/1 (1998).

26   This observation is my own; Griffin does not engage with Finnis' work.

27   Griffin, *Value Judgement*, p.27.

28   Ibid., pp.29-30.

29   Further comparisons of their approaches would be fruitful but lie beyond the scope of this study.

30   Martha Nussbaum, *Women and Human Development: the Capabilities Approach*, the 1998 Seeley Lectures (Cambridge: Cambridge University Press, 2000), pp.70-1.

31   Ibid., p.74. Nussbaum's account of the capabilities approach is developed in M. Nussbaum, "Nature, Function and Capability: Aristotle on Political Distribution," *Oxford Studies in Ancient Philosophy*, 6/Supplementary Volume (1988) pp.145-84; M. Nussbaum, "Aristotelian Social Democracy," in B. Douglass et al. (eds.), *Liberalism and the Good* (London: Routledge, 1990), pp.203-52; M. Nussbaum, "Human Functioning and Social Justice: in Defense of Aristotelian Essentialism," *Political Theory*, 20/2 (1992), pp.202-246; M. Nussbaum and A. Sen (eds.), *The Quality of Life* (Oxford: Clarendon Press, 1993); M. Nussbaum, "Aristotle on Human Nature and the Foundations of Ethics," in J. Altham and R. Harrison (eds.), *World, Mind and Ethics: Essays on the Ethical Philosophy of Bernard Williams* (Cambridge: Cambridge University Press, 1995); M. Nussbaum, "Human Capabilities, Female Human Being", in Martha Nussbaum and Jonathan Glover (eds.), *Women, Culture and Development* (Oxford: Clarendon Press, 1995), pp.61-104; Nussbaum and Estlund, *Sex Preference and Family*; M. Nussbaum, "Public Philosophy and International Feminism", *Ethics*, 108/4 (1998); and most comprehensively in Nussbaum, *Women and Human Development*.

32   Nussbaum, *Women and Human Development*, p.74.

33   Ibid., p.76.

34   Ibid.

35   Ibid., p.77 and p.74, respectively.

36   Like Finnis and Griffin, Nussbaum has developed her list over time. See, for example, Nussbaum, "Non-Relative Virtues: an Aristotelian Approach", in Nussbaum and Sen, *The Quality of Life*; Nussbaum, "Human Capabilities"; Nussbaum, "Good as Discipline, Good as Freedom", in David Crocker and Toby Linden (eds.), *The Ethics of Consumption: the Good Life, Justice, and Global Stewardship* (Lanham, Maryland: Rowman and Littlefield, 1998); and Nussbaum, *Women and Human Development*.

37   Nussbaum, "In Defense of Universal Values", chapter 1 of *Women and Human Development*, pp.78-9.
38   Max Neef, *Human Scale Development*, p.42.
39   From ibid., Table 1, pp.32-3.
40   Ibid., p.18.
41   According to Max-Neef, "It is the satisfiers which define the prevailing mode that a culture of society ascribes to needs. *Satisfiers are not the available economic goods....* Satisfiers may include, among other things, forms of organization, political structures, social practices, subjective conditions, values and norms, spaces, contexts, modes, types of behaviour and attitudes, all of which are in a permanent state of tension between consolidation and change." (ibid., pp.26-27).
42   Ibid., p.31.
43   Likewise, Schwartz, "Universals in the Content and Structure of Values: Theoretical Advances and Empirical Tests in Twenty Countries", *Advances in Experimental Social Psychology*, 25 (1992), pp.1-65.
44   Rokeach, *The Nature of Human Values*, p.3.
45   Ibid., p.3.
46   Ibid., p.30. For criticisms of the arbitrariness and selectivity of Rokeach's choice of values, see V. A. Braithwaite and H. G. Law, "Structure of Human Values: Testing the Adequacy of the Rokeach Value Survey", *Journal of Personality and Social Psychology*, 49/1 (1985), p.251. Braithwaite and Law's work is of particular significance, since they conducted an empirical study to test the extent to which Rokeach's value categories accurately represent the whole value domain.
47   The entire issue of *The Journal of Social Issues*, 50/4 (1994) is devoted to values research in the Rokeachian tradition.
48   Rokeach writes, "Terminal values are motivating because they represent the supergoals beyond immediate, biologically urgent goals. Unlike the more immediate goals, these supergoals do not seem to be periodic in nature; neither do they seem to satiate —we seem to be forever doomed to strive for these ultimate goals without quite ever reaching them" (Rokeach, *The Nature of Human Values*, p. 14).
49   Braithwaite and Law criticised Rokeach for missing "the facets of physical well-being". They also thought terminal values should include individual rights. It does seem possible that the category of 'comfortable life' was intended to cover physical needs ("Structure of Human Values").
50   Schwartz, "Universal Aspects", p.21. See also Schwartz and Bilsky, "Towards a Psychological Structure of Human Values"; and Schwartz, "Universals in the Content and Structure of Values".
51   Schwartz, correspondence with the author, 18 July 1998.
52   The scale is as follows: '7' = of supreme importance; '6' = very important; '5', '4' unlabelled; '3' = important; '2', '1' unlabelled; '0' = not important; '-1' = opposed to my values.
53   Schwartz cites: Rokeach, *The Nature of Human Values*; Braithwaite & Law, "Structure of Human Values"; Chinese Culture Connection, "Chinese Values"; G. Hofstede, *Culture's Consequences: International Differences in Work-Related Values* (Beverly Hills, CA: Sage, 1980); S. Levy & L. Guttman, *Values and Attitudes of Israeli High School Youth* (Jerusalem: Israel Institute of Applied Social

Research, 1974); D. Munro, "A Free-Format Values Inventory: explorations with Zimbabwean student teachers", *South African Journal of Psychology*, 15 (1985), pp. 33-41; and the "examination of texts on comparative religion and from consultations with Muslim and Druze Scholars" (Schwartz, "Universals in the Content and Structure of Values", p.17).

54   The article which summarizes the progress made to date is Schwartz, "Universal Aspects". His work also cross-references other values theories and research. The 64 countries include two African, two North American, four Latin American, eight Asian, two South Asian, eight East European, one Middle Eastern, fourteen European, two Mediterranean, as well as Australia and New Zealand.

55   For an explanation of the test of comprehensiveness see Schwartz, "Universals in the Content and Structure of Values", p.37.

56   Schwartz, "Universal Aspects", p.23. The lists that Schwartz has in mind are those proposed in Braithwaite and Law, "Structure of Human Values"; Chinese Culture Connection, "Chinese Values"; Hofstede, *Culture's Consequences*; Levy and Guttman, *Values and Attitudes*; Munro, "Free-Format Values Inventory"; Rokeach, *Nature of Human Values*.

57   These include: the needs of individuals as biological organisms; the requisites of coordinated social interaction; and the requirements for the smooth functioning and survival of groups. Discussion of the empirical findings of spirituality may be found in Schwartz, "Universals in the Content and Structure of Values".

58   Ibid., pp.15-16, 36-7. The validity of his procedures for testing the terminal-instrumental might be challenged, but discussion of this lies well beyond the boundaries of this chapter.

59   Finnis regards both the principles and the basic human goods to be self-evident; and argues that the principles especially can be related to non-rational motives (see especially his account of the principles in Ruth Chang [ed.], *Incommensurability, Incomparability, and Practical Reason* [Harvard: Harvard University Press, 1997], Chapter IV).

60   Alternatively, one could consider the thirty terminal values tested (see Schwartz, "Universals in the Content and Structure of Values", pp.60-1).

61   The seminal work in social indicators research is Frank M. Andrews and Stephen B. Withey, *Social Indicators of Well-Being: Americans' Perceptions of Life Quality* (New York: Plenum Press, 1976), in which twenty-nine 'concern clusters' for social indicators are identified. The accounts that Cummins reviewed develops their work.

62   A table of these terms and the residual appears in Cummins, "Domains of Life Satisfaction", p.309.

63   Ibid., p.309.

64   Erich Fromm, Kai Nielsen, Robert E. Lane, Johan Galtung, and especially Abraham Maslow are also important because their work informed the Basic Needs Approach to economic development, which arose in the 1970s (see P. Streeten, Shahed Javed Burki, Mahbub ul Haq, Norman Hicks, and Frances Stewart, *First Things First: Meeting Basic Human Needs in Developing Countries* (Oxford: Oxford University Press, 1981); and Frances Stewart, *Basic Needs in Developing Countries* (Baltimore: Johns Hopkins University Press, 1985).

65   Brentano (as reported by Maureen Ramsay in *Human Needs and the Market*) put forward a hierarchy of ten needs, which must be progressively satisfied in human

development: maintenance of life, sexual needs, recognition by others, provision for well-being after death, amusement, provision for the future, healing, cleanliness, education in science and art, the need to create.

66   In "A Theory of Human Motivation", *Psychology Review*, 50 (1943), pp.370-96, Abraham H. Maslow set out five categories of needs, again ordered in a hierarchy: physiological needs, safety needs, 'belongingness' and love needs, esteem needs, self-actualisation needs.

67   Erich Fromm, in *The Sane Society* (London: Routledge & Kegan Paul, 1956), sets out five needs: relatedness; transcendence-creativity; rootedness; a sense of identity and individuality; the need for a frame of orientation and devotion.

68   In 1977 Kai Nielsen tried to identify "some of the central elements" of human need, fourteen in total: love, companionship, security, protection, a sense of community, meaningful work, a sense of involvement, adequate sustenance and shelter, sexual gratification, amusement, rest, recreation, recognition, and respect for one's person (Kai Nielsen, "True Needs, Rationality, and Emancipation", in Ross Fitzgerald [ed.], *Human Needs and Politics* [Sydney: Pergamon, 1977]).

69   Robert E. Lane, in *Political Thinking and Consciousness* (Chicago: Markham Publishers, 1969), presents ten needs which inform human political behaviour: cognitive needs, consistency, social needs, moral needs, esteem, personality, integration and identity; aggression expression, autonomy, self-actualisation, and need for instrumental guide to reality, object appraisal, and attainment.

70   The categories that James Davies offers in *Human Nature in Politics* (New York: Wiley, 1963) are: physical needs, social-affectional needs, self-esteem and dignity needs, self-actualisation needs.

71   Vance Packard "discussed the eight hidden needs towards which marketing theory is orientated". According to Ramsay these are: emotional security, self-esteem, ego gratification, recognition and status, creativity, love, sense of belonging, power and a sense of immortality (*Human Needs and the Market*, p.152).

72   Johan Galtung's list in *True Worlds: a Transnational Perspective* (New York: Free Press, 1980), has twenty-eight rich elements grouped into security needs, welfare needs, identity needs, and freedom needs.

73   According to Ramsay, John Mallman defines need as "a generic requirement that all human beings have in order not to be ill" (*Human Needs and the Market*, p.152). One way he analyses need is in terms of maintenance, protection, love, understanding, self reliance, recreation, creation, meaning, and synergy needs.

74   According to Ramsey, "Lederer ([ed.], *Human Needs: a Contribution to the Current Debate* [Cambridge, Mass.: Oelgeschlager, Gunn and Hain, 1980]) argues that the list of human motives given by Kretch, Crutchfield and Livson, can be analogously applied to needs" (*Human Needs and the Market*, p.152).

75   Ramsey, *Human Needs and the Market*, pp.149-78.

76   Interestingly, she reclassified sexual needs as subsumed under physical survival "in their physical aspects" and partly under each other category 'in their psychological aspects'.

77   For example, "Spitz made a comparative study of infants raised in nurseries by their own mothers and those raised in a foundling home. 100% of the first group survived and developed into normal healthy adults. In the second group there was a 37%

mortality rate by the end of the second year, and those who did survive were more apathetic or hyperexcitable" (*Human Needs and the Market*, pp.154).

78 Brentano's 'provision for well-being after death'; Fromm's 'frame of orientation and devotion'; Packard's 'power and a sense of immortality'; Galtung's 'sense of purpose, of meaning with life, closeness to the transcendental, transpersonal'; Mallman's 'transcendence'; Kretch, Crutchfield, and Livson's 'discovering meaningful place of self in the universe'.

79 *PP*, pp.111-13.

80 Schwartz, Ramsay (security); Rokeach (family security, national security); Cummins (safety); Max-Neef (protection). In this paragraph, as throughout my analysis, the reference to the number of lists is factual only: unanimity or consensus of opinion is not a sufficient ground to propose a change.

81 Schwartz places 'wisdom' under 'understanding', 'curiosity' under 'self-direction', and 'intelligence' under 'achievement'. Cummins places 'education' in his dimension of 'community'; children's education appears in his list of residual domains. Ramsay places 'education or self-expression' among 'self-realisation needs'.

82 Griffin, Rokeach (accomplishment); Schwartz (achievement); Cummins (productivity); Max-Neef (creation).

83 David Wiggins, *Needs, Values, Truth*, 3rd edition (Oxford: Clarendon Press, 1998), p.88. See also *PP*, section XC.

84 Seven of Cummins' source lists, however, included 'marriage' as an element of the quality of life.

85 See Appendix II at the end of this chapter.

86 *NLNR*, p.62.

87 Examples of relevant domains from his sources are 'neighborhood', 'social life', 'social relations', 'belonging to clubs' and so on.

88 Nussbaum (practical reason); Rokeach (inner harmony, self-respect, social recognition); Max-Neef (identity); Ramsay (esteem and identity, self-realisation); Schwartz (self-direction, power, tradition, conformity).

89 Nussbaum (emotions, senses, thought, imagination); Rokeach (happiness); Cummins (emotional well-being).

90 Rokeach (an exciting life); Schwartz (stimulation); Max-Neef (freedom); Nussbaum (control over one's environment).

91 *NLNR*, ch. IV.

92 Griffin (enjoyment); Rokeach (pleasure); Nussbaum (senses, imagination, thought); Schwartz (hedonism).

93 Nussbaum's 1998 Seeley Lectures at Cambridge included one lecture on religion, in which she canvassed the deep need for the protection of religious freedom, especially for marginalised groups. For Finnis' description of his departure from Aristotle, see *NLNR*, ch. XII.

94 Schwartz, correspondence with the author, 18 July 1998.

95 Brentano ('provision for well-being after death'); Packard ('power and a sense of immortality'); Fromm (the need for a frame of orientation and devotion); Galtung (need 'for a sense of purpose, of meaning with life; closeness to the transcendental, transpersonal'); Kretch, Crutchfield, and Livson ('discovering meaningful place of self in the universe').

96   Finnis in Robert P. George, *Making Men Moral* (Oxford: Clarendon Press, 1993), p. 135.

97   This argument is developed in Rufus Black, *Christian Moral Realism* (Oxford: Oxford University Press, forthcoming).

98   Johan Galtung, *Human Rights in Another Key* (Cambridge: Polity Press, 1994), p.71.

99   *CMP*, p.54.

100   *NLNR*, pp.93, 100, 115.

101   Finnis, *FE*, p.90. See also *NLNR*, pp.115f.

102   *NLNR*, p.105; *LCL*, p.292.

103   *CMP*, p.82.

104   Ibid., p.186; cf. pp.131-2.

105   Ibid., p.187.

106   *FE*, p.126.

107   Ibid., p.91.

108   For a discussion of the situations in which all alternatives for action seem to transgress these principles, see *LCL*, ch. 5.

4   John Finnis on Moral Absolutes

Oliver O'Donovan

There are few Christian moralists writing today with whom it is more rewarding to engage than with John Finnis. He has brought to moral-theological discussion, not always noted for the rigour of its proceedings, a demanding level of rational argument and a fruitful cross-fertilisation with contemporary jurisprudence and philosophy. He has stood for a tough-minded conservative Catholic morality, but has usually subordinated the contentious special issues (abortion, contraception, etc.) to the task of defining a moral theory, with the aid of which he has sustained a relentless polemic against the school of Catholic 'proportionalists' which formed the new wave in the decade immediately following the Second Vatican Council. Working in close accord with his American friend Germain Grisez and other sympathetic collaborators, he has helped to propound a comprehensive theory of moral value and decision that has become the hallmark of a new school, but has continued to develop his own theoretical explorations in relation to it. Finally, he has come to be viewed as a representative figure for the Vatican's current thinking on moral questions, so that there are ecumenical as well as intellectual goods to be pursued by a serious response to his thought from other Christian traditions.

The theory common to Finnis and his colleagues has attracted considerable discussion, though only, so far as I am aware, among other Roman Catholics, as a bold attempt to recover the ground of natural moral reason for conservative Catholicism, reversing the slightly unexpected situation in the years following the Council in which the liberals promoted a naturalist interpretation of religious ethics and the conservatives marched, like Protestants, under the banner of Scripture. I do not propose to cover this ground again. Inevitably, this attention to the theory held in common diverted attention away from the development within Finnis' own published views. Without losing his points of reference within the theory he has shifted his centre of gravity, as can be seen from comparing his three theoretical books. In *Natural Law and Natural Rights* (1980), Finnis positioned himself in relation to the Natural Right tradition, an obvious enough opening move for a lawyer to make. In his second book, Fundamentals of Ethics (1983), the emphasis had shifted to the philosophical distinction between practical and theoretical reason; while in his most recent *Moral Absolutes* (1991), a traditional question of moral theology has taken centre-stage. It is with this latest phase of his work that I propose to pursue a discussion here. It brings him to the heartland of moral theology, and finds him occupying positions which are likely to attract the distrust not of modernist Christians only but of some traditionalists too. This makes it especially worthwhile to discuss his latest theses as a matter of ecumenical interest.

At the start of *Moral Absolutes* Finnis adopts two sentences from John-Paul II as a thesis ("to set up the issue, not settle it"):

(a) There exist acts which *per se* and in themselves, independently of circumstances, are always seriously wrong by reason of their object.

(b) There are moral norms that have a precise content which is immutable and unconditioned ... for example the norm which forbids the direct killing of an innocent person.[1]

I shall dispose of the first of these very quickly, by agreeing with it. It defines the area on which I am confident that Finnis and I are at one. It sets us in common opposition to most of what is called 'relativism' in ethics, the view that the moral value of acts inheres in constellations of circumstances surrounding them, by insisting that some kinds of acts are wrong 'by reason of their object'. Finnis later glosses this phrase correctly:. "in terms of the acting person's object; what that person chooses".[2] It sets us in common opposition to the cluster of views loosely described as 'utilitarian', holding that moral value inheres only in the projected consequences of acts.[3] It sets us, finally, in common opposition to subjectivist theories which hold that value inheres only in the interior motives of the agent. The extent and importance of this agreement is, I think, considerable. The exploration of possible disagreements in what follows must be set in the light of it.

Sentence (*b*), then, provides the text for my interrogation of John

Finnis' account of moral absolutes. It is linked to (*a*) in his exposition with the word "correspondingly". This does not imply a claim of synonymity: (*a*) speaks of acts, (*b*) of norms, and Finnis is clear that these are different. Finnis' account of what a 'norm' is, an account which has to be pieced together from a number of scattered observations, requires us to view norms as *propositions*. They "have a precise content". They "identify" acts. They "are true" (even "forceful"!). On their "specificity" Finnis constantly insists. When he refers to norms he cites utterances, either imperative utterances such as "Feed your children", or affirmative utterances such as "adultery is wrong".[4]

What, then, does he take to be asserted in sentence (*b*)? The following paraphrase may come near enough to his meaning: *There are some closely specified moral propositions which are not susceptible of being revised in the light of further moral experience.* Is this true? It depends, I shall argue, on what we mean by 'revision'. And here I shall make a distinction, which may be compatible with Finnis' own views, between an *antithetical* revision and a *complementary* revision.

It is an important part of Finnis' argument that *only some* moral utterances are of this kind; and he takes care to insist that these are not necessarily the most important, though, as a class, they have a special significance as a bulwark against corrupt moral reasoning. Referring to a tag from Thomas, passed on through the moral theological tradition, he says that many other essential (and affirmative) moral norms hold good *semper sed non ad semper* while this class (of negative norms) holds good *semper et ad semper*. With the *semper* ('always') there can, in my view, be no quarrel. All 'perfect' norms have a kind of universality. The question is whether we can distinguish, as something different from this and additional to it, a capacity for *universal reference* or applicability to every conceivable decision. Here I shall argue, as much against the tradition as against Finnis, that there is no universal reference; the *ad semper* ('to all situations') is an illusion. But the *semper* is more than sufficient for Finnis' needs, and will allow him to sustain a class of exceptionless and specific moral norms, safe against antithetical revision.

The following discussion is in two parts. The first addresses his attempt to distinguish specific-and-exceptionless norms from alternatives: non-exceptionless norms on the one hand, trivially exceptionless norms on the other. The second looks more closely at the *ad semper* universal reference. I shall finish with some more general observations on the bearing this may have on ecumenical moral theology.

I

In his opening statement,[5] Finnis gives examples of three kinds of norm. One kind is "not absolute". His example is "Feed your children". There are circumstances in which one cannot apply that norm: when, for example, "the only food available is the body of your neighbour's living child". But in not applying it in those circumstances one does not violate it. The second kind (which exercises Finnis very much at a later stage in the argument) can be called "'exceptionless', but not in an interesting sense of the word". From many examples we select "Do not engage in unjust killing, inordinate sexual intercourse...". These commands *logically* cannot have any exceptions, for they have an evaluative reference ('unjust', 'inordinate') already built into them. And then, thirdly, there is the kind of norm the existence of which Finnis is concerned to defend. "Interestingly exceptionless", it could *logically* be open to exception, but exceptions "are *morally* excluded". The example given in John-Paul's words will suffice: "for example, the norm forbidding the direct killing of an innocent person".

It is the purpose of this part of my discussion to subvert these apparently clear distinctions. I aim to show that the morally binding character of each is essentially the same as that of the others. On the other hand, 'Feed your children' is by no means as vulnerable to exception as Finnis supposes; on the other, 'Do not engage in inordinate sexual intercourse' is by no means so uninteresting. They are all three, in other words, examples of moral propositions which bind *semper*. And more can be made of that universality than Finnis is ready to admit.

(i) On Finnis' account we neither apply nor violate the norm 'Feed your children' when we desist from feeding our children in famine with the flesh of a neighbour's child. The fact that this norm can be not-applied without being violated proves that it is not exceptionless. Exceptionless moral norms have either to be applied or to be violated in every instance. But why do we say that it is not-applied? Because we do not give our starving children human flesh to eat? And if we did, would that 'apply' the norm? *'Misapplied'*, we would surely say. It would show a misunderstanding of what the norm intended. But it is odd to think of 'misapplication' as a species of 'application', and so equally odd to think that if we desist from serving up the cannibal meal we have, in some way, not-applied it.

Finnis makes a disturbing suggestion about *why* we would not kill and serve the neighbour's child: it would, he thinks, violate the norm about direct killing of the innocent.[6] (Alas, on that reckoning there are some school-playgrounds which will always keep the righteous well-fed!). My own reason is more comprehensive: the flesh of my neighbour's child *is not food*. Understand that in the order of creation God has not given human beings as a prey to one another's teeth, and it will follow that no obligation to feed one's children could ever require giving them human flesh to eat. One neither applies the norm nor does one not-apply it. One realises that *it* does not apply. There is no food to give the children, and there is an end of it.

Put another and less harrowing case. Half an hour after lunch the children, having refused a further helping of ice-cream, are playing in the garden. Finding some cake left in the refrigerator my conscience tells me that I ought to take it out to them, lest I should miss a chance of feeding them.... The scruple is clearly absurd; the question is why it is absurd. Finnis would have to say, I think: 'Apply that norm three times a day —at mealtimes!' That seems quite artificial. I know why I would serve a meal three times a day, or take a medicine three times a day; but I don't why I would apply a moral norm three times a day. Does a norm come with a label stating the dosage, like medicine from the chemist's? The simpler way of understanding the matter seems to be that if one understands what 'feeding' means, one knows that it does not include stuffing their faces at every conceivable moment. And so one knows that 'Feed your children' does not apply to needless snacks when they are not hungry.

That norm, like almost every other, is not applicable to every moment of decision. But that does not affect its power to obligate us. Its authority is unvarying: at mealtimes and after mealtimes, in plenty and in famine, when we have children and when we do not yet have children or no longer have them, we are bound to feed (taking cognisance of what feeding means) our (i.e. any that we may have) children. It binds *semper*. But there are very many situations of decision to which it does not refer, to which it has no applicability, and there are, of course, some people who never face a decision to which it does not apply.

The same can be said, in my view, about every norm of the kind which tradition has christened a 'perfect obligation' —more accurately, a *norm that perfectly expresses* an obligation. These are norms to which no exceptions can be conceived. 'Feed your children' strikes me as a rather good example, the exception which Finnis thinks he can identify being, in fact, not an exception but an occasion of non-applicability. But occasions of non-applicability affect, as I shall argue, all exceptionless norms —with the sole exception of those which claim to rule every conscious thought— the command to love God with all one's heart is perhaps the only one of these that Jews and Christians will certainly acknowledge.

But this may prove no more than that Finnis has made an unfortunate choice of example. Let us take a real case of an imperfect obligation, and see how it works. 'Feed children' will serve our turn. This does not bind *semper*. Everyone at all times is obliged to feed *their* children, i.e. such children as they have. But not everybody is obliged at all times to feed children. There are circumstances of emergency in which anyone may have an obligation to feed a child; but most of the time it is a matter of vocation as to whether one does good by feeding children or, let us say, nursing the elderly, rescuing shipwrecked mariners or whatever other forms of doing good there may be open to us. It would make no moral sense to say 'It is not my vocation to feed *my* children'; but it makes perfect moral sense to say, 'Someone else must feed children while I get on with nursing the elderly'.

Or consider an example which fails of exceptionlessness in a different way: 'Give your children one hot meal a day!' To this generally binding rule there really are exceptions: with children feeding at the breast, receiving nourishment through a drip, or simply in a heatwave. Here it is not a question of the rule's not applying to those situations. Nothing in the idea of one hot meal a day will tell you, if you reflect on it, that drip-fed or breast-fed infants are not meant. Its sense extends to those cases too, but its authority does not. Yes, there would be misunderstanding of a kind if you insisted on the steaming plate of steak-and-kidney pie while the mercury stood at 87, but the misunderstanding would not relate to what the norm *meant*, but to the context of its usefulness, the unspoken hypotheses on which it was normally advanced. You would lack 'common sense', which is an ability to locate such useful rules within the context where they have validity.

As a 'perfect obligation' is really a norm that perfectly expresses an obligation, an 'imperfect obligation' arises from the incomplete way in which the obligation is expressed. 'Give your children one hot meal a day' derives its moral authority from the perfect obligation we acknowledge to feed our children. But it is not itself a perfect obligation because it does not fully express the conditions of the narrowly focused obligation it conveys. All kinds of contextual presupposition are left unspoken. If one had the patience to elaborate the proposition to make all the presuppositions explicit, one would have another exceptionless moral rule: 'Give your children one hot meal a day *if* ... *unless*...', and so on, tediously. But its tedious elaboration is in the sharpest contrast to the tight economy of the exceptionless rule, 'Feed your children'.

But that also purchases its formal perfection at a price. Though it succeeds in defining the essential terms of obligation in three pregnant words, it does not develop the possible contextual expressions of the obligation with any specificity. It does not tell us what food is suitable for newborns, what for sick children, what for children with milk allergies, when the food should be hot and when cold, when savoury and when sweet. The detail all remains to be provided. It could be developed in a complementary way for a very long time into a complete science of paediatric nutrition; but no antithetical qualifications will ever have to be made of it. It is, in the Pope's words, 'immutable' and 'unconditioned'; but it is not 'precise'.

Of the two models for an exceptionless moral rule that we have so far identified, one is merely notional: the indefinitely elaborated statement of conditions and circumstances in which some quite specific thing would be obligatory. The other, economical enough in form, is unspecific. As we have seen, Finnis is mistaken to doubt its exceptionlessness. Yet he is right to think it is not what he is searching for. His programme is to locate norms combining the specificity of a typical 'imperfect obligation' with the universality of a 'perfect obligation'. I shall hope to show that this programme is not unreasonable.

(ii) Finnis devotes considerable energy to rebutting the suggestion that the norms he wishes to identify are only *formally* exceptionless, since they contain evaluative terms which make it logically necessary that they should hold in all circumstances. This view of them he attributes to his proportionalist opponents McCormick and Schüller, who maintain (as he understands it) that 'Adultery is wrong' has no exceptions only because 'adultery' *means* unjustified intercourse with another person's spouse. On the contrary, Finnis urges, adultery is defined in morally neutral terms, as "an act of extra-marital intercourse by (or with) a married person, period".[7] In that sense adultery is said to be wrong without exception —meaning that 'justified adultery' is a perfectly intelligible phrase, but not one that refers to any actual moral possibility. His opponents are then taken to allege in reply that this would mean defining adultery in purely 'material' terms, as: performing such and such bodily actions. But, their argument goes on, it is hard to conceive of any set of bodily motions which would not be fitting in some circumstances or other, and the motions involved in adultery are hardly different from those involved in marital intercourse. To which Finnis returns that adultery is not defined in material terms, but in terms of the object of the intention: to commit adultery is to act on the intention of sexual union with another's spouse or with another person than one's own spouse.

The justice of his representation of the dispute lies beyond the scope of this enquiry, which is concerned only to identify the view which he rejects. That view is dependent, for eristic purposes at least, on the traditional dichotomy in Western moral philosophy between fact and value. The logic of the manoeuvre deployed against Finnis is to require him to decide: shall 'adultery' be an *evaluative* term, the negative connotations of which belong to it by linguistic convention, or shall it be a *descriptive* term which identifies certain objective performances? But this decision would cause Finnis no embarrassment unless the descriptive option were characterised in a way that implied a narrowly *factual* content. If 'adultery' describes, it describes certain bare, unqualified material happenings. In overcoming the manoeuvre Finnis challenges this restriction. He points to an element in all human action which can be the object of description but is more than bare 'fact': intention. If we want to say *what* somebody has done, we must speak of what was intended. What was it, for example, that those who fired on columns of Bosnian refugees *did*? They pointed guns at people; they fired them; they acted for the good, as they saw it, of their people. But if we want to say what they did, we must specify the object of their intention: the death of Bosnian refugees.[8]

This line of response is sound. But it carries Finnis further than he is ready to see. For presumably it follows that any norm which has a place in actual moral discourse proposes (or proscribes) an object of intention. Finnis' opponents proposed that his exceptionless norms were mere tautologies. Instead of trying to extricate them from that category, Finnis should boldly have denied the category of moral tautology any place within the sphere of moral discourse, within the world where people actually give advice to one another. Tautologous norms are logicians' abstractions, devised to illustrate the purely formal rational structure of our moral thinking. As such they are innocuous educational diagrams. But they are not things that anyone could say, meaning, that is, to say something. To take an undoubted example: 'What you do in one instance, do the same in all other instances of the same type unless there are significant differences of circumstances or qualifying feature'. *That* is not advice that any father would give his son as he left for the wars! But why should anybody, least of all Finnis, classify as purely formal counsels things which *might* be said by a father, doctor or friend? 'Do not commit adultery', he thinks, is not such a tautology, but 'Do not engage in inordinate sexual intercourse' is. Yet many a worldly father and many a prudent doctor have thought it good advice to give.

A logician, wishing to show how formal structures of moral reason shape our discourse, may extract some norm from its context of use and present it to us as a tautology. 'Do your duty!' is a good candidate for this treatment; its form, uncluttered by specifics, suggests pure definition: your duty is whatever it is that you should do. But we should not be misled by this into thinking that the father who exhorts his son in these terms as he leaves for the wars has become a pure logician himself. In those circumstances 'duty' does not mean 'whatever, if anything, you should do'. It evokes an unspoken reserve of cultural understanding about military virtue, loyalty, compassion, generosity, nobility, and so on. As the word 'duty' points him to this objective cultural content, so the exhortation becomes something more than *mere* exhortation. It directs his attention to moral demands on which he has, or will be, instructed in greater detail at other times, but which require to be conceived as a whole: 'Do what a soldier should do!' *A fortiori* the same point can be made about the less plausible instances of 'formally exceptionless' norms which Finnis offers. 'Do not engage in unjust killing', for example, if addressed to a Serbian irregular, would do rather more than instruct him not to kill whoever it might be (if anybody) that he was not supposed to kill. It would direct his notice to the cultural deposit of law and morality which limits the right of killing in just war. If, then, we were to substitute the epithet 'cruel' for 'unjust', we would altogether change the cultural reference and evoke a *different* constellation of prohibitions for his respect. It is not clear to me how, if they were both tautologous, they could have such different meanings.

The difference, then, between these norms (improperly described as 'formal') and the 'interestingly exceptionless' norms which Finnis defends, is not, as he takes it to be, the difference between a tautology and a synthetic proposition. Yet there is a difference, which we can describe as follows: where the terms 'duty', 'unjust', 'inordinate' and so on gain their sense from an *implicit* reference to cultural commitments, the terms which occur in Finnis' true absolutes arise *explicitly* from institutions and conventions in society. 'Do not engage in the killing of the innocent' and 'Do not engage in extra-marital intercourse' could never be mistaken for tautologies because the terms 'innocent' and 'extra-marital' refer to a social status defined by institutions of judgement and marriage. Yet the difference is only one of degree. The institutions of judgement and marriage are *moral* institutions which exist to protect the *moral* goods of justice and fidelity; and the concepts of injustice and duty also appeal to moral *institutions* to fill out their content. If 'Do your duty!', uttered in a certain context, means, in effect, 'Do what a soldier should do!', 'Do not kill the innocent!' means 'Do not do what an officer of public justice should not do!'. Both norms affirm as valid a corpus of moral demands which is associated with a social role.

If Finnis is wrongly suspicious of the appearance of self-evidence which attaches to the so-called 'formally exceptionless' norms, he may, nevertheless, be right to take a special interest in those norms which lack the appearance of self-evidence. These make explicit demands on the part of moral institutions, such as public judgement and marriage, the value of which may not be perceived immediately but only on reflection. These norms, then, defend us from having to fall back continually upon first principles and invent morality afresh. Here we touch on one of Finnis' broader themes with which I have a special sympathy. The world contains patterns of fulfilling inter-human relations, which we could not invent from scratch but must simply accept as given. To sustain these is the work of divine providence, which it is the wisdom of the anti-revolutionary to respect. Finnis is not mistaken in thinking that one characteristic of moral thought in the modern period is to ignore these preconditions of developed moral wisdom and to undertake to reinvent the world. And he would not be mistaken if he saw it as the particular service of those norms that he finds interesting to commend our assent directly to those instituted patterns of relationship and the laws which define them.

II

So far, then, we have considered two criteria Finnis offers for delimiting the range of true absolute norms: (i) they are never not-applied without being violated; (ii) they are non-tautological. Our response has been that these two criteria allow a far greater number of candidates than he wishes to allow. We are in search, then, of a third criterion which will successfully narrow the field. This criterion, more alluded to by Finnis than explained, can perhaps be summed up as follows: *they are sufficiently specific, or susceptible of sufficient specificity, to rule out any significant question about their applicability.* "Once one has precisely formulated the type", he writes, "one can say that the norm which identifies each chosen act of that type as wrong is true and applicable to every such choice, whatever the (further) circumstances".[9] Further: they are "valid, true and applicable even in circumstances which are neither foreseen nor even implicitly identified in the norm, but which despite their relevance and moral importance (if they arose) would not deflect the norm's applicability".[10] This claim is later reformulated in terms of the traditional *semper* and *ad semper* distinction between negative and positive norms. Moral absolutes are negative norms which hold good always and on every occasion, not, like affirmative propositions, "always somehow relevant but leav(ing) it to your moral judgement to discern the times, places, and other circumstances of their directives".[11]

I think these claims are woven out of three strands, two of which I can confidently defend, the third of which strikes me as problematic.

(i) There is, in the first place, the assertion that exceptionless norms *may be specific*. Finnis rejects the view that highly general exceptionless norms (e.g. the twofold command of love for God and neighbour) have purchased their exceptionlessness by loss of specificity, and that greater specificity must be bought at the cost of exceptionless (or, notionally, economy of expression, since one could imagine in principle a tediously perfect norm telling us in detail all the kinds of things that love of God and neighbour could ever include). If we propose to specify what love of God and neighbour requires of us in *one defined area* of decision —say, Sunday trading— then our specified norm will be hypothetical and subject to revision. No norm specified enough to give precise guidance can be exceptionless; no exceptionless norm can be specified enough to give precise guidance. So runs the view which Finnis rejects.

And he is right to reject it. What is at stake is the existence of those moral institutions to which we have already alluded: structures of active relationship which, while determinate in scope, have a validity that holds good for all human existence because they were not invented by us but given to us. If love for God and neighbour, or some other very general norms, were the only exceptionless principles, then all the structures through which love was mediated in this life would be open to reinvention. Jewish and Christian belief in creation denies that that is possible. The structure of care, for example, by which we show love to our neighbour by protecting and defending her life when she is weak or sick, cannot be replaced by an alternative in which euthanasia will count as a form of loving care. And the structure of marriage, whereby sexual intimacy is tied to monogamous fidelity and openness to parenthood, cannot be replaced by alternative forms of sexually intimate community. The specific demands that one be faithful to one's spouse and that one refrain from (helpfully) taking one's neighbour's life, are exceptionless because they are rooted in unnegotiable structures of creation-order.

Specificity, of course, can be more or less; and the claim that exceptionless norms may be specific does not imply a claim for any greater specificity than the moral institution warrants and requires. The demand that a man be sexually faithful to his wife is exceptionless; but the demand that he never kiss another woman could only be of hypothetical validity within certain variable cultural assumptions. Moral institutions are themselves open to adapting interpretations, and the exceptionless core of their requirements may not be extensive. Nevertheless, they do admit a measure of specificity which is sufficient to define them as institutions and to safeguard against the temptation to reinvent them.

(ii) In the second place there is the assertion that *exceptionless norms are impregnable to changing circumstances*. This is the minimal sense to be ascribed to the word 'exceptionless', and it must apply to all exceptionless norms, specific or otherwise. We need not suppose that Finnis intended the element of ambiguity introduced by the words, "Once one has precisely formulated the type, one can say that the norm ... is true and applicable to every such choice". One does not need to formulate an exceptionless norm *precisely* in order to say that. One can say it of 'Love your neighbour as yourself', and of 'All unloving acts are wrong'. However general, an exceptionless norm is "valid and applicable to circumstances which are neither foreseen nor implicitly identified", so that "no circumstance, whatever its relevance and moral importance, would deflect (its) applicability". Still, one can also say it of the specific ones, and that is what Finnis is concerned to maintain.

But this holds true only of *circumstances*, strictly understood. A 'circumstance' is that which 'stands round' the decision itself; it is not a defining feature of the decision. It is, as Finnis nicely puts it, a "(further) circumstance".[12] To speak about impregnability to circumstances is to insist that decisions under these norms will always be made on their own terms and not in the light of the circumstances. We may decide to have, or not to have, a summer holiday this year 'in the light of the circumstances'; but we could never rightly decide to have, or not to have, an abortion by that dim light, but could only ask if the abortion *in itself* was justified. If there are no types of justified abortion, no circumstance, not even a threat to the mother's life, will justify one. If an abortion to preserve the mother's life is a justified type of abortion, then a threat to the mother's life is not a circumstance, but a defining feature of the case. However, if we lose sight of the strict sense of the term 'circumstance', we may be tempted to think that what is said, when we say that no circumstance deflects the norm's applicability, is that the norm *applies to all situations of decision whatever*.

(iii) This may possibly explain how Finnis came to add the third strand: they *apply not only 'always' (semper) but 'to all situations' (ad semper)*. Surely this is an impossible requirement. Of any exceptionless norm we may say that it binds 'always'. That is the difference we discerned between exceptionless (or 'perfect obligation') and non-exceptionless (or 'imperfect'): the latter may be deemed 'inapplicable' in the sense that it *should not* be applied in some circumstance or other; the former only in the sense that it *does not* apply —but wherever it applies, or refers, it must be applied, or deferred to. But not even exceptionless norms, and especially not precise ones, can refer to all situations of decision whatever. Their meaning tells you what kind of situation they apply to. Understand 'Feed your children' and you know that it will not address the question of how to invest a legacy. Understand 'Do not commit adultery' and you know that you will receive no guidance from it about shooting at refugees.

What Finnis hopes to achieve by this requirement is to remove all question as to whether any given situation is or is not the kind of situation that the norm refers to. His absolutes must refer equally to every situation, so that there can be no cavilling. They must refer to my decision whether to take a holiday, and they must refer to my decision whether to take the bus or the train. And in support of this exceptional demand he resorts to the claim that all interestingly exceptionless norms are negative.[13] Earlier he suggests that all the commands of the Decalogue are exceptionless, and adds mention of "the supreme principles: 'Love God above all things', 'Love your neighbour as yourself' and 'Seek first the Kingdom'".[14] In the light of what follows, however, it appears that these can only be included among those affirmative moral principles which "are always somehow relevant but leave it to your moral judgement to discern the times, places and other circumstances of their directiveness".

It will serve as a first comment to say that this is very much too weak a claim to make for these affirmative exceptionless norms. If there exists a norm which applies as much to my decision to have a holiday as to my decision to have an abortion, surely the twofold command of love for God and neighbour is such a norm. Even if we take a norm which does not apply to all decisions, it is still too weak. It is more than 'always somehow relevant', it is always *binding*; and it is not up to me to discern when and how it becomes *directive* (for it is always directive) but simply to what kind of situation it *applies*. It is a matter of reference, not authority, that may be in question.

Secondly, it is a very strange suggestion that if I perform the grammatical trick of recasting a positive norm in negative form, 'Do not leave your children unfed!', I radically affect the way in which it refers to situations of decision. In its negative form it no more applies to the decision whether to take the bus or train than it did in the positive form. Finnis, led on by Thomas and his subsequent tradition, seems to suppose that not-doing certain expressly prohibited things belongs to the description of any decision I make, so that every decision, on whatever matter, is referred to by the prohibition of these things. Like the passage in Aristophanes' *Clouds* where Euripides is teased by the addition of "then he lost his oil-jar" to every tragic couplet he embarks upon, here we add 'and not to kill the innocent' to every decision to take a train or buy a house: 'I decided to take the train and not to kill the innocent'; 'I decided to buy the house and not to commit adultery' and so on.

It is an understandable but a misguided aim to try to avert cavilling about whether an exceptionless norm refers to any future situation that may arise. We can know in advance that an exceptionless moral norm will never be defeated by any *circumstance*, but we cannot know in advance precisely to which particular situations it will refer, because future particulars are not knowable in advance. Nor can we know to what *kinds* of situations it will apply, other than by thoughtful reflection on the implications of what it says. Discussion of what is included and what not is an inevitable condition of the thoughtful apprehension of the norm, and it cannot be foreclosed. Finnis' own sensitive account of how Jesus handled the Decalogue[15] shows he is aware that such exploratory interpretation may be given to exceptionless norms. And his own willingness to venture upon the interpretation of Jesus's prohibition of adultery shows he does not think this task restricted to the highest authorities. "There are questions to ask about who is indeed married", he observes with perfect justice. "But where there is no doubt ... the Lord's precept applies exceptionlessly".[16] He would have done better to write: 'Where there is no doubt that it *applies*, the Lord's precept *binds* exceptionlessly'. The point is that we cannot forestall legitimate doubts about who is married to whom. Does this open the door to malevolent prevarication? I am afraid it does; but the only cure for malevolent prevarication is honest reasoning, which will always show it up in the end. We cannot close legitimate questions just because someone may employ them to cover up illegitimate evasions.

But perhaps those legitimate questions can be settled decisively. Perhaps Finnis hopes that all the proper doubts as to who is married to whom can be so settled that no further doubts (that are not merely repetitions of old, resolved doubts) will ever arise. The statement beginning "once one has precisely formulated the type ..." could suggest it as his view that a *sufficient* precision will leave no future work to be done in determining which decisions fall, and which do not, within the scope of any norm. I raise this proposal as a possible defence for Finnis' view, not an interpretation of it, and because I think it worth raising for its own sake. The correct answer is, I think, that we may enjoy a reasonable certainty that *major* questions as to who is married, who is innocent and so on, will not arise. For practical purposes, then, we can dismiss those who profess to find these questions exceptionally problematic and hindrance to moral judgement in the ordinary run of cases. They are either very ill-informed about the tradition of deliberative reflection or they are prevaricating.

Still, the possibility of new questions arising from new experience is never absent. By this I do not mean 'radically new experience', such that would make the moral wisdom of the past irrelevant. I mean simply that newness which requires us to press the tradition further and apply it in fresh ways. An example: the policy of nuclear deterrence was new; reflection on the tradition gave Finnis, myself and many others the resources to address remarks to it that will not be found anticipated in Liguori. Another: before the Gulf War of 1991 it never occurred to me to ask whether attacks should be prohibited on water supplies which furnished electric power at once both for civilian and for military uses. I now have a view on that, derived from the tradition but not found in it. And yet another: before *in vitro* fertilisation was in course of development, none of us had cause to ask whether the use of donor gametes was a form of adultery. And so on. Imagination never suffices to envisage all the possible implications of a principle we hold exceptionless; the discovery of such implications is part of what is involved in a serious attempt to apply principles to cases.

For this kind of development of a norm I propose the term 'complementary', in that its role is to fill out the range of the norm's requirements in new kinds of case. It is quite different from an antithetical development. An antithetical development identifies suspensions of the norm, a complementary development identifies new kinds of application. To refuse complementary development when it is needed is to refuse to recognise the claim of the norm itself. For instance, one particularly bad argument about homosexuality, which had some popularity a generation or so ago, ran: "since the Biblical texts did not know of the distinction between 'inversion' and 'perversion' (neither does recent science, of course, but that distinction was still fashionable at the time) they can have no bearing on the behaviour of 'invert' homosexuals". That amounted to little more than a refusal to take up the task of thinking *how* principles enunciated in the texts *might* illumine a situation in which such a distinction could be recognised. It was a purely legalistic manoeuvre, which saw the norms as a kind of statute you might set aside if you could, rather than as a repository of wisdom from which you might learn something for new and different situations.

To sum up: the 'perfectness' or 'exceptionlessness' which can be attributed to some moral norms is: that they express an obligation which can never be superseded by a superior obligation; that they express it with sufficient specificity to give definite guidance for action; and that they express it so aptly that no *antithetical* qualifications need ever be looked for. The perfectness or exceptionlessness which cannot be attributed to any norms is that they express an obligation with such precision that no possible further experience could lead us to add further complementary qualifications to them. I am not sure quite how close this comes to what John Finnis has in mind, but it would seem the gap cannot be very large.

At the risk of disturbing such happy convergence as we have achieved, however, I shall explore in closing some differences of approach which leave me thinking that there remains a major question to address. It has ecumenical implications, and I raise it with a sense of ecumenical responsibility. My concern with John Finnis' programme is not with its capacity to yield conclusions that are, at some moments, almost counter-suggestibly anti-modern, but with whether it confronts modernity with a

Gospel affirmation that will validate his contribution to ethics as a *Christian* witness.

In *Fundamentals of Ethics*, Finnis contended that the good is grasped pre-reflectively and immediately by practical reason. Knowledge of it is not derived from any theoretical account of human nature or the world. In *Natural Law and Natural Rights*, he had argued that this was Thomas's position: "the first principles of natural law ... are not inferred from facts. They are not inferred from metaphysical propositions about human nature, or about the nature of good and evil, or about 'the function of a human being'; nor are they inferred from a teleological conception of nature or any other conception of nature. They are not inferred or derived from anything".[17] In support of the independence of practical reasons from all affirmations about reality, even those of Christian faith, Finnis formerly appealed to the 'is-ought' distinction of twentieth-century moral philosophy. He later became reluctant to speak of this as the 'fact-value' distinction, "for no clear sense can be given to 'factual' other than 'objective and true', and there are many value-judgements that are objective and true".[18] Yet he has kept faith with what is, perhaps, the most distinctive doctrine of post-Enlightenment moral thought, the doctrine of ethical autonomy, though preferring to stress its classical roots by presenting it, in terms of derived from Aristotle and Thomas, as the distinction between practical and theoretical reason.

An observer who undertook to compare Finnis' strategy for defending traditional morality with that adopted by myself in *Resurrection and Moral Order*[19] would, I think, be struck by this difference first of all. I maintained that a Christian morality, to be authentically 'evangelical', had to be founded on the *affirmations* of faith, about creation, redemption, and future consummation. I cannot judge how far this forces me into conflict with St. Thomas' insistence on distinct first principles of practical reason; but I am confident of having the current of New Testament and patristic moral thought flowing in my favour.

It is possible to see Finnis' latest work as offering some kind of resolution to this difficulty. By taking up the category of 'norm', he has strengthened the relation of practical reason, as he understands it, to tradition. *Moral Absolutes* contains extended demonstrations that the norms which Finnis defends are a part of the Christian tradition and of the revelation recognised by that tradition.[20] Here, then, is a serious attempt to overcome the imputation, to which his earlier writing was open, of being uninterested in the relation of morality and faith. Religious tradition has entered to reinforce the immediate deliveries of practical reason.

It is not clear to me how this reinforcement will operate. Practical reasoning cannot recognise the authority of revelation or tradition without ceasing to be practical and setting up a theoretical sideshow of its own. But what this move does is to carry back into revelation and tradition the dichotomy between theoretical and practical. For if revelation discloses authoritative norms, and these norms cannot be derived from the evangelical affirmations which revelation presents to the theoretical reason to enjoy, then revelation contains two distinct and uncompounded elements: evangelical affirmations and norms, the latter independent of the former. This, of course, would be a conclusion of highly-charged ecumenical significance, for it would represent the ambiguous commitment to both Law and Gospel of which the Reformation held late medieval Christendom guilty, and which has been a recurrent element in theological polemics since.

An evangelical morality —using that term in its literal, not its political sense— is one in which the requirement of obedience is authenticated by joyful proclamation of the redemptive goodness of God. Finnis is well aware of one of the corruptions to which this distinctively Christian view of morality is subject: it can lose sight of the requirement of obedience altogether, emphasising the Gospel affirmations without reckoning seriously with their life-transforming implications. The dynamic of salvation through faith then stops still, for the faith with which the proclamation is met is a 'dead' faith, not one actively at work in well-ordered love. This is essentially what reinventing the moral order amounts to. It is a refusal to be grasped by the demanding reality of what God has actually done, preferring to construct a world of meaning in which the only demand will come from the self. As a critic of this corruption, Finnis deserves careful attention.

But there is another way in which Christian morality can be corrupted: by allowing an autonomous morality to qualify and moderate the Gospel proclamation. This has been the temptation of the noble idealists, for whom moral demands have had such a self-standing reality that nothing on earth or in heaven could be allowed to interfere with them, not even the redemptive grace of God. I do not think that John Finnis has succumbed to that temptation, but I do think that he has not fully appreciated the importance of not succumbing to it. And is it not, as much as or more than the other, a temptation to which modernity is prone?

NOTES

1   John Finnis, *Moral Absolutes: Tradition, Revision and Truth* [*MA*] (Washington, DC: Catholic University of America Press, 1991), p.2. The quotations of John Paul II are from the Exhortation, *Reconciliatio et Paenitentia* (1984), para.17.

For the sake of clarity it had better not be left unsaid that the 'acts' of which the Pope speaks are *kinds* of act, not particular acts. What is 'always' wrong is the kind of act we call murder; a particular murder, such as that of the Archbishop of Uganda by the President in 1977, was simply 'wrong'. Similarly, the moral norms which have precise and unconditioned content must be *generic* norms, such as the prohibition of murder, not commands or prohibitions addressed only to a *particular* projected murder.

2   *MA*, p.38.

3   Much of Finnis' polemic energy, in this as in previous books, is directed to arguing that Catholic 'proportionalists' belong to this cluster. I shall not follow him into this polemic, which would involve discussing how well he had understood this school of thinkers.

4   See, for example, *MA*, p.39 n.24: "When the Commandments (sc. of the Decalogue) are considered as they should be, as propositions bearing on human acts understood in terms of their precise intentionality ...". The term 'proposition' includes not only what is said by affirmative utterances, but what is commanded by imperative utterances, questioned by questions, etc. It is not one kind of verbal or grammatical formulation. It is the content of a speech-act of any kind. It has its ontological context within the power of speech to *refer* to reality. It is not itself the moral relation referred to, 'the wrongness of adultery', 'the obscenity of ethnic cleansing', etc. I am grateful to Professor Finnis for clarifying his understanding for me on this point.

5   *MA*, pp.1-6.

6   Ibid., p.2.

7   Ibid., p.3.

8   Professor Finnis has pointed out to me that the use of this fact-value dilemma by the Catholic proportionalists does not commit them to belief that value is merely a matter of attribution. What it would commit them to, in fact, is simply the view that an evaluative term is a composite of (a) a descriptive component and (b) a negative or positive judgement on it. For the sentence 'adultery is wrong' to be tautologous it must be that the negative judgement in 'wrong' *repeats* the negative judgement in 'adultery'. Nothing is said in the term 'adultery' that is not *either* pure factual description or the anticipation of the negative judgement given in 'wrong'. In this sense their account of moral language derives from the fact-value distinction, but without involving them in a constructivist or voluntarist doctrine of moral value.

9   *MA*, p.3.

10   Ibid., p.5.

11   Ibid., p.28.

12   Ibid., p.3.

13   Ibid., pp.27-8.

14   Ibid., pp.10-11.

15   Ibid., p.7.

16   Ibid., p.8.

17   John Finnis, *Natural Law and Natural Rights* (Oxford, Clarendon Press, 1980), pp.33-4.

18   John Finnis, *Fundamentals of Ethics* (Oxford, Clarendon Press, 1983), p.66.

19   Oliver O'Donovan, *Resurrection and Moral Order: an Outline for Evangelical Ethics* (Leicester: IVP; Grand Rapids: Eerdmans, 1986).

20   See *MA*, pp.6-9, 58-67.

Part II:

Theological Dimensions

5   Is Grisez's Moral Theology Rationalistic? Free Choice, the Human Condition, and Christian Ethics

Göran Bexell[1]

Grisez's moral theology, as stated principally in the first two volumes of *The Way of the Lord Jesus*,[2] is a largely Thomistic moral doctrine, faithful to the official teaching of the Roman Catholic Church and of normative Christian character. Grisez, while wishing to remain faithful to the Second Vatican Council, is at the same time critical of much in present-day Roman Catholic moral theology, which he considers to be a series of compromises with secular humanism. Thus he criticises 'proportionalism' and other contemporary Roman Catholic moral theologians who do not adhere closely enough to what he describes as the official teaching of the Church.

His purpose in so doing is clearly not to undertake a comprehensive discussion of alternative ethical ideas, whether philosophical or Christian; this he quickly denies. Important contemporary moral theologians like Bernhard Häring, in his more recent writings, are regarded primarily as dissidents;[3] Richard McCormick he dismisses in an embarrassingly simplistic way.[4] Grisez considers that a good moral theologian ought to be a non-dissident, and it is as such that Grisez states his case, programmatically and without attempting to undertake a dispassionate ethical analysis.

Nevertheless his major work, *The Way of the Lord Jesus*, provides an instructive example of writing in its genre, and is an important contribution to contemporary moral theology. It gives an excellent view of the way in which a traditional Roman Catholic theologian of conservative inclination tackles ethical questions.

Free Choice and the Dominance of Rationality

It is characteristic of Grisez's moral theology that free choice is allocated a dominant function. His moral theory, like many others, begins with the important assumption that human beings can and do make free and rational decisions. He writes: "Perhaps the most important presupposition from philosophical anthropology is that human persons can make free choices".[5] Theologically speaking, according to Grisez, the human being has been created by God, is therefore able to choose freely, and is thereby brought within the moral realm of good and evil.[6] If there were no free choice, there would be no responsibility and therefore no morals: such is the simple presupposition which Grisez shares with many moral theologians and moral philosophers: "Free choice is the central reality in us by which our acts are present in the moral field —that is, are existential".[7] As yet, this is no more than a formal principle. Free choice has to be guided by moral norms. Conclusions are drawn through the judgement of conscience from objectively true moral principles, the meaning and function of which are to be found in the doctrine of natural law: moral norms exist for the betterment of humanity in the sense of the realisation and fulfilment of the essential being of each human person.

Grisez constructs a theory of how correct decisions are arrived at, formally speaking, on certain criteria of responsibility, general and specific norms, adequate reflection, and the character of an enlightened and morally good person endowed with the virtue of prudence. I am happy to affirm the attempt to shape a theory containing a wide range of criteria for true moral choice: it is not dissimilar in principle to the theory of well-grounded moral understanding that I have myself proposed.[8]

However, on the one hand, it is paradoxical to have to record that freedom of choice in a general sense plays a fairly limited role in Grisez's theory, as we see when we compare it with the place of free will in existentialist ethics. On this latter view, it is in the last resort the conditional choice which is the correct one, whereas Grisez maintains that there is a standard of rightness found in natural law and the deliverances of the conscience, which the individual must choose in order to be right. If I have understood Grisez correctly, it is not the act of choosing in itself that determines whether an action is right or wrong. Moral choice is in fact hedged about by so many limiting criteria that the individual is often left with no alternative but to choose what the Church's magisterium declares to be correct, if his or her choice is to be right; but Grisez plays this down. Freedom of choice involves granting the individual responsibility and enabling him or her to choose between alternatives, without prescribing which of them is objectively correct.

On the other hand, there is a great deal in the context and content of ethics which limits the scope of free choice —human conditions, social situations and individual presuppositions restrict the range of human choices, which furthermore are not always rational. Grisez does not deny this, but he gives it no place in his ethical theory.

In this short essay, I cannot argue in detail for and against Grisez's theory as a whole. Instead, I shall focus my critical discussion on the rationality of his ethics and on his view of human being, considering these topics from a number of different angles in order to build up a comprehensive understanding. I shall also hint at an alternative approach.

Nevertheless, let me begin by saying that Grisez's moral theology is extremely interesting, and that it contains numerous valuable distinctions and critical arguments. I agree with him that it is important to acknowledge the importance of free choice and rationality in moral theology. In many ways he has what I regard as a soundly based moral understanding; but I cannot share his blanket criticism of divergent views. I suspect that his ethical system is one-sidedly rationalistic, and that this has caused him to exclude from the moral totality a great deal that is well worth considering and including in both ethical analysis and in a firmly based understanding of morals.

A Rationalistic Theory of Ethics?

The Difference between Rational and Rationalistic Ethics

Grisez's theory, as we have sketched it, demonstrates a number of typical features of a rationalistic theory of ethics. An ethical system having at its heart freedom of choice, free will, and rational reflection will in most cases end up in the vicinity of rationalism.

Although Grisez makes no use of it, there is an important difference between rational and rationalistic ethics. A rational ethic is based on rational considerations and is logically consistent; its opposite is an irrational ethic. That ethics ought to be rational, few would contest. A rationalistic ethic, on the other hand, allows only the reason to determine moral theology, at the expense of other human spiritual capabilities and other ethical phenomena; and it may well presuppose an Aristotelian view of human being as specifically rational. In such a system, feelings, will, or intuition should not override reason, as they may in a rational ethic.

The question is whether Grisez's ethical system is simply rational, or whether it is also rationalistic. In my theory of a soundly based understanding of morals, ethical systems, including religious and Christian ethics, should be rational but not rationalistic. I am not quite sure, but it seems to me that Grisez's ethical views are more rationalistic than rational; certainly they have definite rationalistic characteristics. The argument and illustrations that follow are intended to show this.

Two Views of Human Nature

Grisez and his followers identify themselves with one side of a conflict, which runs throughout the Christian moral tradition, between on the one hand those who affirm humankind's ability to act and choose well and rationally; and on the other hand those who hold that human being is both rational and irrational, constructive and destructive, good and evil. The first line of thought, which we call 'optimistic', is chiefly based on an Aristotelian and Thomistic anthropology: that which distinguishes human being from the animals is that it has a rational soul. This reinforces belief in human reason and capacity for goodness, and in the human ability to become morally more perfect through the living of a virtuous life.

The other line of thought represents the Pauline, Augustinian and Lutheran view of human nature: that it cannot be changed in any significant way merely by exhorting people to behave better. Human being is a mixture of good and evil, morally speaking. No one makes only good and rational decisions, and even when such decisions appear to be made, they are often not so much expressions of deep moral commitment as of shallow personal or social expediency. Human beings are filled not only with longing for God and goodness, but also with selfish and destructive tendencies —indeed, in the last analysis, with rebellion against God. All this has an impact on morals.

This difference in theological anthropology corresponds to the conflict between two other, psychological ways of looking at human behaviour, one based on behavioural science and the other psychodynamic. As a Thomist, Grisez is in the former, behavioural camp. What is defective in this point of view is that it obliterates all the cumulative knowledge of human nature that the other side represents. It would be far preferable instead to create a dialectic capable of preserving the insights of both traditions, allowing both to make a significant contribution to our understanding of human nature and of morals.

Grisez's one-sidedness is evident in the way he deals with Luther and the ethics of Protestantism. For instance, while he is right to emphasise the centrality here of the grace of God in the salvation of humanity, he is wrong to suppose that this excludes human responsibility: "Thus these Protestants denied human free choice".[9] It is not that simple: the way in which Grisez deals with those whose opinions differ from his own is, as we have said, among the weakest features of *The Way of the Lord Jesus*. The question of Luther's controversy with Erasmus about the freedom of the will is one of the most controversial questions in theology, but it is certain that Luther did not deny freedom of choice in people's relations to one another. What he did say, however, was that in relation to God, human beings are subject either to God or to the powers of evil, and cannot remain neutral between them. When a person receives the love of God in his or her heart by faith, good and just works will ensue spontaneously, although there remains an ambivalence, due to their being *simul iustus et peccator*.

Paul writes to the Christians in Philippi, "Work out your own salvation with fear and trembling", and Grisez emphasises this; but in the context of the conflicts of his time Luther stressed the words which follow, "for God is at work in you, both to will and to work for his good pleasure".[10] Both the injunction and the affirmation are found in Paul, and together they indicate on the one hand that the individual has to choose and act, but on the other that God is finally in control. It seems to me that the most fruitful way ahead for Christian moral theology and anthropology is along the lines of a dialectical balance between these two perspectives. Grisez goes to one extreme, Luther occasionally to the other. Nevertheless, a balance between the 'external', breadth perspective and the 'internal', depth one can and should be kept.

Sin and Evil: a Monodimensional Theory

It is always instructive to examine the way in which the doctrine of sin is treated in different ethics. According to Grisez, the cause of sin is the immoral choice made by the first humans, of which death is the consequence. Although he acknowledges briefly that sin is 'mysterious', his main point is that it is caused by the individual's free and immoral choice. Evil is therefore the result of sin, which originates in human free will.

My first objection to this is that Grisez appears to have a monodimensional doctrine of evil. In his attempt to eliminate absolute dualism, Grisez resorts to a rationalistic view of evil, which does not correspond either to human experience or to the witness of tradition and the Bible. A more complex understanding of evil does not necessarily have to accept an absolute dualism or locate evil on God's 'hidden' side; it can simply leave the question open and accept the inexplicable existence of evil in human experience as a reality to which everyone is subject, and which rational choice, for or against, can influence only superficially.

In the Lutheran tradition in particular there is, as we have indicated, a dualistic view, according to which an evil and suprapersonal power stands, in some way that reason cannot grasp, in opposition to God; human beings cannot choose one power rather than the other, but are seized either by God or by evil. The biblical account of the Fall is rich in symbols pointing to the ambiguity and mystery behind the narrator's experience of something evil, tempting humans and drawing them away from the paradisal existence that the creation was meant to be. In the experience and teaching of Jesus, evil is also the dark background against which his life and death are to be seen.

I do not wish, as so often happens in the Lutheran tradition, to place too much emphasis on evil; but it seems to me that Grisez oversimplifies its moral implications. He places all the responsibility for sin on human free will, and takes no account of the notion that after the expulsion from Eden, theologically speaking, human being has fallen under the sway of the 'Evil One'.

This deprives the Fall narrative of much of its meaning. Certainly Grisez admits, as we have said, that there is something 'mysterious' about evil;[11] but this plays no further part in his theory. To choose 'to eat the apple' is on the surface an act of disobedience; but viewed in the light of depth psychology, it is an act of self-assertion on the human being's part, a refusal to accept the goodness of God on the one hand, and human limitations and mortality on the other. Read thus, the narrative is less a statement that a deliberate choice was made to refuse these conditions, than an expression of human mortality and a rationalisation of the desire to escape from it in terms of disobedience. It may therefore be said to illustrate the human lack of freedom: evil in the shape of temptation (the serpent) pre-exists human beings and enters human life from outside. It is not only generated within human nature, and is not only a matter of human free will. It is already in the world, and enters human experience as a fundamental temptation which we are powerless to resist.[12] Grisez appears to take no account of the difference between historical and existential interpretations of the Bible. His one-sided interpretation of the narrative of the Fall as no more than a sequence of events overlooks the function of myth as illustrative of the human condition. Part of this is our subjection to evil.

If it is the case that we are unable to eliminate evil completely from human life by means of rational and enlightened moral choices, this will affect moral action. Sometimes wrong is done without any (rational) choice having been made —though this possibility lies beyond the range of Grisez's system. One recalls Paul's sombre confession: "For I do not do the good I want, but the evil I do not want is what I do".[13]

In my view, maintaining the dialectical tension between evil as a result of man's captivity on the one hand, and his free choice on the other, protects an ethic against becoming one-sidedly rationalistic. But Grisez does not even recognise this tension.

The Theory of the Unconscious Calls Rationalistic Ethics in Question

What is, and what should be, the significance of 'the unconscious' in morals? What would a system of ethics that took full account of psychoanalytical insights look like? These questions can be answered in different ways.

From the point of view of moral psychology, a theory of the unconscious such as Freud's claims to be able to explain the origin, development and function of morals. In Freudian terms, the human being consists of a *superego* (an 'overself'), an *ego* (a 'self') and an *id* (an 'it'): the unconscious is located chiefly in the *id* and the *superego*, and is controlled by desires, painful memories and conflicts which imprison psychic energy. The task of therapy is to make conscious what previously has been hidden in the unconscious, setting free what Freud regarded the two great human capacities —to love and to work.[14] Genuine, effective therapy challenges our defence against freedom, just as salvation challenges our destructive powers. If the *ego* gains ascendancy over the *id* and the *superego*, the freedom of the *ego* can help improve the individual's inner balance; but throughout life the unconscious will exercise a dominant influence on our ethical and religious experiences, thoughts, and actions.

According to this theory, moral commandments are linked to a system of punishment and love, producing a fear that disobedience of norms will lead to the loss of parental love. At the same time, the flouting of norms is a tempting way to mark one's independence. The more we are under the control of the unconscious, the less influence rationality is able to retain. Beginning in infancy, moral ideas are directly linked to, and express, powerful impulses and energies on the unconscious level. For example, the moral injunction against theft serves as a verbal and rational expression for more unconscious energies of anxiety and fear —such as the fear of punishment, and ultimately of forfeiting society's love and being abandoned.

Therapeutic investigations and experience confirm that the idea of the unconscious can help us to understand a complex world of experiences. These days it is generally acknowledged that what appears on the surface to be one thing, may turn out to be an unconscious expression of something entirely different. This also applies in the realms of morals and religion, where an overemphasis upon rational argumentation is suspect of really being a rationalising defence against unconscious anxieties. The greater the anxiety, the stronger the rationalistic defence.

If we accept the theory of the unconscious, we must admit into our interpretation of human phenomena what Ricoeur has called the hermeneutics of suspicion. This bears upon those ethical theories which leave no room for the discovery of the unconscious and the irrational in human behaviour.[15] There is, to be sure, no reason why moral theology should accept a psychoanalytical criticism of morals as a whole; but equally it would be difficult to justify its wholesale neglect of the moral implications of Freud's theory.

According to the hermeneutics of suspicion, many decisions, whose motivation appears to be rooted in admirable social, moral and religious reasons, are in fact driven by entirely different motives and desires in the unconscious depth-dimension. For example, that which seems socially praiseworthy and is regarded as self-effacing altruism may in fact be an expression of unconscious hatred, an anxious defence mechanism against unacknowledged hatreds, a desire for power, or an egoistic craving for love. Or it may be that one who harms others is really revealing a desire for acceptance, while an apparently humble person is hiding a desire for power or thwarted aggressiveness. Or someone who is obedient may be unconsciously demonstrating a low level of personal self-esteem. Thus a 'rational' choice may in fact be an unconscious rationalisation and a defence against anxiety. Naturally enough, explanations of this order seem to the rationalist wholly absurd; and the more he feels the need to defend himself, the more passionate will be his defensive dismissal.

How can one know whether a decision apparently based on acceptable rational motives is what it purports to be, and not merely an expression of other, unconscious motives? It is extremely difficult to know. A person with trained powers of observation, good intuition and an eye for depth-psychological detail may discern something of what will emerge largely in the course of therapeutic relationships and counselling. I do not wish to pursue this matter further. My main purpose has been to point out that it is characteristic of rationalistic ethics to ignore the role of the unconscious in the making of moral decisions, and to assume that the entire moral process is carried out on the rational surface. The depth psychologist, on the other hand, knows that what is most important in a person's life often takes place beneath the surface, on a level to which rational analysis has no access. This can be reached only by a different route, by way of such things as powerful experiences and expressions of love and hate, profound relationships, and therapy. In taking no account of the dimension of depth, rationalistic ethics is unable to cope with a large part of human existence.

Freud's intention, however, was positive as well as critical. The development of psychoanalytical therapy was designed to liberate the individual from the power of the unconscious, so as to render the ego, if not completely free, at least freer in relation to it —and thereby to increase the influence of rationality. Freud himself was a strong believer in the possibilities of rationality, and wanted to help people become more able to make rational decisions, despite their being at the same time somewhat bound by the irrationality of the unconscious. This is the dialectical situation in which human beings find themselves, irrespective of where they deliberately choose to be. On this point Freud's approach has far more in common with that of Luther than with the Thomistic tradition.

Such a view of human nature and its moral consequences supports my thesis that in an ethical theory there ought to be a dialectical relationship between the conscious and the unconscious, between rationality and irrationality. The objective of ethics should be to increase human rationality; but this cannot be successfully pursued without paying full attention to the dialectic. The conscious and rational surface is an essential level of human ethics, but it is also important to recognise that the most powerful moral impulses are perhaps to be found at a deeper level, and that an authentic, well-integrated morality has to take account of both levels.

The theory of the unconscious therefore provides a point of departure for a critical examination of the one-sidedly rationalistic aspect of Grisez's moral theology, although the purpose of therapy nevertheless confirms the importance of free and responsible choice, even if this can never be fully realised. Ernest Wallwork's summary of his brilliant analysis of Freudian ethics supports this view:

> But Freud's assumption is that a person's genuine convictions come from deeper within the self than a mere conscious decision to adopt a set of values or norms. Where these deeper springs are absent, morality lacks a certain authenticity, though what is done may be sufficient for people to relate socially on a superficial basis.[16]

It is interesting that when Grisez makes mention of the phenomenon of rationalisation, it is only in cases where someone chooses to dissent from official Church doctrine: "Indeed, many catholics say their choice to use contraception is not contrary to their conscience. Of course, that assertion could manifest self-deception and rationalisation rather than a genuine judgement of conscience".[17] Grisez seems to assume here that choices contrary to what the Church teaches, made in a situation of ethical tension, cannot really be based on genuine conviction, but must be expressive of covert ignorance or hostility to the Church —in other words, they must be irrational. But surely rationalisation can work in the opposite direction, too. What about the unconscious motives that drive those who always base their moral decisions on some dominant authority? Might it not be that they fear losing approval or their jobs, for example, or damaging their prospects of promotion?

Finally, a brief word in response to the well-worn refrain that the 'psychical determinism' of psychoanalysis renders moral responsibility and free choice impossible. This is not the place to enter into a close textual interpretation of Freud; but, as I have already indicated, he did believe the self (*ego*) to have a certain degree of freedom, and that a certain psychic determinism does not stand in the way of a certain freedom of choice. Freud stressed the importance of moral responsibility, and held that the individual should take responsibility for his or her own unconscious and suppressed desires and conflicts.[18]

Emotion and Reason

A rationalistic ethic typically plays off reason against the emotions, or has an undeveloped theory of the emotions. It is noteworthy, therefore, that Grisez emphasises that decision-making should take place in spite of emotional obstacles, precisely in order to guarantee that the final decision should not rest primarily on emotional impulses. In principle it is reasonable to draw a distinction between decision-making and emotional impulses, but it is typical of a rationalistic ethic that where there is tension between reason and the emotions, reason always gets to hold the upper hand.[19] Whatever Grisez's view of the emotions, it would ruin his system if they were allowed to dominate.

When Grisez dismisses the emotions, it is unclear whether or not he considers them to be morally cognitive; he says nothing explicit on the subject. This in its turn is due to a generally rudimentary theory of the role of the emotions in moral life —a further indication that his ethic is indeed rationalistic. His definition of the emotions is fairly simple: they are "motives at the sensory level which are generically common to humans and other animals. Among them are desire, aversion, fear, anger, and the tendency to rest, which can be called 'tiredness'".[20] Grisez describes the emotions as being mainly a hindrance to change and rational action; he does not consider the possibility that feelings, too, can communicate a moral insight or a signal that something is morally wrong. For example, might not a contemporary married woman's feeling of hostility to a patriarchal ethic that demands that she obey her husband, be a valid indication that there is something wrong with it?[21] The most positive thing Grisez can find to say about the emotions is that: "In general, there is nothing wrong with emotions, and while in themselves they are not rational, neither are they irrational".[22]

It is more satisfactory to work out a theory of the emotions which treats them, not, as Grisez does, merely as elemental and uncontrollable urges like fear, anxiety and hatred, but rather as subtler and more personally formed expressions of the subject's assimilated and interpreted experiences, and hence as morally cognitive. If we regard the emotions as a rich source of moral knowledge, we may rely on them as an alternative to rational choice. In ignoring this possibility, Grisez reveals the rationalism of his ethic. Although his system allows choices to be made in harmony with the emotions, it forbids the emotions themselves to dictate; for that would be to violate the supreme position of rationality in decision-making. The alternative is to allow the emotions —not only the more primitive emotions of fear and anxiety, but also the more refined ones— to take the moral lead, permitting reason test the moral information that they supply, but in the end letting the emotions or 'the heart' decide. Such a method of making ethical decisions can be just as responsible. To summarise: Grisez's simplistic theory of the emotions allows him to play reason off against them, whereas a more developed theory would have supported a dialectic between them.

Varieties of Moral Deliberation

If morals are to become effective in an individual's life, a degree of commitment is needed. In Grisez's view the only basis of such a commitment is free choice. This gives his theory a distinctive profile but is at the same time a weakness, since it overlooks alternatives. A closer analysis of the nature of commitment would have opened up other points of view, as I shall now try to show briefly. Let me begin with some definitions.

(a) In my view, a moral *choice* occurs in the kind of situation in which the individual has to opt for one of two irreconcileable alternatives, leading to totally different consequences. This concept of the act of choosing may be combined with the view that what is chosen thereby becomes morally acceptable, though this is not necessarily so.

(b) Moral *decisions* are choices in more indefinite form, and are always linked with the view that the decision of approval or disapproval does not as such render acts or omissions morally good or morally evil. If I disapprove of euthanasia, it is not my decision that makes it morally wrong; all that it expresses is my moral commitment. Grisez makes no distinction between choice and decision.

(c) Moral *deliberation* is a rational calculation in a situation requiring decision, and involving the weighing against one another of consequences, attitudes, and facts, the result being a reasoned conclusion rather than a clearly delineated decision. Grisez uses the method of deliberation, though never as a final argument in matters of choice.

(d) *Interpretation* (or *Deutung*, in German) is a fourth possibility, the basics of which have been stated by the Danish ethicist, K.E. Løgstrup.[23] This adds another dimension to ethics, one not found in Grisez, namely on the semantic level ethically descriptive statements like, 'John is merciful'. How do I know that John is merciful? Hardly through my choosing so, but nor through sensory perception. My senses tell me that the table is round, but how am I to know that John is merciful? Here the directives of the Church are not of the same objective character as those having to do with norms and values and statements like 'X is right'. The Church can teach what mercy is, but not whether John is merciful or not.

G. E. Moore held that in cases like these, moral awareness comes through intuition, which supplies me with knowledge of a quality John actually possesses, namely mercy. Grisez, on the other hand, has little time for intuition as a source of moral knowledge, because he supposes it to be simply subjective.[24] In Løgstrup's own view, the intuition certainly involves an attitude to John on the subject's part, but this is brought about by John himself.[25] All this, which is neither a choice, nor a statement, nor a perception, nor an intuitive assessment of a quality, Løgstrup calls "interpretation" (in Danish, *tydning*). There seems to be no place for such interpretation in Grisez's ethics, which I take to be further evidence of its rationalism.

Spontaneous Action and Rational Choice

Grisez is forced by his theory of free rational choice to exclude a number of meaningful phenomena as morally uninteresting, or at least non-essential. Among these are not only all those actions carried out on the basis of upbringing, but also spontaneous actions on the part of both children and adults —if you are out rowing and see someone drowning, you will quite spontaneously try to effect a rescue. Much of what we do on a daily basis happens like this —something Grisez duly notes, but without integrating it into his ethical system. In his scheme, it is only the carefully calculated decision, directed by the conscience and tested against facts and feelings, which is allowed to count. This has the additional effect of ruling out those acts that are performed as a direct consequence of faith, when love takes such control that the individual feels directed by a mighty power, without knowing how or why. Ask those who live in this way, whether they have *chosen* to allow love to be outgoing and self-renouncing, and they will answer, No. In Anders Nygren's ethical system, *agape* serves to provide the human individual with an inner motivation to act spontaneously, which faith believes to be the effect of the action of God.

Grisez distinguishes between children's spontaneous play and adults' moral actions; but there are also adult actions which are carried out spontaneously. However, rather than adapt his system to take account of these moral phenomena, he insists on defining morals exclusively in terms of freedom and responsibility, permitting only the subject's own deliberately chosen actions to be morally relevant and excluding in principle those actions that are more or less 'fated'.

Tragedy and the Tragic

This brings us to the category of 'the tragic'. Originally, 'tragedy' was a type of classical drama in which someone was shown to be forced, through no fault of his or her own, into a wrong course of action. Characters in Greek tragedy are compelled by fate to act, despite their best intentions, in a way that everyone knows to be wrong, and which the chorus laments. King Oedipus is the outstanding literary example, but according to didactic Greek tragedy human life as such is tragic.[26] Tragedy, then, implies that individuals are forced against their wishes into situations over which they have no control. This supports the thesis that sometimes things happen to people, that personal choice in many cases changes nothing, and that a feeling of moral guilt ensues nevertheless.

Human life, past and present, is full of such experiences, but this area of morals is nowhere discussed by Grisez, since his ethical system is built on the decisive importance of free choice —precisely the free choice which may come into play superficially in the course of a tragedy, but which cannot influence the outcome, or prevent human guilt. Even when a person apparently chooses and acts correctly, he or she may be doing wrong unwittingly, inevitably incurring guilt.

Another dimension of tragedy is when the individual is forced to choose between alternatives, all of which have evil consequences. For example, take the case of a missionary doctor compelled to choose between performing immediate surgery on the sick son of a chief, who may be expected to give money that will save hundreds of lives in the future, and providing simpler treatment for a dozen children who will otherwise die. This is a tragic choice.

A rationalistic system of ethics, however, seems to presuppose a society consisting of well-balanced individuals, who in situations of moral choice make their rational, non-tragic decisions and then behave in such a way that pure good results. The tragic dimension of what happens to people —through fate, chance, the power of evil, events in history, perhaps even God— is hidden away in Grisez's orderly moral world, in which the wise person chooses in such a way as to avoid insoluble dilemmas. There is little room in a rationalistic ethic for reflection on the tragic dimensions of life.

The Dialectics of Religion's Role in Morals

Another example of the rationalistic nature of Grisez's moral theology is that there is no strong place in it for the dialectics of religion. Religious faith impinges upon morals in a many ways. One feature of its impact, however, is especially important: integrated religious or Christian faith involves all of a person's spiritual capacities and every level of his or her personality. Genuine faith is more than just the result of a free choice; it is also a gift of trust deep in the unconscious, far beneath the level at which rational decisions are made. Whoever believes God to be good is impelled to do good and to interpret life in accordance with that belief. He or she is on the one hand claimed, and on the other hand motivated to choose and act in response to that claim.

A concrete example of this may be found by considering the different ways in which the fundamental Christian commandment to love and the phenomenon of love function in moral life.[27] Jesus taught that one's whole strength, mind and soul should be devoted to the love of God and one's neighbour. This commandment might be viewed as a moral demand, contradicting egoistic impulses; it may be obeyed, but only under external compulsion and in spite of inner resistance. In such a case, free rational choice is without moral significance, if indeed it is present at all. Christians believe that God the Creator can bring out of such reluctantly obedient acts good results from which others can benefit; but these are not the deeds that God really wants. They may be formally correct, but they are not morally good.

Love can also function as the result of a rational and free choice. Here the emphasis lies on the will. Actions can be carried out with or without inward spontaneity. They may be morally both right and good, but there is nothing to say that they have to be: if they are carried out after rational consideration but without inward motivation, though they may still be right, they are not good.

Finally, love can be an expression of a spontaneous state of mind out of which actions emerge freely. In this case the individual has been grasped by love without being compelled by it and without having chosen it; choices follow rather than precede such a welcome state of possession. Here acts may be carried out which Christian ethics regards with approval, since they issue from a pure heart and are therefore good; but they are not necessarily morally correct.

All three possibilities occur from time to time in the life of every human individual, but Grisez restricts himself firmly to the second alternative, emphasising that the 'love' to which the commandment refers is not emotional but volitional.[28] Thereby he fails to distinguish between good and right actions, and regards the second mode of love as a matter of right actions only. Christian ethics, however, admits all three possibilities. But it regards the third as the ideal, because here the individual is grasped by the power of love, while also affirming it and choosing to act lovingly. In other words, the third mode maintains the dialectic between being acted upon and choosing to act.

Conclusion

What is the conclusion of our critical examination of Grisez's moral theology? Is it indeed more rationalistic than rational? Our analysis has produced a number of reasons why it would seem so. It might be that consideration of Grisez's writings in their entirety would modify this result; but scrutiny of the first two volumes of *The Way of the Lord Jesus* certainly justifies it.

Epilogue: the Return of Natural Law as a Global Ethic?

Before I finish, let me make a short excursus on the theme of natural law in contemporary ethics, viewed from a Scandinavian angle. The attempt to bring about the revival of natural law involves both possibilities and problems. In contemporary debate what is mainly at issue is the relationship between universalism and particularism. A doctrine of natural law is universalist, containing as it does a universal claim based on empirical assumptions concerning human nature and the ethical capabilities of reason. But contemporary ethical discussion is dominated by particularist or contextualist theories,[29] which maintain that ethics, whether descriptive or normative, are always totally dependent upon their particular context, which can be that of a tradition, a culture, a society, an ideology, a religion, or a gender. From this point of view, universalist ethical theories are no more than covert attempts to ascribe universal authority to a particular morality. Such attempts, it is claimed, have been a long-standing feature of western and Christian hegemony, though corresponding claims can be found in other religions.

Those who would resurrect the idea of natural law today cannot avoid the problems of universalism and contextualism. Traditional objections must be met in the light of the new contextualist criticism. Is there really something universal which all ethics have in common, whether on the descriptive or the normative level? Why should a Christian ethic with specifically Thomistic character be advanced as something which everyone, everywhere ought in principle to accept? Is a Christian natural law ethic really the same as —or demonstrably superior to— Muslim or Buddhist or all other ethics? Whoever aims to renew the (Christian) idea of natural law must be able to answer these questions in a convincing fashion.

I do not believe that the criticisms brought forward from the side of particularism are so strong that they should lead to the abandonment of the idea of natural law. The title 'natural law' may not be ideal because of its various connotations, but it is nevertheless important to renew this classic tradition of Christian ethics, which has long been a major channel of Christian moral thinking and has done much to bring it into dialogue with humanist ethics.

For this reason, Grisez's approach to this task is of great interest. There are other approaches, of course, and it would have been interesting to have Grisez's comments on them. In this connection, I might mention the work done in recent years in Scandinavian theological ethics. Because of the tragedy of the Nazi years on the one hand, and Barthian influence on the other, German-language theology has long been prevented from renewing an ethic based on a theology of creation. Scandinavian countries, however, have not suffered from this limitation. There has been a powerful tradition of Swedish scholarship in which the question of the relationship of 'natural law' to ethics has been discussed. Gustaf Wingren, for example, developed an ethic, at once Christian and humanist, on the basis of a theology of creation.[30] Together with this a Christian social ethic, largely in line with a universal humanistic ethical system, has been elaborated by Ragnar Holte.[31]   Of Scandinavian scholars the best-known internationally has been Løgstrup,[32] who has used phenomenological methods to argue that the human condition is ethically determined prior to human choosing. This Scandinavian ethical tradition, shaped by Lutheran tradition and reinvigorated in recent years, includes a number of serious proposals for the renewal of the doctrine of natural law.[33] At the present time there is in progress an intensive discussion about the universal versus the particular both in ethics generally, and in Christian ethics especially. In this context I myself have argued for a contemporary ethical system with universal qualities.[34]

There are a number of good reasons why the exaggerated particularism so fashionable in our day deserves to be challenged by an updated universalist ethics, and therefore why the doctrine of natural law needs to be refashioned in the light of today's ethical debates and problems. Grisez's moral theology is accordingly significant as one serious attempt to do just that.

NOTES

1   The present text is an edited version of an English translation, made from the Swedish original by Professor Eric Sharpe.

2   The material on which this article is based consists of Germain Grisez, *The Way of the Lord Jesus*, volumes 1 and 2 (*CMP* and *LCL*) , and Grisez, Joseph Boyle, and John Finnis, "Practical Principles, Moral Truth, and Ultimate Ends" (*PP*).

3   *CMP*, p.37 n.25.

4   Ibid., p.159.

5   *PP*, p.100.

6   *CMP*, ch.2.
7   *CMP*, p.41.
8   Göran Bexell, "En välgrundad moraluppfattning", in *Svensk Teologisk Kvartalsskrift* (1990/4), pp.145 ff.; and (with C.-H. Grenholm) *Teologisk Etik —en introduktion* (Stockholm: Verbum, 1997), ch.13.
9   *CMP*, p.43.
10   Philippians 2.12f. (RSV).
11   *CMP*, ch.13.
12   Cf. Göran Bexell, *Människans befrielse. Psykoanalys och kristen tro* (Lund: Håkon Ohlssons,1975), pp. 82ff., with particular reference to Ricoeur's interpretation.
13   Romans 7.19 (RSV).
14   Bexell, *Människans befrielse*, pp.55 ff., with references to Freud's *Gesammelte Werke*.
15   For an excellent introduction, see Ernest Wallwork, *Psychoanalysis and Ethics* (New Haven: Yale, 1991). See also Bexell, *Människans befrielse*, passim.
16   Wallwork, *Psychoanalysis*, pp.289 f.
17   *LCL*, p.519.
18   Wallwork, *Psychoanalysis*, pp.87 f.
19   *LCL*, p.245.
20   Ibid., p.273.
21   Ibid., p.629: "But in certain cases, the husband-father should make a decision, and his wife and children should obey".
22   Ibid., p.273.
23   K. E. Løgstrup, *Den etiske fordring* (Copenhagen: Gyldendal, 1956); English trans: *The Ethical Demand* (Notre Dame: University of Notre Dame Press, 1997).
24   See *LCL*, p.248 n.2.
25   Göran Bexell, "Ethik zwischen zwei Traditionen", in *Zeitschrift für Evangelische Ethik*, 304 (1986), pp.412 ff.
26   Cf. Martha Nussbaum, "Tragedy", in *Encyclopedia of Ethics*, 2 vols., ed. L.C. Becker and C.B. Becker, vol. II (New York and London: Garland, 1992).
27   Göran Bexell, *Etiken, bibeln och samlevnaden: utformningen av en nutida kristen etik* (Stockholm: Verbum, 1988), pp.120 ff.
28   *CMP*, p.307.
29   Cf. the discussion in Zygmunt Bauman, *Postmodern Ethics* (Oxford: Blackwell, 1993).
30   Wingren, author of *Luther on Vocation, Creation and Law*, and *Theology in Conflict*, was Professor of Theological Ethics in Lund, Sweden from 1951 to 1977.
31   Holte was Professor of Ethics in Uppsala, Sweden from 1966 to 1992.
32   Løgstrup was Professor in Århus, Denmark, and author of *The Ethical Demand*, cited above.
33   Put forward, for example, by Professor Carl-Henrik Grenholm in Uppsala and the present writer. The question of universalism *versus* particularism in ethics is a theme running through the whole of our textbook, *Teologisk etik —en introduktion* .
34   Göran Bexell, "Universalism och partikularism i etiken", *Svensk Teologisk Kvartalskrift*, 1997/2; and "Universalism och partikularism i etiken. Nytt svar till Arne Rasmusson", in *Svensk Teologisk Kvartalskrift*, 1998/2.

6   Is the New Natural Law Theory Christian?

Rufus Black

Natural law theory has had a venerable place in the Protestant tradition of ethics. In the twentieth century, however, for reasons both good and bad, Protestant theology and natural law theory have, on the whole, not travelled well together. A central reason for this difficult relationship has been the influence of Karl Barth's *epistemological challenge* to natural law theories. For Barth, any concept of natural law was insecurely based on a fallen natural knowledge of creation rather than the Word of God, which provides the only hermeneutical key to a secure knowledge of creation. More significantly, Barth considered natural law theories to be too thin theologically. A natural law ethic could, at best, articulate only *one* dimension of the vertical encounter of God, Creator *and* Reconciler and Redeemer, with the acting person in the horizontal field of salvation history.[1] As Barth's influence has moderated over the century, there has been a gradual softening in attitude towards natural law theory —an attitude that was always more open among those beyond the Barthian orbit.[2] This softening in attitude has been aided by sympathisers questioning the adequacy of Barth's doctrine of creation;[3] by the suggestion that Barth gave a larger role to the orderedness of creation in giving shape to ethics than has been recognised;[4] by the renewed interest in the place of natural law in the thought of the founding figures of the Reformation;[5] and by challenges to the monochromatic reading of the ethical significance of the Old Testament through the categories of covenant and command.[6] The leading Lutheran theologian, Carl Braaten, has even gone so far as to argue that, "[a]n ecumenical dialogue on the place of natural law in Christian social ethics is particularly necessary and timely".[7]

Despite this softening in attitude, several central objections —of a Barthian lineage— about natural law theory remain amongst leading contemporary Protestant ethicists. Given that these have largely arisen from

148

reflection upon the very forms of 'scholastic' natural law theory which Grisez has found to be inadequate, it is worth asking whether they apply to Grisez's reformulated natural law theory. In considering this question it will be helpful to focus upon Stanley Hauerwas' formulation of the objections, both because he has made them directly and because his views are very influential in the field of Protestant theological ethics —and beyond. A further reason for considering Hauerwas' work is that the basis of his assessment of Grisez's theory is very inadequate. This inadequacy is perhaps clearest in his unfavourable comment upon recent Catholic natural law theories in which he suggests that Russell Hittinger's book *A Critique of the New Natural Law Theory*[8] —a book centrally concerned with Grisez's and Finnis' natural law theory— provides "an excellent critique".[9] This book, which thanks Hauerwas for reading the manuscript,[10] is anything but an 'an excellent critique'. Both Grisez and Robert George have pointed out that Hittinger's criticisms are, as George says, "based on fundamental misunderstandings of important claims and arguments Grisez and Finnis make".[11]

The Distinctive Epistemology of a Christian Ethic

Hauerwas makes two broad types of objection to natural law theories. The first is essentially epistemological and will be the focus of concern in this chapter. The second comprises a set of objections about the nature of moral deliberation; namely, that all "standard accounts of moral rationality", including natural law theories:

(i) do not give an adequate role to the particularity of the moral agent in shaping the nature of her obligations;[12]

(ii) wrongly oppose reason and emotion as necessarily competing forces, whereas their integral operation is a central feature of virtues;[13] and

(iii) pay insufficient attention to questions of character formation.[14]

In short, Hauerwas believes that natural law theories are not a form of virtue ethics. I have argued elsewhere that the Grisez School's theory is a form of virtue ethics that meets all of his objections.[15]

More challenging are Hauerwas' epistemological concerns. Central to these is his argument is that we articulate all forms of ethics both within, and out of, the world-view of a particular narrative tradition.[16] In other words, the narrative tradition in which an ethic arises necessarily has an epistemological priority. Hence, for Hauerwas, there is no such thing as ethics simply, that is, some system whose truthfulness we could maintain abstracted from any particular tradition of rationality. Rather, every ethic must possess a qualifier, whether "Jewish, Christian, Hindu . . . humanist [etc.]".[17] On this basis, Hauerwas assesses the adequacy of an ethic by examining the extent to which it is shaped by the tradition to which it belongs. It is at this very point, Hauerwas maintains, that Catholic natural law theories are inadequate: "Theological claims set the backdrop that made their work intelligible —e.g., God is the creator of a rational universe and moral law can be thus known without the aid of revelation. Beyond that, little theological reflection was required for explicating the nature of the Christian moral life".[18] Put simply, for an ethic to be a suitable bearer of the qualifier 'Christian', it must arise from and be thoroughly shaped by the world-view of the Christian narrative tradition. My interest here is not in assessing the adequacy of this position —for that would require an assessment of the work of Alasdair MacIntyre, James McClendon and others upon which Hauerwas' analysis relies or builds; rather it is in considering whether the qualifier 'Christian' could, on Hauerwas' terms, be applied to Grisez's natural law theory.

In *Christian Moral Realism*[19] I seek to answer this central epistemological objection to natural law theory, and its elaboration in a series of further related criticisms, in the course of a substantial reworking of the Grisez School's analysis that is designed to reduce their heavy reliance upon self-evidence as the foundation for principles of practical reasonableness and modes of Christian response. Here, I set out to demonstrate that it is also possible to meet Hauerwas' challenge on the basis of their theory as it is currently formulated.

Introducing Grisez's Moral Theology

Given Hauerwas' objections to the broadly Thomistic tradition of natural law theory as a form of *Christian* ethics, the question arises of whether a *rapprochement* with Grisez's natural law theory is possible. At first sight, the prospects are not promising. The starting-point of many of Grisez's and Finnis' works is simply that which is naturally knowable. Here they appear to have signed a Faustian pact with the Enlightenment in an attempt to render natural law intelligible to modern minds by relegating any substantive mention of God to a closing section or chapter[20] or even omitting it altogether.[21] What they have effectively produced in these accounts of their theory is an epistemologically secular natural law theory by which it is possible to know that there is a moral order, while leaving open the question as to the nature of this orderedness. This is not to disparage the enterprise itself —at the very least, it suggests that even fallen humanity is capable of substantial moral knowledge; it is simply to conclude with Hauerwas that it is not a *Christian* ethic.

However —and it is a decisive 'however'— what we really need to consider are the implications of Grisez's seminal work of moral *theology* —*The Way of the Lord Jesus*. In the widely overlooked second two-thirds of the first volume, *Christian Moral Principles*, Grisez discusses the relationship between the distinctive elements of a Christian world-view and moral principles. Indeed, in the opening pages of *Christian Moral Principles*, Grisez explicitly delineates his whole project as being one of systematic moral theology —one which begins by reflecting upon the truths of faith in order "to make clear how faith should shape the Christian life".[22] Such theology, he maintains, arises from the revelation in Scripture and "other authoritative expressions of the Church's faith".[23] The rest of the work is essentially faithful to this approach. Methodologically, therefore, Grisez's whole project takes an unambiguously Christian epistemology as its starting-point.

In unfolding the moral principles related to the Christian affirmations of faith, Grisez's first step is very much in a Thomist mould. He begins by arguing that God has made human creatures capable of natural knowledge about those fundamental moral truths (natural law) that would enable them to participate in his plan for the whole of creation (the eternal law).[24] He also argues that this knowledge is revealed to, and taught by, the Church in order to assist in correcting any errors arising from fallen humanity's flawed natural perceptions of such knowledge.[25] If Grisez's account of moral theology were to stop here — as have many such accounts in the Thomist tradition that Hauerwas criticises— his ethics could be charged with having a very incomplete Christian epistemology, since it would have failed to refer to those very elements of reality that render it specifically Christian. But this is not where Grisez ends. For, from the doctrine of Creation he turns to the story of the Fall and the entry of original sin into the world; and he then unfolds his account of the relationship between God and sinful humankind, culminating in God's redemptive work by covenant, incarnation and Christian participation in the process of redemption. It is not our task, however, to provide an excursus on Grisez's essentially orthodox Catholic theology. Rather, it is to try to understand the way in which Grisez's account of ethics relates to this theological scheme.

Christian Modes of Response: No New Principles

Grisez's theological scheme begins to work itself out as moral theory when he observes that Jesus transforms both the nature and understanding of human fulfilment. By way of his atoning sacrifice,[26] Jesus opens up the possibility of human participation in the divine life[27] through the act of faith.[28] Thus human fulfilment was revealed to consist in human participation in the divine life as mediated by Jesus and the Church. According to Grisez, this participation means contributing to the growth of the Kingdom of God which Jesus inaugurated.[29] He also describes this process as coming to fulfilment in Jesus.[30] In other words, human fulfilment becomes known by the light of revelation as the fulfilment that comes from participating in, and contributing to, the growth of the Kingdom of God.

The question that then arises for Grisez is whether contributing to "the fulfillment of all things in Jesus" brings with it new moral principles and norms. His answer begins with the following general response: "The teachings of faith neither conflict with any of the principles of morality nor add any new principles to them. Yet faith does generate specific norms proper to the Christian life".[31] Grisez pursues this answer in a chapter devoted to the principles or "modes of Christian response" which he considers should guide the Christian life.[32] Each of these modes corresponds to one of the Beatitudes in St Matthew's Gospel because, Grisez argues, "[t]he Beatitudes propose norms of Christian life ... they are Christian moral principles".[33] Grisez does not, however, want to describe these principles as 'new'. Rather, he describes them as "the *transformation*"[34] of the apparently parallel secular moral principles, which he describes as the "modes of responsibility".[35]

In explaining the genesis of the modes of Christian response, Grisez first states a particular Beatitude before very briefly outlining what that Beatitude reveals. He then immediately states the mode of Christian response that he considers, in some sense, to arise from, or correspond to, this revelation. In doing so, he almost always makes the connection between the revelation and the mode of Christian response by beginning the sentence concerning the mode, 'Thus'. His treatment of the first Beatitude should help to make this method clear. To begin, Grisez simply states the first Beatitude: "Blessed are the poor in Spirit for theirs is the kingdom of heaven" (Mt 5:3).[36] His exposition follows: "People whose primary love is charity are disposed to divine goodness before all else. *Perceiving God's goodness as real quite apart from their own effort and action, they understand that their undertakings and achievements are only a share, given freely and generously by God, in his fullness*".[37] "Thus", he continues, "the basic Christian mode of response is to *expect and accept all good, including the good fruits of one's own work, as God's gift*".[38] At this point, the nature of the logical connection between the initial statement about reality and the subsequent mode of response —which is simply described by the adverb 'thus'— is far from obvious. Nor is it clear how this mode is a 'fulfilment' or 'transformation' of the first mode of responsibility.

In seeking to understand the nature of this connection, it is illuminating to consider Grisez's more fully articulated account of how the modes of responsibility arise. He begins by arguing that the fundamental demand of good practical reasoning is that a person should not make choices which are incompatible with a will towards integral human fulfilment.[39] He then observes that our feelings and emotions (which propose definite goals for action) and our practical reason (which identifies the intelligible goods to be pursued in any particular goal) shape our choices.[40] For Grisez, therefore, the general task of practical reason is to ensure that the emotions and feelings do not distort the process of pursuing the human fulfilment realised in the pursuit of these intelligible goods.[41] Preventing such distortions is the function of the modes of responsibility. Hence, these modes appear in his analysis as those self-evident principles for the pursuit of human fulfilment that we recognise in the light of knowledge about human nature, namely, that humans are beings in which reason and emotion both shape the making of choices.

The difficulty with this 'Christian' section of Grisez's analysis is that the modes of Christian response do not appear to arise in response to knowledge about human nature. They arise instead from knowledge about God as Creator and Redeemer. At this point, it is helpful to turn to Finnis' work, because he provides both a broader account and a more explicitly articulated analysis of the origin of what amounts to reasonableness in the pursuit of integral human fulfilment.

Rather than speaking of modes of responsibility, Finnis prefers the language of "the basic requirements of practical reasonableness".[42] He describes these requirements as the "self-evident principles"[43] which are knowable by a person "who has experience (both of human wants and passions and of the conditions of human life) and intelligence and a desire for reasonableness stronger than the desires that might overwhelm it".[44] In other words, the requirements of practical reasonableness arise —in the sense of being self-evident, rather than logically deduced— from knowledge about both human nature and the conditions of human life.

In his explanation of the basic requirements of practical reasonableness, Finnis provides a brief account of the conditions of human life to which particular requirements "respond".[45] For instance, the requirement that "one must have a certain detachment from all the specific and limited projects which one undertakes" responds to the "changing circumstances" of human life and to the fact that, without such detachment, "if one's project failed ... one would consider one's life drained of meaning".[46] This, Finnis maintains, would be an unreasonable course of action.[47] While some of the requirements respond to the conditions of human life, others come as a response to human nature —although Finnis' account of human nature is, at this point, a broader one than Grisez's, encompassing more than just the reasoning and feeling dimensions of a person.[48] Finnis' claim, for example, that one should have no arbitrary preferences amongst persons responds to the fact that the commonality of human nature in total means that there is no reason arising from the nature of a person to justify preferring one person to another.[49] There may, of course, be relational reasons (such as familial commitments) for such preference. The point here is not to defend all the relationships which Finnis draws out, but rather to highlight the integral relationship between an understanding of human nature and the human condition and the basic requirements of practical reasonableness. Given that the requirements of practical reasonableness arise, in part, from a person's understanding of the 'conditions of human life', radically different understandings of these conditions could produce different conceptions of the self-evident requirements of practical reasonableness.

New Visions of Reality and New Moral Principles

Illuminated by Finnis' account, we can now describe Grisez's modes of Christian response as the self-evident basic requirements of practical reasonableness that arise when a person understands the conditions of human life from the perspective of Christian revelation. Such an interpretation finds support in Grisez's own discussion of the modes of Christian response. Here he outlines the nature of reality as it appears to fallen humanity. He then observes that it is when the light of revelation alters our understanding of reality that the Christian modes of responsibility arise. Consider, for example, his treatment of the seventh Beatitude, "Blessed are the peacemakers for they shall be called sons of God" (Matthew 5:9).[50] This, he maintains, reveals that "[t]o love goods mutilated by evil with divine love is to love them as good, not as evil, and so to separate them from their evil and restore them to wholeness".[51] For Grisez this revelation gives rise to the seventh mode of Christian response: "respond to evil with good, not with resistance, much less with destructive action".[52] In explaining how this Christian moral principle relates to the corresponding seventh mode of responsibility —"One should not be moved by hostility to freely accept or choose the destruction, damaging, or impeding of an intelligible human good"[53]— he observes that "[i]n this fallen world ... it really is impossible in many cases to pursue human good effectively without making compromises: violate some goods in order to save others and minimize evil; use bad means to achieve good ends which otherwise will not be achieved".[54] In this fallen world, anything more demanding than the seventh mode of responsibility is unlikely to seem either reasonable or purposeful —unless one's vision is radically transformed by Christian faith, hope, and charity: "the modes of responsibility [are] transformed by faith (which tells us how to live a good life in a fallen world), by hope (which supplies the confidence in God required to make the effort), and by charity (which gives one the power to really live in this way)".[55]

This transformation of the 'conditions of human life' is both epistemological and substantive. It is epistemological in that belief in redemptive nature and the power of divine love, as well as trust in an eschatology that offers the assurance that even apparently futile acts of love are ultimately purposeful, makes loving good that has been mutilated by evil seem reasonable. It is substantive because a response of faith to what was achieved by the Cross actually changes the conditions of human life. The changes that are of particular importance here are eschatological. Death no longer marks the ultimate boundary of human life, and the purposefulness of human action and history are secured by their incorporation into the Kingdom of God.

If we understand Grisez's account as yielding a distinct set of Christian moral principles that arise because "[f]aith sheds a *new* and true light on *the human condition*",[56] what are we to make of his insistence that the Christian faith adds no new moral principles to those which are already naturally knowable?[57] This claim seems difficult to maintain, especially given the extent to which he understands some of the modes of responsibility to be transformed. The seventh mode of Christian response —that a Christian should "respond to evil with good, not with resistance, much less with destructive action"[58]— again provides a good illustration. The seventh mode of responsibility, which Grisez claims is transformed into this mode of Christian response, arises from the possible distortion of practical reasonableness which feelings of hostility might generate, and holds that a person should not choose to harm any human good.[59] However, the mode of Christian response arises not from human nature but from our knowledge of the divine: instead of offering a prohibition not to harm the good, it asserts a positive duty to meet evil with good. Given that this principle arises from (i) knowledge about a different reality and (ii) entirely different epistemological presuppositions, to produce (iii) a practical demand with a distinctively different nature, then the most accurate description of it is as a different or new principle. Correspondingly, it also appears that all the modes of Christian response *insofar as they arise from a Christian understanding of reality* will likewise be 'new' moral principles.

In terms of practical demands, these Christian modes of response will, of course, overlap with those modes of responsibility that arise from a purely secular world-view, because they will both arise in part from common perceptions about certain features of reality. However, Grisez's analysis also suggests that for a Christian at least some of the modes of responsibility will also be shaped by a distinctively Christian perception of reality. Consider, for example, the fifth mode: "One should not, in response to different feelings towards different persons, willingly proceed with a preference for anyone unless the preference is required by intelligible goods themselves".[60] In explicating this mode, Grisez observes that "[d]ivine revelation deepens the foundation for this mode of responsibility even before Jesus",[61] because Scripture reveals that "we are all children of the same Father. Thus, there is a basic equality —in dignity— among all persons".[62] Grisez's language of 'deepening' hinders our recognition of the scriptural understanding of reality as different to that from which the 'secular' mode might arise. Without a scriptural vision of reality, the mode of response arises from knowledge about a common human nature; with a scriptural vision, it arises from knowledge of a shared human relationship — namely, that all people are children of God. This implies that the fifth Christian mode of response is distinct from its secular counterpart because it arises from a quite different world-view. It is, in short, a *new* Christian moral principle which has an independent foundation for its truthfulness, separate from that of its secular 'parallel'. Since Grisez describes how revelation 'deepens' all the modes of responsibility,[63] all of them are susceptible of being transformed by a Christian vision of reality.

Avoiding the Creeping De-Christianisation of Ethics

The interpretation of Grisez's theory offered here provides a more adequate account of the origins and nature of the modes of Christian response —and hence, more generally, of his Christian moral principles— than one based on attempting to sustain his own claim that Christian faith produces no new moral principles. This interpretation should also help to avoid the creeping de-Christianisation of ethics that tends to occur when we do not recognise the epistemological distinctiveness of Christian ethics. It is a tendency that emerges in Grisez's own work. This happens because, when the modes of responsibility and the Christian modes of response are understood in broadly coextensive terms, the 'secular' modes end up being used instead of the Christian principle to analyse moral problems. As a result, the richer understanding invoked by the Christian modes, with their origin in a fuller vision of reality, becomes peripheral rather than central and integral to the application of moral theology to concrete problems.

This removal of Christian insights to the periphery of moral analysis takes a number of forms in Grisez's applied ethics. In one form, the distinctive Christian understanding comes as a preamble with little bearing on the principles and norms used in analysing the problem. A surprising instance of this can be found in Grisez's treatment of abortion in *Living a Christian Life*. After opening with John Paul II's statement that "[h]uman life is precious because it is a gift of God"[64] —a statement which accords with the first mode of Christian response, "accept all goods [including life] ... as God's gift"[65]— Grisez proceeds to frame the discussion entirely within his secular natural law theory. A second form of the problem occurs when the Christian insight merely supervenes onto an already ongoing discussion, when it should actually have been its starting-point. This can be seen, for example, in Grisez's treatment of self-defence, where the Christian insights are almost an afterthought.[66] Finally, specific Christian principles can simply be omitted altogether in favour of 'secular' natural law principles as occurs in Grisez's just war analysis.[67]

Having considered the reasons for dropping Grisez's claim that Christian faith introduces no new moral principles, it is worth briefly examining the strength of his reasons for maintaining it. A rhetorical question which he poses reveals his central reason: "If human nature is not changed, how can there be a distinctive Christian morality?"[68] In other words, Grisez fears that a claim for new principles necessarily involves a claim that different people have different natures. This latter claim is one that he is very keen to avoid because, "[w]hen it is admitted that human nature which is given differs ... the conclusion inevitably follows that ... morality based on it ... changes".[69]

Once Finnis' point —that the basic requirements of practical reasonableness *do not simply arise from human nature but also from the human condition*— is recognised, it is possible to maintain that the new and distinct principles of Christian morality are derived not from a changed human nature but from a changed understanding of the human condition.[70] This application of Finnis' analysis enables Grisez's claim that human nature does not change to be sustained. Grisez, then, has nothing to lose in accepting the full implications of the epistemological priority of theology in Christian ethics and abandoning the claim that faith brings no new moral principles.

Meeting the Demands for an Epistemologically Distinctive Christian Ethic

With this reinterpretation of Grisez's theory before us, we can now return to Hauerwas' concerns and to his first challenge: does Grisez's moral theory arise from a Christian theological understanding of reality? It is true that when it is preceded by a 'secular' description of reality, Grisez's natural law theory certainly does not produce a form of *Christian* ethics. However, when it is employed *in the context of his theological vision of reality*, a distinctly Christian ethic does result. Thus, Grisez's natural law theory emerges as a conceptual framework for ethical analysis, the actual character and content of which will be determined by the understanding of reality —that is, the world-view— of the person who is employing it. In other words, a person's world-view, which we could also describe in terms of the narrative tradition to which she belongs, will have an epistemological priority in moral deliberation. The result is that, *even if* ethics begins simply with practical reason and not with theoretical knowledge (as it does in Grisez's natural law framework in order to avoid the objection that you cannot derive an 'ought' from an 'is'), the nature of that practical reason will still be dependent upon a person's theoretical conception of human nature and the conditions of human life. One way of indicating this epistemological priority is to agree with Hauerwas both that there is no such thing as 'ethics' simply, and that this priority needs to be acknowledged with an epithet denominating the particular world-view from which a given ethic arises.

What may cause confusion is that Grisez and Finnis identify a fundamental structure of practical reasoning that is common to *all* attempts to make practical decisions in accordance with good reason, whatever a person's world-view. Central to this common structure is the claim that good practical reasoning, by its very nature, will be concerned to act in pursuit of what is genuinely fulfilling in human life (basic human goods) by acting in accordance with principles (basic principles of practical reasoning) that coherently direct a person towards that fulfilment, given human nature and the conditions of human life. Crucially, however, the preceding discussion shows that this common structure *per se* can never be the epistemological starting-point for any moral deliberation that aims to produce normative conclusions, because the actual elements of this common structure for moral decision-making (i.e., what the nature of the good is understood to be and what principles should guide its pursuit) are all determined by a person's theoretical understanding of reality. When that account of reality is a Christian one —that is, one founded upon the Gospel's depiction of reality— then ethics will necessarily be Christian.

The common structure of practical reason that Grisez and Finnis identify provides the epistemological superstructure for a bridge between Christian and other forms of ethics. The existence of this common structure means that where Christians and others have a shared understanding of the nature of human life, they are also likely to possess compatible ethical insights. For example, a common recognition of the finitude of life is likely to give rise to similar practical principles concerning the need to make life-plans and stand by commitments. While Hauerwas might doubt the possibility of such shared ethical insight, or suspect it of undermining the distinctiveness of Christian ethics, other leading Protestant ethicists defend the significance of such common understandings. Oliver O'Donovan, for example, considers it important to sustain this possibility that humans have "a certain 'natural knowledge' which is also part of man's created endowment".[71] Without such a possibility, O'Donovan observes, moral disagreements may simply become "ultimate clashes of commitment which are incapable of resolution"[72] so that "all Christian moral duties become analogous to such ecclesiastical house-rules as respect for the clergy ... [e]ven prohibitions of adultery and murder".[73] The possibility of natural knowledge sustains the claim that all people face objective moral realities.[74] In a mark of one of the common genres of disagreement between Protestant and Catholic moral theologians, O'Donovan is much more sceptical than Grisez about the extent to which fallen humanity can accurately perceive this natural order.[75] However, for neither theologian does the essential distinctiveness of Christian ethics lie in the clarification of confusions about 'natural' morality.

In terms of the relationship between secular and Christian accounts of ethics, the Grisez School holds that what is naturally knowable about human life is sufficient to give rise to principles that, first, direct people towards the fullness of their humanity; and, second, prevent people from disfiguring their humanity and that of others. These principles possess their own integrity. Grisez's Christian modes of response do not contradict such principles but set them in the 'vertical' context of eschatology.[76] From such an eschatological perspective, the fullness of humanity is now understood to consist in a transformation in which "[g]oods shared in imperfectly in this life will be shared in more perfectly in everlasting life"[77] and the "[e]vil, which now disrupts Christian life, will be eliminated from creation or wholly overcome".[78] Human fulfilment is now fulfilment in the Kingdom of God, or, as Grisez speaks more frequently of it, as "fulfillment of all things in Jesus".[79] The Christian modes of response spell out what it is to participate in the redemptive work of the Kingdom of God: they call Christians to treat all goods as a gift of God; to discern their particular role, or vocation, in a community called to anticipate the eschatological fulfilment of humanity; and to engage in the confrontation with evil and the redemption of the good that has been disfigured.[80]

The distinctiveness of this vision of the Christian moral life enables us to conclude, with some confidence, that the Grisez School's theory is able to meet the central challenge posed to natural law by Protestant moral theology.[81] With this conclusion, new vistas open up for what may be an important ecumenical conversation between Roman Catholic and Protestant moral theologians about the place of natural law in Christian ethics.[82]

NOTES

1   See especially, Karl Barth, "The Doctrine of Creation", vol. III/4 of *Church Dogmatics* (Edinburgh: T & T Clark, 1961), pp.3-46.

2   See, for example, D. Little, "Calvin and the Prospects for a Christian Theory of Natural Law", in *Norm and Context in Christian Ethics*, ed. Gene Outka and Paul Ramsey (New York: Charles Scribner's Sons, 1968), pp.175-197; I.T. Ramsey, "Towards a Rehabilitation of Natural Law", in *Christian Ethics and Contemporary Philosophy*, ed. I.T. Ramsey (New York: Macmillan, 1966), pp.382-96; John Macquarrie, *Three Issues in Ethics* (London: SCM, 1970); and Keith Ward, *The Divine Image* (London: SPCK, 1976).

3   Oliver O'Donovan, *Resurrection and Moral Order*, 2nd ed. (Leicester: Inter-Varsity Press, 1994), pp.86-87.

4   Nigel Biggar, *The Hastening that Waits* (Oxford: Clarendon Press, 1993), pp.49-62, 164-65.

5   See, for example, J. McNeill, "Natural Law and the Teaching of the Reformers", *Journal of Religion*, 26 (1946), pp.168-82; K. Collins, "John Wesley's Platonic Conception of the Moral Law", *Wesleyan Theological Journal*, 21, pp.116-28; E.A. Dowey, "Law in Luther and Calvin", *Theology Today*, 41 (1984), pp.146-47; P. Helm, "Calvin and Natural Law", *The Scottish Bulletin of Evangelical Theology*, 2 (1984), pp.5-22.

6   See, for example, John Barton, "Natural Law and Poetic Justice in the Old Testament", *Journal of Theological Studies*, 30 (1979), pp.1-14.

7   Carl Braaten, "Protestants and Natural Law", *First Things*, 19 (1992), p.23.

8   Russell Hittinger, *A Critique of the New Natural Law Theory* (Notre Dame: University of Notre Dame Press, 1987).

9   Stanley Hauerwas, "The Importance of Being Catholic: Unsolicited Advice from a Protestant Bystander", *Listening*, 25 (1990), p.32.

10   Hittinger, *Critique*, p.9.

11   Robert George, "Recent Criticism of Natural Law Theory", *The University of Chicago Law Review*, 55 (1988), p.1429; Germain Grisez, "A Critique of Russell Hittinger's Book, *A Critique of the New Natural Law Theory*," *New Scholasticism*, 62 (1988), pp.438-65.

12   See, for example, Stanley Hauerwas and David Burrell, "From Story to Story: an Alternative Pattern for Rationality in Ethics" in Stanley Hauerwas, Richard Bondi

and David Burrell, *Truthfulness and Tragedy* (Notre Dame: University of Notre Dame Press, 1977), p.17.

13   See for example, Stanley Hauerwas, *A Community of Character: Toward a Constructive Christian Social Ethic* (Notre Dame: University of Notre Dame Press, 1981), pp.111-28, especially, pp.124-25.

14   See for example, ibid., p.129-35.

15   Rufus Black, "Towards an Ecumenical Ethic: Reconciling the Work of Stanley Hauerwas, Germain Grisez, and Oliver O'Donovan", D.Phil. Thesis, University of Oxford, 1996. See also the last section of Chapter 1 in this book.

16   For the most sustained development of this argument see Stanley Hauerwas, *The Peaceable Kingdom* (Notre Dame: University of Notre Dame Press, 1983).

17   Ibid., p.1.

18   Ibid., p.51.

19   Rufus Black, *Christian Moral Realism* (Oxford University Press, forthcoming).

20   This is particularly evident in G. Grisez, J.M. Boyle, and J. Finnis, "Practical Principles, Moral Truth and Ultimate Ends", *American Journal of Jurisprudence*, 32 (1987), pp.99-151; Germain Grisez and Russell Shaw, *Beyond the New Morality*, 3rd ed. (Notre Dame: University of Notre Dame Press, 1988); Finnis, *NLNR*; and Grisez, *NDMR*.

21   Grisez, *LCL*; and Finnis, *FE*.

22   Grisez, *CMP*, p.6.

23   Ibid., p.4.

24   Ibid., pp.173-75.

25   Ibid., p.176.

26   Ibid., pp.539-41.

27   Ibid., p.395.

28   "Following Scripture, the Catholic Church also teaches definitively that faith is the foundation of all justification and the beginning of our salvation ... which must shape a life of good works" (ibid., p.394).

29   Ibid., pp.468, 470.

30   Ibid., p.471.

31   Ibid., p.607.

32   Ibid., pp.627-59.

33   Ibid., p.628.

34   Ibid., p.627; my emphasis.

35   Ibid., p.205.

36   Ibid., p.634.

37   Ibid., Grisez's emphasis.

38   Ibid., Grisez's emphasis.

39   Ibid., pp.178-89. See Chapter 1 for an explanation of this portion of Grisez's theory.

40   Ibid., pp.189-91.

41   Ibid., p.189.

42   *NLNR*, p.100.

43   Ibid., p.101.

44   Ibid.

45   *FE*, p.75.

46   *NLNR*, p.110.

47   Ibid.
48   For a further discussion of this aspect of Finnis' analysis see Chapter 1.
49   *NLNR*, pp.106-9.
50   *CMP*, p.649-50.
51   Ibid., p.649.
52   Ibid.
53   Ibid., p.215; Grisez's emphasis has been removed.
54   Germain Grisez and Russell Shaw, *Fulfillment in Christ* (Notre Dame: University of Notre Dame Press, 1991), p.313. This work summarises *Christian Moral Principles* and sometimes, especially on this topic of the nature of *Christian* moral principles, states the essentials of Grisez's argument more clearly than the larger volume.
55   Grisez, *Fulfillment*, pp.304-5.
56   Ibid., pp.313-14; my emphasis.
57   *CMP*, p.607.
58   Ibid., p.649.
59   Ibid., pp.215-16.
60   Ibid., p.211.
61   Ibid., p.212.
62   Grisez, *Fulfillment*, p.91.
63   *CMP*, pp.205-24.
64   John Paul II, Homily at Mass for Families (Cebu City, Philippines, 1976) quoted by Grisez in *LCL*, p.498.
65   *CMP*, p.634.
66   Ibid., pp.483-84.
67   Ibid., pp.897-911; see also, Germain Grisez, "Toward a Consistent Natural-Law Ethic of Killing", *American Journal of Jurisprudence*, 15 (1970), pp.64-96.
68   Grisez, *Fulfillment*, p.298.
69   *CMP*, p.620.
70   The suggestion that general moral principles arise not only from a person's understanding of human nature (an understanding that the Grisez School would agree does not change with faith) *but also* from her understanding of the conditions of human life (which, we will argue, does change as a result of faith), calls into question the position adopted by Richard McCormick and others, that the general demands of Christian ethics cannot be distinctive because ethics arises only from our essentially unchanging knowledge of human nature (Richard McCormick, "Does Religious Faith Add to Ethical Perception", in Charles Curran and Richard McCormick, *Readings in Moral Theology No. 2: The Distinctiveness of Christian Ethics* [New York: Paulist Press, 1980], pp.164-69).
71   O'Donovan, *Resurrection*, p.20.
72   Ibid., p.16.
73   Ibid.
74   Ibid., p.17.
75   Ibid., p.19.
76   Grisez's analysis suggests that a distinctive account of Christian ethics need not involve maintaining a radical discontinuity between creation and redemption, as some have thought it must (e.g., Charles Curran, *Catholic Theology in Dialogue* [Notre Dame: Fides Publishers, 1972], pp.18-19).

77   *CMP*, p.817.

78   Ibid.

79   Ibid., p.627.

80   Ibid., pp.634-53.

81   The position developed in this chapter on the question of the distinctiveness of a Christian ethic is, in its broad structure, similar to that developed by James Gustafson (James Gustafson, *Can Ethics be Christian?* [Chicago: University of Chicago Press, 1975], especially pp.163-68), with the vital distinction that his reductive account of distinctly Christian beliefs removes any substantive epistemological or practical significance from his account of the distinctiveness of a Christian ethic.

82   Some of the possibilities for such a *rapprochement* are developed in my doctoral thesis, "Towards an Ecumenical Ethic".

7 Karl Barth and Germain Grisez on the Human Good: An Ecumenical *Rapprochement*

Nigel Biggar

At first glance, the omens for fruitful ethical dialogue between Karl Barth and Germain Grisez do not look promising. After all, Barth is usually taken to be extremely Protestant in his rejection of the concept of natural law, his affirmation of Scripture as the primary source of ethics, his use of a Christological canon within the Canon, and the central place he gives to hearing a command of God (the Holy Spirit); whereas Grisez stands firmly in the tradition of natural law, which is commonly accused by Protestant critics of exalting the role of natural reason to the point of marginalising the ethical contributions of Scripture, Christology, and the Spirit.[1] It might seem, therefore, that an exchange between Barth and Grisez could only be described euphemistically as a dialogue, since it would consist of little but the mutual contradiction of fundamental premises. Faced with such an unedifying prospect, one could easily be forgiven for doubting its value.

Here, however, appearances deceive. For, on the one hand, a concept of natural law (covertly) plays a fundamental role in Barth's more mature ethical thinking, where it assumes the guise of 'created structures' of relationship between human beings and God, and between humans and their fellows. And, on the other hand, in the post-Vatican II thought of Grisez, the natural law ethic is significantly qualified by the life and teaching of Jesus, as conveyed by Scripture, and by a concept of personal vocation (issued by God the Holy Spirit). In fact, then, there are sufficient points of convergence to make ethical dialogue between Barth and Grisez possible, as well as sufficient points of difference to make it interesting and fruitful.

My aim in this essay is to compare the two ethics, to distinguish significant from superficial points of difference, and to make a critical evaluation of the former. By so doing I hope to show that there are things that Barth and Grisez should learn from one another, and thereby to effect a measure of *rapprochement* between the two traditions that they represent.

I have chosen to concentrate my comparative analysis on their respective conceptions of the human good and its relation to morality —that is, on their versions of the natural law[2]— and I have done so for several reasons: because this is an ethically decisive matter, because Protestant and Roman Catholic ethicists are usually understood to diverge sharply over it, because in fact Barth is much closer here to Grisez than their stereotypes would predict, and because it therefore provides a fruitful point at which to assess their significant differences.

We begin with Barth.

Barth and Natural Law [3]

There are several places where Barth explicitly repudiated the concept of natural law. In his wartime *Letter to Great Britain from Switzerland* (1941), for example, he argued that natural law could not provide an adequate basis for opposition to Nazism, because it could easily be interpreted in such a way as to support it: "All arguments based on Natural Law are Janus-headed. They lead to Munich".[4] Five years later, he wrote along the same lines in "The Christian Community and the Civil Community" (1946) that natural law cannot provide "any certain knowledge of the trustworthy standards of political decisions", or any firm grounds for them.[5] What lay immediately behind Barth's view here was his experience of German politics in the 1920s, when the Protestant equivalent of the concept of natural law —that of 'created orders' or 'orders of creation'— was used by the 'German Christians', so-called, to support the ideology of National Socialism. That this political experience did indeed shape his thinking Barth himself virtually admitted when, in *Church Dogmatics* III/4, he attributed N.H. Søe's repudiation of the notion of created orders to his fear of "any traces of the German theology of orders current in the twenties", and judged that this fear was "not without good cause".[6]

Barth's objection to natural law, however, was not entirely founded on this particular historical experience. It also rested on deeper theological foundations. One of these was the typically Protestant conviction that the power of human reason to apprehend God's natural law or created order is radically compromised —and not merely weakened— by sin. The fact that this law or order has been created by God does not mean that humans are naturally able to discern it: "How can we know to what extent we really have to do with God's creation, and therefore with a valid standard for understanding the ethical event, in what we claim to recognise here as reality?"[7]

A less typically Protestant, but very typically Barthian, ground for rejecting natural law was Christological. Here the argument is that, since God the Creator is none other than the God who is gracious to humankind in Jesus Christ, it is only when we know about the grace of God in Christ that we can know for certain what creation is, who the Creator is, and what it means to be the creature of this Creator.[8] In other words, even apart from sin, we would need God's self-revelation in Christ, and not just natural reason, to grasp the natural law or the created orders.

A further ground for Barth's objection was simply theological; namely, that concepts of created orders are *a*theological, entirely neglecting the 'vertical' dimension of reality for the 'horizontal' one. In their haste to establish "the general truth ... of certain laws of life and existence", they completely overlook the most fundamental order of all —the one that obtains in the vertical relationship between God the Creator and His human creatures.[9]

Barth's opposition to natural law and its Protestant equivalents is well-known. Less well-known is his covert endorsement of a certain concept of it. In *Church Dogmatics* III/4 he affirms that human being has a given, created nature that is characterised by a four-fold structure of responsibility: to God the Creator, to fellow humans, for life, and within the limits of a certain time. Each of these forms of responsibility is susceptible of specification in terms of certain obligations. Responsibility to God involves keeping Sunday as a day of worship, bearing express witness to God, and turning to Him in prayer. Responsibility to fellow humans involves: a voluntary interdependence between the two sexes, in which it is nevertheless given to the male to 'lead' and the female to 'follow'; a mutual honouring between parents and children, in which parents should guide and children should obey; and a reciprocity between neighbours, whether near or distant, in which national loyalties are held to be radically provisional. Responsibility for life involves respecting and protecting one's own life and that of one's fellows as a loan made by God to be used through the Christian community in the service of the sanctification of the world. Responsibility within the limits of a certain time involves cooperating in this task by heeding one's own special vocation to seize a few unique opportunities.

Barth's ethic, then, does involve a concept of human nature that generates certain kinds of moral responsibility or obligation. But this created, natural law is set within a larger, complex theological context, which qualifies it in significant respects. The primary responsibility of the human being, with her creaturely nature, is to God her Creator. But this God is not just her Creator, and she is not simply God's creature. She is also a sinner, and God is also the one who has sought in Jesus Christ to overcome her sin and reconcile her to Himself. Therefore the natural *law* —the responsibilities generated by created human nature— should not be understood legalistically; that is, as obligations whose end is simply to command conformity and which must be met on pain of punishment. Rather, these natural responsibilities are properly viewed as liberating, enabling human beings to live freely and gladly *as the creatures they are*, instead of exhausting and damaging both themselves and their fellows in trying (sinfully) to become like gods —or, in other, unBarthian terms: moral obligations or laws are designed to enable human beings to flourish according to their creaturely nature. Further, since God is not simply our Creator but also a gracious Father who has acted in Jesus Christ to reconcile sinners to Himself, our responsibility toward Him involves a basic attitude that moves beyond a creaturely awareness of absolute dependence to a reconciled sinner's commitment to absolute trust. According to Barth, this commitment involves baptism, participation in the Lord's Supper, and prayer for the coming of God's kingdom and therefore the securing of just relations between human beings. Such prayer should lead to corresponding engagement, through the Christian community, in the struggle for human justice. This struggle should take its cue from the example of Jesus and assume the form of a revolt against "the lordless powers" —human potentialities that, in rebellion against the primary creaturely responsibility (the worship of God), have become oppressive idols. Of these, Barth mentions four species: political absolutism, materialism, ideological dogmatism, and what he calls the 'chthonic' powers (such as technology, fashion, sport, pleasure, and transportation).[10]

In the light of God's reconciling work in Jesus Christ, then, living according to the structure of our creaturely nature amounts to this: that, worshipping God as Creator and gracious Reconciler, we should devote our lives to the service of His kingdom and so revolt against the lordless powers, within the moral terms set by the natural structures of relationships between man and woman, parents and children, and all human neighbours, and within the limits set by our time and place. Implicit in this account is an eschatological reference: final victory over the lordless powers has yet to be secured. The advent of God's kingdom has begun, but it is not yet complete. Redemption as a completed state lies in the future. Our situation, then, is one of standing 'between the times' in an ambiguous mixture of light and darkness, encouraged by the manifestation of

God's reconciling grace in the past, but still radically dependent upon the final manifestation of His redemptive grace yet to come. So, as we hasten toward the consummation of God's kingdom, we should not imagine that this is something simply within our power to realise. Our activity may correspond to God's, but it is not identical with it. Thus, our devotion to the service of God's kingdom, within the responsibilities engendered by the structure of our creaturely nature, is subject to a radical eschatological qualification. If we hasten as we should, we do so toward a future that is finally God's gift, not our own achievement. Our hastening, then, should always be one that is also a prayerful waiting upon God's gracious initiative.

Our outline of Barth's theological ethic, and the place within it of a certain concept of natural law, is almost complete. What remains is to introduce and locate the concept of hearing a command of God, which looms very large in Barth's thinking. Here, a command should be distinguished from a law; it is not a universal obligation, binding all members of a community, or at least all members of a certain kind, and rationally deducible from first ethical principles. A command is a unique obligation, binding a particular individual, and communicated by God the Spirit. As I have argued elsewhere,[11] Barth's concept of hearing a command of God is best understood in terms of apprehending a personal vocation. The role it plays in Barth's ethic is as follows. Reflection upon Jesus Christ, upon the Bible in the light of Christ, and upon human experience in the light of both, will enable us to acquire general information about our responsibilities as beings created by God, graciously reconciled to Him, and awaiting His gift of final redemption. But what it will not tell us is precisely what we should do as individuals in our particular situations. This final determination of our responsibilities is made by the call of God to each individual to devote her peculiar set of gifts to the service of His kingdom at a unique point of time and space.

Grisez and Barth on the Priority of the Good

In contrast to classic, Counter-Reformation moral theology, Grisez takes pains to assert the priority of the concept of the human good to that of moral law.[12] What he intends thereby is to make clear that the point, the obligatory force, the authority of moral laws or norms consists in the fact that they maintain or promote the human good. Grisez is therefore unequivocally anti-legalist and eudaimonist: living morally is not about obeying laws blindly and simply because

God wills them, but rather with reason and for the sake of furthering human *eudaimonia* or well-being.

Barth is also eudaimonist, but less unequivocally. He makes it clear enough that the God who commands us, whether in created structures or personal callings, is motivated by love and intends human 'freedom'. After all, for him, God is never other than the One who manifested Himself in Jesus Christ in order to reconcile us to Himself: the Creator is also always the Reconciler.[13] Nevertheless, Barth's decision to conceive of moral life basically in terms of human response to God's commands[14] does tend to give the impression that right action is *simply* a matter of blind human obedience to the will of an infinitely more powerful Deity; and although, when other aspects of his thought are taken into account, this can be seen to be false,[15] there are still particular moments when Barth takes a voluntarist's delight in underscoring how God's commanding confounds human reason absolutely.

Grisez is prepared to say that divine revelation can transcend the moral conclusions of human reason and posit norms that would otherwise not be formulated; but he maintains that our obeying this 'divine positive law' is nevertheless reasonable —that is, that it sustains or promotes the human good.[16] It might be said that Barth presupposes the true reasonableness of obedience to God (grounded in God's irreducible love for us), but he is certainly not inclined to assert it. Rather, what he is inclined to assert is the contradictory relationship between God's wisdom and what passes for moral reason among humans: God's commands, according to Barth, do not merely transcend and supplement natural, rational morality —they confound it.

The difference between Barth and Grisez here lies partly in what they mean by 'reason'. Barth means the actual understanding of human sinners, whose sinfulness takes the modernist form of the aspiration to moral autonomy —or, better, autarky; and at the heart of which lies the refusal to acknowledge any moral authority external to the human self.[17] Grisez, on the other hand, means by 'reason' the accurate grasp of real, irreducible human goods and their implications —and among these goods is that of religion or friendship with God. In other words, Grisez focuses on the genuine article, where Barth concentrates on the distorted version. An examination of the reasons for this divergence in focus will furnish some insight into the nature of the difference between them.

One reason lies straightforwardly in their allegiance to different Christian traditions. Barth is a Protestant, Grisez a Roman Catholic. Typically, Protestants are more sceptical than Roman Catholics of the ability of sinful human beings to grasp religious or moral truth apart from spiritual conversion and enlightenment by the Word of God. But this divergence in traditional allegiance is less explanatory than appears at first. It may be fair to characterise Roman Catholic theology as typically Thomist, but the thought of Thomas Aquinas is susceptible of being read and developed in different Thomist ways. In particular, Aquinas' assertion that human reason is not only limited by nature but 'wounded' by sin, and that it therefore needs correction as well as supplementation by divine revelation,[18] can be given more or less emphasis — and since the Second Vatican Council it has generally received more. Further, if there are different Thomisms, there are certainly different Protestantisms. Luther may sometimes have viewed 'reason' as the tool of sinful self-justification,[19] and Arminian Calvinists may have subscribed to the doctrine of the total depravity of human beings; but Luther (as well as Calvin) recognised at least the politico-ethical wisdom of pagan Romans,[20] Melanchthon identified the moral law basically with the law of nature and assigned its exposition to philosophy,[21] and Kant and his liberal Protestant followers regarded the ethic of Jesus as simply representing the pronouncements of autonomous reason.[22] The mere fact, then, that Barth was Protestant did not fully determine his view of moral reason, any more that Grisez's being Thomist does his. Another explanation for the difference between them is required.

In part, this can be found in the cultural contexts in which each of their ethics is situated. Barth's thinking was profoundly shaped by his experience of the outbreak in Europe of the First World War, which he read as exposing the hollow pretensions of modern, post-Enlightenment culture.[23] Since this culture was characterised above all by its confidence in the power of autonomous human reason, not only to make sense of the world but also to govern it, Barth's reaction was to stress the corruption by sinful interests of what purports to be 'reason' and therefore the absolute degree to which this is at odds with, and is confounded by, the wisdom of God. Thus Barth's rhetoric often makes his ethic appear anti-rational, whereas it is really best understood as anti-rational*ist*.

In contrast, Grisez's cultural context —the United States at the end of the twentieth century— is *post*modern, in the sense that it is characterised, not by excessive confidence in 'objective' reason, but by subjective sentimentality.[24] In response to this context, he propounds an ethic that is unashamedly rational, but not rationalist in the sense of ignoring the data of divine revelation.

In provisional summary, it may be said that for both Grisez and Barth *eudaimonia* or human well-being or the human good furnishes the ultimate justification for acting rightly. Where they differ —partly because of religious tradition, but more so because of cultural context— is over how we *know* what the human good consists of and what actions promote it and are therefore right —by 'reason' or by 'revelation'? We will intensify our scrutiny of this epistemological divergence later; but in the meantime, let us turn to consider the different ways in which the human good is deployed by the two authors.

The Deployment of the Good by Grisez and Barth

In Grisez's ethic, of course, the concept and theory of the good are explicitly basic. The very first chapter of *Christian Moral Principles* asserts the need for contemporary moral theology to make clear that the end of moral life is human fulfilment, in this life as well as in the next.[25] Then, following arguments for the reality of free moral choice and for judgements of conscience that are derived from objectively true principles, Chapters Five to Eleven lay out a complex theory of the goods that fulfil human persons and of the moral norms that derive from them.

In contrast, explicit reference to the human good or goods in the sense of the state of human fulfilment and its aspects is almost entirely lacking in Barth's ethic;[26] and there is no equivalent of Grisez's carefully elaborated theory of them. What this signifies is not that Barth denied that acting rightly is good for humans,[27] but that he resisted any focus upon the human good as the end of right human action. The reasons for this are several. One is his tendency, following Anders Nygren, to regard *eros* —the desire to realise one's natural, specific potential— as simply selfish, and therefore to suppose that the realisation of one's own good cannot be a properly moral intention.[28] A second reason is his conviction that, partly because creaturely life "belongs to God" and partly because sinners can live "only in the power of His mercy",

> it is obviously outside our power to try to discover unequivocally and conclusively what constitutes the real pleasure of our real life, and in what the fulfilment which summons us to gratitude actually consists. We think we should seek them here or there because this thing or that appears as light or alleviation, as warmth, benefit, refreshment, consolation and encouragement, promising us renewal and the attainment of that which hovers before us as the true good of all that we do and refrain from doing. But do we really know this true goal and therefore our true joy? God knows it. God decides it. But this means that our will for joy, our preparedness for it, must be wide open in this direction, in the direction of His unknown and even obscure disposing,...[29]

Then there is his conviction that the human good is realised only as a by-product of right relating to God; and that therefore the focus of our attention should not be on our own self-fulfilment as such, but upon the nature of God and upon appropriate human responses to him.[30]

However, although Barth is shy of explicit reference to the human good and its components, these are nevertheless present in his ethical system. In general, the human good or the state of human flourishing is characterised as 'freedom' —the freedom of humans to act and to be in a manner befitting their status as sinful creatures whom God has reconciled to himself and whose redemption he is completing. The decision to think of the human good primarily in terms of 'freedom' is indicative of the anti-legalism of Barth's conception of Christian life: from the Christian point of view, moral life is not simply about obedience to God or conformity to created structures. It does involve these, but they are not its end. The end of living rightly is a dynamic, vital state where the human being's will is so consonant with God's that she does not need to be constrained by law to act according to it, but does so freely; she herself will spontaneously and naturally what God wills. But this freedom is not merely negative; it is not just the condition of lacking constraints. It is also the vital freedom of self-fulfilment or flourishing or *eudaimonia* —as is well indicated by another word that Barth frequently uses to refer to the human good: 'gladness'.[31]

This general characterisation of the good in terms of freedom or gladness is not simply empty and formal; from the context in which they are used, they clearly imply that human flourishing involves friendship with God (Grisez's 'religion'). But this is not all. Other distinct goods are prominent in Barth's analysis of human 'freedom' in the *Church Dogmatics* III/4. For this involves, not only freedom "before God", but also freedom "in fellowship" with other humans (Grisez's 'friendship') and freedom "for life";[32] and freedom for life itself involves freedom for play and art (Grisez's 'playful activities').[33] Further, elsewhere in the *Church Dogmatics* the unification of the human self or 'inward harmony' (Grisez's 'self-integration') appears as one of the good effects of the divine command.[34]

However, a number of Grisez's basic human goods are missing from Barth's account altogether. Knowledge of the truth and appreciation of beauty *as distinct from* friendship with God[35] receive no consideration. Skilful performance also goes unmentioned. Marriage, which Grisez has proposed as an eighth basic good,[36] Barth explicitly rejects as a created order. Most important of all, there is no equivalent in Barth's ethic of the complex good of practical reasonableness.

How should we assess the difference between Barth and Grisez in their treatment of the human good? To start with, I judge Barth's reluctance to make explicit reference to it to be unwarranted. His Nygrenesque assumption that self-interested desire is necessarily selfish is mistaken. Whether or not the desire for self-fulfilment or the realisation of one's good is selfish, depends on how that good is conceived. It might be conceived as a state of being where the individual's natural focus of concern is outside of himself; and since the statement, "It is in my interest not to be selfish and to learn to grow strong in care for others", is not a logical self-contradiction, such a conception of the human good is not nonsense.

The second reason adduced for Barth's coyness with regard to the human good is also, in my opinion, inadequate. Part of his argument is that we cannot know what our own good is; and one of the reasons that he gives for this is that creaturely life belongs to God and He alone has the power to decide what its good consists in. Barth gives the impression here of subscribing to a voluntarist understanding of divine sovereignty, according to which God, being God, has the power to do whatever He wills and what He wills is entirely free and unconstrained. God may then decide the content of the human good from moment to moment, reinventing it at will and rendering it unpredictable. However, this impression is given in the course of an exposition of the command of God the Creator that clearly asserts that this command has certain constant features that correspond to the "definite structure"[37] of creaturely being: it always enjoins freedom —before God, in fellowship, for life, and in limitation. Certainly, God in his sovereignty has decided that this is to be the nature of the human good; but the implication of the phrase "definite structure" is that this is a decision that God will not reverse. If that is so, and the human good has a stable, God-given nature, then in principle it is *there* to be known independently of direct reference to God.

But Barth also suggests a second reason why we cannot know our own good: not God's untrammelled power to reinvent reality at will, but human sinfulness. Whatever might be the case in principle, in fact sinfulness distorts our knowledge; this would seem to be the implication of what Barth says in the quotation above about sinners being able to live "only in the power of [God's] mercy". Even so, this passage does not say that apart from God's mercy (in Christ) —apart from the Word of God— we can know nothing about the human good; it says only that our knowledge cannot be unequivocal and conclusive. So Barth is not saying that the effect of sin is such that the human good simply cannot be known, but that it cannot be known properly except through the Word of God.[38] Therefore his objection should not be to the very attempt to discover the nature of the human good, but only to those attempts at discovery that proceed without primary reference to God's Word.

The third reason for Barth's reluctance to make direct reference to the human good is psychological rather than epistemological; namely, that the good is realised only as a by-product of right relating to God, and that to think about it separately from God is to risk succumbing to the fantasy that it can be realised independently of Him.[39] Barth adopted such a principle because he believed that, to avoid the illusion of human autarky, we must keep our attention fixed on the human creature in its religious relationship. However, Barth's own tripartite differentiation of his special ethics implies that he recognised the possibility of considering separately the parts of an ontic whole, without forgetting their status as parts. The same is implied by the distinction that Barth makes between the human freedom, on the one hand, to be before God (and in limitation) and, on the other hand, to be in fellowship and to be for life. The latter are not in fact independent of the former and their dependence is made explicit; but they are nevertheless considered separately. My concluding judgement on this point, then, is that Barth had insufficient reason not to refer to the human good directly and not to elaborate a theory of it.

As we have seen, Barth does have a particular concept of the human good —although he does not call it by that name— and he does analyse this into a number of discrete parts or dimensions. I have argued that all of these have their counterparts in Grisez's theory; but that there are several elements of the human good as Grisez conceives it that are absent from Barth's account. What are we to make of this difference?

Barth rejected marriage as a created order for two reasons: because he finds that Scripture affirms it only as a vocation and not as a universal obligation,[40] and because he suspects that to accord it the status of a created order is to render normative what is really only a particular cultural construct.[41] His concern about giving normative status to a particular cultural construct could be dealt with straightforwardly by acknowledging that the universal social institution of marriage takes diverse cultural forms. But his reluctance to affirm it as a universal obligation —or, in Grisez's terms, as a *basic* human good— is not unreasonable. The New Testament, while not denigrating marriage, nevertheless relativises it; and it is not at all clear to me why it should be considered a necessary component of human flourishing.

The absence in Barth of any equivalent of Grisez's practical reasonableness can be explained, as I suggested above, by his suspicion of the casuistical formulation and application of moral principles as an exercise in rational autarky, and so as an expression of practical atheism.[42] I have argued at length elsewhere that this suspicion is unfounded.[43] In brief, my argument amounts to this: that Barth was wrong to assume that methodical and systematic moral reasoning must be closed, autarkic, rationalist. On the contrary, moral reasoning is quite capable of being open to new data that requires the more or less radical reformation —sometimes even the wholesale jettisoning— of a ruling theory. Now, it could well be argued that the ethic that Grisez builds out of his concept of practical reasonableness is an example of a rationally derived system that is excessively deductive and insufficiently open to revision under pressure from empirical data. But that does not excuse Barth for expressly denying the value of practical reason altogether and thereby failing to lay open to inspection the reasoned system of principles and derivate rules that he covertly develops.

To some extent Barth's theoretical objection to systematic reasoning in ethics was driven by his desire to maintain space in moral life for a personal vocation —a calling by God of an individual to play a unique part in the Grand Project of redeeming the world. But Grisez's ethic is precisely an example of a highly determined rational system that is nevertheless sufficiently open-ended to leave space for personal vocation —"a unique share in the Church's mission".[44]

The absence in Barth's ethic of any recognition of knowledge of the truth and appreciation of beauty —insofar as truth and beauty are distinct from God— and of skill in performance as elements of the human good is symptomatic of his reluctance to consider the value of created things except in *direct* relationship with their Creator.[45] Here Barth moves within range of the criticism that Grisez levels against Augustine. Grisez finds that Augustine's theology "narrows human life to its religious dimension"; and in focusing so strongly on the existential goods of peace with God, within oneself, and with others, he overlooks substantive goods —including knowledge of the truth and skill in performance.[46] Although it would not be fair to say of Barth what could be said of Augustine (at least in *De Doctrina Christiana*) —that he regarded the enjoyment of God in heaven as the only intrinsic good to which all other, secular goods are mere means[47]— it is nevertheless true that the religious (or, to use Barth's metaphor, 'vertical') dimension of the human good so overshadows its secular (or 'horizontal') components as to eclipse some of them altogether.

Certainly, Barth is Augustinian in his unequivocal assertion that friendship with God is primary and basic to the human good: participation in any of its other dimensions depends on participation in this one. At first glance, it would seem that on this point Grisez diverges sharply; for in his exposition of the basic human goods, he tells us that "the human good of religion —that harmony with God which perfects human persons as human— is only one human good alongside others".[48] However, closer inspection discloses that Grisez distinguishes between 'harmony with God' and 'the divine life in which Christians share by adoption'[49] or 'the covenant relationship';[50] and that the light of revelation reveals that this relationship has primacy —"[i]f its perfection is pursued consistently and diligently, every other human good will be served; but if harmony with God is not placed first, nothing else in life will go well".[51] From a Christian point of view, according to Grisez, friendship with God is indeed primary and basic. Accordingly, Grisez agrees with Barth that prayer is "the fundamental category of Christian action" and that the sacraments are "organizing principles of Christian life".[52] This, then, is not exactly where Grisez and Barth diverge.

Grisez and Barth on Reason and Revelation

Where they do part company, however, is over the relationship of reason and revelation. Grisez's distinction between the good of religion and the covenant relationship implies two views of the good of harmony with God, one according to natural reason, the other illumined by revelation; and as with this particular good, so it is with all the others. The exposition of the basic good at the beginning of Grisez's system, before the themes of sin and redemption are introduced, gives the impression that these can be grasped —at least accurately, if not completely— through reason alone, unaided by revelation. This impression is confirmed when we read that one can come to know the goods by rational reflection on the experience of "privations which mutilate them" (in the case of existential goods)[53] and on the experience of natural or spontaneous inclinations toward them (in the case of substantive goods).[54]

However, the further one reads in *Christian Moral Principles*, the more complicated this impression becomes. On one occasion we are told that in the light of revelation "natural law is *restored*, completed, and elevated ...".[55] The words 'completed' and 'elevated' are consistent with our initial impression: reason can grasp a body of moral knowledge (the natural law) that may need supplementation, even transformation, but which is nevertheless sound in itself. However, the word 'restored' implies something significantly different: that reason's knowledge is not only incomplete, but defective —in some respects at least, unsound. The nature of this defect becomes clearer when Grisez explains how he thinks Christian revelation transforms the modes of responsibility implied by practical reasonableness.[56] Apart from revelation, he tells us, "no widely accepted morality is free of gaps, misunderstandings, and false norms"; and these defects appear especially "in dealing with moral evil and its consequences, and in interacting with individuals and groups beyond one's own clan, tribe, caste, or nation".[57] This is because the fallen human condition is one characterised by sin, whose species include: lack of confidence that action for good will be efficacious;[58] fear of pain, suffering, and death;[59] lack of trust in other people;[60] partiality toward one's own people;[61] and the resentful pursuit of vengeful 'justice' against wrongdoers.[62] In these various forms, sin under-mines "an upright and energetic pursuit of human goods" and causes us to be "constantly tempted to deal with evil inappropriately —for example by destructive methods or renunciation of human hope for a good life in this world".[63] What Christian revelation does is to read the human condition as at once fallen and redeemed.[64] Christian moral life, then, is distinctively characterised by its holding in tension both realism and hope.[65] On the one hand, Christians may not overlook the fact of wrongdoing or evil; and they must expect to suffer on account of it.[66] On the other hand, the Resurrection of Jesus gives them reason to hope that integral human fulfilment is (by the grace of God) possible,[67] and therefore that unswerving commitment to the human good —and especially friendship with God— is not futile.[68] Such hope then fuels in each Christian the patient and strenuous following of their personal vocation,[69] the acceptance of a limited role for oneself in the world's redemption,[70] the compassionate respect for others as equal subjects of a personal vocation,[71] the will not to resort to evil means of combating evil,[72] and so the eschewal of vengeance for conciliatoriness.[73]

To some extent, the defect that revelation remedies is one, not of knowledge, but of commitment. What sin —or lack of faith in God— does is to undermine commitment to the claims of practical reasonableness, leading people into inertia; into impatient individualism; into 'tribalism';[74] into action driven by the myopic desire for a particular satisfaction, by the frantic desire for immediate satisfactions, by the fear of pain and death, or by resentment; and into compromising with evil. According to this reading, what those living without revelation and faith lack is not knowledge of the good and (especially in the case of practical reasonableness) their implications, but the ability to behave in a manner that is truly respectful of them. Such an account is consistent with the claim, which Grisez appears to make, that 'natural' human reason is in fact capable of an accurate —if incomplete— understanding of the human good and its constituents.

Further reflection, however, suggests that the defect from which human morality suffers apart from revelation and faith is not just voluntary but also cognitive. For surely those who lack faith in God, and therefore hope in the possibility of the realisation of integral human fulfilment, cease to see the requirements of 'practical reasonableness' *as reasonable*. In a world where there appears to be no God and no hope for integral fulfilment, the requirements of 'practical reasonableness', by ceasing to appear practicable, thereby come to seem practically *un*reasonable. The grand implication of this is that there really is no sound body of moral knowledge grasped by reason 'naturally' and occupying some neutral spot in between sinful and redeemed perspectives. The presence or absence of faith in God and hope for the realisation of integral fulfilment determines what seems morally 'reasonable'. In other words, moral reason cannot be detached from particular metaphysical commitments; it cannot avoid being set in the particular context of one metanarrative or another.

This is not at all to say that the content of theistic and atheistic moralities are entirely different. Theists and atheists alike are human, sharing experience of the constant features of human being, which gives rise to points of common understanding of the human good and the conduct that it requires. The point is not that the adherents of different metanarratives espouse entirely different moralities, but rather that the particular moral beliefs that they share are differently located in larger wholes that qualify —sometimes slightly, sometimes radically— the significance of each of their parts.

Barth's understanding of the relation of moral 'reason' and revelation is far closer to this than is Grisez's. One of the great virtues of Barth's ethic is that it makes quite clear that its understanding of the human good and its requirements is significantly determined by Christian theological premises; and that there is no metaphysically neutral body of moral knowledge —'natural reason'— to which revelation or non-revelation merely 'adds'. Where Barth is weaker —and where Grisez is stronger— is in acknowledging that, not-withstanding this metaphysical determination, common human experience does give rise to common moral beliefs that are shared by Christians and non-Christians, while being construed more or less differently. Much of the time Barth gives the impression of supposing that a truly Christian ethic is one that is exclusively *derived* from theological premises; and this goes some way toward explaining why certain obvious dimensions of the human good —knowledge of the truth and appreciation of beauty, where truth and beauty are distinct from God— are simply absent from his account. Nevertheless, there are other occasions where Barth implies that what he is trying to do is something rather more complex and dialectical: on the one hand, explicating how Christian theological beliefs shape our understanding of the human good and of conduct that accords with it; while on the other hand, drawing material discriminately from other sources of moral knowledge —empirical, behavioural- or social-scientific, and philosophical— and locating it, duly qualified, within his theological system.[75]

Conclusion

In conclusion, it seems to me that Barth had some good rhetorical reason to let the language of divine command dominate his ethic. It emphasises the obligatory force of right action to an extent that talk about its rationality does not; for it implies that failure to act rightly involves not merely error, but penalty. Further, it urges attention to the Word of God, and thereby critical reflection upon the body of moral assumptions that bear the title of 'reason'.

Nevertheless, Barth was mistaken to let talk of divine commanding virtually drown out talk of the human good. He had insufficient reason to avoid direct reference to it; and in particular he had insufficient reason to deny the value of practical reason, and to fail to give independent consideration to those components of the human good other than friendship with God. He was also mistaken to treat the Word of God as the sole source of moral knowledge, and not just the primary point of reference in our moral thinking.

Correspondingly, Grisez's rhetoric of rationality is, arguably, appropriate to his context. He is correct to assert unequivocally the logical priority of the good to the right, to elaborate explicitly a theory of the human good, and to give independent consideration to those of its components other than friendship with God. He is also correct to recognise both that Christian revelation makes a significant difference to how the human good and its moral implications are conceived, and that nevertheless Christians and non-Christians, theists and atheists, share fragments of moral material.

Where Grisez is wrong is to suppose, as he sometimes does, that there is a coherent body of knowledge about the human good, its components and its moral implications, which is sound per se, and to which reason can in fact attain 'naturally' —that is, without illumination by revelation. The theory of the good and the moral law that Grisez presents as attainable 'naturally' is actually formed by specifically Christian presuppositions. It is in fact a Christian theory, formally abstracted from the theological context in which alone it makes sense. This flaw in Grisez's ethic inadvertently confirms Barth's contention that theological presuppositions radically determine the whole of a Christian ethic — although there may be isolated fragments that Christians and non-Christians share alike.

The implication of this is not at all that moral debate between Christians and others is reduced to the dogmatic declamation of rival metanarratives. Nor is it relegated to argument over whether natural morality needs the sheer addition of a supernatural dimension. Rather, the implication is that moral debate should be about whether a Christian theological ethic can 'outnarrate' its alternatives — that is, whether it has the resources with which to make better sense of common moral data and so to transcend the theoretical cul-de-sacs of its rivals.

NOTES

1   For a contemporary instance of Protestant criticism of natural law, see Stanley Hauerwas, *The Peaceable Kingdom* (Notre Dame: Notre Dame University Press, 1983), pp.55-59,

where Hauerwas tells us that the result of basing ethics on "a natural law methodology ... [is] that theological convictions about Jesus are not directly relevant to concrete ethical analysis" (p.55).

2   According to Grisez's conception, with which I agree, right conduct (morality) is that which maintains or promotes the kind of flourishing that is proper to the nature of human beings (the human good). This is correct sense in which the moral law is 'natural'.

3   For fuller accounts of Barth's thinking on natural law and its Protestant equivalents, see Nigel Biggar, *The Hastening that Waits: Karl Barth's Ethics* (Oxford: Oxford University Press, 1993, 1995), pp.49-62; and Nigel Biggar, "Barth's Trinitarian Ethic", in *The Cambridge Companion to Barth*, ed. J.B. Webster (Cambridge: Cambridge University Press, 2000), section IV.

4   Karl Barth, *A Letter to Great Britain from Switzerland* (London: Sheldon Press, 1941), p.17.

5   Karl Barth, "The Christian Community and the Civil Community", in *Community, State, and Church*, ed. and intro. Will Herberg (Gloucester, Mass.: Peter Smith, 1968), pp.163-4.

6   Karl Barth, *Church Dogmatics* (henceforth, *CD*), III/4, p.22.

7   Ibid., p.28.

8   Ibid., p.39.

9   Ibid, pp.136-8.

10   Karl Barth, *The Christian Life: Church Dogmatics*, IV/4, Lecture Fragments (Grand Rapids: Eerdmans, 1981), pp.213-33.

11   See Biggar, *Hastening*, pp.7-45, 163-4.

12   *CMP*, pp.12-13; *LCL*, p.xiv.

13   The assumption here is that the fact that God is our Creator does not in itself imply that He is benevolent. This is true: the Creator also needs to demonstrate His benevolence by acting to promote human well-being or salvation —by becoming Saviour or Reconciler. Nevertheless, it is untrue to say that God can only be known as benevolent insofar as He is known in Jesus Christ; for God's benevolence was hardly unknown to the authors of the Old Testament.

14   The first ethical section of the *Church Dogmatics* (II/2, chapter VIII) is entitled "The Command of God"; the second (III/4), "The Command of God the Creator"; the third (IV/4), "The Command of God the Reconciler"; and the fourth —had Barth had time to write it— would have been "The Command of God the Redeemer".

15   For a fuller discussion of this complicated issue in the interpretation of Barth, see Biggar, *Hastening*, chapter 1.

16   *CMP*, pp.278-79.

17   Biggar, *Hastening*, p.8 n.2.

18   Thomas Aquinas, *Summa Theologiae*, I-II, q.85, a.1,2,3 ("in so far as reason is deprived [by sin] of its direction towards truth, we have the 'wound of ignorance' ..." [Blackfriars edition, 1965]); q.94, a.6 ("natural law ... can be missing from a particular course of action when the reason is stopped from applying the general principle there, because of lust or some other passion, ..." [Blackfriars edition, 1966]; q.77, a.2.

19   See Brian Gerrish, *Grace and Reason: a Study in the Theology of Luther*, Midway Reprint (Chicago: University of Chicago Press, 1979), ch. VI ("Reason and Law") and Conclusion.

20   John T. McNeill, "Natural Law in the Teaching of the Reformers", *Journal of Religion*, XXVI (1946), pp.168-82.

21   In his *Epitome philosophiae moralis* (1541).

22   See, for example, Kant's *Religion within the Limits of Reason Alone* (New York: Harper & Row, 1960), especially pp.146-47.

23   See Biggar, "Barth's Trinitarian Ethic", sections I and II.

24   *CMP*, 3-G; 4-A; 6-H.5.

25   Ibid., 1-D, F.

26   When Barth does talk about 'the good', he understands it in Kantian fashion as "the perfect correctness and therefore morality of human will and conduct, ... the sum of all that is required and commanded" (*CD*, II/2, pp.665-66), and not —following Aristotle— as the ontological state of *eudaimonia* or flourishing. "The question of the good [is] the question what [*sic*] man should do" (ibid., p.564) —not the question of what he should become. What Barth means by 'good', I mean by 'right'.

27   Barth is in no doubt that what God intends through his commanding, and what is achieved through our obeying, is "man's welfare" (*CD*, II/2, p.709).

28   See *CD*, IV/2, pp.734-5 ("a grasping, taking, possessive love —self-love— ... is the direct opposite of Christian love"). Barth's view of self-love, however, was more nuanced than Nygren's: see Gene Outka, *Agape: an Ethical Analysis* (New Haven & London: Yale University Press, 1972), pp.221-29.

29   *CD*, III/4, pp.382-83.

30   *CD*, II/2, p.556: "Of course, the command of God is also a promise. Its fulfilment produces fruit. It yields a reward. That is something which we must not, of course, overlook or deny. But we cannot and must not seek the basis of its claim in the fact that its fulfilment has these consequences, that along with blessedness, the fellowship of man with God, it brings with it the answer to the problem of human life —the only possible answer to it. The divine command, whose fulfilment has this promise, must be known and understood as grounded in itself, as having a divine basis ...".

31   *CD*, III/2, pp.265-85 ("being in encounter, in which we have seen the basic form of humanity, is a being which is gladly actualised by man. I think that this unpretentious word 'gladly', while it does not penetrate the secret [of humanity] before which we stand, does at least indicate it correctly as the *conditio sine qua non* of humanity" [p.266]).

32   The fourth species of freedom that Barth treats here —'freedom in limitation'— is not so easily rendered as a distinct good; however, insofar as it consists in the glad acceptance of one's status as a creature, and therefore of one's personal vocation by God to play modest role in the redeeming of the world, it could be subsumed under the category of the good of friendship with God or 'religion'.

33   *CD*, III/4, pp.553-54. Barth's discussion of play and art here is brief in the extreme. But since, in his Münster-Bonn lecture on ethics of 1928-31, he discussed these topics much more extensively under the rubric of "The Command of God the Redeemer", it is possible that they would have received much fuller treatment in the equivalent section of the *Church Dogmatics* (that is, Volume V), had Barth lived to complete it.

34   CD, II/2, pp.726-32.

35   It could well be argued that knowledge of the truth about God and appreciation of his beauty is basic to the human good as Barth conceives it; but while knowledge of other kinds of truth or appreciation of other kinds of beauty may not be separable from or independent of this knowledge and appreciation, they are nevertheless distinguishable from them.

36   *LCL*, 9.A.1.

37   *CD*, III/4, p.44: "Real man, man himself, is the being reflected in the grace of God addressed to man in Jesus Christ. This being is indeed a sinner, a pardoned sinner, and a child of God in hope. *But this being does not start with the sinner. It is also the creature*

of God, participating as such in a definite structure [einer bestimmten Struktur], and knowable in this structure in the Word of God". The emphasis is mine.

38   See the footnote immediately above: the creaturely being of man is "knowable in this structure in the Word of God".

39   This is an instance of a general methodological principle of Barth's that what has no independent existence should not become an independent object of thought. For further discussion, see Biggar, *The Hastening*, pp.158-9.

40   *CD*, III/4, pp.141, 148.

41   Certainly, this is how he judged Bonhoeffer's concept of marriage as a divine 'mandate': see ibid., pp.21-22.

42   Ibid., pp.7-8. For detailed discussion, see Biggar, *Hastening*, pp.40-1.

43   See ibid., ch.1; Biggar, "Barth's Trinitarian Ethic", section V.

44   *CMP*, 23.E; *LCL*, 2.

45   It may also be symptomatic of the limitations of an ethical method that focusses too exclusively on Christology and Scripture.

46   *CMP*, 5.F.2,4.

47   Ibid., 34.A.   Grisez is careful to note here that Augustine himself later recognised the inadequacy of the distinction —introduced in *De Doctrina Christiana*— between the one good that is to be 'enjoyed' (God) and all the others that should only be 'used' (all temporal goods). "However," he comments, "a system which must stretch its own categories to accommodate the minimal requirements of Christian humanism leaves something to be desired" (ibid., 34 n.3).

48   Ibid., 5.D.9.

49   Ibid.

50   Ibid., 21.C.1.

51   Ibid.

52   Ibid., 29: "Prayer: the Fundamental Category of Christian Action"; 30, Introduction (p.725). Barth says of prayer that it "must be the perennial undertone, basis and support accompanying and upholding all other human actions", and he describes it as "the primal and basic form of the whole Christian life" (*Christian Life*, p.89); and the centre-piece of his ethical system in the *Church Dogmatics* —the treatise on the command of God the Reconciler— begins with baptism, has at its heart the Lord's Prayer, and was planned to conclude with the Lord's Supper (see *Church Dogmatics*, IV/4 and *Christian Life*).

53   Ibid., 5.D.7.

54   Ibid., 7.D.4.

55   Ibid., 7.B.8. My emphasis.

56   Ibid., 26: "Modes of Christian Response".

57   Ibid., 25.E.11.

58   Ibid., 26.D.1, F.1, I.1, K.1.

59   Ibid., 26.G.1, F.1.

60   Ibid., 26.E.1, I.1.

61   Ibid., 26.H.1.

62   Ibid., J.1.

63   Ibid., 27.A.4.

64   Ibid., 25, Summary (p.617).

65   Ibid., 25.E.13: "The distinctiveness of Christian morality is clearest in its linking together seeming opposites.   For example, one must love enemies, but absolutely refuse to compromise with them; one must suffer for the sake of uprightness, but not passively

regard the world as broken beyond human repair, one must concede nothing to anyone's moral error, yet judge no one wicked".

66   Ibid., 26.G, K.
67   Ibid., 7.F.2; 19, Introduction; 27.A.3.
68   Ibid., 22, Summary (p.544); 21.D.8. As in Barth, so in Grisez, eschatological hope functions to inspire at once modest expectations about the possibilities of human achievement, and yet (through faith in God) motivation to committed service of the human good (Grisez) or the Kingdom of God (Barth).
69   Ibid., 26.F.1.; G.1; I.1.
70   Ibid., 26.E.
71   Ibid., 26.H. Grisez himself does not quite establish the (psycho)logical connexion between accepting one's own role in the world's redemption as a limited one, respecting the roles of others, and treating them with compassion and generosity.
72   Ibid., 21.D.8; 26.J.1, K.1; 27.A.4-6; 28.G.6.
73   Ibid., 26.J.
74   The term is mine, not Grisez's.
75   The word that Barth himself used to denote the second movement of his project was 'annexation' (*CD*, II/2, p 524). For further discussion of Barth's methodology and its ambiguity, see Biggar, *Hastening*, pp.152-60, 163.

8 Grisez's Ecclesiology, the Role of Moral Theologians, and the Scope for Responsible Dissent

Bernard Hoose

In these ecumenical days most theologians, it would seem, use the word 'Church' (preceded by the definite article and often with a capital 'C') to refer to the whole community of Christians. As Max Stackhouse puts it, "More theologically, the term may be applied to the 'mystical body of Christ', to the company of believers of all times and places (church universal) or to those within and without the institutional church (including 'anonymous Christians' who belong to other religions) who are known by (or 'elected' by) God to be faithful (church invisible)".[1] Inevitably, perhaps, writers who use the word in this way (and, of course, as a name for certain kinds of buildings in which Christians gather for worship) also apply it to the various branches or denominations of Christianity. This is not usually a problem if suitable adjectives are added, as in 'the United Reformed Church' or 'the Roman Catholic Church'. Such, however, is not always the case. It is not unusual, for instance, to find Roman Catholic writers occasionally referring to their particular denomination simply as 'the Church'. One such is Germain Grisez.

In his case, this practice appears to be the expression of a conviction that "the perfect unity of Jesus' Church requires the full communion of all Christians in the Catholic Church".[2] Such a claim would be unlikely to raise many eyebrows, even among Protestants, Anglicans and Orthodox Christians, if the term 'catholic' were taken to mean simply 'universal'. Clearly, however, Grisez is here referring to the Roman Catholic Church.[3] The unique Church of Jesus, he states, "subsists in the

Catholic Church, governed by the pope and the other bishops who are in communion with him". That Church is divided because many of those who are baptized are not in full communion. Most of these people, he notes, are in other churches or ecclesial communities. Those who are members of such churches and communities do, in practice, "enjoy many things that come from Jesus and lead back to him". However, Grisez goes on to say, "all these things which build up and enliven the Church, belong by right to the Catholic Church, and the fulness of the means of salvation can be obtained only in her".[4] There is, of course, no hint here that disaster necessarily looms for Christians who are not Roman Catholics. In a discussion of baptism, Grisez says that nothing extrinsic is added by the other sacraments. They develop what is already present in embryonic form in baptism. This he sees as explaining why people who die at a very young age "and those who fail to appreciate the fulness of Catholic truth (for example, Protestants of good will) can enjoy a true sacramental life by baptism alone".[5] Nevertheless, those whom Grisez refers to as separated brothers and sisters "lack some essential truths of Christian faith and morality and are deprived of some means of salvation available in the Catholic Church".[6] In spite of his use of the word 'separated', however, Grisez regards Christians to whom he attributes that label as being in imperfect but real communion with the Roman Catholic Church:

> It follows that without excluding non-Christians and separated Christians from salvation, we must find the oneness of the only Church of Jesus in the enduring unity of the Catholic Church (see *LG* 8). She alone recognizes the principle of unity and cooperation established by Jesus: the collegial episcopacy centered upon the successor of Peter, who is the vicar of the Lord Jesus and head of the whole Church (see *LG* 18). To put the matter bluntly: Christians who do not regard themselves as Catholics are so despite themselves, just insofar as they truly are Christians. (Although the purpose of this bluntness is clarity, not offensiveness, it obviously is not likely to be appreciated by our separated brothers and sisters.)[7]

Grisez and Russell Shaw express themselves with similar bluntness when discussing lawmaking in the Church. The obligation to obey Church law, they say, is more serious than the obligation to obey other law because the governing authority of the (Roman Catholic) Church is divinely grounded. Only members, of course, are obliged to obey:

> Non-Catholics do nothing wrong in not observing this law. But in disregarding the Church's moral teaching, non-Catholics are, whether they know it or not,

violating moral truth. Even so, they may be less guilty than Catholics because, not accepting the Church and its teaching, they know less clearly what the truth is.[8]

This leads us on to a topic concerning which Grisez's writings have provoked a fair amount of debate, the issue of authority in the Church.

Authority in the Church

Over the centuries there has been a good deal of controversy concerning the question of where precisely authority is located in the Church. Some, for instance, have said that it is simply in the Holy Spirit. Others have located it in a kind of consensus of the faithful or in the tradition of the Church. Classical Protestantism, of course, emphasised the role of the Bible. In view of what we have already observed about Grisez's ecclesiology, however, we shall confine our discussion to authority within Roman Catholicism.

In recent centuries there has been a growing tendency within that church to lay emphasis upon the teaching authority of the Pope and the other bishops, who are seen as the successors of the apostles. Indeed, until the 1960s, it would seem, there was a tendency, as Avery Dulles puts it, to reduce all other kinds of theological authority to that one font. The term 'magisterium' came to be applied exclusively to the teaching office of the episcopate.[9] The Pope, moreover, came to be seen as having as much authority as the whole body of bishops. He was also seen as being equipped with the infallibility with which Christ endowed the Church. Dulles refers to this theory of authority as hierocratic or institutional. It has the advantage, he accepts, of helping to safeguard unity as well as doctrinal continuity with the Church of apostolic times. The hierocratic model, moreover, provides a way of gathering together "a body of clearly identifiable, self-consistent, and certified teachings". A negative point, however, is that, because this model emphasises the juridical and formal aspects of authority, it encourages what Dulles refers to as "the 'blank check' theory of assent". Moreover, it does not give sufficient attention to the fact that no official teaching would have power or credibility unless it emanated from a community of faith: "The doctrine of infallibility, in particular, becomes incredible if set forth in an automatic or mechanistic way, without taking account of the human and Christian character of the process by which faith is gathered up and distilled into doctrine". In place of this hierocratic model of authority, Dulles proposes a pluralistic theory.

He holds that numerous distinct organs of authority are necessary if the Church is to maintain its health and vigour. These various authorities, moreover, act as checks and balances to each other. There is tension and dialogue among them, "and only when they spontaneously converge can authority make itself fully felt". Among these authorities are Scripture, sacred tradition, the general sense of the faithful, people with special gifts (such as those with prophetic insight or learning), and people who hold offices within the Church.[10]

Even within the confines of Roman Catholicism, Dulles is far from being alone in displaying wariness of the hierocratic model of authority in the Church.[11] Grisez, however, sees things somewhat differently. The infallibility invested in the Church by Christ needs, he says, an instrument or organ through which it can be exercised. This instrument is the Roman Catholic magisterium, which, he claims, is competent to decide what belongs to revelation, although he is keen to point out that the word 'decide' here has the sense of judging, and not of choosing. The magisterium receives, guards and explains revealed truth, which has to be communicated in every age. Those who exercise the magisterial function, continues Grisez, are not qualified to do so because of expertise or scholarly competence. They simply have divine authority. Indeed their authority belongs to the same category as the authority of Jesus. Doctrinal decisions of the bishops, as well as their judgements concerning matters of faith and morals, "have the authority of truth, the personal truth revealed in Jesus".[12]

Writing with Russell Shaw, Grisez does not claim that all statements by bishops, or even popes, concerning matters of faith or morals are infallible. Suppose, however, that there has been no solemn definition concerning a certain matter and that there is no unity of teaching on the issue by the whole episcopal college in union with the pope. If the pope and/or a number of bishops propose a teaching on that same issue as certainly true, say Grisez and Shaw, "religious assent short of faith is required". They expand on this, explaining that, although the teaching could be erroneous, one accepts it simply because it has been proposed authoritatively by one's bishop or the pope (but especially so in the latter case). They cite the example of *in vitro* fertilisation. Clear teaching on this matter has been given by Pope Pius XII, the Congregation for the Doctrine of the Faith, and by some bishops and groups of bishops. Up to the time of writing, the college of bishops as a whole had not been involved. Teachings such as this, however, might eventually be seen to pertain to revelation and thus turn out to be matters of faith. Knowing that the pope and the bishops are responsible for safeguarding the faith of the Church and for directing

Christian life, Catholics, they say, will assent to what is taught.[13] Elsewhere Grisez says that, when people give religious assent to a papal teaching, they submit their own judgement to that of the pope. This amounts to agreeing with him, even if they would have thought such a teaching to be untrue had it not emanated from the pope. Foreseeing objections, Grisez admits that, since what is concerned in such teachings are not matters of faith, it would be wrong for people to submit their judgement to that of the pope or bishops if the teachings concerned were not consistent with relevant evidence and convincing reasons. However, he claims, papal and episcopal teachings hardly ever give rise to problems of that kind. Moreover, he sees it as reasonable to believe that, when the popes and bishops fulfil their role as teachers, God arranges things so that anybody who submits his or her judgement to what is taught does not fall into serious and harmful error.[14]

History reveals, he admits, that it is not unusual for a single bishop, or, indeed, a number of bishops, to propose as certain a doctrine that is erroneous. In such cases, he says, members of the faithful can seek clarification from the Holy See, "since there is a basis in Catholic faith for preferring the pope's judgment in such a matter". As for papal teaching, itself, however, it is unlikely, he asserts, that the normal ground for religious assent will be undercut by a superior source —such sources being Scripture, an already defined doctrine, or a teaching that has been proposed infallibly by the ordinary magisterium— "since popes ordinarily try hard to avoid proposing as certain any moral norm which might be shown false from such a source".[15]

It might be objected that, Grisez's assurances notwithstanding, anybody who accepted and acted upon certain papal teachings in bygone days would most certainly have fallen into serious and harmful error. After all, the record of the popes as far as moral teachings are concerned is by no means unblemished. In 1864, for example, Pius IX declared that it is erroneous to claim it is no longer beneficial for the Catholic Church to be considered the only religion of the state to the exclusion of all other forms of worship. The same pope went on to describe as equally erroneous the claim that laws promulgated in some so-called Catholic countries are wise in permitting visitors to them to participate in the public exercise of other forms of worship.[16] All of this is, of course, in stark contrast to the contents of the *Declaration on Religious Liberty* of the Second Vatican Council. Another example is provided by Pope Innocent IV. His predecessor Nicholas I, in a letter to the Bulgars written in the year 866, had declared that it is wrong to beat people in order to extract confessions from them. In 1252, however, in his *Ad extirpanda*, Innocent allowed that heretics be tortured (barring amputation and death) so that they might reveal information about their own wrongdoing and even accuse others of misdemeanours. This, he noted, was already the case with thieves and marauders.[17] A third instance is one noted by Grisez himself. It is true, he admits, that "Leo X condemned Martin Luther's proposition that the burning of heretics is against the will of God (see *DS* 1483/773). But this condemnation was not proposed infallibly, and Vatican II clearly excludes the practice (see *DH* 6)".[18]

A somewhat similar defence could be applied, of course, to the previous two examples, and, indeed to other instances of papal error. The fact remains, however, that Grisez lays a great deal of emphasis on the requirement of religious assent to non-infallible teachings. Indeed, his theory of religious assent appears to come very close to what Dulles was referring to in his comments about a blank cheque type of assent. When there were instances of error in the past, says Grisez, Roman Catholics of the time, theologians included, acted rightly in trusting the judgement of the magisterium. If similar cases were to occur again, we would not have the clarity that comes with hindsight. We should therefore adopt the teaching of the magisterium:

> Responsibly following the possibly erroneous judgment of the magisterium is the same as responsibly following one's sincere conscience in other cases; it is possible to go wrong in this way, but one has no better norm than one's best judgment. Thus, when a faithful Catholic's best judgment is formed, as it should be, by the Church's noninfallible teaching, the Catholic might possibly be following a false norm. Yet God has provided no better norm for his or her current belief and practice.[19]

A few years ago, in reacting to the last sentence of the above quotation, the present writer referred to the condemnation by Leo X of Luther's affirmation that burning heretics at the stake is against the will of God:

> Surely it is incredible to claim that nobody could have had a better judgement than Leo on that matter before a later pope received enlightenment directly from God or otherwise. On the same page on which he refers to this case Grisez notes that the practice of burning heretics was clearly excluded by the Second Vatican Council. I imagine, however, that many an individual had come to exclude it long before the announcement of any such conciliar exclusion. Indeed, I would say it is very likely that, even if Luther himself is left out of the discussion, there were many people, both Catholic and Protestant, in fifteenth-century Europe whose 'best judgement' regarding the burning of heretics was far superior to that of Leo X. Such people would have needed to do violence to their consciences in order to accept papal teaching on the matter.[20]

Responding to similar comments I had made in an earlier work,[21] Robert P. George sought to defend Grisez's position by pointing to the latter's assertion, referred to above, that one may judge a teaching of the magisterium to be false if a superior theological source requires such a conclusion. Anybody around at the time of Leo's condemnation who was persuaded by scriptural arguments that it was wrong to burn heretics, he said, should have refused to do such a thing, and should have done whatever was appropriate to resist the practice.[22]

This might seem to be a reasonable comment, but a certain circularity comes into the discussion when one finds Grisez quoting with approval from chapter 10 of *Dei verbum*, a document of the Second Vatican Council: "The task of authentically interpreting the word of God, whether written or handed on, has been entrusted exclusively to the living teaching office (magisterium) of the Church, whose authority is exercised in the name of Jesus Christ".[23] Again this might be considered, at least by some Roman Catholics, not to present a problem. This merely highlights the fact that the magisterium is the authentic teacher, it could be said, and any pope who teaches something contrary to what has already been taught authoritatively by the magisterium is in error. Thus it could be said that the teaching of Innocent IV in favour of torture was opposed to the teaching of Nicholas I, and was therefore wrong. On the other hand, using the same type of reasoning, it could be claimed that Pius XII was wrong in speaking against torture in the middle of the twentieth century because he was thereby opposing the teaching of his predecessor Innocent IV. Or is it just a matter of finding out which pope spoke first on the subject (in this case Nicholas), and accepting his teaching as the authentic one? It might seem so to some people, but on what grounds could we accept such a scheme? No rational ones, it would appear. Moreover, it may even be the case that some pope or other spoke or wrote in favour of torture before Nicholas I wrote his letter opposing it. This author has certainly not made an exhaustive search to ascertain whether or not that is so. If we take up the subject of religious liberty, moreover, we find we have a case in which the Second Vatican Council not only opposed the clear teaching of a pope, but acted against what appears to have been a long tradition. Indeed, some years ago, W.F. Hogan wrote in regard to the *Syllabus of Errors*, the document referred to above in which Pius IX spoke against religious liberty:

> Many theologians attribute infallible teaching authority to the syllabus itself, whilst others deny this. Nevertheless, the syllabus must be accepted by all Catholics, since it comes from the Pope as universal teacher and judge, according to the official communication from Cardinal Antonelli accompanying

it. Its contents cannot be challenged by Catholics, and they are to give assent to it, holding the opposite of the condemned propositions.[24]

I imagine that, in this case, Grisez, like most of us, would uphold the teaching of the Council and not that of Pius IX. If that is so, however, he has to explain why the teaching of a Council should be regarded, in this case, as superior to that of a pope who apparently claimed that he was speaking with authority.

Infallibility

In practice, the magisterium has rarely claimed infallibility for specific proclamations on matters of faith and morals. Concerning concrete moral questions, moreover, it would seem that there has never been any such proclamation. The mere absence of a solemnly proclaimed definition, however, does not suffice to bring to an end all argument within Roman Catholicism about the infallibility or otherwise of teachings regarding concrete behavioural norms. This is so because of ongoing debate concerning the power of the so-called 'ordinary' magisterium. Daniel Maguire explains matters succinctly thus:

> Customarily, the magisterium is spoken of as either *ordinary* or *extraordinary*. The extraordinary magisterium comprises the *ex cathedra* statements of the Pope and the solemn statements of bishops convoked in council in union with the Pope to define the faith. The ordinary magisterium refers to the normal daily teaching of the bishops throughout the world. As regards infallibility, the ordinary magisterium is considered infallible when there is "unanimity of the episcopal magisterium".

Maguire goes on to point out that special problems surround the concept of an infallible ordinary magisterium. How, for instance, does one determine unanimity, especially in regard to specific questions of morality?

> Secondly, unanimity or consensus can be of various kinds. There can be reflective or non-reflective consensus. Unanimity on some moral matters might represent only a legacy received uncritically from another age, a non-reflective consensus, which has serious limitations.[25]

In spite of such difficulties, however, Grisez argues that certain teachings of the ordinary magisterium have been taught infallibly. Indeed, some years ago, he and John C. Ford wrote a long article in which they argued that the official Roman Catholic teaching on contraception has been proposed infallibly by the ordinary magisterium.[26] Their arguments are centred on the following extract from the Vatican II document *Lumen gentium*:

> Although the bishops individually do not enjoy the prerogative of infallibility, they nevertheless proclaim the teaching of Christ infallibly, even when they are dispersed throughout the world, provided that they remain in communion with each other and with the successor of Peter and that in authoritatively teaching on a matter of faith and morals they agree in one judgement as that to be held definitively.[27]

Commenting on this text, after having studied its evolution, Ford and Grisez conclude that, although the ordinary magisterium must be universal, and although the infallibility of the Church is to be found in the teaching of the bishops in union with the pope *as a whole*, total mathematical unanimity among the bishops is not required. If, moreover, the requisite universality were attained at some point in the past, a present-day lack of consensus among the bishops would not nullify it: "What is once infallibly proposed must always afterward be accepted with absolute assurance of its truth". This does not, of course, mean that it cannot later be explained in new ways. An indication that such universality has been achieved would be that the teaching in question has been taught by bishops repeatedly at different times and in different places, responding to different challenges. Further required evidence of universality would be "that the bishops have articulated and defended this point of teaching in different intellectual frameworks, perhaps reinforcing it with varying disciplinary measures". In spite of the point about there being no need of total unanimity, Ford and Grisez go on to say that there should not be any evidence that the teaching in question has ever been challenged by a bishop or other person authorized to take part in the teaching mission of the Church, except where such challenging resulted in an admonition and a restatement of what had already been universally taught.[28] They then set out to demonstrate that the teaching on contraception meets the conditions laid down in the text of *Lumen gentium* cited above, and conclude that there is an extremely strong case that it has been proposed infallibly.[29]

In the same issue of the same journal, Joseph A. Komonchak wrote an article in which he pointed out that a teaching could not meet the requirements for infallibility unless it was divinely revealed or was necessary for the defence or explanation of what has been so revealed.[30] Having taken that into account as well as the conditions spelled out in the text of *Lumen gentium* referred to above, he says that he does not see "how one can reply to the question of the infallibility of the magisterial condemnation of artificial contraception with anything but a *non constat*". Referring specifically to the teaching of Paul VI in the encyclical letter *Humanae vitae*, he says he finds that "there is something like a *consensus theologorum* that the magisterial tradition behind *HV*'s condemnation does not constitute an infallible exercise of the teaching office".[31]

Grisez does not, in fact, confine his claim about infallible teaching of concrete norms of behaviour to the matter of artificial contraception. In a more recent publication, he states that "having been proposed with one voice by Catholic bishops as a requirement for eternal salvation, the whole body of common Catholic moral teaching concerning acts which constitute grave matter meets the requirements articulated by Vatican II for teaching proposed infallibly by the ordinary magisterium".[32] To be convincing, however, he has to deal adequately with Komonchak's point concerning revelation. A similar point has been made more recently by Frank Mobbs. There is, he points out, no limit to the area over which the magisterium might teach with the authority of natural expertise. However, he argues, matters of natural law which are not revealed simply cannot be a part of *de fide* or authoritative teachings of the magisterium. If they are claiming to teach Christ's requirements, the bishops should confine themselves to what Christ has taught us. Matters of natural law, he says, are not part of what Christ has taught us and the magisterium does not have a divine commission to teach them.[33] In accordance with the teaching of the two Vatican Councils, Mobbs accepts that there is a secondary object of the magisterium's authority. In other words, he accepts that the magisterium has authority in regard to matters which are not part of revelation but are necessary for the defence and exposition of the same. Thus it seems to him that the magisterium has authority to teach that anything which contradicts revealed propositions is false. It does not follow from this, however, that it has divine authority to teach that unrevealed propositions which do *not* contradict revealed ones are true.[34] Given the subject matter of his book, it would seem that Mobbs is principally concerned here with unrevealed propositions concerning natural law. Indeed, he declares that the magisterium has acted *ultra vires* in teaching on natural law as if it had divine authority. Its teachings on that subject, therefore, "do not count as teachings of the Catholic Church".[35]

Some years earlier Grisez had claimed that matters of natural law do fall within the secondary object of the magisterium's authority. He argued that this must be the case because the magisterium has taught definitively certain moral propositions expressing precepts of natural law, and anything that is taught infallibly must pertain to revelation, "at least by being a truth required to safeguard and develop revelation itself".[36] There is a circularity in this argument which did not escape Mobbs: "This means that a sufficient condition for one's being able to know that a moral proposition is one the magisterium may teach with divine authority, is knowing that the magisterium has taught it definitively".[37] It might seem at first sight that, if such is the case, the magisterium could teach definitively on any matter from tennis to astrophysics. Grisez, however, would be quick to point out that only matters of faith and morals fall within the competence of the magisterium. 'Faith and morals' here is, of course a translation of the Latin phrase *'fides et mores'*, which was used in the original decree on papal infallibility at the First Vatican Council. Since that Council there has been a considerable amount of debate concerning the exact meaning to be attributed to the words —most especially, it would seem, to *'mores'*. Mobbs, however, points out that, traditionally, the phrase has been used as equivalent to 'deposit of faith'. Grisez, he believes, has failed to notice that the magisterium is divinely authorized to teach morals which are of the *depositum fidei*, what God has revealed: "There are not two objects of the magisterium's divine authority, faith *and* morals. The morals are those which are known through faith".[38] He also notes that the teaching of the Second Vatican Council that there is a secondary object, is not taught as a revealed truth and has not been taught definitively.

Dissent and the Role of Moral Theologians

In writing his book, Mobbs appears to have joined the growing ranks of those Roman Catholic scholars described by Grisez as 'dissenting theologians'. Given his convictions concerning the limits of the magisterium's authority, however, it would seem safe to assume that Mobbs would see himself more accurately described merely as one who disagrees with the holders of magisterial office in regard to certain matters. Surely, moreover, such is part of the role of a theologian. Is that not one of the ways in which development in teaching comes about? That would seem to have been the case, for instance, where religious liberty is concerned. Grisez, however, sees the role of theologians as somewhat more passive. We have already noted his saying that, when real instances of error on the part of the magisterium occurred in the past, theologians of the time acted rightly in trusting the judgement of that same magisterium. He also claims that, even in cases in which it is not clear that an item of episcopal or papal teaching is proposed infallibly, there is good reason for assuming that such teaching pertains to revelation. The good reason, he adds, is the office which is divinely given and the grace that accompanies it.[39] If Grisez were correct, it would seem that any theologian who campaigned in favour of religious liberty (John Courtney Murray, for instance) before the magisterium changed its teaching, was wrong to do so. Some years ago, Richard McCormick addressed this very issue. Was the teaching of Pius IX in the *Syllabus of Errors* and his encyclical *Mirari vos* right, he asked, until corrected by the Vatican II document *Dignitatis humanae*?

> Or is it not that we came to see through experience and theological reflection what is right and then it could be authenticated by the magisterium? Even more concretely, what was John Courtney Murray to say when he was convinced of the truth of the doctrine eventually enshrined in *Dignitatis humanae*? Should he have said that it is not the doctrine of the Church but it is right —or it is not the doctrine of the Church and *therefore not right*? Surely not this latter. But unilateral emphasis on past formulated doctrine too easily leads to this cul-de-sac.[40]

Kevin Kelly points away from the cul-de-sac by highlighting the importance of the process of learning within the Church's life. We must, he says, respect the dynamism of this process. This dynamism requires that all the riches of genuine experience, interpretation and understanding which are to be found in the Church be shared as widely as possible. The good teacher is one who enables people to share. As collective understanding on particular issues develops, he or she will occasionally attempt to articulate it "in a way that does justice to the level of learning the group feels it has achieved". The teacher will, of course, have his or her own contribution to make, but that is incidental to the main teaching role just described. In fact, in cases where there are great riches to be shared within a group, the teacher's own contribution might be quite small:

> This is not to deny that within the Church the Pope, as supreme teacher, does not need the permission of the Church before he articulates its faith. However, it does mean that his articulation is binding because it is the faith of the Church that it articulates. His own personal viewpoint, as personal to him and not as an expression of the faith of the Church, will be listened to with respect, but individuals may disagree.

When well founded, appropriate, and honest, publicly expressed dissent seems to Kelly to be a way of positively and responsibly participating in the Church's learning process. In fact, maintaining silence could be seen as an avoidance of personal responsibility and as a form of disloyalty to the Church. Indeed, we might lead people astray if we maintained silence whilst believing that the guidance being given was not true or at least did not do full justice to the truth.[41]

As Kelly sees things, it would seem, dissent could be, at least in certain circumstances, a necessary part of the role of the moral theologian (and, indeed, of other kinds of theologian). That, no doubt, is also true of Charles Curran. In the latter half of the 1980s he noted that probably the majority of Catholic theologians who had written on the subject round about that time saw the role of the Roman Catholic theologian as "somewhat independent and cooperative in relationship to the hierarchical office and not delegated or derivative from the role of pope and bishops". He or she should theologise within the context of Catholic faith and should give due importance to the various *loci theologici*, included among which are the teachings of the magisterium. This somewhat independent and cooperative role, he notes, seems to be indicated too in the general ecclesiology of Vatican II and in the general understanding of theologians presented by that Council. In the Code of Canon Law which came into effect in 1983, however, the role of the theologian is seen "as primarily derived from the hierarchical teaching office and functioning by reason of delegation given by the hierarchical teaching office".[42]

Grisez's vision of the role of the theologian would seem to be closer to that expressed in the Code of Canon Law than to that favoured by Curran. He does not expect theologians to be mere puppets in the hands of the hierarchy, and accepts that, before Vatican II, too much conformity was required of them. They have an active role to play in eliciting "the testimony of witnesses of faith on matters about which the magisterium must judge". In doing so, theologians act with the authority that comes from scholarly expertise, an authority which the magisterium should respect. However, he says, it is not for theologians to judge. Only the magisterium may decide whether and when to make a judgement.[43] At first sight, this may seem to be not too far removed from Kelly's comments about the Pope's articulation of the faith of the Church. Many (perhaps most) Roman Catholic moral theologians, however, lay some emphasis on the importance of individual assessment of magisterial statements. This raises the subject of conscience. Josef Fuchs points out that the magisterium can achieve significance in a person's life only via his or her responsibly formed conscience. He also recalls Thomas Aquinas' affirmation that an ecclesiastical decision judged in conscience to be certainly unacceptable should not be followed, even if such refusal will result in one's dying excommunicated.[44] Like Fuchs, most of the moral theologians whom Grisez labels as dissenters appear to lay greater emphasis than he does on the importance of the individual conscience when faced with hierarchical teaching. Here, it would seem, lies the core of much of the difference between his ecclesiology and theirs. More than a few, one imagines would endorse the following words of Robert J. Smith:

> Rather than conscience serving the final decision-making process of individuals who are striving to reason from universal natural law principles to practical possibilities, Grisez regards conscience as that which helps individuals make the "Church's teaching one's own". In fact, "this work of appropriation is a task for conscience". This would seem to place the cart before the horse. Taking Grisez at his word, individual decisions of conscience must give way to church teachings. Individuals must conform to the church's teaching even before it is genuinely and truly their own. Such an approach abdicates personal responsibility —personal responsibility, not moral subjectivism— and implies that one might or even ought to go against one's own freely and maturely formed conscience.[45]

Grisez might respond to all this by claiming that his ecclesiology is closer to that of John Paul II than is that of those moral theologians he describes as dissenters. That may even be the case, but it is not a sufficient argument to condemn their disagreeing with the magisterium. A glance at the New Testament reminds us that tension arising from disagreement has been in the Church since the early days. It is not necessarily the cancer that Grisez seems to think it is. Expressed in love, it can contribute to the growth of the Church and to our common search for truth. One's openness to other opinions, moreover, should surely stretch far beyond the boundaries of one's own denomination.

NOTES

1   Max L. Stackhouse, "Church", in *A New Dictionary of Christian Ethics*, edited by John Macquarrie and James Childress (London: SCM Press, 1990), p.90.
2   *LCL*, p.174.
3   In fact, Grisez seldom uses the full title 'Roman Catholic Church'. He usually refers simply to 'the Catholic Church'.
4   *LCL*, pp.173-74.
5   *CMP*, pp.737-38.
6   *LCL*, p.174. On page 2 of *DMQ* Grisez states that Catholic faith includes two beliefs: "that only someone invincibly ignorant of the obligation to belong to Christ's Church can be saved outside her (see *LG* 14, *AG* 7), and that Christ's Church subsists fully in the Catholic Church, but not fully in the Orthodox churches, although they are, in most respects, truly and richly Christian (see *UR* 2-3, 13-18; *CCC* 838)". The first three

abbreviations refer to documents of the Second Vatican Council: *Lumen gentium, Ad gentes*, and *Unitatis redintegratio*. The fourth refers to *Catechism of the Catholic Church*.

7   *CMP*, p.745.
8   Germain Grisez and Russell Shaw, *Fulfillment in Christ: a Summary of Christian Moral Principles* (Notre Dame: University of Notre Dame Press, 1991), p.135.
9   Recently it has also been applied to the pope and bishops themselves.
10   Avery Dulles, "Doctrinal Authority for a Pilgrim Church", in *Readings in Moral Theology No. 3: the Magisterium and Morality*, edited by Charles E. Curran and Richard A. McCormick (New York: Paulist Press, 1982), pp.251ff.
11   Various points of view concerning the role of the magisterium in regard to moral teachings are expressed in the above mentioned *Readings in Moral Theology No. 3*.
12   *CMP*, pp.840-42.
13   Germain Grisez and Russell Shaw, *Fulfillment in Christ*, pp.416-17. Here they are apparently interpreting the teaching of *Lumen gentium* that the faithful should accept and adhere to the teaching of the bishops with *religioso obsequio*, and that *religiosum obsequium* of will and intellect should be shown in a special way to the authentic teaching authority of the pope, even when he is not speaking ex cathedra (*Lumen gentium*, 25). There has been some debate among Roman Catholic theologians during the last three decades concerning the exact meaning to be attributed to '*religiosum obsequium*'. Grisez and Shaw translate it here as 'religious assent'. Such a translation would seem to be acceptable to many, but it would also seem to be the case that some of those who accept it dispute the weight and exact meanings to be attributed to 'religious' and 'assent'.
14   *LCL*, pp.47-8. Grisez states that there are five cases in which people are not required to give religious assent: "(i) when popes and bishops express opinions on matters outside faith and morals, (ii) when they speak or write on matters of faith and morals but as individual believers or private theologians rather than in their official capacity, (iii) when they teach officially but only tentatively, (iv) when they put forward observations and arguments, without calling for acceptance in themselves, but as incidental to a truth of faith or a teaching which calls for religious assent, or (v) when they give merely disciplinary directives, for example, that certain opinions should not be taught while certain others may be. In all these cases, one's responsibility is not to assent, but to listen respectfully, try to understand what the pastors are saying, and obey any disciplinary directives" (ibid., p.49).
15   *CMP*, p.854.
16   Pius IX, *Syllabus of Errors*, 77 and 78.
17   For more information see Francesco Compagnoni, "Capital Punishment and Torture in the Tradition of the Roman Catholic Church", *Concilium*, 120 (1979), pp.39-53. In an address to the Sixth Congress of International Penal Law in October 1953, Pope Pius XII said that physical and psychic torture must be excluded from judicial investigation. He quoted from the letter of Nicholas I, but made no reference to the contrary teaching of Innocent IV or of any other pope who had permitted torture.
18   *CMP*, p.220. 'DS' refers to Henricus Denzinger and Adolfus Schönmetzer, *Enchiridion symbolorum definitionum et declarationum de rebus fidei et morum*, ed.

34 (Freiburg im Breisgau: Herder, 1967). 'DH' refers to *Dignitatis humanae*, the Declaration on Religious Liberty of the Second Vatican Council.

19   *CMP*, p.884.

20   Bernard Hoose, *Received Wisdom?: Reviewing the Role of Tradition in Christian Ethics* (London: Geoffrey Chapman, 1994), pp.20-21.

21   Bernard Hoose, "Proportionalists, Deontologists and the Human Good", *Heythrop Journal*, 33 (1992), pp.175-91.

22   Robert P. George, "Liberty under the Moral Law: B. Hoose's Critique of the Grisez-Finnis Theory of Human Good", *Heythrop Journal* 34 (1993), pp.178-179.

23   *CMP*, p.840.

24   W.F. Hogan, "Syllabus of Errors", in *New Catholic Encyclopedia* (New York: McGraw-Hill, 1967), p.855. One imagines the editors had not noticed the clash between this and the contents of the then quite recently published document *Dignitatis humanae* (December, 1965), which had presumably appeared after the time of Hogan's writing, but before the date of publication of this edition of the encyclopedia.

25   Daniel C. Maguire, "Morality and Magisterium", *Readings in Moral Theology No. 3*, p.35.

26   John C. Ford and Germain Grisez, "Contraception and the Infallibility of the Ordinary Magisterium", *Theological Studies*, 39 (1978), pp.258-312.

27   *Lumen gentium* 25. The translation is by Ford and Grisez, "Contraception", p.263.

28   Ford and Grisez, "Contraception", pp.273-74.

29   Ibid., p.312.

30   Joseph Komonchak, "*Humanae vitae* and its Reception: Ecclesiological Reflections", *Theological Studies*, 39 (1978), p.247.

31   Ibid., p.250.

32   *CMP*, p.847.

33   Frank Mobbs, *Beyond its Authority: the Magisterium and Matters of Natural Law* (Alexandria, New South Wales: E.J. Dwyer, 1997), pp.300-1.

34   Ibid., p.234.

35   Ibid., pp.2-3.

36   Germain Grisez, "Infallibility and Specific Moral Norms: a Review Discussion", in *The Thomist*, 49 (1985), p.250.

37   Mobbs, *Beyond its Authority*, p.273.

38   Ibid., pp.281-85. His emphasis.

39   Ibid., p.852.

40   Richard A. McCormick, *Notes on Moral Theology 1965 through 1980* (Washington D.C.: University Press of America, 1981), p.660.

41   Kevin Kelly, "Comments on the Curran Case: PRO the Learning Church", in *Readings in Moral Theology No. 6: Dissent in the Church*, edited by Charles E. Curran and Richard A. McCormick (New York: Paulist Press, 1988), pp.475-77.

42   Charles E. Curran, "Public Dissent in the Church", in *Readings in Moral Theology No. 6*, pp.391-92.

43   Germain Grisez, "How to Deal with Theological Dissent", in *Readings in Moral Theology No. 6*, pp.456-60.

44   Josef Fuchs, "Conscience and Conscientious Fidelity", in *Moral Theology:*

     Challenges for the Future, ed. Charles E. Curran (New York: Paulist Press, 1990), p.120.

45   Robert J. Smith, *Conscience and Catholicism: the Nature and Function of Conscience in Contemporary Roman Catholic Moral Theology* (Lanham, Maryland: University Press of America, 1998), p.61.

Part III:

Moral Fields

9 Respect for Life in Germain Grisez's Moral Theology

Dave Leal

Introduction

The most superficial acquaintance with Germain Grisez's writings will give a strong sense of the significance within his work of the theme of respect for life. Apart from books on the specific themes of abortion and euthanasia, large parts of the *Way of the Lord Jesus* series comprise theoretical expositions of the nature of proper respect for life, as well as continuing and developing reflections on abortion, euthanasia, warfare, capital punishment and the control of human reproductive capacities.

A superficial acquaintance may convince one of this much, but it may not indicate the specific understanding of respect for life which is contained within these works. A few aspects may be familiar. 'Life' is one of the eight basic goods or values identified by Grisez.[1] These values, being incommensurable, cannot be used to serve the theoretical requirements of a system of moral judgement founded upon consequences or outcomes. Thus, life may not be traded for some other good in any form of ethically grounded exchange. Secondary instances of primary goods —knowledge relating to human health and the treatment of disease, for example, as a specific instance of the good of knowledge— cannot legitimately be derived from any process in which the destruction of life is a means to that end of knowledge. Now, there will be much to discuss in any practical example falling under such a description, including such matters as the discriminability of means from any other effects of an action, and the discernment of whether a specific action does indeed constitute a destruction of life. (We would need to ask whether, for example, destroying an early conceptus or pre-embryo[2] is an attack on the good of

203

life.) We shall begin our investigation with an account of the way in which respect for life operates in the broader context of Grisez's moral theology, and of the understanding of 'life' which is at stake.[3]

Respect for Life as Love of God

A characteristic feature of Grisez's moral thought is its acceptance of the rôle of moral norms, of lawlike generalisations applicable without exception to human action. There is, specifically, a class of moral norms which constitute absolute prohibitions; norms which specify classes of action which ought never to be actualised in human conduct. Some of these norms relate to respect for life, such as 'do not murder', 'do not contracept' (that is, do not act against the potential fecundity of sexual intercourse); they are specifications of the norm (a norm which can be stated universally but in practice requires such further articulation) that one should not attack the good of life. This is an exemplification of the principle that no basic good be directly attacked; these prohibitions are not, then, instrumentally related to some further or higher good.

To make this last point is not simply to express the distance between Grisez's approach and some forms of rule utilitarianism, where subordinate norms are claimed to coexist with and to serve a higher source of moral value. The difficulties of developing a robust form of rule utilitarianism are well enough known. In practice, many utilitarian moral philosophers betray a commitment to more than one value in their work (say, autonomy *and* happiness), having no clear standard of commensuration to resolve cases of conflict. Their 'rules' (for example, 'respect autonomy') serve a much more informal and episodic purpose than might have been hoped. Even if an adequate rule utilitarianism were possible, it would still be the case that the rules, and obedience to the rules, would have an instrumental rôle. The justification of the rules will require access by human reason to a universally applicable scale of evaluation, a common 'moral metric', against which all human action, indeed the value of all human life, must be measured. There are good philosophical arguments against such commensurability, but a theologically more decisive argument against it lies in its impersonal value-monism. What doctrine of creation, what doctrine of God, does it imply or leave room for? The answer 'none' is potentially ambiguous between on the one hand a moral-theological neutrality (ethics and theology are distinct) and on the other of an implicit, untheological idolatry of *something* (and here, for 'something', we may insert whatever name the value happens to be given at the time of reading;

pleasure and happiness are familiar examples, but they by no means exhaust the field).

In contrast to this, Grisez's moral thinking is, at least its foundations, unambiguously Christian, informed throughout by a recognition of the particular creative and redemptive activity of the Trinitarian God of Christian orthodoxy.[4] If norms are derivable from goods, goods are themselves the result of God's free expression of Himself in creation. The purpose of that creation involves its fulfilment in the free realisation of itself through love of God and love of neighbour. The fulfilment of *itself*, not of some abstract value independent of itself. Its fulfilment through *love*; insofar as its acts serve this fulfilment, they are, in and of themselves, acts of love.

This last point, which I take to be vital for Grisez, and to mark a distance between himself and some Protestant moral theologians, is worthy of further comment. *Moral* obligation, at least, is not arbitrary, as if God were simply to make some whimsical demand which human beings would be obliged to obey, albeit out of love for Him. The particularity of God's creative act implies something of moral substance, and human activity in accordance with that moral substance *is* love for God.

A couple of reflections are needed on this. Firstly, a frequent concern in Grisez's reflection upon practical cases is the way in which behaviour may *appear* to proceed in accordance with, or against, some moral norm, whilst the correct evaluation of the human act needs to take the agent's intention into account. A couple of examples will make the point well enough. If killing in war is ever legitimate, a particular and otherwise licit instance of such killing could be vitiated purely by personal malice. If contraception is illegitimate, the taking of a 'contraceptive' pill[5] under medical supervision in order to control health-endangering menstrual problems could be, in appropriate circumstances, morally obligatory. So 'human activity' is a complex notion, bound up with the inner life of the individual. Secondly, and to extend this, it might even turn out to be the case that any and all authentically good moral action could require a *conscious* acknowledgement of God as author and goal of human life, though this is to go beyond what is required for an account of Grisez's work, and is an implication which I do not think he himself would draw.

So, on this view, it appears that moral action *is* (an aspect of) love of God, and not an instrumental means towards a higher good of loving God, though the question of consciousness of God as a criterion of moral action remains to be faced, and could constitute a significant point of discussion. Now, if loving God is (at least in this aspect of moral action) respect for goods, it remains to be stated that respect for goods is not accomplished solely by the performance of particular acts in the service of those goods.

A core element of the theory of goods is that *each and every* human action be carried out respecting *all* of the goods. Respect for life, then, may have a special significance in the decisions of the government roads minister, or of the engineer planning the decommissioning of a nuclear power station, but it carries a pervasive significance for each of us in all of our actions. 'Respect' here amounts to a criterion of non-violation, but this is in itself significant, because it may serve to draw our attention to aspects of our lives which require closer scrutiny. Perhaps it amounts to the wearing of a cycle helmet when travelling to work by bicycle. Perhaps it involves not using certain aromatherapy oils for massage during pregnancy. Central to this general observation is the broadening of our understanding of 'respect for life' from the particular preserve of specialists in medicine or defence policy and enactment; a broadening not simply to less obvious categories of professional, but to *all* people in *all* of their actions.

Where Do Moral Norms Come From?

Central to the above account was a claim that respect for life (and for the other goods central to Grisez's account of moral reality) is grounded in the right ordering of creation, and therefore ultimately in the ground of creation, which is to say in God.[6] If this is the case, the way seems to be open for a radically *theological* account of the discernment of moral norms.[7] Yet what we actually find is an account of the discernment of moral norms which renders them knowable in a theologically neutral fashion, which is to say *via* a particular account of (or form of) 'natural law'. In this account, the perception of the basic goods *as* good is something which is accessible to human reason, though not by any process of *a priori* reasoning, or by derivation from biological or medical data. The central account of the process is in *Christian Moral Principles*, 5D, and involves (in its more schematic presentation) "noticing the assumptions implicit in one's practical reasoning and that of other individuals and deliberative assemblies".[8] *Noticing the implicit assumptions* — assumptions which, as it were, ground the intelligibility of one's practical reasoning by expressing the perception(s) of good which informs its particular judgements. At a more specific level, an indication of the names of the goods may be had by noticing the point where one's justifications of one's actions —one's responses to the question 'why?', asked successively to each justification— reach an end.

As Grisez notes, this may be a problematic procedure in a number of ways.[9] There is, for example, the possibility that a response offered could admit of a number of interpretations or classifications whilst still appearing appropriately 'final', and here a degree of imaginative investigation will be required. There is also the possibility that a good may be justified instrumentally when it is *supposed* to be (according to Grisez) a *basic* human good. I may justify my pursuit of life and health, not as goods in themselves, but as instrumental means to the obtaining of some other perceived good, such as the fulfillment of an artistic goal, or the pursuit of a vendetta against an enemy. I can say, with sincerity and intelligibility, "If I thought I'd never finish composing the symphony, I'd commit suicide tomorrow; it's the only thing which gives purpose to living".

Reflections of this sort may *seem* to relativise the supposed basicality of the good of life, and the norms associated with it. We may recognise the important distinction which Grisez makes between sensible and intelligible goods[10] and account for some of the above as a prioritising of sensible over intelligible goods, yet the issue seems to run deeper. Are the intelligible goods constituted as good by our perception of them, so that differing perceptions of the goods or their basicality undermine the supposed universality of Grisez's list of eight? As suggested above,[11] he himself has licensed a modest expansion of the list, which might raise suspicions. In fact, it appears that the rationality of the list of goods resides in their proving plausible, *both* at first sight *and* on reflection, to Grisez's readership. This is an important test; the only test, indeed, which seems available to anyone with a continuing commitment to the distinction of 'is' and 'ought'. It need not follow that there is no other 'ground' for the goods. The nature of the "requirement set by a judgment upon free choice between open alternatives" which is necessary for "moral normativity"[12] may be a *perception* of good, but that good must be in some importantly independent and objective sense a *real* good.[13]

This summary and incomplete exposition of Grisez's thought[14] raises many questions which cannot be pursued but merely mentioned here. The model of freedom envisaged, in which free choice is exercised as an abstract consideration of alternatives, raises questions both for action theory and the narrower issue of the nature of human freedom. The acceptance and adoption of a version of the fact-value distinction, so called, raises important issues in its own right.[15] It seems entirely possible for Christian thinking to pursue the question of moral norms on the basis of its own theological resources, and to trust in their intelligibility more directly on the basis of a theology of God and of creation. The importance of this point is not that such a grounding could serve as an alternative account of the nature and basis of such norms, where either account would (for practical purposes) do just as well. The extent to which we are able correctly to discern goods, and to reason on the basis of them, are matters which themselves demand to be subjected to theological scrutiny, and concerning which it scarcely needs to be added that there is great controversy. In any event, Grisez's own thought is determined by its faithfulness to a particular understanding of ecclesiology, so that the resources for discerning moral norms are by no means limited to his 'natural law' moral epistemology. All of the matters discussed above serve as a background to the issue of respect for life in Grisez's thought.

The Meaning of 'Life'

A. *When Grisez speaks of respect for (human) life, this is not identical with pure respect for earthly bodily life.* The fullest meaning of 'life' is not exhausted by human bodily life as currently experienced in the world. 'Life' as a basic human good is about more than this. This 'more' is not an historical 'more', a 'something else to look forward to', but is part of the meaning of 'life' in the present (see *Christian Moral Principles*, 1G.4 and *Living a Christian Life*, 8A.2a, where the phrases "a unity of coprinciples" [of body and soul], and "constitutive *part*" [italics mine] are used).

B. *Respect for life is not respect for something other than bodily life.* Whatever the good of life amounts to, it at least includes the good of bodily life.[16] This is an important point to note, because it offers a point of resistance to any claim that 'spiritual' life, or the life of the soul, might be set over against bodily life. The soul is (for Grisez) conceptually distinct from the body, but human life *is* (at least) bodily life, and the eternal life to which Christians look forward is or includes physical life. The hope of resurrection is an integral part of the hope of eternal life, not an arbitrary fact of the kind of life which God happens to have chosen for human beings to enjoy.

C. *Respect for life appears to be respect for* human *life.* The goods are presented as basic *human* goods, goods which fulfil (human) persons, and life is one of them. This means at least that life is among those goods which are discerned as the non-arbitrary basis of our judgements of practical reasoning. It also (a further point which need not belong with that first observation) appears to place *human* life at the heart of concern over respect for life.

The Meaning of Life

From the indications A to C set out in the previous section, along with the observations that one must never act against any good directly, and that one must respect all the goods in all one's actions, we may begin to trace an outline of Grisez's views of respect for life. Clearly, one aspect of this will be the insistence that human bodily life is an aspect of life, and worthy of respect. To attack bodily life —to kill— is to attack the good of life, so no forms of proportionate or utilitarian reasoning can legitimately weigh bodily life against any other good in an attempt to judge right or wrong action. A temptation for some Christians might be rather different; to view bodily life as being *other than* 'real' life, even to the point where martyrdom is seen as a sacrifice of bodily life for eternal life. Yet such a transactional approach is ruled out. It fails to respect the good of bodily life, reducing its destruction to a means by which to obtain some *other* good thing (eternal life). It is bad action because it attacks a good, but there is an ironic dimension to this particular action, too; it fails to recognise the intimate relation of the good sacrificed and the good sought. The good of eternal life is actually much more intimately linked to bodily life than such an agent could comprehend. In the tradition of the analysis and categorisation of actions, such an act of seeking or even accepting bodily death *for the sake of* eternal life could not be counted as a genuine martyrdom.

Respect for Life and Environmental Responsibility

The importance of noting that respect for life appears to constitute respect for *human* life is most obviously seen in the way in which questions of environmental responsibility are handled. It is true that the question of environmental responsibility should not be reduced narrowly to questions of respect for life; the insistence that human beings respect all goods in all their acts makes the inclusion of possible aesthetic violations integral to our handling of such issues, for example. Even acknowledging this, it must be admitted that there is a strong possibility that the closure of 'goods' to 'goods perceived by humans' may relax the Christian's sense of an injunction to stewardship-of-the-creation as a thing of value for reasons other than its instrumental importance to human beings. Given that questions of responsibility in the fields of ecology and environment have become both pervasive and pressing in just about every area of human activity for some decades now, the relatively slender place given to such issues in Grisez's works is something calling for comment.

It may be that the comment which needs making simply is that these were not the questions dealt with in the published volumes. The absence of comment does not imply that there is no comment worth making, nor that the theory may not provide a natural law basis for some radical revisions of human activity as it relates to and affects the environment and non-human creatures in it. We do not have the space here to do more than point up a contrast between two approaches.[17]   One is that of instrumental justification; it really matters how we behave towards our environment, but it does so because it has a real effect upon human life, positively or negatively. Deforestation matters because it diminishes the health of the planet, where that phrase 'health of the planet' is cashed out as constituted by certain facts regarding the planet's capacity to sustain human life. It is sometimes claimed that the justification for not harming non-human animals lies in our capacity to be seduced by such harm into more easily sliding into cruelty to human beings; the reason to not harm animals is, then, instrumentally justified by its further effects on *human* relationships.

An alternative is to see all of the creation as due respect, and animal life as valuable *in itself*. The cashing out of that 'in itself' is not such an easy task, but it is likely at least to assert the value of *each* animal. A contrast can be made between that and those who give value to animal life only through the value of each *species*. Those who support the species as the bearer of value may do so by commitment to biodiversity; and the value of biodiversity may be seen in its contribution to human well-being by (say) providing the broadest possible resource for exploitation by medical science. (It would also be possible to have a specifically 'religious' vision underwriting a commitment to biodiversity, a kind of moral-ecological cosmology.) If Christians were to take the value of the creation to be grounded in its createdness and thus in its relationship to God the Creator, the value of each animal, and of the life-supporting qualities of the environment, would be justified in an entirely non-instrumental way. This need not imply an attitude of environmental quietism; stewardship may have positive implications of tending and caring. Nor, quite specifically, need it imply vegetarianism, though it may do so where this is possible and consistent with other duties.

The important distinction here is between a pure instrumentality which sees human fulfilment as a thing to be achieved even over against the rest of the creation (which serves as a resource for aspects of that fulfilment), and a proper stewardship which may admit of some hierarchy of values but in which, by a suitable admission of the distinction of wants and needs, and a recognition of the satisfaction of *need* as a proper limit, humans see that respect for life may both be, first of all, respect for human life, but then, secondly, and in a way which bears a close relation to the first, respect for life in the whole of creation. It has been admitted that environmental responsibility will be more than 'respect for life', but it may surely include this. Intriguingly, Margaret Atkins[18] identifies the more instrumental view with Thomas Aquinas, and the alternative view with Augustine. Perhaps the influence of Thomas on Grisez's thought is a significant factor here? In any event, the application of Grisez's thought to this area of moral inquiry would be a matter of great interest.

Respect for Life and Control of Conception

Enough has been said already to indicate that specific themes in the area of respect for life range much more widely than standard discussion topics of abortion, euthanasia and reproduction technologies might indicate. It is also worth adding that 'life' is not treated as an isolated good by Grisez, but associated with health and bodily integrity, and a complete treatment of his discussion would need to do justice to these related concerns. However, there is value in including in our treatment an indication of the shape of his discussion of a particular area of respect for life.

Control of conception has been selected as offering an opportunity to discuss some special aspects of Grisez's approach to these questions, whilst also being an area of deep disagreement between Christian authors. It is also an area where health service developments, at least in the United Kingdom, raise serious questions of public policy. An experiment has been announced for the Lothian area of Scotland in which women are given 'medicine cabinet' supplies (five doses) of an abortifacient drug.[19] The public policy justification for this experiment lies in an attempt to reduce the number of abortions; which is to say (depending on one's classification of the effects of the drug) to reduce the number of *later* abortions.[20] It seems quite possible that other Catholic theologians could justify such a move, as (a) mitigated in moral seriousness by the status of the conceptus, and (b) having the potential to constitute an affirmation of personal autonomy for the woman concerned. I take it that a view of this kind might be the logical outcome of some of Jean Porter's commitments, expressed at different points in her book *Moral Action and Christian Ethics*, though whether she draws this conclusion herself I am not sure.[21]

Now, it is clear that such a move cannot be expected from Grisez. Insofar as there is human life deserving of moral respect (and in particular, deserving of the respect which consists in the non-violation of life), that respect is due from the moment of conception. That respect is not to be identified with a commitment to the furtherance of 'bodily life at all costs' for the developing foetus, any more than it would be for an adult human being. Presuming the context to be one where the users of health care services and medical practitioners are all people of good will, there seems no reason why ante-natal scanning should not be used to assist in the diagnosis of poor foetal development, nor why the results of such investigations should not lead to a judgement that some treatment, though possible, is unreasonable in the circumstances.

We will return to the problem of abortifacient drugs in the next section. We now turn to the use of contraceptive techniques properly so-called. In so doing, we will agree with Grisez that the proper context for this discussion is that of marriage, and the question to be asked is whether married couples may properly utilise contraceptive techniques, which might be (for example) barrier methods or chemical-hormonal ones, in an attempt to render their sexual intercourse non-fecund. Grisez interprets this as an attack on the good of *life*. A natural first reaction to this claim is to imagine that, whatever sort of attack on the good of life it is, it must be one quite different in kind from the attack sub-categorised as abortion. In the latter, a *particular* human life is attacked. In the former, there is no particular life to attack. The attempted prevention of a life is not the attempted prevention of any particular life, and that not because there is a random, though specific, life which is prevented, so that it is merely one's *intention* which is not focused on a specific individual!

Surprisingly, though, Grisez is inclined to assimilate the cases of abortion and contraception. Contraception does indeed constitute a failure to respect life, in his view, in a way quite closely analogous to abortion. The thought appears to be as follows:

> A married couple determine that their sexual intercourse be rendered infertile, insofar as available techniques, and their skill in using them, permit. The intention which they form is an intention to prevent a life occurring. It makes no sense to ask, "Which life are they preventing?"; insofar as they are successful, there is no life (or: are no lives) to point at as the life which forms the object of any failure of respect. Yet their intention is still that *something* be prevented. Imagine that they failed in their intention. (This act of imagination need not depend upon the dependability of the technique, or the capacity for the couple's utilisation of it, to fail; even if both were 100% guaranteed, the argument would have the same status.) The 'failure' here would take practical shape in the form of the conception of a particular human individual. This failure

cannot be vague, but only exist in this quite specific form. Because of this, we can only characterise their intention (in terms of its concrete outcome) as the intention to *prevent a particular occurrence* —that is, the coming to be of a particular life —and therefore their intention is precisely lacking in respect for life.[22]

This is an intriguing claim, and one which deserves to be taken seriously. Though there is no specifiable human individual whose life is attacked by contraceptive practice,[23] it makes no sense to discuss contraceptive practice without acknowledging that the lives prevented must be *particular* lives (albeit, because prevented, not the lives of particular nameable human individuals).

That there is a problem with this argument can be brought out by the presentation of a situation which is, I suggest, entirely plausible. Imagine a couple to have decided (perhaps for the present time only, leaving their decisions in, say, a decade's time entirely open) that for now they will engage in sexual intercourse in such a way that, and with the intention that, conception be prevented. However, they discover that in spite of their contraceptive practice their intercourse has resulted in pregnancy. It is, of course, possible for them to regard this as a 'wholly new situation'. Whatever their intentions were, their intentions now will be directed towards the health and well-being of the child. I take it that Grisez will hold that this must constitute a change of intention; there could be no fixed intention, sustained through the conception, first to prevent the conception but then to accept the conception and nurture it. It is certainly the case, by contrast, that there are couples who, having experienced 'failure' in their contraceptive practice, feel justified in seeking to procure an abortion, and thereby demonstrate some consistency in their intentions.

Such is not the case with the couple we are interested in, however. It may be that they recognise the possibility of contraceptive failure in advance, so that they self-consciously accept that engaging in sexual intercourse using contraceptive techniques may still result in pregnancy. Yet even this degree of consciousness is not required. What *is* required is the distinction drawn between 'the conception' which they are trying to prevent, and 'the conception' which has actually occurred. Their activity in contraceptive intercourse might be claimed to be activity designed to prevent *any* conception, and that universal must include the particular conception which actually occurs; thus, this conception is against their intention. That is, I think, Grisez's picture of the situation, and it is certainly an accurate picture of the couple who then resort to an abortion.

Our couple, however shocked they may have been by the news, never even considered abortion a possibility. Having discovered the pregnancy, finding themselves in the presence of developing life, their actions have been oriented towards nurture and care. If we do not say that their intention has changed, what can we say? We can say that their intention is shown to have been an intention to prevent conception whilst engaging in sexual intercourse; but also that their intention can be clumsily expressed as an intention to prevent any conception except that which actually occurs! They may, in other words, engage in sexual intercourse hoping that there will be no conception as a result, and even praying this (leaving to one side whether this ought to be prayed or not), whilst not foreclosing the possibility that the answer to their prayers may be a child. This must, after all, surely be the practical situation of the Catholic couple who engage in forms of 'natural family planning'.[24] Their intention, at least for the present, is to engage in sexual intercourse and yet do so in such a way as to minimise the likelihood of pregnancy, and yet they will surely be expected to embrace any pregnancy which comes. The apparently significant moral difference is in the choice of method: periodic abstinence, or such 'artificial' devices as hormonal regulation or barrier methods.

There are actually two questions to be asked here: first of all, whether the difference is morally significant; and secondly, whether Grisez is correct to identify its significance as lying in its relationship to the good of life. It seems quite possible to answer these question, in turn, 'yes' and 'no'. A defence of such a view might take the following form. Grisez acknowledges there to be two 'goods' of sexual intercourse, which we can label 'unitive' and 'procreative'.[25] These goods are held to be conceptually separable, but practically inseparable; for the unitive good to be available, the couple must fully respect the good of procreation. Now, the proof of 'openness' to the latter good might be seen in the refusal of the couple to seek to prevent conception. If the couple take the greatest of care to abstain from sexual intercourse when they believe conception to be biologically possible, their action looks like a certain form of respect for biological reality, but it is not in any obvious sense respect for life.

Oliver O'Donovan complains of at least certain expressions of the Catholic attitude towards contraceptive intercourse that they threaten an individuating of sexual acts, carrying with them "an unmistakeable hint of the pornographic".[26] Yet his own preferred way of approaching these questions, which appears to be seeing the whole marriage as the context for a history of sexual intercourse (in which perhaps contraceptive methods may have their place), faces an opposite danger. The goods of sexual intercourse in the life of the couple are seen to arise through their actual life of sexual intimacy, which is not separable from the physical reality of their individuated expressions of that intimacy in sexual intercourse. There is no 'broad view' of the couple's sexual life which is the bearer of the good. It is for this reason that Catholic critics of contraceptive methods are surely right to point out their effects upon the sexual intimacy of married people. If we leave to one side the possibility of voluntarily childless marriage, about which much more would need to be said than there is space for here, it will be enough to reflect upon the influence of contraceptive methods on the sexual intercourse of couples who have stopped using it, having decided that now they would like to 'start a family'. The experience of such couples seems often to be that their sexual intercourse has taken on a kind of either/or quality. *Now* it is for the sake of possible children (and must be suitably rationed to ensure quality and quantity of sperm); *once* it was for fun, maybe, or because something was desired which may have been the spouse but may just as easily have been the act of sexual intercourse objectified.

It seems that there is no easy way with these reflections. The Catholic couple who, in good conscience, regard the present time as a bad one for them to start a family, either abstain from intercourse or engage in it with the potential anxiety of anticipating infertile periods (by whatever permissible means). Their intention must not, of course, be contraceptive, though precisely what form of moral consciousness this imposes upon them is another matter. Couples who have used contraceptive methods may come to find that their sexual intercourse, when they stop using those methods, becomes solely 'for' an anticipated pregnancy (which is, note, no more specific than the pregnancy which contraception is designed to prevent!) The Catholic couple may have a better opportunity to experience the twin goods of sexual intercourse, in that their refusal of contraceptive intent may have made it less likely (*pace* O'Donovan?) that their intercourse will be 'objectified'. Yet for both couples the experience is a difficult one. If it seems likely that the couple who refuse contraceptive intercourse are closer to 'respecting all the basic goods in their actions', it is not because the other couple are necessarily acting against the good of *life*. It seems much more plausible that there is a threat to the integrity of sexual intercourse as a characteristic formative aspect of *marriage* present in the couple who embrace contraceptive practices. And to that extent Grisez's acceptance of marriage as a distinct good may help us to see something significant in the traditional Catholic prohibition.

The conclusion of this section of our reasoning must be as follows. The specific norms of action concerning contraceptive practice which are discussed in volume 2 of *The Way of the Lord Jesus* are claimed in that place to be supported specifically by respect for the good of life. If our discussion is correct this claim seems implausible, even on Grisez's own terms. By adding the good of marriage to the original list of seven goods, we find a more plausible justification emerging for the same norm. There can be no complaint, I think, regarding the revisability of the list of goods; this list is, after all, not 'given' immediately in moral intuition, but disclosed by reflection on our commitments and judgements. The revision may merely point to the difficulty involved in performing the task, which is itself a deeply significant matter. What is at least clear is the extent to which moral commitment and perception of goods must be mutually informative; for how, otherwise, could we come to the belief that our list of goods is not in fact a true representation of that part of moral reality which it claims to disclose?

Prevention of Implantation as an Attack on the Good of Life

We return at last to the question of the morality of those forms of 'contraception' often so-called which are effective in preventing implantation rather than conception.[27] To those who see the value of life, or life itself, as emergent through the development from conceptus to child, there may be no problem with interruption of the process at such a very early stage. For those who, with Grisez, regard the moment of conception as the point where life begins, and where therefore any direct attack on the developing life will be an attack on the good of life, the intention to perform such an action is clearly ruled out.[28] It is possible, of course, that the running together in medical educational literature of differing forms of prevention of pregnancy under the title 'contraceptive' might make those who would otherwise take exception to the particular effects of (say) the intra-uterine device (IUD) ignore those effects; indeed, they may be ignorant of the distinction altogether.

It is sometimes urged in support of the use of anti-implantation ('contragestive') techniques, and especially of the so-called 'morning after pill' when viewed in such a way, that the supposed high number of pre-embryos spontaneously evacuated pre-implantation reduce the moral significance of the intervention. How such an argument is intended to work is, however, obscure. Presumably there are two options: that the intervention in *this* case is rendered licit by the above observation; and that the apparent carelessness of 'nature' in the protection of the pre-embryo renders human beings less liable for any conscious and intended interruption of the process leading to implantation.

As to the first of these, the counter-argument is quick and decisive. Whatever may be the case following a large number of conceptions, this particular conception constitutes a life, and as such should be immune from intentional attack. The possible argument that, as we do not know whether a conception has occurred, the medication may not be doing anything, is of course ridiculous; if a conception has occurred then the contragestive substance should not be taken, and if it has not then there is no point in taking it at all.

The obvious complication lies in the possibility that the 'contragestive' may also have a potential contraceptive function if used at an opportune moment, for example by the prevention of ovulation. Now, by a suitable act of the imagination we may be able to conceive of a situation where prevention of pregnancy is regarded as necessary for a woman's health (it would be life-endangering), and where she has been raped. Here, the health-endangering aspect of any resulting pregnancy appears to count against certain alternative counsels which might be offered, such as to wait and see what will follow, and to accept a pregnancy if one should arise.

What might follow if the result were to be a pregnancy —the probable evaluation of life against life, perhaps of two deaths against one— is not the subject of our present inquiry, though it is clearly a limit case of moral reasoning, and quite plausibly one where moral reason (though not, of course, responsibility to God) runs out. What is rather to our purpose is to ask whether, if a woman were to be placed in a situation where she believed ovulation to be imminent, and to be preventable by some medication, she could be advised to take the medication, knowing that if ovulation had in fact occurred she could instead be preventing implantation and gestation. The decision might always be one made on balance of probabilities, and the moral seriousness of the decision might be gauged by the extent to which likelihood of ovulation having already occurred were consciously entertained and regarded as a genuine limit on the acceptability of the action. However, given that the act, even *qua* contraceptive act, can hardly be an attack on the good of *marriage* (which we suggested above, *contra* Grisez, to be the most plausible good to be directly at issue in reflection on contraceptive practice),[29] there seems no reason why a decision to take the medication could not be a responsible one, and proportionate in an appropriate sense.[30] This could be so, even within only a very modestly re-configured account of Grisez's reasoning on contraception, and utilising forms of moral thinking already implicit or explicit in his work.

The second possible avenue for embracing the use of contragestives on the basis of spontaneous evacuation of pre-embryos lay in the claim that the moral significance of such human intervention was diminished by the large number of such events in nature. It is worth remarking that the statistics often cited in this regard are highly speculative (agreeing with *LCL*, p. 497, though rejecting the 'probably' there as without foundation), and the reasons behind these claimed non-implantations are in any event little understood. If the reason were normally to lie in some defect of potential in the pre-embryo, this would certainly be no basis for intentional intervention in any case where the potential of the pre-embryo is as yet quite unknown.

In effect, the strongest argument here seems to be that nature exhibits a carelessness (or even a malice) which can justify intentional mimicry by human agents. Yet however a non-Christian might feel happy to resort to such a personification of nature, to the Christian this route is not open. Somehow the providential hand of God is to be seen in the operation of nature, whether by permission or positive action, but that word 'somehow' is not to be taken as an easy invitation to read off any convenient explanation whatever. In the face of events in nature which can be properly thought of as mysterious, it can hardly be judged reasonable to act in purported imitation of those events as we choose to interpret them, if in so doing we may be engaged in acts against life. Whether the unreasonableness of this is grounded in an abstract perception of basic goods, or in concrete moral norms grounded elsewhere (say, in 'the created order' or in special revelation), is another question.[31]

Conclusion

Two major things have been attempted in this essay: a review of Germain Grisez's moral theory as it contributes to an understanding of the good of life; and a discussion of an aspect of that theory specifically in relation to moral questions in the area of contraception and the prevention of pregnancy. This latter discussion has shown something of the importance to Grisez's theory, in arriving at and understanding particular moral norms, of getting the characterisation of those basic goods, of which life is claimed to be one, right. It has served as a reminder that the characterisation of the goods is always to some extent provisional, though not at all because of any provisionality or historicisation of that moral reality to which those perceptions of goods relate.

It is true, of course, that many people who would not wish to follow the moral theory outlined in Volume 1 of *The Way of the Lord Jesus* do nonetheless adopt (apparently quite intuitively) the language of life as a good, or speak of its 'sacredness' or 'intrinsic value'. However much they may instrumentalise the other goods in Grisez's list (knowledge or play, for example), this one at least is often held to have absolute value. The relationship of perception of norms and of the perception of basic goods in general as they appear in Grisez's theory constitutes an important avenue of inquiry, and the observation just made implies that there is an interesting range of data to be worked on in relation to the good of life. Regarding the specific theme of this paper, this relationship or norms to goods is important not simply for Grisez but for anyone who wishes to make the claim that life is a good, and that respect for life is required of us.

NOTES

1 The number eight (to include marriage as a distinct good, accountable independently of the other seven goods) follows the revisions of *The Way of the Lord Jesus*, vol 1: "Christian Moral Principles" (Chicago: Franciscan Herald Press, 1983), chapter 5, contained in Germain Grisez and Russell Shaw, *Fulfilment in Christ* (Notre Dame: University of Notre Dame Press, 1991), 5D and note 3 on p.439.

2 The 'pre-embryo' constitutes the developmental phase up to about 14 days after conception, when the so-called 'primitive streak' emerges. See (for example) Peter R. Braude and Martin H. Johnson, "The Embryo in Contemporary Medical Science", in G.R. Dunstan (ed.), *The Human Embryo* (Exeter: Exeter University Press, 1990). For Grisez's views, see *LCL*, 8D.1, "It is Reasonable to Hold that Human Persons Begin at Fertilization".

3 This essay is not an attempt to provide a general critique of Grisez's moral theology as a whole; in particular, the discussions in sections 7 and 8 try to provide an approach broadly sympathetic to that theory. This should not be taken as an endorsement of that theory, however.

4 Note the grounding of the sacredness of human life at *LCL*, 8A.1, "Human Life is Sacred because of its Relation to God".

5 It is important to note that the description of something as a contraceptive pill is grounded in expectations which we have regarding its labelling or normal usage; it does not exhaust the range of functions which the substance has. It could be used to regulate health-endangering irregularities in menstruation. A drug to deal with blood pressure problems may turn out to have an impact on problems of sexual impotence; what we *call* the drug (a 'blood pressure treatment' or 'an impotence treatment') depends on a variety of factors.

6 See especially *CMP*, p.122, where we are told: "... goods which can be sought for their own sake can also be regarded as means to an ulterior purpose or, more importantly, as contributions to a larger whole, all the way to the largest whole which is the consummation of everything in Christ (see Ephesians 1:9-10)".

7 For the importance of the thoroughly theological nature of moral reality to Grisez, see *CMP*, 1F.

8 *CMP*, 5D.3.

9 Ibid., p.124f.

10 Ibid., 5B.

11 In note 1.

12 *CMP*, p.113 n.21.

13 See Grisez's discussion of conscience in *CMP*, 3, and the relation of goods to human fulfilment given summary expression at ibid. 5D.4f.

14   An exposition which has had to omit (for example) discussions of such important themes as Grisez's use of the so-called 'principle of double effect' (*CMP*, 9F, 12F, 12: Appendix 3); see the discussion in the review of *Living a Christian Life* by Nigel Biggar in *Studies in Christian Ethics*, 8/1 (1995), pp.110ff.

15   For an exposition, see Finnis, *NLNR*, II.4, 5. For a skeptical voice, see G.E.M. Anscombe, "Modern Moral Philosophy", in her *Collected Philosophical Papers*, vol. III: "Ethics, Religion and Politics" (Oxford: Blackwells, 1981). See also O.M.T. O'Donovan, "John Finnis on Moral Absolutes", *Studies in Christian Ethics*, 6/2 (1993), pp.50ff., especially pp. 64-66 (republished in this volume as Chapter 4). These questions may strike to the heart, not of the content but of the epistemology inherent in Grisez's work; but they do so in a way which appears quite indifferent to the special question of respect for life.

16   See *CMP*, 5: Appendix 4; *LCL*, 8A.2, D.1c. See also the criticism of Grisez by Nigel Biggar, in his review in *Studies in Christian Ethics*, pp.113f.: "But surely he is wrong to argue that bodily life which no longer supports personal life *and cannot support it ever again* (because, for example, the upper part of the brain has been destroyed), remains intrinsically valuable?" (author's emphasis). What kind of 'cannot' is that? It could be, for example, that Grisez is perceiving the language of modality here through the eyes of the New Testament, and refuses the premise marked by the 'because' not on philosophico-medical grounds, but on specifically theological ones. If that is so, though, it surely compromises our capacity to discern in Grisez's moral writings an approach to questions of respect-for-life based upon anything recognisable as natural law reasoning.

17   The contrast is drawn from the paper "Flawed Beauty and Wise Use: Conservation and the Christian Tradition" by Margaret Atkins, *Studies in Christian Ethics*, 7/1 (1994), pp.1-16.

18   In the article cited in the previous note.

19   An early reaction to this experiment was reported in *The Times* newspaper for 9 July 1999 ("'Morning after' pill available on demand"). It contains the paragraph (presumably reporting the aspirations of 'pregnancy advisory services') that "Fifteen per cent of British women have used emergency contraception in the past two years, according to government figures. It is hoped that with the availability of the pills, the figure will increase to as much as 50 per cent to counter a rising abortion rate". See also "French schools to provide morning-after pill", *The Times*, 1 December 1999.

20   The British Medical Association, through their literature, and some General Practitioners, have developed a habit of terming such potentially abortifacient drugs 'contraceptives'. This raises important questions regarding their effects, because it appears possible that they may indeed prevent conception if it has not yet occurred. (The earlier report mentioned in the previous footnote presents the delay of ovulation as the only immediate effect.) If it *has* occurred, however, the effect of the drug is potentially abortifacient. By classifying the drug as 'contraceptive', we may find our attention drawn towards one aspect of its potential, quite legitimately. Equally, we may (whether deliberately or not) find our attention distracted from an obvious aspect of the range of effects which the drug may have.

21   Jean Porter, *Moral Action and Christian Ethics* (Cambridge: CUP, 1996), pp.54-8, 114-15. I take it that, however restricted a rôle autonomy is allowed to play in her understanding of the moral life, there is at least a serious question whether the value of the very early conceptus (see pp.119-24) is such as to override any restriction of autonomy.

22   See, for example, the phrase used in the "Summary" on p. 459 of *Living a Christian Life*: "But even true contraceptive acts, considered in moral terms, are contralife, since one who chooses to contracept chooses to prevent *a new instance of the basic good of life*". The emphasis here is mine. I am trying in the above paragraph to capture the thought of *LC L*, 8E.2d.

23   Perhaps where contraceptive practice *has* failed, and conception has resulted, one may feel inclined to describe the outcome as the coming-to-be of a specific individual whose life the parents were intending to prevent. This is precisely the point where issue should be taken with the argument.

24   See the discussion in *LCL*, 8E.2e, where Grisez acknowledges the possibility that abstinence may (through the contraceptive intention of the couple) amount to contraception in his terms. On p.511 of this discussion he introduces an argument regarding episodic natural infertility which seems clearly related to Oliver O'Donovan's objections (see below). It appears, in any event, that the acceptability of marital intercourse when good reasons to avoid pregnancy are present is reduced to those times when the couple may be *certain* that pregnancy will not occur. It is only sexual intercourse at such times which *cannot* be contraceptive in intent, for they realise that no conception is *possible*. At the least we may say that any legitimate reasons for avoiding pregnancy impose limits on the legitimacy of intercourse; where pregnancy is even the remotest risk, if pregnancy must be avoided, so must sexual intercourse. Thus the Catholic prohibition, at least read in this fashion, is not particularly or especially 'about' so-called artificial means of contraception; contraceptive intent may be present even in so-called natural methods, too.

25   See "The Christian Family as the Fulfilment of Sacramental Marriage", in *Studies in Christian Ethics*, 9/1 (1996), pp.23-33, especially pp. 29-30 n.20. (I am not sure that the 'part of' language in this expression of the relation of the two goods is an accurate reflection of that relationship.)

26   O.M.T. O'Donovan, *Resurrection and Moral Order* (Leicester: IVP, 1986), p.210. The specific target in view here is "the teaching of Paul VI's encyclical *Humanae Vitae*".

27   The argument of the immediately preceding section has offered some basis from within Grisez's theory for regarding *all* positive prevention of conception as illicit; so here we may simply be drawing distinctions within the range of things which are not allowed, and showing how even if the argument regarding violation of the basic good of *marriage* is not accepted, certain so-called contraceptive techniques may nonetheless violate the good of *life*.

28   The extent of the literature on this subject makes a quick treatment of it dangerous; but as an argument supportive of Grisez's position, the following may be helpful. Certain reflections on the end of life lead may us to imagine that life is *constituted* by the presence of a range of criteria —brain function, for example. The temptation then is to regard life as a property, synchronically, rather than as a form of being, diachronically, and to deny the 'property' of life to something which fails to possess those criteria. This is a typical move on the part of those favouring early abortion (and even infanticide in some cases). We could instead insist that the presence or absence of criteria are *indicative* of the state of a process; and here the absence of such criteria on the part of a human adult may properly serve as indicative of death (of the end of a process, which is how one such criterion is used by Nigel Biggar in the example in note 16 above). Their absence in the conceptus could hardly serve the same purpose! Here, the moment of conception serves as the non-arbitrary

starting point for *living,* and a deliberate interruption of that process appears very naturally as a lack of respect for life. The temptation to see life as a synchronic *property* of things is surely fuelled by the pervasiveness of utilitarian forms of moral thought.

29   Sexual intercourse outside marriage may constitute an attack on the good of marriage whether 'contraceptive' or not.

30   That is, implying no proportionate attachment to or violation of goods, but a proper proportionate analysis of risks and goods. I take it that this is Grisez's own account (see *LCL*, p.512 n.103). It may appear puzzling there that the notion that the we are told the "slight risk of abortion [may be] accepted as a side effect". Why the risk, rather than any actual abortion which may happen to occur? Because the moral status belongs to the action and the intentions of the agent. What is *prima facie* bad is the willingness to embrace an action which carries a risk of abortion. That it is (claimed to be) acceptable in a particular circumstance is justified by appeal to the principle of 'double effect', from whence comes the language of side-effects. See note 14 of this essay for references. See also *LCL*, 8C.2, "Norms for Risking Death as a Side Effect", noting especially the charming sky-diving example on p.487, where the possible specificity of divine vocation to individuals, and its effects on the limits of acceptable action, is delightfully expressed.

31   The basic analysis here is in agreement with *LCL*, 8D.1h.

10   Natural Sex: Germain Grisez, Sex, and Natural Law

Gareth Moore, O.P.

In this paper I will examine some aspects of Germain Grisez's philosophical treatment of questions surrounding marriage and sexual behaviour. I will concentrate on Chapter 9 of Volume 2 of his manual, *The Way of the Lord Jesus*, entitled *Living a Christian Life*, as being his most recent and fully worked out treatment.

In this work Grisez devotes much energy to expounding recent Church teaching on these matters, and to showing that his own position as here developed is consonant with this teaching. But he also seeks to establish a great deal of his position independently of Church authority, revelation or Christian faith, simply by using human reason. Arguments based on reason alone will not establish everything that Grisez wants to hold in this area, but they will, he hopes, carry him, and us, quite a long way. It is Grisez's use of reason which I wish to examine in this paper, to see how successful he is in establishing, as he claims, a sexual ethic of limited but still considerable extent by appeal to human reason as applied to the natural facts of human existence. My aim will be to see how successful is his treatment considered as a series of natural law arguments, to examine how cogently he thinks about sex and marriage on the purely natural level.

In so far as natural arguments can be found in support of Christian sexual ethics, it will be possible to show Christians that the sexual norms they subscribe to as part of their faith are not arbitrary (and mostly arbitrary restrictions) but rational ways of achieving and safeguarding human goods. They will thus be able to understand themselves, when they attempt to follow these norms, as living freely and reasonably, rather than as subject to a cramping law. Grisez rightly rejects a legalistic attitude to chastity and insists on the importance of understanding sexual norms.[1] Grisez's arguments throughout this chapter are precisely designed to furnish people with an understanding of what is really at stake in sexual behaviour of various kinds. It is by reflecting on the considerations he puts forward that they can come, Grisez hopes, to an informed and rational conviction of the rightness and desirability of the norms taught by the Church.

While this is a laudable aim, Grisez does not achieve it. I shall attempt to show that, in so far as Grisez's writing represents an attempt to derive a sexual ethic from reason alone and without dependence on faith, it fails irretrievably. For all that it has the appearance of a carefully reasoned case, and at times of a series of proofs, many of the arguments which make it up are radically fallacious and some are based on false premises. In the space available to me I am unable to demonstrate the invalidity of all his arguments, so I will concentrate on what appear to me to be the major difficulties and incoherences of his most important contentions.

Marriage has a central place in Grisez's exposition. Its nature and properties will determine for him not only the kind of sexual behaviour appropriate for married couples but also that (*viz.* none) fitting for the unmarried. It will also govern his explanations of why the various forms of inappropriate sexual activity are to be avoided. He therefore begins by treating of marriage, and my criticism will follow him there.

"One-flesh Union" and the Indissolubility of Marriage

My first major topic is Grisez's account of the indissolubility of marriage, but it will be necessary to make some preliminary remarks about Grisez's characterisation of marriage as a "one-flesh union", an idea that will become central in the exposition of many of his arguments about sex. For Grisez marriage is a basic human good, which can be further specified as "the communion of married life itself". This refers "to the couple's *being* married, that is, their being united as complementary, bodily persons, so really and so completely that they are two in one flesh".[2] The mention of 'one flesh' here is clearly an allusion to Genesis 2:23-24, a text referred to by Jesus in his dictum on marriage and divorce in Matthew 19:4-6, traditionally interpreted as asserting the indissolubility of marriage. The argument that Grisez will go on to develop will thus appear, by means of this allusion, to be a natural law vindication of the biblically founded doctrine of the Church. (Whether there is actually any link between the biblical use of the phrase and Grisez's is another question which there is not space to pursue.)

There is an evident problem with this conception of marital union: it is not quite clear in what sense two people can be one person; it seems, on the contrary, clear *prima facie* that however the unity of marriage is described the two spouses do remain two persons and do not become one person. This appears to be a minor point, since the qualifying phrase "as it were" makes the idea of two spouses as one person seem intended to be metaphorical. But in fact it is put to serious work in Grisez's argument. It will function in fact as the central element of that argument.

To give the notion a clearer sense, Grisez makes appeal to the faculty of reproduction. There is, according to Grisez, an important difference between reproduction and any other animal function. The initial contention is that biologically, "every animal, whether male or female, is a complete individual with respect to most functions: growth, nutrition, sensation, emotion, local movement, and so on". When it comes to reproduction, however,

> each animal is incomplete, for a male or a female individual is only a potential part of the mated pair, which is the complete organism that is capable of reproducing sexually. This is true also of men and women: as mates who engage in sexual intercourse suited to initiate new life, they complete each other and become an organic unit. In doing so, it is literally true that "they become one flesh".[3]

From this, it appears that becoming one flesh, in Grisez's sense, is equivalent to engaging in sexual intercourse suited to initiate new life. This looks promising, for sexual intercourse and procreation are evidently linked in some way to the institution of marriage. But again there are problems. Principally, this approach confuses two very different things: the automatic *functioning* of glands, organs and other parts of an animal, and the *voluntary activity* of an animal.

Generally speaking, reproduction, in species which reproduce sexually, is dependent on the cooperation of two members, a male and a female, of that species. Males and females possess glands, organs, etc., which have a reproductive function, but to perform that function they have to be brought into appropriate contact with a reproductive element of a member of the opposite sex. The usual way in which this happens is by the sexual intercourse of two animals, a joint activity of those animals. Animal reproduction is not a function of an animal or of a pair of animals, but the result of the successful functioning, in combination, of the products of their organs. While this normally happens as a result also of the joint sexual activity of the two animals in question, it is possible for human beings to intervene in the process, through techniques of artificial insemination, etc., to bring about animal reproduction without the direct cooperation of two members of a species. The functioning of the reproductive parts can be set in motion without the joint activity of two animals. We might at a pinch speak of male and female reproductive organs as incomplete, if by that is meant that one cannot achieve reproduction without the other, but the male and female animals are in no sense incomplete. So neither is a mating pair a single complete organism; it is simply two organisms cooperating in a joint activity of mating.

Grisez has, then, failed to make out a significant sense in which a mating couple is a single organism, "one flesh" or "as it were one person". This failure has serious consequences for the rest of his argument, for the idea of one-flesh unity plays a central role in everything that follows. Its incoherence vitiates his later attempts to distinguish which sexual activities are and which are not legitimate. More immediately, it is one of the things which contributes to the failure of his bid to show that the exclusivity and indissolubility of marriage is evident from the very intention of the marrying partners.

The Marriage Intention

Grisez's belief in one-flesh union gives him the illusion of a way of developing the argument at this point: "Since they complete each other to become, as it were, one person, a man and a woman truly joined in marital communion cannot attempt to divide without severe trauma, analogous to, and in some respects even worse than, the loss of a substantial part of one's own body".[4] This has consequences for a couple about to marry:

> If they anticipate that they might intentionally attempt to separate from each other, they either must be prepared to cause the trauma divorce would involve or must will to limit their unity in order to avoid that trauma. But doing either is at odds with conjugal love. If, therefore, in attempting to marry the parties reserve the right to divorce, they act inconsistently with the conjugal love necessary for marriage.[5]

Grisez's argument centres on the intention to cause the trauma which divorce necessarily involves. The reason why he thinks it is necessarily traumatic is that two who are truly joined in marriage become "as it were, one person". Because they are one person, one flesh, trying to separate them is like trying to sever a limb from an individual. The highly metaphorical 'one person' language, which originally served to contrast the human pair capable of reproduction from individual people allegedly "incomplete with respect to reproduction", is now being used, without justification, for a totally different purpose, to imply the necessary pain and damage of separation. But the two who have married do not in fact become as it were one person; they are two individuals who have joined to become one couple. In divorcing, a couple lose, not part of themselves, but each other. That divorce often is a trauma is not to be doubted. But it plainly is not necessarily so, since couples do in fact divorce with relief. Further, if there is pain, there is no reason to think that this has anything to do with the putative one-flesh union: unmarried couples, including same-sex couples, who cannot share one-flesh union, can also suffer trauma on separation.

Even if Grisez were right on the point that divorce is necessarily traumatic, his conclusion —that somebody who reserves the right to divorce at the point of marriage either is prepared to cause this trauma or intends to limit the couple's commitment in order to avoid it— would not follow. For it does not rely on the putatively objective fact of the one-person unity of a married couple, but on the *intention* of one or both of the marrying partners. It may be an objective fact that if I lace your tea with strychnine your death will soon result. But I can only intend to cause your death in this way if I also *believe* that strychnine in tea causes death. In the same way, even if Grisez were right in holding that divorce is necessarily traumatic, a marrying person who anticipated that he might later divorce would only necessarily intend, in any sense however weak, to cause trauma if he held the same view as Grisez himself. That is, he would necessarily intend to cause trauma only if he thought that any divorce must be traumatic. If he does not agree with Grisez (and he would be right not to do so), he can envisage the possibility of divorce without envisaging causing trauma.

According to Grisez, common experience shows that "people can wish for and pledge undying friendship, but cannot preclude a future choice to end a relationship which either or both parties have come to consider undesirable."[6] He claims that this observation has the following consequence:

> even if couples planning to marry understand and accept that the good they desire calls for a truly mutual and entirely dependable relationship, they will realize, if they are clearheaded, that they themselves cannot make their marital union exclusive and indissoluble. If the union they are about to form is to have these properties, they will see, it cannot be by their own wills but must be by virtue of something about one-flesh union itself which they must accept, so that once they enter into that union, nothing they subsequently choose or do will be able to divide them from each other and/or unite them simultaneously in a similar union with someone else.[7]

But this is not what such couples see if they are clear-headed. To begin with, when Grisez claims that a marrying couple cannot make their union exclusive and indissoluble, there is an important ambiguity in the word 'make'. If the meaning is, roughly, 'determine in advance', so that the exclusivity and permanence of the union is guaranteed, then Grisez's observation is correct but does not get very far. It is simply a general fact about human life that we cannot determine the future, and because this is well known, it is not to be supposed that any marrying couple will think that the exclusivity and permanence of their relationship can be guaranteed in any way, either by themselves or by another.[8] But if the meaning of 'make' here is closer to 'construct', if the claim is that a couple cannot make or build a relationship which is exclusive and permanent, then this is more interesting as a claim, but it is false, for people do make such relationships. If they thought Grisez's claim true, they could not possibly intend to embark on an exclusive and permanent relationship. Reflection on common experience does not, then, show clear-headed couples that they cannot make their marital union exclusive and permanent. What it shows is merely that their present intentions and feelings for each other are not sufficient to make it so. If it is to be so, they will have to work at their relationship and not take it or each other for granted; they will have to take care to avoid the pitfalls into which others have fallen: to maintain their physical and emotional intimacy, avoid getting too close to others, be prepared to face problems when they arise, to be patient with each other in difficult times, etc. They will also need a certain amount of luck. No human project is guaranteed success; if a marrying couple are looking for a relationship which is guaranteed to be exclusive and permanent, they are confused and looking for a chimera. But we have no reason to think that couples do think of marriage in this way.

If the union they are about to form is to be exclusive and permanent, then it will be because they work to make it so. It will not be by virtue of the nature of one-flesh union as such. This is partly because, as previously shown, there is no one-flesh union in Grisez's sense. Even if there were, it would not do the job it is supposed to in this context. According to Grisez, once they enter into this union nothing they subsequently do will separate them from each other. But, first, nothing we have seen shows that this one-flesh union, even if we accept its existence, is itself indissoluble. Even if two married people are as it were one person, and even if they cannot be separated again without a trauma comparable to the amputation of a limb, still limbs can be amputated; the couple complete with respect to reproduction can revert to being two separate individuals incapable of reproducing on their own. Second, this putatively unbreakable unity is supposed to persist whatever the couple subsequently do. They can hate each other, have affairs, live as far apart as possible, go through divorce proceedings, go through a form of marriage with others, and still have this unbreakable one-flesh unity. But what the marrying couple want is to share their lives together in mutual love and trust, and they realise from their share of common experience that they cannot of themselves guarantee that they will continue to enjoy such a relationship throughout their lives. What they want to be sure of, and what they cannot be sure of, is that they will *not* end up hating each other, having affairs, living apart, getting divorced, etc. The purported one-flesh union cannot give this assurance. It is said to guarantee the future unity of the couple *whatever* they later choose and do, and this is just not the kind of unity they are interested in. Instead of a real personal relationship involving a loving sharing of life, which is what they want, it offers only a guarantee that even if they do not have this they will have some kind of metaphysical unity. While the purported one-flesh union is presented as guaranteeing the couple what they want, it assures them only something they do not want.

The Variety of Sexual Acts

Enough has been said by now to show that Grisez's argument attempting to prove the exclusivity and indissolubility of marriage does not work. I turn now to a consideration of his treatment of sexual acts. The general schema is as follows: Any non-marital sexual act violates the good of marriage, and is therefore inappropriate and to be avoided.[9] A married couple's community depends on mutual consent, each partner seeking the other's good. Therefore genuine marital sexual acts must be performed willingly and lovingly, without coercion, and must not be for selfish satisfaction or the selfish manipulation of a partner. Further, this activity must allow for the possibility of procreation.[10] Any sexual activity which does not conform to these requirements is not marital. Hence all non-loving and necessarily non-procreative sexual activity within the communion of marriage, such as intercourse using any method of contraception, is to be avoided.[11] The same is true of all sexual activity outside that communion, such as adultery, the intercourse of an unmarried heterosexual couple, masturbation, and all homosexual activity.[12]

There are two main areas of difficulty in all this: first, the assertion that non-procreative sexual activity is necessarily non-marital; and second, the contention that any non-marital sexual activity violates the good of marriage.

Any married couple's willing and loving sexual behaviour must, according to Grisez, "constitute the cooperation appropriate to realize their organic complementarity in respect to reproduction".[13] Because they are as a couple fitted to reproduce, they must not in their sexual act itself deliberately exclude the possibility of reproduction. For Grisez, this is not a separate requirement from that of mutual love in the sexual activity of marriage partners, but an element of it:

> A marital act expresses and fosters the couple's marital communion precisely because, when they willingly and lovingly cooperate with each other in an act of itself suited to procreating, their mutual self-giving actualizes their one-flesh unity. If one or both spouses engage in a sexual act which does not realize one-flesh unity in this way, that act is not marital.[14]

It is evident that this view of the sexual activity of the married is heavily dependent on Grisez's theory of one-flesh unity. The collapse of the theory leaves Grisez without any basis for his current assertions. Since the married couple do not have this kind of unity, such unity is not actualised by any act of theirs, sexual or otherwise.

But suppose all my criticisms of Grisez's theory are wrong, and that the 'one-flesh' theory is correct. Still, why should we think that an act must foster marital communion in order to be a marital act or that an act's being of itself suited to procreation is essential to its ability to foster marital communion? It may well be that a couple's willing and loving act of intercourse open to new life strengthens their marital communion, but the same would appear to be true of any willing and loving joint activity. Going shopping together, playing tennis together, or any other joint activity performed in the same spirit, with the same mutual regard, attentive to each other's good and each other's enjoyment, are not activities which make a communion marital, but they can foster any personal communion, marital or otherwise.[15]

Why should a joint sexual act not suited to procreation achieve the same effect? Grisez has arguments to hand. These centre on showing that if a sexual act is not of itself suited to procreation it is undertaken for motives at odds with that communion. Thus, for example, he claims that

> when husband and wife cooperate in a sexual act which is not a marital act, what they do cannot be an act of conjugal love, that is, the reciprocal self-giving which brings about one-flesh unity. So, their actions must have other motives, which, even if they include mutual affectionate feelings, are unintegrated with conjugal love and more or less at odds with it.[16]

The sexual act in question is held to be non-marital by reason of its form: it does not bring about one-flesh unity, that is, it is not suited to procreation. But, apart from the failure of the argument due to its reliance on the theory of one-flesh unity, the form of the act implies nothing whatever about the motives of the couple. They may even, if they are sexually ignorant, perform a sexual act not suited to procreation in the belief that it is so suited, and with the intention of procreating. Any sexual act, even though not suited to procreation, may be an act of reciprocal self-giving, an act undertaken willingly and lovingly, and Grisez is not entitled to infer otherwise. The act may of course be selfish on both sides; but it may perfectly well not be. If it is, then it is unlikely to strengthen marital communion; if it is not selfish, but undertaken in a context of mutual affectionate feelings, it surely is likely to strengthen marital communion. It is hard to see how mutual affectionate feelings can be unintegrated with conjugal love, and still harder to understand how they can be at odds with it.

Non-Marital Sex

Having, to his satisfaction, placed limits on the legitimate sexual activity of married couples, Grisez proceeds to comment on other sexual activities, principally of the unmarried. He divides these acts into three basic kinds, commenting on each in turn: masturbation, extramarital full heterosexual vaginal intercourse ("fornication"), and the oral or anal intercourse of two unmarried men ("sodomy"). There are a number of questions that might be raised about this classification and this vocabulary, but for want of space I shall accept it and confine myself to examining his comments on each of these categories.

Masturbation Grisez's basic objection to masturbation is that somebody who masturbates violates the body's capacity for self-giving because the choice to masturbate is the choice to alienate oneself from one's body: "In the choice to masturbate, the immediate intention is to have a sentient and emotional experience: the sensation of orgasm and the accompanying emotional satisfaction".[17] The reason why this is wrong is that:

> In choosing to actuate one's sexual capacity in order to have the conscious experience of the process and its culmination, one chooses to use one's body as an instrument to bring about that experience in the conscious self. Thus, the body becomes an instrument used and the conscious self its user. In most cases, using one's body as an instrument is not problematic. This is done when one works and plays, and also when one communicates, using the tongue to speak, the finger to point, the genitals to engage in marital intercourse. In such cases the body functions as part of oneself, serving the whole and sharing in the resulting benefits. By contrast, in choosing to masturbate, one does not choose to act for a goal which fulfills oneself as a unified, bodily person. The only immediate goal is satisfaction for the conscious self; and so the body, not being part of the whole for whose sake the act is done, serves only as an extrinsic instrument. Thus, in choosing to masturbate one chooses to alienate one's body from one's conscious subjectivity.[18]

There are, once again, a number of things wrong with this. First, here, as elsewhere in his treatment of sex, Grisez assumes that he knows about the intentions and motives of others. With what right does he speak as if he had knowledge of the immediate intention of a masturbator? And what Grisez says about intention and motive is not obviously coherent. He posits a case of somebody who masturbates in order to get a night's rest. If that is the motive, then whether the orgasm will be a nice sensation or not will be irrelevant. The immediate intention is certainly to masturbate, but it is a crude and false assumption that every time somebody masturbates they do it in order to have the pleasurable sensation of an orgasm.[19]

But the principal problem with this argument is the strange dualism on the basis of which masturbation is supposed to effect an alienation between the body and the "conscious self". It is certainly possible to make sense of the idea of being alienated from oneself, and that this alienation might find expression in masturbation. You might dislike yourself and express your self-contempt by masturbating. It is even possible that you might specifically hate your body, and express this alienation by masturbating. But these are particular psychological states, not truths about masturbation in general. Neither do they involve the kind of dualism that Grisez thinks is inherent in masturbation as such, of the conscious self over against the body. It is in fact not at all clear what Grisez is getting at here. The notion of a conscious self is not transparent. Grisez goes on to say that there is no metaphysical dualism between conscious self and body, yet he claims that masturbation brings about an "existential dualism".[20] How the one might be possible without the other is not explained. And he gives us no reason to accept what he asserts. An experience of masturbation, like any other experience, is not an experience of a conscious self but of a whole person. It might indeed be said that masturbation is in a certain sense reflexive: the masturbator acts on himself or herself. This *might* be put by saying that the masturbator acts on his or her own body. But this is a whole person acting on himself or herself, not a conscious self acting on a body. It is a bodily act. There is no existential alienation from the body here. Neither is any implied by the possibility that an act of masturbation might be a pleasant activity, or by the possibility that part of its pleasurability might consist in its affording pleasant sensations. In this respect masturbation is parallel to scratching an itch. A scratcher acts upon himself or herself, with the motive of removing the itch; such an activity is often pleasant, and part of the pleasure of the activity lies in the sensations it produces. It would seem to follow from Grisez's reasoning that scratching also is immoral because it implies an existential alienation of the conscious self from the body.

Things are not made clearer by the examples of unproblematic use of the body that Grisez gives. We use the tongue to speak and the finger to point, as we might use the hand to masturbate. But how is the body meant to share in the benefit of the whole person from this use in the first two cases in a way that it does not benefit in the third? How does my tongue benefit if I use it to speak? It is true that *I* might benefit as a result of speaking, though I might also suffer; but only in exceptional circumstances might my tongue be said to benefit or suffer. If anything, it makes clearer sense to say that my body shares in the benefit of the whole if I masturbate, for, if it is a pleasant activity for me, my pleasure may be in an obvious sense a bodily pleasure, and one of which pleasant bodily sensations are an important element. If I am preoccupied with such pleasures, this may be reprehensible, for I will be selfish, less disposed to attend to others to the extent that I concentrate on myself. This simple observation is an important one for a moral consideration of pleasure. But it is a general point about preoccupation with pleasure, and has nothing to do with the bodily nature of sexual pleasure.

In the case of masturbation, as often elsewhere, Grisez locates the moral deficiency not in the act performed but in the choice to perform the action. This involves him in further problems. Because to masturbate is, according to him, to fall into existential self-alienation, in choosing to masturbate "one chooses to alienate one's body from one's conscious subjectivity"; to choose to masturbate is "to choose a specific kind of self-disintegrity", and to choose self-disintegrity is always wrong, because it damages the basic good of self-integration and therefore violates the eighth mode of responsibility.[21] But this is false. It neglects the 'intensional' element in choice, that element which relates to the aspect under which the object of choice is chosen. In choosing to drink from the cup I may end up drinking strychnine, but to choose to drink from the cup is not to choose to drink strychnine. It becomes a choice to drink strychnine only if I know that the cup contains strychnine. If I do not know that, my choice will certainly be unfortunate, but this shows nothing about my will; it will not be a choice to commit suicide. Similarly, it may be, if Grisez is right, that if I masturbate I fall into self-disintegrity, but my choice to masturbate is a choice to fall into self-integrity only if I know that masturbating has this effect. It may be that my choice to masturbate is an unfortunate one, since I will end up damaging my self-integrity, but again this shows nothing about my will; if I masturbate, it will not be morally reprehensible or violate any modes of responsibility unless I actually hold the same view about masturbation as Grisez does. I may, mistakenly according to Grisez, believe on the contrary that masturbation promotes my self-integrity, in which case my choice to masturbate is a choice in favour of a basic good.

A further area of difficulty with Grisez's argument is his claim that those who masturbate "violate the body's capacity for self-giving". A capacity for self-giving is not a capacity of the human body. It is *people* who have a capacity for self-giving, and they give themselves in various ways, such as by dedicating themselves to a political or religious cause. A person can also make a gift of self by dying for other people, or by working hard to build and maintain an intimate relationship with one other person, labouring to provide that other person with affection and with physical, economic and emotional security and well-being.

There are reasons for thinking that physical and sexual intimacy is particularly at home in an intimate personal relationship between adults, and that sexual activity between partners in such a relationship is naturally suited to expressing and fostering the bond between them.[22] For these reasons we can say that the intercourse of such partners expresses their mutual self-giving. But it would be misleading to say that such intercourse *is* a self-giving, unless it is made clear that this is a kind of shorthand, and that the context of an intimate personal relationship is assumed, a relationship in which the partners give themselves to each other in a number of ways. In the context of personal relationships, if people have a capacity for self-giving, that is not a capacity to engage in sexual intercourse but a capacity to dedicate themselves —their time, energy, affection, attention, resources, etc.— to another person. The capacity to dedicate oneself in this way to another (as well as the capacity to devote oneself to a cause) is an important part of human life, as is the ability, within an intimate relationship, to express committed affection through sexual intimacy, and the loss of both these abilities is correspondingly something to be avoided.

What Grisez has to show, then, is that when people masturbate they diminish either their capacity to dedicate themselves to another in an intimate personal relationship or their ability, if a partner to such a relationship, to express such dedication sexually. None of the arguments he presents, of which the main ones are presented above, have any tendency to show this, and it is difficult to see how it could be demonstrated.

Extramarital Heterosexual Activity Much of Grisez's treatment of heterosexual activity outside marriage is concerned with those who wish to marry. For the sake of space, I will pass over this and go to what should be the most clear-cut part of the argument, that concerning the case where the couple involved have no wish to marry, but are simply friends. Grisez approaches this case in the following way:

> The unitive meaning of sexual intercourse, insofar as it makes the couple into a single reproductive principle, is part of the good of marriage; but precisely insofar as intercourse is not chosen for any aspect of that good, it does not communicate anything definite by itself, and therefore can communicate good-will, affection, and so on only insofar as the couple use their own and each other's bodies as one uses one's tongue to speak, one's finger to point, and so on. But the motive for choosing sexual intercourse to communicate is not that it is especially apt for expressing good-will and affection, since modes of communication commonly used by friends —conversation joined with actions conferring benefits (that is, real instantiations of one of more intelligible goods)— are far more expressive. The true motive is sexual desire and the pleasure of satisfying it. Hence, insofar as fornicators are not interested in the marital good, their intercourse is masturbatory.[23]

In so far as it depends for its validity on the idea of a married couple as "as it were one person", which we have already seen to be incoherent, this passage fails to give us a proper reason for saying that there is anything wrong with extramarital sex. However, Grisez plainly has other points to make here. The first concerns sexual activity as communicative. Sexual intercourse is apt for the communication of affection, just as (we might say) punching somebody is apt for the communication of hostility. But, contrary to what Grisez appears to think, these are not meanings inherent in the acts of intercourse and punching. Intercourse can sometimes communicate nothing between the partners, because there is nothing between them to communicate and they know it; a punch can sometimes be given as part of a boxing match or friendly horseplay, and be accepted as such. Thus it is true, as Grisez says, that the sexual intercourse of unmarried partners does not communicate anything of itself. This, however, does not show the intercourse of unmarried couples to be inferior to that of the married, for the same is true of the intercourse of a married couple.

But we may ask: what is the point of introducing the factor of communication here? Grisez's purpose seems to be to set up a contrast between the intercourse of married couples and that of the unmarried. The former, it seems, communicates of itself, whereas the latter does not. But unmarried people cannot want to make love in order to communicate their good-will and affection for each other, since there are obviously better ways of doing it than sexual intercourse; they can, for example, tell each other of their love. The true motive for wanting intercourse must therefore be sexual desire, the desire for sexual pleasure. But, even accepting Grisez's claim that marital intercourse sometimes signifies of itself in a way that non-marital intercourse does not, why should we be tempted to think this a significant distinction? Why should it be thought that whether an act communicates of itself, or at all, is important? The impression is being given that sexual acts are or might be performed in order to communicate something, but this is in general not so; a false standard of comparison is being set up. As a result, a false idea of sexual desire is implied.

Although people sometimes communicate feelings and attitudes to each other through their acts, and although therefore many acts may be said to communicate, people rarely perform any act *in order* to communicate, apart from acts obviously designed to impart information, such as some acts of speaking, writing and signalling. I may, if I dislike you enough, punch you in the face. You will probably gather from this act that I dislike you, and in this sense my act may be said to communicate to you that I dislike you. However, I do not punch you in order to communicate this fact to you. I punch you because I want to hit you and thereby hurt you. Thus if I throw a punch at you and miss, you will still gather that I dislike you very much, but I will nevertheless be disappointed to have missed. It was not my aim to communicate, even though the act communicates.

What is true of punching is true of making love. I may want to make love to you because I love you, and the attempt to do so may convey to you the fact of my love. But I am unlikely to want to make love to you simply in order to communicate that fact. Normally, I will want to make love to you because I love you, not because I want to let you know that I love you. Making love may be the expression of love, but not normally of the desire to communicate love. Grisez claims that conversation joined with the conferring of benefits is a better form of communication than sexual intercourse. This *may* be true, but it is irrelevant. Sexual intercourse is normally not chosen as a mode of communication, either inside marriage or outside, and it was a mistake to characterise it as such in the first place. It is better seen, like throwing a punch, as expressive behaviour.

Because a false emphasis has been placed on communication in sexual activity, a similarly false picture is implied of sexual desire. Because, it is claimed, unmarried people do not engage in sexual intercourse because they want to communicate good-will and affection, the 'true' motive for their intercourse is "sexual desire and the pleasure of satisfying it". Their intercourse is therefore 'masturbatory'. As before, Grisez wrongly assumes he is entitled to make generalising assumptions about people's motives. Even if his analysis so far is correct, this would tell us nothing at all about the motives that unmarried people have for intercourse; what would follow is only that, if somebody believes the same things as Grisez does about sexual intercourse, then he or she cannot have certain motives for engaging in extramarital sex. If that person thinks, like Grisez, that (only) the sexual intercourse of married couples realises one-flesh unity, then his or her motive for desiring sexual intercourse outside marriage cannot rationally be to realise one-flesh unity. If his beliefs are different, that person may even desire to engage in extramarital intercourse precisely as a way of achieving one-flesh unity with his partner.

Together with this unwarranted presumption of knowledge on Grisez's part goes a failure to recognise the complexities of sexual desire. From the way he links extra-marital intercourse with masturbation (no attempt being made to justify this link), and from his earlier[24] characterisation of masturbation as something done to bring about one's own orgasm, it is clear that he thinks of sexual desire as the desire for an orgasm, and the orgasm is the pleasure that is the satisfaction of sexual desire. But this is jejune in the extreme. An unmarried couple might have sex because both of them want an orgasm, because they want to give each other physical pleasure, because they want to rebel against parental authority, or want a baby, or because it is what everybody else at the party is doing, or because they are bored, or because they are curious to know what it is like, or because it is what they always do on a Saturday evening, etc.. Grisez takes no account of this. Indeed, on his account it will be difficult to explain why anybody should go to all the trouble of finding a partner for sexual intercourse when they could obtain their pleasure more conveniently by masturbating. It is also hard to see why people should seek out, as they often do, one particular partner for their sexual activity. All the evidence is that on the whole people's sexual desires and sexual pleasures are *much* more complicated than Grisez represents them, and often make little or no reference to orgasm. Sexual desire often includes the desire for physical intimacy with another person, or with one particular person, to penetrate or be penetrated, to reassure oneself that one can be sexually desirable to another, to give various kinds of pleasure to one's partner, to play out a particular role, etc.; and the pleasures of sex are, among others, the pleasures of doing those things. Sex, between married partners or unmarried, is a very various thing, and it just will not do to ignore almost all possibilities of sexual desire and sexual pleasure as Grisez does here. By over-simplifying and caricaturing in the way that he does, Grisez ensures that his treatment bears little relation to reality.

Male Homosexual Relationships Grisez's objections to homosexual activities are in part the same as those to extramarital heterosexual intercourse, and are invalid to the extent that the latter are. But he has additional objections. One of these is again dependent on the idea of one-flesh union. He concedes that two men could "conceivably" have a committed relationship of mutual affection; but of their sexual intercourse he says, "The coupling of two bodies of the same sex cannot form one complete organism and so cannot contribute to a bodily communion of persons. Hence, the experience of intimacy of the partners in sodomy cannot be the experience of any real unity between them".[25] We have already seen that Grisez's conception of two bodies as one complete organism is confused. This stops the current argument dead. But even if that idea were logical and true, Grisez's conclusion would still not follow. Even if there were such a thing as one-flesh union, which was unavailable to partners in homosexual intercourse, what Grisez would also have to show is that such union is the *only* form of bodily communion of persons. Otherwise it would be open to homosexuals to enjoy through their sexual activity a form of bodily communion other than one-flesh unity. But Grisez would have a hard time showing this, for, *prima facie*, the simple bodily joining of two people bound together in a committed relationship of mutual affection, be they both male, both female or a mixed couple, is just the sort of thing we would call a form of bodily communion of persons. The experience of intimacy they have in their intercourse may not be the experience of marital union, but it by no means follows that it is not the experience of any real unity between them. That could only be so if marital union were the only real unity between people, which is plainly not the case.

Perhaps sensing that appeal to one-flesh unity is not enough here, Grisez introduces another consideration: "Each one's experience of intimacy is private and incommunicable, and is no more a common good than is the mere experience of sexual arousal and orgasm. Therefore, the choice to engage in sodomy for the sake of the experience of intimacy in no way contributes to the partners' real common good as committed friends". There has been reference to the privacy and incommunicability of experience earlier; Grisez has claimed that "the pleasurable sensations of sexual activity culminating in orgasm are in themselves a private and incommunicable experience".[26] Grisez does not explain what he means by claims like this, but it seems as if what he is alluding and subscribing to is the philosophical theory of the privacy of sensations. According to this theory, each person's sensations —of pain, sound, colour, etc.— are held to be private in that they are accessible to that person alone and cannot be shown or communicated to another person: I cannot show you my headache as I can show you my umbrella. I have direct knowledge of my sensations, whereas you only have indirect evidence, the testimony of what I say and do.

This is a controversial theory with many difficulties in it, and this is not the place to go into it.[27] Even if the theory is true, however, it does not have the relevance that Grisez thinks it has. Even if sensations can in some sense not be shared, it is not the sense that Grisez needs in order to make his point. There is an obvious sense in which sensations and experiences *can* be shared: two people can have them together. You and I can share a delicious meal. It may be that your taste sensations are yours and mine are mine, but I can share my experience with you by sharing my food with you; I can give you the taste of mushrooms by giving you my mushrooms. If this is true at the level of sensations, it is true even more in the present case, in which Grisez speaks of the homosexual partners' "experience of intimacy". Intimacy is often an important element of the pleasure of sexual intercourse, and not only homosexual intercourse. That somebody is experiencing intimacy is not private and incommunicable, but can be communicated by word and gesture. It can be shared, and the enjoyment of sharing it also shared, just as can the taste of mushrooms. For this reason alone, the sharing of experiences of intimacy is indeed, *pace* Grisez, a common good, just like the sharing of any good experience. This is as true of homosexual men as it is of anybody else. If they are friends and enjoy sex together, their joint enjoyment and their desire to provide enjoyment for each other will contribute to the strength of their friendship and their mutual commitment.

But it is an additional important point, which Grisez appears to miss, that the experience of intimacy is significantly different from the taste of mushrooms. It may only take one person to taste a mushroom, but it takes two to be intimate. I cannot procure the experience of intimacy as I might procure the sensation of the taste of mushrooms by eating a mushroom. I can only have it if I perceive the world around me in such a way that I believe certain things about it. If I am in bed with you, I can have an experience of intimacy only if I believe that there is an intimacy to experience, which implies believing that you too are having a similar experience. If I think that for you this is a moment of intimate communion, that will enable me to think in the same way, and so to have the experience of intimacy. If, on the other hand, I think that our joint sexual activity is irksome to you, and that you are impatient to get it over with, or that you are all the time thinking of somebody else, then, whatever orgasms and other sensations I have, I will realise that there is no intimacy, and I therefore cannot have an experience of intimacy; if I had expected intimacy, I will experience the lack of it as alienation.

Conclusion

If the considerations presented in the course of this article are broadly correct, they amount to a demonstration that Grisez's attempt to derive a sexual ethic from reason and nature fails catastrophically. The lapses of logic and factual inaccuracies are not minor and remediable, but systemic and fatal. This is not to imply that all of the conclusions towards which he is arguing are false (though it will be clear that I think a number of them are). Some of the values which he supports are clearly admirable; the mutual dedication of married people, devotion to the good of their children, and fidelity are excellent things to strive for. But sympathy with conclusions should not make one sentimental about the arguments alleged to support them. The overwhelming impression is that Grisez simply tries to do too much on the basis of reason.

If we then ask why he is tempted to try to make reason achieve so much, the answer seems clear: his agenda is preset by an adherence to a particular strand of modern Catholic teaching. There is no reason why Grisez should not be so attached; he is a Catholic and the teaching to which he subscribes comes from authoritative Catholic sources. But it is questionable whether it is wise to let such attachment set the goals for natural reason unaided by revelation. The overwhelming impression is given that Grisez is determined to appear to prove by philosophical means the truth of modern Catholic teaching. He does not follow where the logic of his arguments leads him, but is determined to get to where, on the basis of his faith, he wants to arrive, and arguments appear constructed with the sole purpose of leading to a predetermined conclusion. This procedure does not inspire confidence. The resulting arguments may convince the converted, i.e. those who do not need much convincing; but the suspicions of those who need genuine arguments are bound to be aroused —as it turns out, with some considerable justification. Inconvenient facts are ignored, and elementary logical and philosophical points overlooked in the effort to get to the desired conclusion. It looks as if any old specious argument is being drummed up in order to give an appearance of credibility to the Catholic position to which, *a priori*, Grisez subscribes. This is surely far from what Grisez, or anybody who, like him, wishes to think seriously about Christian sexual morality, wants. The catastrophic failure of such a massive and designedly rigorous attempt to give Catholic sexual ethics a basis in natural reason is also bound to leave the uncommitted reader with the impression that it will be difficult to find any rational basis for that ethic; the result of the attempt is somewhat counterproductive.

This is a great pity, for there must after all be something right in Grisez's approach. Christian sexual ethics must have some grounding in human nature and human reason. But it is a mistake to try to predetermine where that reason will take us, particularly when the goals set are so ambitious. We must surely follow Grisez in his project of trying to think seriously at a philosophical level about sex and marriage, but should learn the lesson of his failure and set our sights more modestly, being more open to take account of the complexities of human sexuality, and being more prepared go where the logic of our arguments leads, and no further. It may be too that certain elements of Christian sexual morality turn out to be rationally indefensible, and in so far as this is so Christians will have to look and think again, and be prepared to remedy what may turn out to be the errors of centuries.

NOTES

1　*LCL*, p.672.
2　*LCL*, p.568.
3　*LCL*, p.570.
4　*LCL*, p.577.
5　Ibid.
6　*LCL*, p.578.
7　Ibid.
8　For the same reason Grisez's choice of the word 'indissoluble' is out of place. A clearheaded marrying couple do not want to make their relationship *impossible* to dissolve, for they know that marriages, like other human relationships, are very soluble indeed. What they want is a union which *does* not dissolve. They want, not an indissoluble union but, more humbly, a permanent one.
9　*LCL*, p.633.
10　*LCL*, p.634.
11　*LCL*, pp.643ff.
12　*LCL*, pp.648ff.
13　*LCL*, p.634.
14　*LCL*, p.635.
15　This is not to deny that joint sexual activity can on occasion have a particularly strong effect, the physical intimacy being at once expressive of a couple's unity of life and a reinforcement of that unity. For a lengthier development of this point, see my *The Body in Context* (London, SCM Press, 1992), chapter 6.
16　*LCL*, p.635 n.162.
17　*LCL*, p.649.
18　*LCL*, p.650.
19　Plus the "emotional satisfaction" that Grisez thinks goes with an orgasm, though he never explains this. Behind this assumption of Grisez that he knows without further ado what people masturbate for (namely, orgasms), I suspect, lies the more general erroneous assumption that people, at least people not joined in a one-flesh union, undertake sexual activity because of the sensations they expect to get from it, those sensations themselves

being conceived in a minimalist sense, stripped of the cognitive element normally attaching to them. For a criticism of such a view see my *The Body in Context*, pp.51-63.

20   Ibid.

21   Ibid.

22   I have tried to present such reasons in *The Body in Context*, chapter 6.

23   *LCL*, p.653.

24   *LCL*, p.649.

25   *LCL*, p.653.

26   *LCL*, p.637. There is a further reference to "individual and incommunicable enjoyable sensations" at *LCL*, p.664.

27   The classic critique of it is to be found in Ludwig Wittgenstein, *Philosophical Investigations*, §§243-315.

11 Grisez on Sex and Gender: A Feminist Theological Perspective

Lisa Sowle Cahill

The approach to ethics represented in this essay is indebted to Thomas Aquinas, to Catholic moral traditions, and to feminist theology. Its fundamental method will be Thomistic in the general sense of venturing objective, potentially universalizable moral claims on the basis of practical experiences of human goods and needs. It will be Catholic specifically on sexual morality by affirming the unity of sexual expression, interpersonal commitment, and responsibility for children (i.e., sex, love, and procreation).

Its critical edge will be theologically feminist. Feminism is committed to women's and men's equal personal dignity, equal mutual respect, and equal social power. In theological perspective, gender equality is entailed not only by the recognition of women's humanity and agency, emerging so forcefully in the modern period, but also by the central message of the New Testament. The teaching of Jesus, including his parables and the Sermon on the Mount, reverses worldly criteria of status and unites all members in a new inclusive community. Some of the social effects of the kingdom of God are illustrated in Paul's imagery of the Body of Christ, and in the baptismal formula of Galatians 3:28 ("there is neither Jew nor Greek, there is neither slave nor free person, there is not male and female, for you are all one in Christ Jesus").

The renewal of natural law represented by the work of Germain Grisez holds promise as a form of critical realism in ethics. In my view, the recovery of some sort of realist foundations and objectivity in ethics is especially important from a feminist point of view. Although liberal feminism centering on 'equal rights' for women provided the momentum for the women's movement of the 1960s and 1970s, feminist theory in the past couple of decades has increasingly drawn its power from postmodern deconstructions of accepted realms of knowledge and social practice. Claiming that conceptions of women's nature and proper roles have been fabricated to serve the interests and maintain the hegemony of patriarchal institutions, feminists such as Judith Butler, Jane Flax, Catherine MacKinnon, Iris Marion Young, and María Lugones attack gender, heterosexual marriage, and even sexuality itself as dominatively 'constructed'.[1] Such critiques rightly resist distorted, constricting and oppressive definitions of women's nature. But their force —especially in a cross-cultural context— is limited by their instrinsic and explicit social relativism. Unless it is possible to make at least some basic claims about the goods and practices which constitute human flourishing as such, it will be impossible to make a coherent argument that some actions or relationships are dehumanizing or unjust to women, and should be prohibited and resisted no matter what the contexts in which they occur.

Interestingly, many Roman Catholic feminists and 'third world' feminists (women who speak out of concrete experiences of oppression) do advance such claims, even though they also affirm differences among women and among cultures as necessary and valuable. The 'full humanity of women' is a key critical norm, which in turn presupposes that humanity is a widely recognizable category implying certain fundamental goods for humans which moral behavior ought to recognize and pursue. In the words of Rosemary Radford Ruether, "The critical principle of feminist theology is the promotion of the full humanity of women".[2] She adds:

> This principle is hardly new. In fact, the correlation of original, authentic human nature (*imago dei*/Christ) and diminished, fallen humanity provided the basic structure of classical Christian theology. The uniqueness of feminist theology is not the critical principle, full humanity, but the fact that women claim this principle for themselves. Women name themselves as subjects of authentic and full humanity.[3]

To argue that both men and women are fully human is not necessarily to assert that there are no differences between them. Yet the point of feminist criticism is that so-called 'innate' or 'natural' differences have been articulated, justified, and institutionalized in ways that are in fact demeaning to women and amount to a denial in practice that women deserve the same degree of respect, social participation, and influence as men. Women in virtually all cultural traditions have been understood predominantly in terms of their sexuality, and respected for fulfilling reproductive and domestic roles. Women are thus relegated to a household sphere of influence which is not only socially devalued relative to public economic and political spheres, but is not in itself expressive of women's full range of capacities and contributions. (The separation of masculine and feminine spheres has deleterious consequences for men's full development as well.)

In a recent review, Patricia DeFerrari sees official Roman Catholic social teaching as accomplishing a gradual advance in its valuation of women's work both inside and outside the home, and in its critique of gender bias. At the same time, Catholic teaching is still plagued by a "dual anthropology which effectively limits women's role in society despite assertions to the contrary".[4] According to the experience of many women, and in much feminist theory, including feminist theology, definitions of women's 'special nature' have actually served to diminish women's full humanity.[5] Total elimination of male-female difference is not the only alternative. Rather, as DeFerrari emphasizes, the task is to recognize that some gender differences may accompany sexual differentiation for reproduction, while still upholding the moral mandate to embody in theology, ethics, and social policy women's radical equality with men.

As I read Germain Grisez's work on gender and sexuality, I appreciate his interest in defining sex, procreation, and marriage as important spheres of moral experience, related to basic goods that exert a claim on all human beings, no matter what their culture, time, or circumstances. At the same time, I am ever cognizant of Aquinas's caveat that it is easier to attain certainty and universality at the more general levels of natural law precepts than it is in the particulars, where contingent circumstances may affect both what is objectively right to do and what our perception of the good may be.[6] For instance, in the case of gender and sexuality, I would take male-female social and sexual cooperation, the bearing and nurturing of children, and the institutionalization of kin identity and responsibility in the intergenerational family to be fundamental human goods recognized in all cultures. What that implies for the specific structures of gender, sexual morality, marriage, and family are different and more ambiguous matters.

I question Grisez's specification of a 'natural' ethics of sex and gender which essentially puts women in a subordinate position, and tends to define the moral demands of sex, gender, and family in terms of reproduction. But, perhaps more importantly, I concur in his retrieval of natural law, understood as a critical realism in ethics. I too am committed to his and the recent Roman Catholic teaching tradition's essential defense of the unity of sex, mutual commitment, and family responsibility as constituting a positive ideal for moral behavior. Note that the area of 'assent' linking my views (and those of many other theologians often labelled 'dissenters') with magisterial teaching on sex, marriage, and family is much greater than the area of disagreement. To categorize all critics of subsidiary points of such teaching as dissenting theologians (or even 'radical' dissenting theologians, in Grisez's phrase[7]) effectively distances proponents of supposedly more orthodox positions from the need to take proposed revisions seriously. The same goes for simplistic characterizations of 'radical' feminists, which fail to take into account the variety within feminism and the commitment of theological feminists to essential values in Scripture and Christian tradition.[8]

Grisez's Position: Marriage as a Basic Good

For Grisez, the foundation of ethics is an association of seven basic goods, to which marriage is added in *Living a Christian Life*.[9] The initial seven are self-integration; practical reasonableness; justice and friendship; life, including health and the handing on of life; knowledge of truth and appreciation of beauty; work and play.[10] Grisez calls these goods equally basic and incommensurable; they cannot be prioritized and no one of them can be sacrificed directly for any other.

As Jean Porter has noted, the trouble arises in this theory just at the point at which these goods are stated to make equally important and irreducible claims on our moral attention. If the thesis of Grisez and his colleagues were simply that "there are certain broad classes of generally acknowledged goods, which are of significance for moral reflection, then their analysis would be unassailable".[11] But, as Grisez, Finnis, and Boyle allow, these goods correspond to diverse and complex aspects of human nature and its fulfillments.[12] If so, it seems reasonable to conclude that they are not all on the same level all of the time, and are in fact often compared, weighed, and even sacrificed in non-controversial moral decisions.[13] The association of goods identified by Grisez certainly does represent a fundamental, cross-cultural sense of what constitutes human well-being, and could well serve as a base for negotiating situations of moral conflict and for positively forming social institutions and policies that further such goods. But it may not provide answers to conflict-situations at the specific level as readily as is implied when the absolute equality of such goods is asserted.

All of the seven basic goods could to some extent be realized in and through sexual relationships, especially those characterized by marital commitment and shared parenthood. Among them, life, justice and friendship, self-integration and practical reasonableness seem to bear most centrally and importantly on sexual, marital, and family ethics. Eventually, though, Grisez adds marriage itself to the association of intrinsic, incommensurable goods. His definitive statement is that

> marriage is a basic human good, and the married couple's common good is, not any extrinsic end to which marriage is instrumental, but the communion of married life itself. The *communion of married life* refers to the couple's being married, that is, their being united as complementary, bodily persons, so really and so completely that they are two in one flesh. This form of interpersonal unity is actualized by conjugal love when that love takes shape in the couple's acts of mutual marital consent, loving consummation, and their whole life together, not least in the parenthood of couples whose marriages are fruitful. Thus in considering marriage as a basic human good, none of its traditional ends and goods is set aside; rather, all of them are included in the intrinsically good communion of married life itself.[14]

Does marriage belong as an eighth in Grisez's set of goods? One difference between marriage and the other seven is that no human life could be called genuinely happy or complete without some share in each of the original seven goods; but marriage seems both experientially and conceptually distinct in that it is a relationship, practice, or institution within which other goods may be realized, without being essential to their realization, or itself essential to a happy and virtuous life. Experientially and morally, it is not immediately clear that the marriage relation is in the same category as the other seven goods; or that, if it is, other roles and relations, such as parenthood, priesthood, or political office ought not to be in the group too. This unclarity demonstrates the difficulty of placing all these goods in precisely the same category, for the same reasons, and with the same results for moral judgment and choice.

A more problematic point is Grisez's countering the traditional (Augustinian) language of the goods of marriage by a revision in which the goods become intrinsic aspects of the being of a marriage itself. Grisez does not say that where these goods cease to be, so also does a marriage. Quite the opposite: mutual consent establishes a "one-flesh" unity such that it is indissoluble. Moreover, the goods of marriage, as intrinsic, exist in any and every marriage, no matter what its practical condition. The purpose of Grisez's argument that the goods of marriage constitute the very being of marriage is evidently to bolster his view that marriage is a basic good, and not only a realm in which goods may be enjoyed; and to refute the possibility that it could ever be right to act directly against a marriage, for example, by seeking to dissolve it. The nugget of the above cited definition is that marriage is a basic good by virtue of the couple's being married as such, *whether or not* that union is in fact characterized by love or parenthood, or is an existential communion of persons. Certainly this proviso permits Grisez to prepare the way to a reaffirmation of traditional Catholic teaching against divorce.

No doubt having in view another controversy (about contraception), Grisez also stipulates that the marital communion is ordered and determined by the conditions necessary for the "begetting and raising of children". Procreation is the "specific perfection" of marriage.[15] Grisez insists that "a married couple's fulfillment in parenthood intrinsically perfects their spousal relationship",[16] and that sexual acts which do not replicate the biological pattern which can lead to procreation are not "marital acts" at all.[17] What otherwise might be considered subsidiary goods are thus placed on the same footing as the basic good of marriage, reinforcing the implication of the original formulation of seven goods that it is always wrong to act against the good of procreation (as attached to the fundamental good of life and accorded the same weight).[18] In support , Grisez cites *Gaudium et spes*: "the institution of marriage and conjugal love are directed to the procreation and raising of children and find their culmination in this".[19] This conciliar document does not, however, seem closed to the interpretation that marriage as good in itself is ordered to the further, distinct goods of procreation and family, if one sees these goods as derivative rather than merely 'extrinsic' to marriage.

According to Grisez, the roles of spouses in marriage are "sexually differentiated", though not with excessive rigidity. Grisez regards complementary gender roles as necessary to the care of children.[20] In this division, women are more responsible than men for the practical support of the good of procreation, for their key role is caring for children: "By differentiating the sexes, God plainly intends to differentiate the spouses' roles; and because this natural differentiation serves the good of marriage and family, it should be endorsed willingly, not resisted and limited as much as possible".[21] The telling points are how one knows 'plainly' the divine intention by observing biological facts; how far 'natural' differentiation actually extends beyond pure reproductive biology; how the 'good' of marriage is defined exactly; and whether any biological facts or tendencies (such as hormonally stimulated aggressiveness or moodiness) should in fact be resisted or limited.

One could concur in Grisez's statement above and interpret it to mean merely that men and women cooperate biologically in a complementary way to initiate pregnancy which results in birth. To add that "not only physiologically but psychologically, women naturally are adapted to this nurturing role" goes far beyond this minimum. The socially restrictive effects for women of strongly contrasting gender roles become apparent when women's role is contrasted to that of the "husband-father", who "also is naturally adapted for his role". The father "deals with the wider world outside the home in order to obtain the necessities of life and defend his family against threats to its security ... he must set and pursue goals, make and execute plans and strive to meet standards for success".[22] A woman, on the other hand, "is made to be a mother" (quoting Pius XII[23]), and to assume primary responsibility for young children in the home. Despite the greater appreciation for the dignity of women that Grisez shares with recent popes, he vehemently defends teachings on sexuality, including contraception and abortion, which were originally proposed on the assumption that women are inferior beings created primarily to be reproductive helpers to men.[24]

The unitive value of sexual intercourse is theoretically on a par with procreation in *Humanae vitae*, and is experientially so in marriages characterized by genuine love and mutuality. Yet, as is evident in their joint work on the birth control encyclical, the Grisez School tends to place individual control of sex drives (often idealized as 'self-mastery') as the critical issue in determining the morality of intercourse not aimed at procreation. They seem to see the hedonistic venting of physical urges as the most common reason why married people seek non-procreative sex: "Plainly, sexual frustration is the only factor essentially related to intercourse that causes all the bad effects some people suffer due to marital abstinence".[25] The proper role of sex in a loving marital friendship is sparingly prescribed.

Granting that "the satisfaction of sexual desire" is related to love in some way, Grisez and associated authors carefully enumerate "three kinds of occasions" on which marital intercourse is appropriate. These are: first, to consummate the marriage; second, "on the part of those who desire children"; and third, events on "the calendar of each married couple's special occasions", such as anniversaries.[26] This does not go much beyond the views of my five-year-old nephew, who on one occasion suddenly spoke up from the back seat of the family car and said to his mother (who was driving), "We have three kids, so you and daddy had to have sex three times, right?".

I would venture that the sex lives of many married couples with children are more in need of a little encouragement and *joie de vivre* than of discipline and mastery. I suspect that more, not less, generous and companionable sex would improve the *moral* quality of most marriages.

The guiding questions which I shall put to the Grisez School's position on sex and gender are whether it advances or undermines the basic goods of friendship and justice between women and men; and whether it advances or undermines the self-integration of women. My thesis is that the basic moral goods of friendship, justice, and self-integration are not well served by the way Grisez (and his colleagues) define 'life' as the centerpiece, not only of sex, but of marriage and of women's roles as well. Subsuming procreation under life, Grisez defines the former as the culminating meaning of marriage, makes contraception the moral equivalent of murder, and differentiates male and female roles so that women have primary responsibility for children but are to submit to their husband's authority even in the family.

Over the past three decades, Roman Catholic teaching on sex and marriage has ceased to call procreation the primary purpose of either sex or marriage, making love an equal purpose. Moreover, Catholic teaching does not equate the value of procreation with the value of life. While teaching since the Second Vatican Council has outlined a special maternal role for women, it has also affirmed women's social participation and has ceased to portray marital roles in an explicitly hierarchical fashion. What I see in Grisez as an unbalanced emphasis on procreation, in a context of female subordination, reverts from the themes guiding the teaching of John Paul II to those of Pius XI and Pius XII. The integration of sex, love, and procreation could be much more successfully advocated in many contemporary cultures within an approach which made love the grounding value and treated the sexes as fully equal in defining sexual, marital, and parental relationships. Gender equality (though not necessarily identity) is intrinsic to male-female friendship, justice, and self-integration for either sex. This fact is widely appreciated in North Atlantic, industrialized societies, and is becoming more and more evident in cultures around the world, as women gain education, economic resources, and a public voice.

Gender and Authority

Demonstrating a critical approach to past philosophical, theological, and magisterial teaching about the 'nature' of women, Grisez rejects unjust male domination, and supports women's objections to it. But he also rejects the idea of an 'egalitarian' relation between the sexes. Those who do not see sex differences as socially significant are said to view sex as "merely biological", "to despise the diverse gifts of different sorts of people", and to advocate a view which "manifests hatred" toward "a communion of many members in one body". They are termed "radical feminists" and distinguished from "sound efforts to ... achieve justice for women". "Catholic radical feminists" favor women's ordination.[27]

In Grisez's view, justice for women is compatible with the complementarity of the sexes in distinct gender roles in family, society, and church. Difference is not the end of the matter, however; women are to be subject to the authority of their husbands, at least in the case of inability to reach mutual agreement on a joint decision. The background of this proposal is an interpretation of authority as demanded by communal good order and the differentiation of tasks. Grisez's paradigm example is the case of four male students who decide to go camping together and determine by common agreement that each will assume responsibility for part of the preparations. They are all subsequently obedient to the group decision, whether the particular tasks assumed continue to have appeal or not: "This example makes it clear that authority and obedience are necessary if there is to be any community and cooperation whatsoever".[28]

It will be immediately evident to most readers that this case substantiates rather than refutes the feminist critique of hierarchical gender authority. When four equal individuals come together freely and by mutual consent commit themselves to equitably apportioned duties, there can hardly arise accusations of injustice. If, on the other hand, two of those students were informed by the others that they are by nature subordinate; that it is their 'special gift' to perform duties which are less desirable to and less valued by the group as a whole, as well as more time-consuming; that these special roles would, further, give them less say in the planning of the trip as a whole; *and* that their performance of these duties would be supervised and guaranteed by their two more 'authoritative' colleagues, they would very likely decide not to go camping. Now feminists do not necessarily advocate liberal individualism; many advance a vision of community in which authority is indeed the mandate of a communal process of discernment. But the conclusion drawn by most feminists is that the exercise of authority which respects the participation of all members and serves the common good cannot be premised on a notion of natural subordination which deprives some members of a decision-making voice on the basis of hypothetical and morally irrelevant 'differences'.

Sexual differentiation is closely linked to Grisez's understanding of authority in the family. He highly commends mutual understanding, generosity, forgiveness, and forbearance. Yet only a few pages after his camping example, he sets authority in a much more hierarchical framework by observing that "the moral basis of any genuine use of authority is that the one in authority reasonably decides what is required", that obedience imitates Christ, and that disobedience can be a grave sin.[29] The hierarchical rather than the consensual model seems to be operative in the section entitled "The Husband-Father has a Special Role in Decision-Making". It is the father who finally undertakes the "unified decisions" needed for cooperation in family life: "To make decisions for any group is to function as the authority in that group". Although the father is not to "dominate", there are "certain cases" in which "the husband-father should make a decision, and his wife and children should obey".[30] Although family members are able to make decisions in their "proper spheres", the father has final say even in the supposedly female domestic sphere in situations where no consensus emerges, and "neither spouse recognizes special competence in the other to make the decision".[31] In other words, if neither spouse agrees that the other is right, the man always has the prerogative to decide the issue: "The authority of the husband-father in precisely such cases is the irreducible core of the traditional Christian teaching which Pius XI summarizes as "the primacy of the husband with regard to the wife and children, the ready subjection of the wife and her willing obedience".[32] Grisez holds that John Paul II, who writes of the "mutual subjection" of spouses, does not reject this traditional view. But none of the texts he cites from *Familiaris consortio* or *Mulieris dignitatem* require such an interpretation, though the pope certainly defends women's *maternal* role as unique and indispensable, and even as structuring the feminine personality. Yet Grisez's argument for the agreement of John Paul II with Pius XI on the subordination of women amounts to the *assertion* that "mutual subjection" entails a subordinate role for the wife: "The unstated implication [of John Paul II] is that while a wife need not submit to her husband's selfish domination, she remains subject to his rightly exercised authority".[33] This interpretation is not only unwarranted; it is counteracted by the pope's assertion that women's dignity mandates "real equality in every area", including "equality of spouses with regard to family rights".[34]

I can hardly disagree with Grisez's beautiful avowal that "marriage is like friendship: the spouses enter it freely and as equals, and undertake to form an open-ended communion and to cooperate in mutually fulfilling activities. Each therefore is entitled to the other's respect, love, support, and availability for the interpersonal relationship".[35] Yet a fundamental question is whether mutually respectful and loving friendship, characterized by freedom and equality, is really compatible with the 'natural' subordination of one of the friends to the other. It is doubtful that a hierarchical model of marital friendship can be tolerated, much less required, by a vision of marriage as "total mutual self-giving".[36]

Abortion and Gender

Both official Roman Catholic teaching and Grisez present the morality of abortion primarily in terms of the destruction of the unborn child, arguing that it must be considered a person from conception, and that directly killing it must therefore be classified as murder. *Gaudium et spes* speaks of abortion as an "unspeakable crime", a characterization repeated in much pro-life literature. The more compassionate attitude toward desperate women found in recent papal teaching illustrates its greater cognizance of the pressures and social conditions leading to abortion. For instance, John Paul II reflects on the situation of many an unexpectedly pregnant woman:

> How often is she abandoned with her pregnancy, when the man, the child's father, is unwilling to accept responsibility for it? And besides the many 'unwed mothers' in our society, we also must consider all those who, as a result of various pressures, even on the part of the guilty man, very often 'get rid of' the child before it is born.[37]

The abortion question is a useful lens through which to view the tacit views of women still operative in Catholic teaching about sex-related matters. Abortion brings together the factors of life, procreation, sex, and gender, but those who debate its morality often limit attention to one or two of these aspects. Pro-choice advocates downplay the value of fetal life in favor of gender equality and the right of women to sexual and reproductive self-determination. Pro-life advocates often style the issue as one of life alone, ignoring the seriousness of the situations of women who lack the ability or social support to carry out responsible decisions about sex, pregnancy, and rearing a child, as well as the sexist and punitive tenor of many arguments about women's duty to endure the consequences of burdensome pregnancy. I agree with Grisez that the status of the fetus is a crucial question in the abortion debate, and would furthermore hold that the unborn child deserves strong moral and social protection. Yet I also believe that the most important missing piece in the Catholic abortion platform is a serious, demonstrable, and effective commitment to the equality and well-being of women. In fact, women's full moral agency and responsibility in sexual and family matters is a *sine qua non* of reducing abortion. Women's sense of self-integration, including bodily integrity and self-determination, should be wholeheartedly supported by ecclesial and theological opponents of abortion. This would not only gain public credibility for their moral and policy arguments, but would help create the actual conditions of virtuous and just childbearing.[38]

Germain Grisez authored a massive work on abortion not long before US abortion law was changed by the Supreme Court decisions of 1973. In that book, he identifies the "central issue" as whether "the unborn should be regarded as persons", argues that life begins at conception, opines that women's expectation that their offspring "are going to be a burden for a long time" is the motive for abortion, and sees reasons favoring legal abortion as no more than "shifty excuses".[39] Grisez constantly (though not without exception[40]) refers to the pregnant woman as "the mother", an identifier conducive to the equation of women's welfare and social contribution with a maternal role. He tends to identify proponents of legal abortion as extremists; a repeated refrain is that abortion permitted in a few cases will lead to abortion promoted in many. He tells us that two wide justifications of abortion access (by Havelock Ellis in 1910 and Frederick J. Taussig in 1934) have each become "a bible" for American "pro-abortionists".[41]

Referring to a 1938 case concerning the rape of a fourteen-year-old girl by soldiers in London, Grisez reports that the governmental committee which studied the matter affirmed the inviolability of innocent life, but was willing to make exceptions in limited cases. Grisez passes over the question whether limited exceptions could be justified in their own right, and refers not at all to the plight of the young girl, possible connections between military and sexual violence, or social attitudes and policies which might encourage or deter such violence or alleviate its effects. He moves on to a minority report which held that abortion does not differ essentially from contraception and urged liberalization of the abortion laws. He focuses on the report as representing a movement for acceptance of abortion to be realized in the post-war years:[42] "Loosening the abortion laws is a step toward an evolution toward legalized abortion, available to all without discrimination".[43] The real issue avoided here is the appropriate moral resolution of situations in which the value of unborn life is in direct conflict with the serious well-being or even life of a woman or young girl.

As far as moral theology is concerned, Grisez argues that abortion amounts to turning directly against the basic good of life, and so is always a sin. He grounds his argument in Aquinas's justification of self-defense, in which indirect intention is required; in killing the aggressor, one's intention is focused on saving one's own life.[44] Since in itself, Aquinas's use of the principle of 'double effect' would justify killing the fetus to save the mother's life, Grisez conjoins it (without explicitly noting the difference) to the 'third condition' of double effect as formulated in the manuals, namely, that the evil effect may not be the means to the good effect. On this ground, abortion to save life is excluded. Noting that this conclusion was not only disputed in the 1800s, but that life-saving abortion was "strongly and plausibly defended", Grisez settles the question negatively by introducing "the intervention of the Holy See" (1895) as "the decisive factor in the controversy".[45]

Some of these issues are revisited in *Living a Christian Life*, particularly the 'life against life' dilemma. In a conclusion which is more consistent with Thomas Aquinas's original use of the principle of double effect than with the casuistry of later manuals of moral theology, Grisez concludes that an operation like craniotomy is morally permissible to save the mother's life. Instead of calling such a remedy direct abortion, however, he redescribes the act as a "proposal ... to alter the child's physical dimensions and remove him or her, because, as a physical object, this body cannot remain where it is without ending in both the baby's and the mother's deaths".[46] This, he believes, permits him to retain the requirement that in an act with a good and evil effect, the latter may not be the means to the former. While I agree with Grisez's more recent moral instincts on the point of direct abortion in extreme cases, I find his argumentation implausible and evasive. On the one hand, he rightly realizes that it is callous and inhumane to accept a woman's death as the price of avoiding 'dirty hands' sullied by killing the life within her. On the other, his rewording of the moral stakes veils the overriding value of the woman's life and masks the responsibility we do bear for taking life in a tragic situation.

Grisez's new acceptance of direct (redescribed) abortion reflects sensitivity to the devastating consequences of some pregnancies for women. A feminist reader is gratified to find note that "women often choose abortion with great anguish and reluctance, under pressure from a social worker, a parent, a husband, a lover, an employer, a landlord, her own desperate need; reluctantly consenting to abortion, a woman may suffer it with great anguish as the only way to avoid what appears to be some disaster". Yet the same reader is dismayed to find in the very next paragraph that if women know abortion destroys fetal life (how could they not?), then they "usually intend the baby's death. Almost always there are other ways to forestall or deal with the problems which lead to the choice of abortion, but they would require self-control and self-sacrifice, and it is easy to see these as greater evils than ending incipient life 'when necessary'".[47] The final section on abortion heightens the note of blame by concluding that when a woman might save her unborn baby by risking her own life, "a Christian mother rightly does this work of mercy for her child".[48]

Biological Nature as a Norm

Like Aquinas, Grisez takes reproductive function to be largely determinative of the *moral* nature of sex and gender.[49] Empirical observation and scientific studies are employed in specifying what social arrangements successful reproduction demands.[50] Yet the 'givens' of biological nature are pliable in the face of distinctively human potentialities and needs. What would fully humanized sex, gender, and family look like? Grisez would never say that the merely biological in and of itself provides the human moral dimension of sex or procreation; but for him, the *structure* of gender and family relationships is defined by their functions in facilitating reproduction.

Sociobiology can provide a point of comparison with Grisez's use of descriptive information about human reproductive behavior. Sociobiologists and evolutionary psychologists interpret virtually all human behavior in terms of passing one's genes on effectively into the next generation (and so they account for the biological 'necessity' of male infidelity).[51] Although they often imply very different moral standards than those Grisez adopts, they veer close to biological determinism and reductionism in treating sexual morality and gendered behavior. To both the sociobiologists and Grisez, I would say that a morality which is consistent with our full and distinctive human nature subsumes biological drives and capacities under intelligence, freedom, and our capacities for love, mutuality, and fidelity. While love and friendship in sex and marriage ought to build on the continuities of human embodiment, the psychosocial dimensions of our being as female and male are fairly pliable.

Thus the equality of male and female, their intimacy and mutual communion in marriage, their reciprocal support in parenthood, and their formation of a family as a sphere of interpersonal commitment and social contribution, should control the ways in which physical sex and biological reproduction are defined and shaped morally. This is not to say that freedom totally overrides the moral value of human reproductive embodiment. The question is, rather, whether the genuine dignity, equality, and mutuality of woman and man can be served adequately by a theory of their relationship contoured primarily by their biological reproductive roles, rather than by the distinctively human qualities of their interpersonal communion.

Concluding Reflections

In conclusion, I want to introduce briefly two elements for explicit reflection which have been largely implicit in my treatment of a renewed natural law approach to sex and gender. One of these elements is epistemological and the other biblical. The first is the redefinition of objectivity in a late modern or postmodern age; the second is the relevance of biblical narratives and ideals to reasonable moral thinking.

Since the Enlightenment and for most of this century, a scientific model of knowledge has been in possession in Western cultures and especially in academe. On this model, knowledge of the truth is attained and demonstrated on the basis of empirical evidence or strict logical deduction. Aspects of moral knowing such as its communal context, its reliance on the emotions and on embodied experiences, its inferential character, and its practical origins, have been under-appreciated when not denied outright. Beyond the fact that Grisez speaks of the emotions as "weakening" the will and contributing to practical irrationality,[52] he has in general been committed to defending truth in ethics from historical contingency and relativistic viewpoints.[53] For instance, he rejects the notion that "[a]bortion is right for those who think it is right and wrong for those who think it is wrong"[54] —a rejection with which I could not agree more. But defining the precise conditions under which it is right or wrong, *objectively*, is not a simple matter of deduction from clear first principles such as the value of life. It requires a more rounded and complete attunement to the conditions of human life and to the complexity of some human experiences, even an acknowledgment that there may be some moral dilemmas demanding practical action whose objective morality we may never be able to discern clearly or unambiguously at all. Above all, it requires the critical assimilation of personal, cultural, and historical variations on the experience of being human, even while acknowledging a fundamental commonality of human goods. More careful attention to the human experiences of women — as well as of ethnic, racial, and social groups who have not in the past enjoyed wide cultural and religious authority— will reward us with a more, not less, objective understanding of moral goods, opportunities, and obligations.

This objective understanding will, of course, be partial, provisional, and revisable, just as moral teaching has been in the past, however little that fact has been acknowledged. As demonstrated already in developments in papal teaching and in the views of Germain Grisez himself, more equal familial and public roles for women and men have already changed our perceptions of what 'objectively right' gender relationships might be.

Finally, it has been characteristic of Roman Catholic theology to see Scripture and natural law as coexisting in a complementary and mutually critical relationship. Grisez repeatedly uses marriage as an example when elaborating on the Christian duties of cross-bearing and self-denial.[55] The Cross is certainly a central New Testament image. But it is debatable whether the Christian life should be formed primarily around it, rather than around the inclusive and compassionate solidarity which seems more at the heart of Jesus' teaching and deeds, and informs the earliest Christian communities.[56]

What is "following the way of the Lord Jesus" mostly about, and what impact could this 'way' be expected to have on gender, sex, and marriage? Although a full exploration of this question —in Grisez's writings and much more so in related literature— would exceed the possibilities of the present essay, Grisez does write of Jesus' "personal vocation", as well as his preaching of the kingdom of God. Grisez's interpretation of Jesus' mission, with its emphasis on individual freedom, commitment, and perseverance, has an almost existentialist tone.[57] The kingdom of God and the command to love one's enemies[58] are associated with overcoming evil, but the social meaning of the evil overcome and thus also of the kingdom are not fully developed.[59] Rather, "to follow Jesus means to accept and carry out our own personal vocations faithfully", and to "live a good life".[60] Although the Christian act of faith is community-forming, structural change in society is not addressed at any length as a moral outcome of "the way of the Lord Jesus". Rather, the individual Christian, like Jesus, should give up "a pleasant life of self-satisfaction" and face personal responsibilities in marriage, family, or business, however difficult or unappealing.

Yet recent biblical scholarship, including research on the social history of the first Christian communities, suggests an alternative view of the implications of discipleship for human relations, including sex and gender.[61] The kingdom of God embodies a new experience of God as 'Abba' which flows outward in mercy, forgiveness and compassion toward one's fellow human beings. The kingdom of God overturns cultural status hierarchies, establishes a socially radical community which cuts across boundaries of race, class, and gender, and embodies a special commitment to inclusion of the marginalized. The early Christians, by holding up virginity as an ideal, offered a critical alternative to the Greco-Roman patriarchal family, which oriented social prestige and material wealth around procreation within politically advantageous marriages. A highly procreation-centered ethic which holds women's place to be subordinate reverts to family models which the early Christians struggled to resist.

The biblical models disrupt 'natural' sex, gender, and family patterns, as focused on reproduction and social competition, and sensitize us to more 'humane' forms of gender and family behavior. In their original setting, even the *Haustafeln* or 'household codes',[62] commanding submission of family members to the *paterfamilias*, had this effect. While in today's more gender-equal societies, the reiteration of these instructions can and does represent the tenacity of patriarchal bias (hence John Paul II's reinterpretation in terms of 'mutual subjection'), the codes originally functioned to moderate even more strongly worded and less reciprocal pagan versions. The challenge for Christians today is likewise to modify our own cultures toward greater gender-equality than we now find around us.

On the whole, New Testament portrayals of₃ Christian moral behavior encourage us to develop the empathetic and inclusive potentials of human nature, built over a natural substructure of biological and social survival strategies strongly colored by the drive to assert dominance over other individuals and groups. Parenthood is certainly an important meaning of sex and marriage, and even of gender roles. Yet it is even more important to ensure that sex, gender, and marriage are realized socially in terms of their distinctively human, relational meanings. This means full equality of men and women in family and in public roles. Gender differentiation need not and should not be so pronounced as to preclude social equality (domestic, ecclesial and public). This more egalitarian interpretation is supported both by New Testament models of discipleship-community, and by the modern worldwide revolution in women's roles as expressive of a new consciousness of women's full humanity.

NOTES

1   Many draw on the work of Michel Foucault. Some central representatives are Jane Flax, *Psychoanalysis, Feminism, and Postmodernism in the Contemporary West* (Berkeley, California: University of California Press, 1990); Judith Butler, *Gender Trouble: Feminism and the Subversion of Identity* (New York and London: Routledge, 1990); Judith Butler, *Bodies that Matter: On the Discursive Limits of 'Sex'* (New York and London: Routledge, 1993); Linda Singer, *Erotic Welfare: Sexual Theory and Politics in the Age of Epidemic*, edited and introduced by Judith Butler and Maureen MacGrogan (New York and London: Routledge, 1993); Jana Sawicki, *Disciplining Foucault: Feminism, Power and the Body* (New York and London: Routledge, 1991); Iris Marion Young, "The Ideal of Community and the Politics of Difference", *Social Theory and Practice*, 12/1 (Spring 1986); Susan Bordo, *Unbearable Weight: Feminism, Western Culture, and the Body* (Berkeley, Los Angeles, London: University of California Press, 1993); and Catharine MacKinnon, *Toward a Feminist Theory of the State* (Cambridge, Mass.: Harvard University Press, 1989). Theological examples of the deconstructionist mood in feminism include Sheila Greave Devaney, who urges feminists to reject the ideal of objective, universal knowledge, as well as evaluative norms ("Problems with Feminist Theory: Historicity and the Search for Sure Foundations", in Paula M. Cooey, Sharon A. Farmer, and Mary Ellen Ross [eds.], *Embodied Love: Sensuality and Relationship as Feminist Values* [San Francisco: Harper and Row, 1987], p.92; see also her "A Historicist Model for Theology", in Jeffrey Carlson and Robert A. Ludwig [eds.], *Jesus and Faith: a Conversation on the Work of John Dominic Crossan* [Maryknoll, NY: Orbis, 1994], pp.44-56); and Rebecca Chopp ("Seeing and Naming the World Anew: the Works of Rosemary Radford Ruether", *Religious Studies Review*, 15 [1989],

pp.8-11).

2   Rosemary Radford Reuther, *Sexism and God-Talk: Toward a Feminist Theology*
        (Boston; Beacon Press, 1983), p.18.

3   Ibid., p.19. The full humanity of women is a central theme, developed from a
        Latin American liberationist perspective, in María Pilar Aquino, *Our Cry for
        Life: Feminist Theology from Latin America* (Maryknoll, NY; Orbis Books,
        1994). Both Ruether and Aquino are Catholics.

4   Patricia De Ferrari, "Seeking Full Dignity: Catholic Social Teaching and Women
        in the Third World", *Horizons*, 22 (Fall, 1992), p.259. DeFerrari cites Maria
        Riley, "Catholic, Feminist, Committed to Justice and Peace", *Concilium*, 5
        (1991).

5   See Anne Carr and Elisabeth Schüssler Fiorenza (eds.), *The Special Nature of
        Women?*, *Concilium*, 6 (1991).

6   *ST*, IaIIae, q.94, aa.4, 5.

7   Grisez entitles the concluding section of *CMP*, "A Critical Examination of
        Radical Theological Dissent". He asserts that dissenters reject "many" infallible
        norms and characterizes their claims as "gratuitous" and "specious".

8   A major recent statement of feminist theology by a Roman Catholic is Elizabeth
        A. Johnson, *She Who Is: the Mystery of God in Feminist Theological Discourse*
        (New York: Crossroad, 1994). Others are Anne E. Carr, *Transforming Grace:
        Christian Tradition and Women's Experience* (San Francisco; Harper and Row,
        1988); Catherine Mowry LaCugna (ed.), *Freeing Theology: the Essentials of
        Theology in Feminist Perspective* (San Francisco; Harper, 1993); and Ann
        O'Hara Graff (ed.), *In the Embrace of God: Feminist Approaches to Theological
        Anthropology* (Maryknoll, NY; Orbis Books, 1995).

9   *LCL*, p.568.

10   *CMP*, p.124; *LCL*, pp.567-8, including footnotes 40,42, 43. See also *PP*, pp.107-
        8.

11   Jean Porter, "Basic Goods and the Human Good in Recent Catholic Moral
        Theology", *The Thomist*, 57/1 (1993), p.36.

12   *PP*, p.33.

13   Porter mentions halting the Superbowl game in response to a bomb threat; simply
        choosing not to find out more about the love life of Princess Di despite an easily
        accessible newpaper article proffering that knowledge; and declining life-
        supports which could keep one alive in a coma. Moreover she regards as
        "fantastic" the idea that the "contra-life" mentalities of a murderer and of a
        person who uses contraceptives are the same (ibid., pp.38-40).

14   *LCL*, p.568.

15   Ibid., p.570.

16   Ibid., p.572.

17   Ibid., pp.634-5.

18   See also John C Ford, Germain Grisez, Joseph Boyle, John Finnis, William E
        May, *The Teaching of Humanae vitae: a Defense* (San Francisco: Ignatius Press,
        1988), where the following judgment is quite confidently advanced: "Those who
        deliberately make the contralife choice of contraception and maintain that choice
        have contralife hearts Married couples who make this choice and maintain it do

not merely commit isolated acts of contraception but have hearts that are not marital.... Rather than sanctifying one another, they slip together toward spiritual self-destruction" (pp.106-7).

19   *Gaudium et spes*, 48.

20   *LCL*, pp.570-71.

21   Ibid., p.626.

22   Ibid., p.628.

23   Ibid., p.388.

24   See Thomas Aquinas, *ST*, Ia, q. 92: "On the Production of Woman".

25   Ford et al., *Humanae vitae: a Defense*, p.71.

26   Ibid., pp.71-2.

27   *LCL*, pp.386-87.

28   Ibid., p.432.

29   Ibid., pp.437-39.

30   Ibid., p.629.

31   Ibid., p.630.

32   Ibid., p.631. The citation is from *Casti connubii* (1930), from which Grisez also quotes: "Within the family, the father stands in God's place. He must lead and guide the rest by his authority and the example of his good life" (ibid., p.615 n.140). He refers to this document as a *"doctrinal* encyclical" (p.616, my emphasis), whatever that is meant to imply.

33   *LCL*, p.617.

34   *Letter of Pope John Paul II to Women* (Vatican City: Libreria Editrice Vaticana, 1995), 4.

35   *LCL*, p.618.

36   John Paul II, *Familiaris Consortio*, 19.

37   *Mulieris Dignitatem*, 14.

38   In *LCL*, Grisez recognizes the importance of embodiment in personal and sexual identity, and hence repudiates sexual assault, of which rape is said to be the paradigm case. Nonetheless, he speaks of women's occasional "responsibility" for rape, and views forced intercourse in marriage as not true rape because the wife's body is no longer autonomous (pp.546, 548, 645)!

39   Germain Grisez, *Abortion: the Myths, the Realities, the Arguments* (New York and Cleveland: Corpus Books, 1970), pp.361, 274, and 468, respectively.

40   Ibid., p.6.

41   Ibid., pp.210 and 226, respectively.

42   Ibid., p.224.

43   Ibid., p.65.

44   Ibid., p.326. The text in Aquinas is the *ST*, IIaIIae, q.64, a.7.

45   Ibid., p.179.

46   *LCL*, p.502.

47   Ibid., p.500.

48   Ibid., p.503.

49   Ibid., p.570.

50   Ibid., p.388 n.13 (on anthropology).

51   See, for example, Donald Symons, *The Evolution of Human Sexuality* (New

York: Oxford University Press, 1979); David Buss, *The Evolution of Desire* (New York: Basic Books, 1994); and Robert Wright, *The Moral Animal: Why We Are the Way We Are —the New Science of Evolutionary Psychology* (New York: Pantheon, 1994).

52   *CMP*, p.413.

53   See Germain Grisez and Russell Shaw, *Beyond the New Morality: the Responsibilities of Freedom* (Notre Dame: University of Notre Dame Press, 1974).

54   Grisez, *Abortion*, p.270.

55   *CMP*, p.558.

56   I Corinthians 13.

57   Ibid., p.536: "Jesus freely accepts death because in doing so he carries out his personal vocation".

58   Matthew 5.43.

59   Ibid., pp.535-36, 555-59.

60   Ibid., pp.557, 559.

61   For further development of the extremely abbreviated ideas in this section, see my "Sexual Ethics: a Feminist Perspective", *Interpretation*, 49 (1995), pp.5-16; and *Sex,Gender and Christian Ethics* (Cambridge: Cambridge University Press, 1996), chapter 5, "Sex and Gender Ethics as New Testament Social Ethics".

62   Ephesians 5.21-6.9.

12 The Moral Standing of Nature and the New Natural Law

Michael Northcott

Introduction

In 1972 one of the world's oldest conservation societies, the Sierra Club, took out a legal action against Rogers Morton, the United States Secretary of the Interior, in order to prevent the United States Forest Service from permitting Walt Disney to build a theme park in Mineral King Valley, part of the Sierra Nevada Mountains, a region which the Club was originally established to preserve from economic development. The lower courts challenged the standing of the Sierra Club in relation to the disputed land; and in consequence Professor Christopher Stone published an article in the *Southern California Law Review* in defence of the Sierra Club's legal status.[1]

The central thesis of Stone's now classic paper, "Should Trees Have Standing?", was that rights should be conferred on the natural environment, and on objects in the environment such as the Sequoia trees and water catchment areas that would be despoiled by the proposed development at Mineral King, in the same way that legal entities such as corporations are accorded rights that grant them the status of legal persons. Stone argued that this extension of legal rights to inanimate objects was the only sure legal mechanism for advancing environmental conservation because, until such rights were recognised in relation to the environment, it would be difficult for parties wishing to defend particular parts of it to do so in a court of law. The conferral of rights would permit a guardianship approach to objects in the environment, thus conferring on them the status of legal persons analogous to those already recognised in relation to public institutions, trusts and corporations.

Stone also proposed that the extension of rights to the environment would influence the framing of future State and Federal laws concerning economic development and environmental conservation analogously to the successive advancements in the conferral of rights on slaves, then commoners, then women, and most recently the disabled —advancements that have pioneered the reform of institutional, corporate and community behaviour towards such classes of persons.

I begin with reference to this (ultimately unsuccessful) legal action because, while the natural law tradition is widely recognised as having provided the ideological grounds for the original delineation of the rights of persons in the constitutions of the Republics of the United States of America and France, and more recently in the Universal Declaration of Human Rights made by the United Nations in 1948, it has not been engaged in the modern struggle for the recognition of the moral standing or rights of the natural world. It is the central intention of this essay to demonstrate that the natural law tradition provides uniquely powerful resources for grounding such recognition.

I first explored the possible advantages of a natural law approach to the moral standing of nature over other philosophical approaches in my book, *The Environment and Christian Ethics,* where I drew on the Grisez-Finnis theory of natural law.[2] While noting their anthropocentric orientation, and their denials of the existence of natural rights beyond the human community, I argued there that, suitably modified, their account of natural law could be pressed into service in relation to environmental ethics. Here, however, I shall argue that the Grisez-Finnis restatement of the natural law tradition is more flawed than I earlier proposed, and in particular that their uniquely modern reconceptualisation of natural law in deontological terms seriously disables the tradition as a vehicle for establishing the moral standing of nature and the duties we owe to the natural world.

My argument will proceed as follows. First, I will consider the status of nature —human and non-human— in the Grisez-Finnis theory. I will contend that its relatively low status is related to the theory's deontological denial of a natural or metaphysical foundation for natural law. Secondly, I will review alternative restatements of the natural law tradition by Henry Veatch, Anthony Lisska, and Pamela Hall, all of whom reject the rationalist and transcendentalist approach of post-Enlightenment philosophy embraced by Finnis and Grisez, and instead repristinate a metaphysical approach to natural law. Finally, I will argue that these metaphysical restatements, when combined with elements in modern ecology and animal ethology, are suggestive of an ecological extension of the natural law tradition, one prefigured both in the Old Testament and in Aquinas' natural law theory.

The Standing of Nature in the Grisez-Finnis Natural Law Theory

The anthropocentric account given by Grisez and Finnis of the moral standing of subpersonal things represents these lower orders of life as being dependent on human nature for their fulfilment and ultimate value.[3] It is therefore appropriate to begin by considering the theory of the origin of moral value in human nature, and then to consider the status of non-human being in relation to this. The central thesis of Finnis concerning the relationship between nature and value is that the determination of value, and hence of the good or goods, does not rest upon factual judgements or observations of nature. Rather the determination of values or goods, and of priorities among them, rests upon one irreducible human good, which is knowledge itself. That knowledge is a good is said to be unarguable, since to argue against it is already to demonstrate its truthfulness.[4] The putatively fundamental priority of knowledge (and reason) over all other values or goods provides Finnis and Grisez with the rational and objective bedrock on which they build the rest of their system. It also provides a key principle for assessing relationships between human and subpersonal creatures. As Grisez puts it, a fundamental reason why misuse of subpersonal creatures is bad is because it enhances the alienation of the human body, and of the misused subpersonal creature, from reason.[5]

The category of the personal, which is identified by capacities for knowledge and reason, is crucial for distinguishing between the goods of persons and the interests of subpersons. Thus Finnis argues that although subpersons may appear to instantiate goods which are analogous to human goods (as proposed by advocates of animal rights), they do not truly do so, because in persons these goods are not just aspects of life or conscious life; rather, "they are good as aspects of the flourishing of a person".[6] Human goods must therefore always trounce subpersonal goods where there is any reasonable conflict of interest.

In the opening chapter of *The Fundamentals of Ethics*, Finnis distinguishes his approach to natural law and the good from two other approaches: naturalism, or the attempt to reduce moral judgements to properties in nature such as pleasure or pain; and intuitionism, or the attempt to reduce moral judgements to human intuitions, gut feelings, or cultural consensus about the good. Finnis makes clear in both *Natural Law and Natural Rights* and *The Fundamentals of Ethics* that he is developing his account of objective value in contradistinction to accounts that attempt to ground claims about value or the good in factual statements about human nature. In other words, he eschews two of the traditional enterprises of natural law theory and two of its key features: the enterprises of philosophical anthropology and metaphysics, and the features of teleology and fact-value claims.

In a critical exposition of this approach, Anthony Lisska characterises Finnis' position as 'transcendentalism', by which he means that Finnis shares with Hume and Kant in the Enlightenment attempt to base value or the good on an analysis of the ways of human knowing —that is, on epistemology— in contradistinction to medieval philosophy, which sought to ground ethics in the structure of reality, including nature itself, as well as in the capacities of the human mind.[7]

As Finnis acknowledges, this Enlightenment approach to ethics arises from and confirms the modern scientific claim that nature —human and non-human— does not express inherent purposiveness or teleology, and that therefore ascriptions of value or goodness cannot be properly connected with factual accounts of the world. In other words, Finnis —and Grisez with him— accept the logic of Enlightenment deconstructions of teleology, realism, natural theology and metaphysics, and therefore attempt to find a basis for their natural law theory apart from any account of nature, and in the only transcendent category acceptable to modern analytic philosophers (and for that matter modern scientists and legal scholars): the human mind itself. The is-ought distinction is a fundamental tenet of modern thought with which Finnis and Grisez do not wish to contend. Instead, they seek to demonstrate that there are objective grounds for key features of the natural law tradition within the universal structure of human consciousness and cultural experience, grounds which are so unarguable and *a priori* that they are self-evident to all conscious persons and therefore do not constitute statements of fact.

In an extensive review of *Natural Law and Natural Rights*, Henry Veatch argues that in their attempt to concur with post-Enlightenment philosophy, Finnis and Grisez make a virtue out of a necessity, and present an entirely deontological, non-naturalistic and non-metaphysical account of natural law. Like their utilitarian and deontological dialogue partners, they present a theory of ethics which avoids any foundational reference to nature.[8]

As Pamela Hall puts it, they present us with a theory of "natural law without nature".[9]

There is widespread agreement that Finnis and Grisez are of major significance in rehabilitating the natural law tradition in modern ethical and legal debates. Their Thomist critics argue, however, that by subtracting nature they effectively empty the tradition of constitutive elements —to such an extent that Hall asks whether their use of the term 'natural law' is any more than a "nostalgic acknowledgement of the philosophical home they have departed"; while Veatch suggests that one who contends, as Finnis does, that the norms referred to in a theory of natural law should not be taken as based on judgements about nature, "must surely be an opponent of natural law doctrines in ethics, not their defender!"[10]

Finnis and Grisez offer a number of replies to their critics. The first and central one is already present in their restatement of the natural law position; namely, that neither Aristotle nor Thomas ever claimed that their accounts of the human good or flourishing rested on factual statements about human nature. Thus Finnis contends that "from end to end of his ethical discourses, the primary categories for Aquinas are the 'good' and the 'reasonable'; the 'natural' is, from the point of view of his ethics, a speculative appendage added by way of metaphysical reflection".[11] A second defence involves the contention that, despite the focus of their account of moral judgement on certain features of human consciousness, they do at times also represent nature as an objective realm where potential goodness and fulfilment are not simply imputed by human minds but are constituted by nature.

As to the first defence, Lisska, in a notable and thorough exposition of Thomas' natural law theory, identifies unambiguous metaphysical and naturalistic claims at the heart of Thomas' enunciation of natural law in the *Summa*. He demonstrates that disposition is the key to Thomas' derivation of natural law. Humans and other kinds of being are disposed to live and develop in certain ways and not in others. These dispositions are inherent in the nature of their being and include as their ends (in the case of humans): life, sexual union, the nurture of children, the knowledge of God, and the avoidance of harm to others in their social group.[12] In contrast to the Finnis-Grisez claim that pre-moral goods are self-evident, Lisska, Hall, and Veatch contend that Thomas' account of these goods relies on their observable presence in the lives of classes of being, and on the claim that beings are directed by their nature to certain goods as developmental potentialities or goals. Therefore factual accounts of teleological nature are a central, and not a disposable, feature of Thomistic accounts of the natural law.[13]

The second element of Finnis' and Grisez's riposte to their critics is rooted in their accounts of the substantive goods which are located in natural orders other than the human, and of the extent to which these natural orders may be said to present limits and boundaries to human activity. Thus they point out that in *Beyond the New Theism* Grisez presents "a thoroughly objectivist theory of value as *fulfilment of possibility*, in each order of reality";[14] and that Finnis in *Natural Law and Natural Rights* considers the significance of the order of nature as an order of being which is external to human understanding while still amenable to it. But these passages, of course, do not gainsay or undo the non-naturalistic character of their ethical theory, nor are they designed to do so. Certain aspects of the natural world —climate, biology, psychology— may, according to Finnis, "affect the realization of human well-being in discoverable ways", but they do not constitute a moral order.[15] On the contrary, he contends that the whole of nature is so wasteful and lacking in internal logic and wisdom that it presents, in words which he quotes from the protagonist in Hume's *Dialogues concerning Natural Religion*, "nothing but the idea of a blind Nature, impregnated by a great vivifying principle, and pouring forth from her lap, without discernment or parental care, her maimed and abortive children".[16] Finnis concludes, with Hume:

> the proposition that the cause or causes of order in the universe probably bear some remote analogy to human intelligence, while acceptable, is "ambiguous, at least undefined" and "not capable of extension, variation or more particular explication" and "affords no inference that affects human life, or [that] can be the source of any action or forbearance".[17]

Given this espousal of the Humean view of nature as blind, undiscerning and wasteful, it is unsurprising that when we turn to a consideration of their regard for the non-human world, we find Grisez and Finnis arguing that it is primarily created as a site for the realisation of human goods, that the realisation of goods in subhuman things is entirely derivative, and that therefore any conflict between human goods and the interests of non-human beings should be resolved in favour of humans.[18] The primary orientation which Grisez adopts with regard to the place of subpersonal reality arises from a strong interpretation of the reference to human dominion over creation in the book of Genesis: "included in the dominion God gives humans over subpersonal creatures is the authority to use them to meet human needs".[19] In using portions of land or other creatures, humans draw these things into relationship with their bodies. Thereby "subpersonal creation becomes humanized and personalized. Pieces of territory and things acquire new meaning and value; they are no longer merely parts of the natural world, but pertain to the human subject".[20] In other words, by coming into relationship with human persons, subpersonal reality acquires value in addition to that which it has inherently as part of the order of creation that God has judged to be good. In using material things Christians draw them into the holiness of their lives and thereby restore them to God through Christ. There are, however, limits to this process. Christians are not to use material things without restraint or for motives other than those of meeting human needs: thus "people should never disturb natural things except to serve some human good, their own or others', in a reasonable way; but they always may deal with nature as that purpose requires".[21]

Grisez's position is a restatement of classic Christian anthropocentrism, which has traditionally involved the exaltation of the theme of dominion over other themes which also find biblical warrant —such as those of stewardship, asceticism, and community between nature and humans.[22] Lynn White was the first among many scholars to draw attention to the implication of this anthropocentrism in the origins of the current global crisis of the environment.[23] Despite Grisez's principal qualification of this position (that subpersonal creatures have God-given, inherent value), his approach gives weak moral grounds for ascribing weight to the inherent value of nature independently of human needs. Therefore it gives insufficient support to attempts by lawyers, philosophers, and citizens to resist the ecological depradations of corporations and governments through economic developments that are said to meet human needs. While Grisez might concede that, in particular cases such as the Sierra Nevada or Sarawak, clear-cutting forests to feed the human demand for paper and plywood is not a reasonable use of nature, his insistence that the ultimate good of trees is dependent on their potential for use by (redeemed) persons prevents their being granted the moral and legal standing necessary for the general regulation of such use.[24]

The weakness of Grisez's position from an environmental perspective is even more clearly manifest in his treatment of the status of animals. He begins by dismissing the concept of animal rights, arguing that their ascription to animals undermines their ascription to humans, since animals have no sense of moral obligation and cannot therefore share moral status analogous to that of persons.[25] The priority in the consideration of the treatment of animals is therefore the needs of persons, and not of animals themselves. Although they are part of God's good creation, cruelty towards them is intrinsically bad only when this treatment does not clearly serve human benefit: "it is cruel to cause animals pain by misusing them for activities which serve no basic good of persons, for example, purported experiments which offer no reasonable prospect of advancing scientific knowledge".[26] However, the clear implication is that it is not cruel to cause animals pain when there is such a prospect. The reason why pain has no determinate moral significance for animals as it does for persons, is because "animals' lives are not sacred as human life is" and hence "their suffering cannot have the spiritual and moral meaning human suffering has".[27]

The fundamental premise of Grisez's account of moral obligation, like Finnis' account of natural law, is a reductionist, denatured, and deontological one: "one can account plausibly for moral obligation by reducing it to the first principles of practical reason, which shape human actions toward the basic intelligible human goods".[28] Since both Finnis and Grisez deny the practical quest for these goods by any creatures beyond humans, they exclude the realisation of goods in subpersonal creatures. But, as Carol Gilligan argues, this denatured and rationalist approach to morality is insufficiently rich to account for the complexities of human patterns of moral development that empirical observation reveals.[29] More importantly for our purposes here, it offers no grounds for dialogue with the growing body of scientific accounts of analogies between forms of moral behaviour and good evident among humans and those evident among other animals, accounts which have clear, ancient —and for Grisez (and presumably Finnis) authoritative— precursors in the Old Testament, especially the Book of Proverbs.[30]

Henry Veatch argues that Finnis' creation of a denaturalised natural law theory, his rejection of teleology, and his affirmation of the is-ought distinction, has been deeply influenced by the scientistic and anti-metaphysical philosophical culture of his academic environment in Oxford. As Veatch puts it, "no so-called scientific study or investigation of nature is ever going to be able to turn up evidence of the existence of real norms or values right within the facts of nature".[31] Finnis' aim has been to advance the case for a key feature of the medieval philosophical tradition without challenging the modern scientific and philosophical shibboleth of the fact-value distinction.

Given the formative influence of this university culture on his project, it is unsurprising, Veatch argues, that Finnis also shares with Kant, Hume, and most contemporary analytic philosophers that other great shibboleth of

Enlightenment thinking: the assumption that our knowledge and judgements about the real world of phenomena are always distorted by cultural and mental processing, and that therefore the only sure foundation for values and ethics is an account of the process of understanding, or an analysis of the specific linguistic features of moral claims. Veatch describes this Enlightenment shift to epistemology, and the more recent philosophical and ethical vogue for linguistic analysis, as the 'transcendental turn' whose import is "that neither science nor philosophy can any longer claim to be in any way a knowledge of things in themselves —i.e., of things as they really are".[32]

This turn is also manifest in the Cartesian dualism between mind and matter, rationality and the body, which many environmental philosophers also identify as a key element in the causation of the modern environmental crisis. Veatch is again perspicacious in this regard when he quotes Kant to the effect that the consequence of the transcendental turn is that "the understanding is enabled not so much to draw its laws from nature, as rather to prescribe them to nature".[33] The environmental philosopher Holmes Rolston suggests that instead of the prescription of laws to nature, the environmental crisis requires a resensitisation to the values that already exist within the natural world — values that may be said to precede human processing and from which duties toward the natural world may therefore be said to arise.[34] According to Rolston and other environmental philosophers, the resolution of the environmental crisis requires, first of all, criticism of the core assumptions of modernity, especially Cartesianism and its anthropocentric implications; and then the development of a new philosophical project to discover goods or values in the non-human as well as the human environment. It is my contention that the natural law tradition provides unique and important resources for environmental philosophy at this point; but that it can only perform this service in the ontological mode originally advanced by Thomas, which clearly grounds natural law in theological metaphysics and a theological account of creation, and not in the 'transcendental' mode proposed by Finnis and Grisez.

A New Naturalist Version of Natural Law

Anthony Lisska commences a systematic ontological restatement of Aquinas' naturalist natural law theory with an examination of the metaphysics of essence: "An essence determines the nature of a particular individual belonging to a natural kind".[35] But essences are not fixed; they are constituted by developmental properties or dispositions in the expression of which each individual of each kind has the potential to grow. Not all individuals may realise their full developmental potential, but this potentiality is already present in their being. Lisska understands Aquinas' frequently used words *inclinatio* and *appetitus* as meaning developmental dispositions, and he arranges Aquinas' enumeration of these dispositions in the central text on natural law in the *Summa Theologiae* as follows:

1. dispositions or inclinations towards living, continuing in existence, seeking nutrition and growth;
2. dispositions or inclinations towards sensory apprehensions, having sense experiences, caring for offspring;
3. dispositions or inclinations towards rational cognitivity, understanding (rational curiosity), living together in communities.[36]

Lisska contends that once we have determined which of these kinds of disposition —biological, sensory and rational— personal or subpersonal beings possess, then we know what their natures are. He argues that Aquinas is not a teleologist in the sense he is often construed (and dismissed) as being by modern philosophers. For Aquinas, natural kinds can be said to 'act for an end', not consciously, but by virtue of their inherent dispositions: the end or 'telos' is the point at which the dispositional properties in the primary substance reach their development or perfection, and where the individual functions well as a member of a natural species. In Thomistic terminology, it is where the potency or disposition has reached a state of actualisation. But this is not a conscious development on the part of beings themselves, for the acorn is not 'consciously driven' to become an oak tree.[37] Whereas, Lisska contends, Cartesian logic sees universals and essences as essentially static and unchanging, Aquinas sees them as in process, in becoming, and hence containing within themselves a direction toward an end.

According to Lisska, natural law for Aquinas is a description of those dispositional properties (non-rational and rational) that different kinds of being possess (and that human beings alone possess fully), combined with the recognition that these dispositions also have a moral character, indicating the goods towards which individuals and communities, human and non-human, are by their nature directed. Each good is an end, but it is an end which is already present as potential in the dispositional property, and hence in the essence, of each individual kind. It is in these terms that *beatitudo*, Aquinas' version of Aristotle's *eudaimonia*, should be understood: to function well is to realise the developmental potential of one's essential properties.[38]

It is on the basis of this theory of essence, disposition, and potential in nature that Aquinas develops what Lisska, *contra* Finnis and Grisez, identifies as his ethical naturalism. Morality has its foundation in the nature of human being. An act is morally wrong, not because God commands that 'A is wrong', but rather because the act prevents the completion —the self-actualisation of the dispositional properties which constitute the content of human nature.[39] In Lisska's reading of Thomist natural law, nature has a central place because it determines those dispositions whose realisation comprises the goods that make for fulfilment.

In his original enunciation of the first principle of natural law, Aquinas expressed the belief that natural law is universally present and discernible in the structure of the universe, just as God, the cause of all that is, is present and discernible throughout the cosmos, and in everything that lives: "the first principle of practical reason is founded on the notion of good, viz. that good is that which all things seek after".[40] This universal natural law is specified in his enumeration of the dispositions or inclinations towards which creatures are variously directed: dispositions to continue in existence and to seek nutrition and growth; dispositions towards sensory experiences and towards care for offspring; dispositions towards curiosity and elementary rationality, and towards living together in community. Whereas the first two categories of disposition are common to all animals, Thomas believed that the third category —rationality and community— is the exclusive property of human animals, since only they act rationally in their discernment and keeping of the natural law. Whereas for humans the keeping of the natural law involves the action of reason and the will, all other animals keep it by instinct and appetite.[41] For humans, in other words, observance is voluntary, whereas for animals it is involuntary.

The operation of natural law finds more universal, cosmological expression in the thought of the sixteenth-century English divine, Richard Hooker, than in Aquinas' *Summa*. Hooker's assertion that "all things that are have some operation not violent or causal; nor doth any thing ever begin to exercise the same without some foreconceived end for which it worketh" indicates a view of natural dispositions or ends, such that they can be seen at work in rivers or trees as much as in animals, rational or otherwise.[42]

In his little-known *Commentary on Dionysius*, Aquinas also seems to hint at this same kind of universal conceptualisation when he proposes that all beings should have rendered to them what is their due according to natural law, and that the principles of equity and distributive justice that arise from the natural law are not therefore limited to humans but are part of God's ordering of the cosmos as a whole: "just as through the ordering of distributive justice in a city governed by a first citizen, the entire political order is preserved, so through this ordering of justice the entire universe is preserved by God".[43] And again: "(divine) justice truly consists in this: that it gives to all things according to their proper worth and that it preserves the nature of each thing in its proper order and power".[44] In these passages we see that those natural rights or dues which arise from the recognition of the natural law in humans are not simply confined to humans; and in this we may discern a prefiguring of an ecological revision of natural law that gives moral standing to creatures according to the richness of goods that they have the potential to realise.

The Ecological Significance of Naturalist Natural Law

Finnis' and Grisez's rejection of the naturalistic character of natural law, and their limitation of morally significant natural rights and goods to human being, reflect their affirmation of a modern scientific worldview that rejects the idea of natural teleology and the idea that individual members of subpersonal species or particular ecosystems are engaged in anything that could be described as working for certain ends or goods.[45] However, a growing number of scientists and philosophers are questioning this received post-Enlightenment scepticism about natural teleology. As Veatch argues, some have even readopted the ancient Aristotelian causal scheme of material, formal, efficient, and final causes, which underlies the natural law thinking of Thomas and Hooker.[46]

From an environmental perspective, this challenge to received scientific wisdom is crucial because, as can be seen in Finnis' approving quotation of Hume above, the modern refusal to discern ends or goods in nature that can be valued independently of human ends or goods, sustains an attitude of control toward nature which is deeply anthropocentric and damaging to the interests of non-human creatures and ecosystems. As Veatch argues, in reducing the knowledge of nature to purely hypothetical and deductive reasoning, the scientist has reduced such knowledge merely to those appearances which manifest themselves in the particular terms within which the scientist happens to be operating in any given procedure: "in other words, the objective of science is to control and manipulate nature, and not necessarily to know it as it is in itself at all".[47]

Naturalist natural law offers important ontological grounds from within the Christian tradition for revising Christian anthropocentrism, and for taking more seriously the effects of human economic development on the morally-considerable interests of non-human creatures. There are three areas in the growing discipline of environmental ethics which resonate with a naturalist account of natural law, and where the debate might be enhanced by a fuller exploration of the natural law approach. The first of these is James Lovelock's *Gaia* hypothesis and the growing perception of the interaction between human flourishing, human communities, and the well-being of ecosystems. The second is in the area of primatology and animal welfare. And the third is the issue of the moral standing of objects in the environment, such as trees, and the duties that may be said to arise from the recognition of this standing.

The essential idea represented by Lovelock's *Gaia* hypothesis is that the earth as a whole is a living organism in which chemical and biotic processes and pathways interact in such a way as to maintain the conditions essential for life.[48] Thus, for example, the interaction between oceans, trees and other plants, clouds and air currents maintains a level of oxygen in the earth's climate that is essential to human and other forms of life. Lovelock suggests that it is partly because modern urban humans have lost touch with the delicate sensitivities and balances of such complex natural processes that modern urban industrial societies are so destructive of natural resources.

Lovelock's thesis represents a biochemical extension of a much older idea in ecological science and philosophy, which is the interconnectivity of all kinds and systems of life on the planet. I have proposed elsewhere that this supposedly modern understanding of planetary interconnectivity may also be discerned in the natural law tradition as we encounter it in the Old and New Testaments, and in the thought of Aquinas and Hooker. The strongest pointers to this tradition in the Old Testament include: the tradition that the covenant between God and Israel includes the land and its creatures and not just persons; the idea commonly found in the Psalms and Prophets that the justice of the king and of Israelite society, the fertility of the land, and the reliability of the climate and seasons are all interrelated; the prophetic observation that nature goes awry, land turns to desert, and the climate warms because of the rebellion of the people of Israel against divine justice and the righteous commandments of Yahweh; the connection made in the later prophets between economic injustice, inequality and the lost fertility of the land; the observation in the Wisdom tradition of the wisdom and moral goods that are manifested by non-human creatures and from which humans might learn about their own flourishing.[49]

Natural law was not invented by the Stoics or Aquinas. It has its origin in the deep connections which the ancient Hebrews, like contemporary primal or aboriginal peoples, saw between human and non-human forms of life, and their belief that the divinely revealed moral commands which make for human fulfilment are of cosmic, and not just human significance. The Torah and the Prophets witness that the human quest for right relationships with God and with fellow humans has vital implications for the condition of the cosmos and the non-human creatures among whom they live. Natural law here is deeply rooted in the purposes of God for the fulfilment of creation, both human and non-human. This recognition of the rootedness of natural law in the physical structure of the theistically originated creation, as well as in human moral and social dispositions, involves the idea that human and non-human life are bound together in a complex web of relationships and interactions. The theological recognition in the Old Testament of the moral significance of these relationships acts as a vital corrective to anthropocentric interpretations of human responsibility for creation, such as that advanced by Grisez. It also renders problematic Grisez's isolation of human life as the sole locus of spiritual and sacred significance in the physical world.

A natural law approach to ecological relationality, which is theistic as well as naturalist, has considerable advantages over purely naturalist conceptions of relationality, for it suggests that right relations and balances between creatures are connected to incipient moral qualities which may be said to have been expressed in the original divine distribution of the material goods of creation (not least land) —qualities such as justice, equity, compassion and peaceableness. It therefore involves the recognition of the growing responsibility of humans for the condition of the planet as human populations, and especially affluent populations and their heightened demands on natural resources, grow. It also involves the idea that these moral qualities are to be expressed in human relations with the non-human world, and that their expression is not confined to human society.[50]

Modern studies of primates have given increasing substance to this latter claim. As the biologist Frans de Waal shows in *Good Natured: The*

Origins of Right and Wrong in Humans and Other Animals, reciprocal altruism, compassion, empathy, nurture and desire for community are as characteristic of relations between kin and between friends among elephants, dolphins, monkeys, and even vampire bats as they are among humans. In a series of empirical studies of empathy in animal groups, de Waal describes the behaviour of a group of chimpanzees around the body of one of their number who had fallen from a tree breaking its neck. The male chimpanzees went into a frenzy of wailing and calling around the gully where their companion's body had fallen. Several stopped to stare at the body and one sat looking at it for a whole hour. Other chimpanzees were "embracing, mounting, touching, and patting one another with big, nervous grins on their faces".[51]

The expression of empathy and grief by chimpanzees, who are genetically and in other ways so close to humans, may be less surprising than its appearance among other groups of animals much more distant from us. A group of lemurs, for example, was observed in the process of helping one of their young who had mounted an electric fence, received a shock, and been thrown off. Infant lemurs, who do not normally groom one another, groomed the injured infant intensively after its injury. Its grandmother, who did not normally allow infants to ride on her back, carried this infant for some time after the incident, and also persuaded its reluctant mother to carry it for longer. De Waal assembles a whole range of accounts of empathy and care, and also of grieving, among elephants, dolphins, whales, and other mammals. A photograph in his book shows an elephant caressing the skull of its mother at the place where the latter had died eighteen months previously. Whales frequently beach themselves in a large group rather than abandon one of their number who is too ill to return to deep water in time for the tide. Even more remarkable than these accounts of in-species empathy and care are observations of inter-species altruism, such as an incident involving an elephant coming to the aid of an infant goat that had been abandoned by its parents in the face of an approaching group of adult elephants. Seeing the danger to the goat, the elephant picked it up with its trunk and carried it back to its parents.[52]

Evolutionary biologists have tended to explain all animal behaviour in competitive, selfish, and survivalist terms. Modern theologians and ethicists have tended to ascribe moral behaviours such as empathy, care, and the quest for community exclusively to humans, and to resist the idea that morality might also be expressed in the non-human world. Increasingly, however, ethicists and biologists are coming to the realisation that there is a great deal of common ground between humans and their mammalian relatives in moral behaviour; and that in both cases such behaviour is essential to the flourishing of the societies in which it is expressed, even though for the individuals who express it there may be no direct or obvious short-term pay-backs. De Waal enumerates four key elements in human moral community which ethologists have also found in mammalian groups: sympathy and empathy; learning and the enforcement of social rules and norms; reciprocal exchange and giving, and punishment of individuals who violate reciprocal rules; and peacemaking, avoidance of conflict and community concern.

Community concern and social restraints on excessive self-interest and aggression are as common among some groups of non-human mammals as among humans, and ethologists observe that in both cases the end result is a collective improvement in welfare and peaceableness: "the higher a species' level of social awareness, the more completely its members realize how events around them ricochet through the community until they land at their own doorstep".[53] Such collective concern may sometimes be in the interests of the individuals who practice it, particularly in higher mammals, but its widespread expression gives the lie to the dualism between the morality of personal being and the amorality of subpersonal being, which Grisez and others seek to sustain; for as de Waal notes, "conscious community concern is at the heart of human morality".[54]

This extension of the field of moral considerability is by no means a uniquely modern project. Indeed, primal peoples, including the ancient Israelites, express a much greater sense of the common bonds of life and blood that they share with other animals, than do we moderns. This sense of common life-bonds is expressed, for example, in rituals commonly found among primal peoples around the killing of an animal, rituals which express a sense of reverence for life and a recognition that the taking of it is always a weighty issue. It is also expressed in the self-imposed limits on hunting commonly found in the social systems and rules of these peoples. And such self-regulation is not confined to humans. Ethologists have often observed the tendency of animal predators to hunt older and weaker individuals, perhaps because they are easier targets, but perhaps also from some deeper instinct that their prey's kind deserves to continue to live.

This growing recognition of the moral sensibilities and capacities of sub-human beings is accompanied by the rediscovery of a moral community between humans and other animals which, while common in primal societies, has largely disappeared in modern societies —as witness the widespread modern practices of vivisection, animal experimentation and factory farming.

De Waal's study suggests that the ground for ending the vast array of modern practices and behaviours which involve systematic cruelty to other animals is larger than a mere recognition of their sensate capacity to feel pain as we do. De Waal himself resists the ascription of rights to animals, since they are not capable of the corresponding expression of responsibility. His concern here is that the ascription of rights to beings that are not conscious moral agents may result in the extension of this ascription to creatures lower down the scale of consciousness —from crows to cockroaches— with impossible practical consequences. However, he does argue that we should either phase out the use of apes in experimentation, or take steps to "enrich and enhance their lives in captivity and reduce their suffering".[55]

Natural Law and the Global Ecological Crisis

The recognition of key moral traits such as conscience, care, compassion and community beyond human society challenges the traditional boundaries that advocates of natural law, including Grisez and Finnis, have erected between rational and non-rational creatures in the expression of moral purposes and goods. It is my counter-proposal that natural law may be said to be operative at a number of levels in the created order. Animal instincts that value reciprocity over unbridled competition may serve a moral purpose, just as much as the more conscious desire of most humans for peaceableness instead of conflict. This recognition also brings us back to my earlier observation that natural law is set in the structure of the cosmos. Societies that sustain unfair patterns of resource-distribution, and which dedicate their trading systems to the global spread of weapons of war, do not only threaten their own internal security and foment international conflict. They also infringe a deeper cosmic law that has become manifest in the global climate changes and extinction of species of the late twentieth century.

An ecologically revised approach to natural law, such as that outlined in this chapter, highlights the importance of relationships of proximity and reciprocity in both human and non-human communities. It also indicates the importance of finding legal and political discourses for the expression of the moral standing of all life-forms that are capable of sustaining community. As mentioned at the outset of this essay, modern legal and political systems have, since the eighteenth century, granted to transnational corporations the status of legal persons. Currently transnational corporations and Western governments are involved in the construction of a new body of international law around the World Trade Organisation, along the lines of the proposed Multilateral Agreement on Investment, which will raise the legal claims of private corporations above those of local and national public communities of persons —to say nothing of the claims of communities of sub-human life, such as rainforest trees or the apes that may inhabit them.

The discourse of natural law has played an important role in the growing universal recognition of human rights. Equally it has played a role in the growth of the body of law that governs international relations and international conflict, such as international labour law (which outlaws slavery and bonded labour) and the Geneva Convention. The growing threat to this body of law from free trade law, as represented by the newly established court of the World Trade Organisation, which disregards both human rights and labour and environmental conditions, suggests the need for a revival of natural law theory as a discourse about the origins of morality in face-to-face communities, which should also inform the legal regulation of regional and international relations between communities. Equally, the increasing scale and pace of the ecological crisis requires a rediscovery of the local and global inter-species connections and balances, which tie together the different life-groups that inhabit the planet.

While philosophers, and in particular Grisez and Finnis, may not wish to ascribe rights to apes or trees because they are not responsible moral agents, this argument has not prevented the modern ascription of legal rights to commercial corporations that are not moral agents, and which are first and foremost dedicated not to responsible moral ends or the common good but to commercial profit, frequently gained at the cost of the destruction of human communities and ecosystems. The extension of natural rights to all human communities would itself be a considerable advance over present economic arrangements governing control of natural resources between nations and within them. Its extension to beings and communities of life which also express richness in their nurturing and preservation of life —from groups of apes to stands of broad-leaf boreal or tropical trees that provide homes to communities of thousands of species— is a logical extension of the recognition of the moral significance of communities of non-human beings. It is also an urgently needed corrective to the conferral upon corporations of rights that carry more legal weight than those of human and sub-human communities of life.[56]

NOTES

1   Christopher D. Stone, *Should Trees Have Standing? Toward Legal Rights for Natural Objects* (Los Altos, California: William Kaufman, 1974). The original article first appeared in the *Southern California Law Review* in 1972.
2   Michael S. Northcott, *The Environment and Christian Ethics* (Cambridge: Cambridge University Press, 1996), esp. ch.6.
3   Grisez, *LCL*, p.778.
4   Finnis, *NLNR*, p.75.
5   *LCL*, p.779.
6   *NLNR*, p.195.
7   Anthony J Lisska, *Aquinas' Theory of Natural Law: an Analytic Reconstruction* (Oxford: Clarendon Press, 1996). Finnis argues that he shares with Aquinas the location of natural law in an examination of epistemology, but this reading of Aquinas is not uncontentious (*NLNR*, pp.33-35).
8   Henry B. Veatch, *Swimming Against the Current in Contemporary Philosophy: Occasional Essays and Papers* (Washington, DC: Catholic University of America Press, 1990).
9   Pamela M. Hall, *Narrative and the Natural Law: an Interpretation of Thomistic Ethics* (Notre Dame: University of Notre Dame Press, 1994).
10   Hall, *Narrative and Natural Law*, p.18; and Veatch, *Swimming Against the Current*, p.294.
11   *NLNR*, p.36.
12   Thomas Aquinas, *Summa Theologiae*, IaIIae, q.94, a.2, cited and translated in Lisska, *Aquinas' Theory*, p.101.
13   Hall, *Narrative and Natural Law*, p.19. See also Northcott, *Environment and Christian Ethics*, pp.268-9.
14   John Finnis and Germain Grisez, "The Basic Principles of Natural Law: a Reply to Ralph McInerny", in Charles E. Curran and Richard A. McCormick (eds.), *Natural Law and Theology: Readings in Moral Theology No. 7* (Mahwah, New Jersey: Paulist Press, 1991), p.161.
15   *NLNR*, p.380.
16   David Hume, *Dialogues concerning Natural Religion*, cited in *NLNR*, p.381.
17   *NLNR*, pp.381-2. Finnis' citations in quotation marks are from Hume, *Dialogues concerning Natural Religion*.
18   *NLNR*, p.111; and *LCL*, pp.771-82.
19   *LCL*, p.777.
20   Ibid., p 778.
21   Ibid., p 781.
22   See further Northcott, *Environment and Christian Ethics*, chs.4 and 5.
23   Lynn White, "The Historical Roots of our Ecologic Crisis", *Science*, 155 (1967), pp.1203-7.
24   Clear-cutting is the practice, commonly used in the timber industry, of cutting down all trees in a given forest area, rather than extracting mature examples of trees for lumber. Unlike clear-cutting, selective extraction, when done carefully, need not involve the wholesale destruction of forest ecosystems, and the species loss and erosion that this destruction entails.
25   *LCL*, p.784.
26   Ibid., p.786.

27   Ibid., p.786.
28   Ibid., p.785.
29   Carol Gilligan, *In a Different Voice: Psychological Theory and Women's Development* (Cambridge, Mass.: Harvard University Press, 1982).
30   See further Northcott, *Environment and Christian Ethics*, ch.5.
31   Veatch, *Swimming Against the Current*, p.97.
32   Ibid., p.172.
33   Ibid., p.143.
34   Holmes Rolston III, *Environmental Ethics: Duties to and Values in the Natural Environment* (Philadelphia: Temple University Press, 1988).
35   Lisska, *Aquinas' Theory*, p.86.
36   Ibid., p.101.
37   Ibid., p.99.
38   Ibid., p.103.
39   Ibid., p.104.
40   Aquinas, *ST*, IIaIIae, q.99, a.2.
41   Aquinas, *ST*, IaIIae, q.94. a.2.
42   Richard Hooker, *Laws of Ecclesiastical Polity*, cited in Veatch, *Swimming Against the Current*, p.276.
43   Aquinas, *Commentary on Dionysius' "De Divinis Nominibus"*, 22; cited in Northcott, *Environment and Christian Ethics*, p.268.
44   Aquinas, *Commentary*, 781; cited in Northcott, *Environment and Christian Ethics*, p.268.
45   Richard Dawkins, of course, takes this view even further in his hugely influential 'Selfish Gene' hypothesis, contending that the only units of life which can consistently be said to be working for ends are genes, which work unconsciously through their carriers to replicate themselves in future generations (*River Out of Eden* [Oxford: Oxford University Press, 1989], pp.27-9).
46   Veatch, *Swimming Against the Current*, p.277.
47   Ibid., p.278.
48   James Lovelock, *Gaia: A New Look at Life on Earth* (Oxford: Oxford University Press, 1979).
49   See further, Northcott, *Environment and Christian Ethics*, pp.167-74.
50   See further, ibid., pp.179 ff.
51   Frans de Waal, *Good Natured: the Origins of Right and Wrong in Humans and Other Animals* (Cambridge, Mass.: Harvard University Press, 1996), p.56.
52   Northcott, *Environment and Christian Ethics*, p.251.
53   De Waal, *Good Natured*, p.207.
54   Ibid., p.208.
55   Ibid., p.216.
56   See further Michael Northcott, "Christians, Environment and Society", in *Transformation*, 16/3 (1999), pp.102-9.

Conclusion

Nigel Biggar

We conclude with some reflections on eight important topics that have each recurred in several of the essays contributed to this volume. These are: the status of ethical realism in the contemporary intellectual climate; whether realism should be conceived in rationalist or naturalist terms; whether marriage is really a basic good; whether physical pleasure should not be counted a basic good; whether it is always wrong to act deliberately against a basic good; the problems of moral certainty and authority; the *rapprochement* between Protestant and Roman Catholic ethics; and, finally, whether ethical understanding is independent of one's anthropological point of view.

The Contemporary Status of Ethical Realism

The fact that all the contributors to this book endorse (explicitly or implicitly) the Grisez School's ethical realism, tells us that the notion that morality is grounded in a reality that is prior to human choosing finds *some* support among other contemporary philosophers and theologians. Timothy Chappell provides this support with historical depth by finding in Aristotle, Hume, and Mill something of a classical "philosophical consensus" about the given reality of certain basic goods (pp. 33-4). Sabina Alkire adds backing from contemporary Anglo-American philosophy in the form of James Griffin's theory of objective, "prudential values" and Martha Nussbaum's universal "basic human capabilities" (pp. 77-81). Lisa Cahill then broadens the ranks of philosophical support when she argues that "the recovery of some sort of realist foundations and objectivity in ethics" is necessary to sustain feminist critiques of 'unjust' social institutions and conventions (pp. 242-3). Evidence that Cahill represents a wider body of opinion within contemporary feminist theory may be found, for example, in Grace Jantzen's book, *Grace, Gender, and Mysticism.*[1] Here Jantzen deconstructs deconstructionism to reveal that "it is precisely the demand of justice" which calls forth its efforts. In support she cites no less than Derrida himself who, in an essay with the uncharacteristic title, "The Mystical Foundation of Authority", affirms that "deconstruction is justice", and justice, unlike law, is *not* deconstructible; rather, it is an "infinite" idea, "infinite because it is irreducible, irreducible because owed to the other, owed to the other *before any contract* ...".[2] But perhaps the most telling indication that the philosophical future lies with ethical realism rather than (deconstructionist) relativism, and that the Grisez School are on the right track here, can be found in the work of one of the foremost representatives of postmodernist ethics, Zygmunt Baumann. In his *Postmodern Ethics*, Baumann argues passionately that moral responsibility "has ... no foundation" and "that a non-aporetic, non-ambivalent morality, an ethics that is universal and 'objectively founded', is a practical impossibility".[3] Nevertheless, four pages later we encounter the claim that the postmodern perspective has succeeded in piercing through to "the *common* moral condition that *precedes* all diversifying effects of the social administration of moral capacity"; and, later on, the assertion that responsibility for the other is "an unfounded [that is, absolutely 'basic'] *foundation*".[4] If the likes of Baumann —and Derrida— cannot help but resort to realist claims, then we have reason to suspect that ethical realism 'outnarrates' its alternative —that is, that realism can do better justice to the valid concerns of non-realism than vice-versa.

Realism: Rationalist or Naturalist?

In Michael Northcott's chapter we are reminded that the rationalist form of ethical realism that Grisez and Finnis espouse has long brought them into contention with certain other Thomists —for egregious example, Henry Veatch— who prefer a naturalist version (pp. 265-6). To some extent, this dispute is about who can lay best claim to the mantle of Thomas Aquinas; and as such it is of limited importance (pp. 266-7). What would be of much greater importance is the claim that the rationalism of the Grisez School suffers from a serious deficiency that a certain ethical naturalism can supply. And, indeed, this is what Northcott himself asserts, when he argues that the School's rationalism is expressive of an anthropocentrism that, unable to recognise the inherent value of non-human being, encourages human abuse of the environment; and that the prevention of this abuse requires the recovery of a notion of natural teleology as a basis for the ascription of rights to non-human species (pp. 268, 273, 279-80).

How cogent is this criticism depends, of course, on whether *all* forms of anthropocentrism do encourage environmental irresponsibility; how much sense it makes to think of inanimate beings such as trees having 'inherent value' and therefore 'rights'; and, crucially, whether a notion of natural teleology can be made philosophically credible.

Enter Chappell, who, tacitly representing a considerable body of contemporary philosophers (among them, Peter Geach and Alasdair MacIntyre),[5] contends that it is possible to move 'non-fallaciously' from an 'is' to an 'ought', or from the 'natural' as statistically normal to the 'natural' as morally normative. The crucial mediating concept in such a move is the natural teleological one of an essential function or tendency of a certain species of being —a concept without which, Chappell claims, (biological) science would be incapable of explaining anything (p. 45).

What remains unclear (at least to this reader) is how we are to distinguish 'essential' tendencies from the full range of actual or existing ones. Chappell tells us that the former are characterised by their "salience", but denies that this salience is statistical. So what other kind of salience is this, and by what criteria can we establish it?

Is Marriage Really a Basic Good?

If one criticism of the Grisez School's theory of basic goods is that it has been arrived at by the wrong route, another bears upon its components. Three of our authors —one philosopher, one moral theologian, and one representative of social science— object to the inclusion of marriage in the list of basic goods. Timothy Chappell describes this proposal as "extraordinarily unpromising" (p. 38), arguing that 'marriage' does not complete any action-explanation in the way that 'friendship' does, and that it is reducible to other goods such as "friendship, self-integration, play, aesthetic good ..., physical health and well-being —and, dare one say it, physical pleasure" (pp. 38-9). Similarly, Lisa Cahill denies that marriage is essential to the making of a happy or virtuous life, and suggests that it is better considered *one* context for the realisation of other goods such as "life, justice and friendship, self-integration and practical reasonableness" (pp. 245-6). Finally, Sabina Alkire reports that in all the lists of basic human goods that she has surveyed, Grisez' and Finnis' 'marriage' finds no corroboration (pp. 92-3).

Should not Physical Pleasure be Counted a Basic Good?

A second objection to the Grisez School's current list of goods that also wins explicit support from some of our authors, is the exclusion from its ranks of physical pleasure. Noting in his Introduction to the School's theory that pleasure in general is integral (albeit secondary) to the experience of the realisation of any good, Rufus Black explains why "purely physical pleasure" is denied the status of a basic good Central to the School's argument, he tells us, is their affirmation —against Robert Nozick's notion of a life totally absorbed by the experience of pleasure— that a genuinely fulfilling human life is one built out of personal commitments to worthwhile things (pp. 11-12).

One response to this could be to point out that Nozick's notion is of a life that is committed to physical pleasure as the *one and only* good; whereas what is being proposed is only that physical pleasure be recognised as *one of several* goods. However, Grisez and Finnis could reply that the weight of their objection bears on the *passivity* of the experience of pleasure —that it is merely experienced, rather than achieved. As Finnis puts it: "one wants to *do* certain things (not just have the experience of doing them); one wants to *be* a certain sort of person, through one's own authentic, free-self-determination and self-realisation; one wants to *live* (in the active sense) oneself ...".[6]

Nevertheless, it is also true that the terms in which Grisez and Finnis describe what they are objecting to, often speak of *hedonism* more than pleasure as such. For example, the section in *Natural Law and Natural Rights* where Finnis discusses the matter is entitled "Is pleasure the point of it all?" Note: "*the* point of it *all*". And it is clear from his subsequent discussion that what he is resisting is the 'modern' *reduction* of human well-being to "some form of experience". Likewise, in the relevant section of *Christian Moral Principles*, Grisez refers explicitly and repeatedly to 'hedonism', which he associates with "an *emphasis* upon pleasure and pain".[7]

With regard to the point about human fulfilment being the result of voluntary, self-committing, human *acts*, one might ask whether this must be true of every aspect of fulfilment. Finnis himself admits that aesthetic experience, the fourth of his basic goods in *Natural Law and Natural Rights*, "need not involve an action of one's own; what is sought after and valued for its own sake may simply be the beautiful form 'outside' one, and the 'inner' experience of appreciation of its beauty".[8] Alternatively, we might agree that all human fulfilment is the result of acts, but insist that there are acts of appreciation as well as acts of achievement. But what is the difference, then, between an act of appreciation of natural beauty and Chappell's example of an act of stepping into a coffee shop simply in order to enjoy the pleasure of the aroma of coffee (p. 36)?

Chappell identifies a further reason why the Grisez School resists according physical pleasure the status of a basic good: namely, that the absence of such pleasure does not always detract from the realisation of integral human fulfilment, whereas that is not true of any other good (p. 35). His own response is to point out that pain can sometimes be lethal, and more often so all-absorbing as to detract from one's participation in other goods (p. 35). That, however, does not quite meet the point that pain is sometimes salutary.

Chappell concludes his discussion of this matter by recommending that the Grisez School drop its distinction between basic 'intelligible' and non-basic 'sensible' goods (p. 37). Jean Porter reached the same conclusion some years ago, but for different reasons that are worth quoting here:

> Grisez's argument for [the] exclusion [of physical pleasure from the list of basic goods] is that pleasure cannot be an *intelligible* good, and therefore cannot be an object of practical reason. But he equivocates. If by "intelligible" good he means something that has a necessary intellectual component, like knowledge, then neither is human life, taken by itself, an intelligible good; on the other hand, if he means something that can be the object of thought and planning, then certainly pleasure can be an intelligible good (just as much as life itself can be). It begins to seem that underlying Grisez's argument at this point is a hunch that pleasure is just not worthy to be a basic human good, that poetry must somehow be better than pushpin if the human race is to maintain its dignity.[9]

Is it Always Wrong to Act Deliberately Against a Basic Good?

Some of the most controversial features of the Grisez School's theory of basic goods lie in their articulation of the content of the good of practical reasonableness, by which they make the transition from basic values to moral norms.

Among our own authors, Chappell raises logical questions about the alleged 'self-evidence' of the first principle of practical reasonableness (pp. 32-3). He also detects a certain ambiguity in the (in)famous seventh "requirement of practical reasonableness" (Finnis) or "mode of responsibility" (Grisez) —namely, that "One should not be moved by hostility to freely accept or choose the destruction, damaging, or impeding of any intelligible human good".[10] Chappell locates the ambiguity in the meaning of "'destroying, damaging or impeding' 'an instance of an intelligible good'" (p. 32). I am more inclined to locate it in whether or not the principle acknowledges that the deliberate acceptance or choice to destroy etc. could be motivated by something other than 'hostility'. As formulated, the principle could fairly be taken to imply such acknowledgement; but my impression is that when Grisez and his colleagues apply it, they assume that any deliberate harm or hindrance of a good must be malevolent. If that is so, it is a mistake; because it is possible to choose deliberately to harm something while 'honouring' it. Michael Northcott supplies an example of this in relation to the taking of life, when he mentions the "rituals commonly found among primal peoples around the killing of an animal, rituals which express a sense of reverence for life and a recognition that the taking of it is always a weighty issue" (p. 277).

Dave Leal also questions the identification of deliberate harm (or impediment) with malevolence in Grisez's treatment of contraception, where Grisez tends to identify the deliberate choice to impede procreation with hostility to children in general or to any child that dares to be born in spite of the contraceptive measures taken. Leal rightly affirms the possibility of a wider range of more complex motives —in particular, that it is quite possible to choose not to have children for a certain period, but *at the same time* to be ready to love any child that should be conceived against one's will (pp. 212-16). Likewise, Gareth Moore argues against Grisez that the choice to masturbate is not necessarily a choice to harm one's self-integrity (pp. 231-4).

The Grisez School's tendency to identify acts that harm or impede a good with an ill will, causes them to offer some rather disingenuous —or at least incomplete— action-descriptions. For example, as Lisa Cahill reports, Grisez can be found describing the choice of an act of fetal craniotomy, undertaken as the only way of saving the mother's life, as a "'proposal ... to alter the child's physical dimensions and remove him or her, because, as a physical object, this body cannot remain where it is without ending in both the baby's and the mother's deaths'" (p. 254). What this description passes over is that "to alter the child's physical dimensions" will, given the current limitations of surgical skill, certainly kill the child, so that to choose the former is at one and the same time to choose the latter (provided, of course, that one *knows* that the inevitable effect of physical alteration will be lethal). An act of fetal craniotomy involves a deliberate choice to take life —albeit not at all out of 'hostility' toward the child.

Another example may be found in Joseph Boyle's[11] treatment of the famous case of Captain Oates. Oates was a member of Scott's expedition to the South Pole in 1912, which was dangerously delayed and became weatherbound: "Lamed by severe frostbite, Oates, convinced that his crippled condition would fatally handicap his companions' prospect of winning through, walked out into the blizzard, deliberately sacrificing his life to enhance his comrades' chances of survival".[12] Adhering to the Grisez School's (effective) principle that a deliberate act against a good must be expressive of a 'hostile' will, and unwilling to pronounce Oates' action immoral, Boyle argues that "actions like that of Captain Oates need not be suicide, but can be the acceptance of death as a side-effect of choices to do other things (e.g., removing oneself from the group), which have death as a predictable result".[13] However, to describe Oates' action as an unintended 'side-effect' of 'removing oneself from the group' is to omit certain significant data; namely, that Oates removed himself as a severely sick man into an Antarctic blizzard, knowing (presumably) that to do so would be lethal. In other words, his act was at one and the same time one of self-removal and of suicide —albeit not a suicide motivated by any 'hostility' to his own life. One might demur at describing what Oates did as 'suicide', since he did not die 'at his own hand'. In this respect his case is different from that of Henning von Tresckow, one of the conspirators in the von Stauffenberg plot to kill Hitler on 20 July 1944. Upon learning that the plot had failed, Tresckow told his cousin "in a totally calm, collected way" that he would take his own life because he feared that he would betray his accomplices under torture. The next morning he drove out past the German lines into no man's land, where he killed himself.[14] Here is a case of altruistic 'self-removal' that was indubitably suicidal. Is the difference between this and the case of Captain Oates a morally significant one? I think not. Both chose to save their comrades by means that they knew would result in their own deaths —deaths that *under the circumstances* were necessary to achieve their aims. Whether the means chosen were self-exposure to Antarctic weather or pulling the pin on a hand-grenade makes no moral difference.[15] The problem with the kind of redescription that the

Grisez School finds itself forced to make by its identification of acts of harming goods with 'hostility' toward them, is succinctly expressed by Cahill in her verdict on Grisez: "his rewording of the moral stakes ... masks the responsibility we do bear for taking life in a tragic situation" (p. 254).

The Problems of Moral Certainty and Authority

Several of the problems that our authors find with the Grisez School's ethic they attribute to the School's unswerving adherence to certain specific moral conclusions —or, to be more exact, to the teaching of the Magisterium. Ralph McInerny says of Grisez that "he long ago accepted the role of the paladin of the Magisterium" (p. 53). Leal observes generally "that Grisez's ... thought is determined by its faithfulness to a particular understanding of ecclesiology ..." (p. 208). More critically, Chappell worries "that the modes of responsibility [especially the seventh and eighth] have simply been generated *ad hoc* to give certain conclusions in applied ethics" (p. 32). Regarding Grisez's treatment of sexual matters, Moore complains unequivocally that "he does not follow where the logic of his arguments leads him, but is determined to get to where, on the basis of his faith, he wants to arrive ..." (p. 239). And Cahill notes that Grisez's not very persuasive assertion of marriage as a basic good in its very constitution serves to reaffirm traditional Catholic teaching against divorce by "refut[ing] the possibility that it could ever be right to act directly against a marriage — e.g., by seeking to dissolve it" (pp. 246-7).

Insofar as the fault here is an assumption that moral realism implies moral fixity and certainty, Cahill reminds us of Aquinas' caveat "that it is easier to attain certainty and universality at the more general levels of natural law precepts than it is in the particulars, where contingent circumstances may affect both what is objectively right to do and what our perception of the good may be" —thereby implicitly urging Grisez to be more open to the revision of more specific moral norms and particular moral judgements (p. 244). Oliver O'Donovan advises Finnis along similar lines, though in more conservative terms, when he writes that since "the possibility of new questions arising from new experience is never absent", one must be open to the "complementary development" of moral norms (pp. 124-5).

Insofar as the fault is an unwillingness to admit error in received (or authorised) wisdom, Moore boldly urges a greater willingness "to look and think again, and be prepared to remedy what may turn out to be the errors of centuries" (p. 240). Of such errors Bernard Hoose provides some papal examples, in order to show why a responsible regard for the authority of Magisterial teaching ought to be critical and may take the form of loyal dissent (pp. 188-91).

The *Rapprochement* between Protestant and Roman Catholic Ethics

There is little evidence in the Grisez School's ecclesiology of a readiness to acknowledge the validity of Protestant concerns. However, in other respects Grisez's own moral theology displays features that —thanks to the influence of Vatican II— satisfy some historic Protestant complaints. One of these features is its pronounced eudaimonistic character, which, clearly subordinating moral law to the service of the human good, acquits it from certain charges of 'legalism'. Another point where Grisez's 'natural' ethic approximates historic Protestant thought —as I observe in Chapter Seven— is its considerable theological qualification "by the life and teaching of Jesus, as conveyed by Scripture, and by a concept of personal vocation (issued by God the Holy Spirit)" (p. 164).

On the other hand, three of the contributions to this volume provide evidence of Protestant movement toward the natural law tradition, which the Grisez School represents (albeit in rationalist form). Göran Bexell mentions that since the Second World War "a number of serious proposals for the renewal of the doctrine of natural law" have been developed in Lutheran circles in Scandinavia (p. 146). Rufus Black refers to "the renewed interest in the place of natural law in the thought of the founding figures of the Reformation" (p. 148). He also quotes the (Protestant) Anglican, Oliver O'Donovan, as affirming the importance of sustaining the possibility that humans have "a certain 'natural knowledge' which is also part of man's created endowment" (p. 159); and he cites the leading American Lutheran theologian, Carl Braaten, as saying that "[a]n ecumenical dialogue on the place of natural law in Christian social ethics is particularly necessary and timely" (p. 148). In my own contribution I point out that, throughout history, eminent Protestants may be found affirming the natural derivation of moral truth (p. 170).

The main contribution of this volume to ecumenical *rapprochement*, however, appears in the dialogues created by myself and Black between Grisez on the one hand, and two famously anti-natural law Protestants — Karl Barth and Stanley Hauerwas— on the other. Although, as both Bexell

and Black aver, Barth was responsible for the poor regard in which natural
law has been held in certain Protestant circles since the 1930s (pp. 146, 148-
9), I argue that he himself was unable to avoid using a form of it in his own
ethic; and that his reasons for repudiating it are wanting (pp. 166-7, 172-5,
178-9). I also argue that the basic moral norms that Grisez develops under
the name of 'modes of responsibility' are sometimes more decisively shaped
by a specifically Christian vision of the human condition than their
supposedly 'natural' character permits (pp. 176-7). Independently arriving
at the same observation, Black uses it to answer Hauerwas' objection to
Grisez's ethic that it is unformed by the world-view that issues from the
Christian 'narrative' (p. 158-60). Each of us then concludes with a qualified
affirmation of the natural law project. We affirm the possibility, validity,
and necessity of deriving a body of moral insights from reflection on
common human nature and experience —but with the proviso that at certain
points, some of them basic, this body of moral common sense will be shaped
by the particular anthropological beliefs of those who hold it (pp. 158-60,
177-9).

Is Basic Ethical Understanding Independent of Anthropology?

This brings us to one of the most basic points upon which several of our
Protestant authors take issue with Grisez and Finnis: the alleged
independence of genuine understanding of ethical foundations from any
anthropological commitment; that is, from any particular understanding of
the nature of human being and the human condition. According to the
Grisez School, the basic goods, the first principle of morality, and "the
modes of responsibility" or "the basic requirements of practical
reasonableness" are all 'self-evident' in the sense of being graspable simply
by reflection upon practical reason. Göran Bexell, standing in the tradition
of Paul, Augustine, and Luther over against that of Aristotle and Aquinas,
denies the possibility of a neutral ethical understanding (or 'reason') that is
not shaped either by the presence of religious faith or by its absence (pp.
134-5). Advancing this line of criticism, Rufus Black observes that, since
Finnis asserts that knowledge of the basic requirements of practical
reasonableness arises, in part, from an understanding of the "conditions of
human life", different such understandings will produce different
conceptions of what is practically 'reasonable'; and that, *pace* Grisez, a
Christian vision of those conditions does add new basic moral principles to

those that are naturally knowable (pp. 153-6). Pushing the point one step further, I argue that even some of what Grisez (and Finnis) present as being elements of practical reason simply, only appear reasonable in the light of Christian faith and hope; and that therefore their 'natural morality' is actually formed by Christian presuppositions (pp. 176-7, 179). However, as I have said (pp. 177-8), this need not mean that different anthropologies yield *absolutely* different ethics. On the contrary, they may well share common elements, more or less differently qualified. Nor does it mean that there is no scope for critical dialogue between different ethics, and no reason to hope for eventual (even if eschatological) consensus. What it does mean, however, is that at certain points ethical dialogue will grind to a halt unless it is willing to grapple with larger issues about the nature of human being and the universe in which it is set.

NOTES

1   Grace Jantzen, *Power, Gender, and Mysticism* (Cambridge: Cambridge University Press, 1995).
2   Jacques Derrida, "The Mystical Foundation of Authority", in Drucilla Cornell, M. Rosenfeld, and D.G. Carlson (eds.), *Deconstruction and the Possibility of Justice* (New York and London: Routledge,1992), pp.15, 25; cited in Jantzen, *Power, Gender and Mysticism*, p.351. My emphasis.
3   Zygmunt Baumann, *Postmodern Ethics* (Oxford: Blackwell, 1993), pp.13, 10.
4   Ibid., pp.14, 74.
5   For an efficient introduction to the debate in moral philosophy about whether or not any move from an 'is' to an 'ought' necessarily commits the 'naturalistic fallacy', see W.H. Hudson, *Modern Moral Philosophy* (London: Macmillan, 1983), chs.6, 7.
6   Finnis, *NLNR*, pp.95-6.
7   Grisez, *CMP*, 5C. My italics.
8   *NLNR*, pp.87-8.
9   Jean Porter, "Basic Goods and the Human Good in Recent Catholic Moral Theology", *The Thomist*, 57 (January 1993), p.41.
10   *CMP*, 8G.1. Cp. *NLNR*, pp.118-25.
11   Joseph Boyle is another member of the Grisez School.
12   *Chambers Dictionary of Biography*, 6th edition, ed. Melanie Parry (Edinburgh: Chambers, 1997), s.v. "Oates, Lawrence Edward Grace".
13   Joseph Boyle, "Sanctity of Life and Suicide: Tensions and Developments within Common Morality", in *Suicide and Euthanasia: Historical and Contemporary Themes*, ed. Baruch Brody (Dordrecht and London: Kluwer, 1989), p.233.
14   Joachim Fest, *Plotting Hitler's Death: the German Resistance to Hitler, 1933-45* (London: Weidenfield and Nicholson, 1996), p.289. As he took final leave of his cousin, von Tresckow gave this additional reason for his choice of suicide: "The whole world will vilify us now, but I am totally convinced that we did the right

thing. Hitler is the archenemy not only of Germany but of the world. When, in a few hours' time, I go before God to account for what I have done and left undone, I know I will be able to justify in good conscience what I did in the struggle against Hitler. God promised Abraham that He would not destroy Sodom if just ten righteous men could be found in the city, and so I hope that for our sake God will not destroy Germany. None of us can bewail his own death; those who consented to join our circle put on the robe of Nessus. A human being's moral integrity begins when he is prepared to sacrifice his life for his convictions" (ibid., pp.289-90).

15   I believe that von Tresckow blew himself up with a hand-grenade, but I have been unable to find confirmation of this.

Index